THE LOEB CLASSICAL LIBRARY

FOUNDED BY JAMES LOEB, LL.D.

EDITED BY

† T. E. PAGE, C.H., LITT.D.

† E. CAPPS, PH.D., LL.D.   † W. H. D. ROUSE, LITT.D.

L. A. POST, L.H.D.   E. H. WARMINGTON, M.A., F.R.HIST.SOC.

PAUSANIAS

V

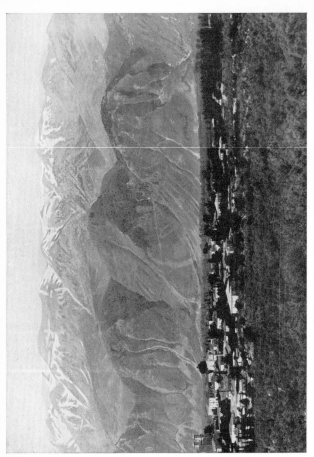

MODERN SPARTA AND MT. TAYGETUS.

PAUSANIAS,

DESCRIPTION OF GREECE

WITH AN ENGLISH TRANSLATION BY

W. H. S. JONES, Litt.D.

ST. CATHARINE'S COLLEGE, CAMBRIDGE

IN FOUR VOLUMES
WITH A COMPANION VOLUME CONTAINING
MAPS, PLANS AND INDICES

V

COMPANION VOLUME, CONTAINING ILLUSTRATIONS
AND INDEX

PREPARED BY

R. E. WYCHERLEY, M.A.

PROFESSOR OF GREEK, UNIVERSITY COLLEGE OF NORTH WALES

CAMBRIDGE, MASSACHUSETTS
HARVARD UNIVERSITY PRESS
LONDON
WILLIAM HEINEMANN LTD
MCMLXV

First printed 1935
Revised and reprinted 1955
Reprinted 1961, 1965

Printed in Great Britain

CONTENTS

v

PREFACE

This volume cannot, of course, illustrate Pausanias fully, or provide a full archaeological commentary. Its object is to give a representative selection which should illustrate the most important sections and enable the reader to follow the rest of the *Description* with greater interest and understanding; and which may at the same time be of some use independently of the author. The maps explain themselves, though it should perhaps be pointed out that the routes are indicated exactly as Pausanias describes them; in practice he may have linked them up more than appears. Plans have been included of sites where illustration is helpful in following the description, in cases where appreciable material is to be had. On the other hand, no attempt has been made to include sites such as Sparta, where the topography has not been sufficiently ascertained to bring it into close relation with Pausanias' description. Particular buildings which Pausanias describes with great care or mentions with great interest have been illustrated independently. The photographs in all cases show things actually seen by Pausanias. An attempt has been made to include at some point a good representative of each class of monument, so that the plates may enable the reader to appreciate similar things not actually shown, and may in a sense illustrate the *Description* as a whole. Few

PREFACE

photographs of sculpture have been included, since these are easily accessible elsewhere. The Mantineia basis (60, 61, 62) has been illustrated in full, however, since it provides an interesting commentary on Pausanias' methods of description; Pl. 57 (a) and (b) provide a curious contrast; and the Lycosura torsos (66(a) and (b)) are unfamiliar, though the heads are often shown.

For permission to use material for maps and plans, thanks are due to the following :—the American School at Athens, (12, 15, 16, 17) (in particular, Professor T. L. Shear, director of the excavations in the Athenian agora, has very generously supplied a photograph of an unpublished plan, which it has been possible to include at the last moment); the Archaeological Society of Athens (25); K. Baedeker, Leipzig (18, 27); W. Dörpfeld (19); C. Dugas (26); Paul Geuthner, Paris (26); the Society for the Promotion of Hellenic Studies (24, 85(c)); W. de Gruyter, Berlin (85(a), (b)); W. Judeich, and his publishers C. H. Beck, Munich (10, 11); Alfred Kröner, Leipzig (23(b)); Macmillan and Co., London (13); J. Murray, London (1–9); R. Oldenburg, Munich (28); Weidmannsche Buchhandlung, Berlin (14). Thanks are also due to the following, for permission to reproduce photographs :—Fratelli Alinari, Florence (39, 54, 74); Deutscher Kunstverlag, Berlin (34); Deutsches Archaeologisches Institut, Athen (33, 35, 48, 50, 53, 56, 60, 61, 62, 64, 67, 70, 71, 73); the Society for the Promotion of Hellenic Studies (Frontispiece, 41, 44, 46, 47, 49, 52, 57(a), 63(a), 69, 75, 77, 78, 80, 81, 82, 83, 84) (apart from the actual photographs used, the facilities of the Society and the help of the Librarian have been invaluable);

viii

PREFACE

Kunstgeschichtl. Seminar, Marburg (30, 31, 36, 37, 43, 51, 53, 57(*b*), 58, 65, 66(*a*), 68, 71); Neue Photographische Gesellschaft, Berlin (32, 38); J. van der Woude, formerly student of the French School at Athens (29, 79); S. C. Atchley, Esq., British Legation, Athens (63). Acknowledgement in detail is also made in the list of illustrations. The Cambridge University Press prepared the plates for reproduction and made the blocks, and their staff was very generous with help and advice on technical points.

R. E. W.

PREFACE TO REVISED EDITION

THE purpose of this volume remains the same— to provide a representative set of illustrations of Pausanias, and incidentally, by carrying further the author's principles of selectivity, to give some guidance to the visitor to Greece, confronted by a bewildering profusion of monuments. I leave the old preface unchanged, though it is no longer applicable in every detail. In particular I do not wish to delete any record of assistance formerly received.

Pl. 12, Pl. 16 and Pl. 28 are new, and a slight change has been made in Pl. 11, which though sketchy will still be adequate, I hope, if supplemented by Pl. 12. Twelve new photos have been substituted. Some pages of the text have been completely rewritten; in many, minor changes have been made.

Besides renewing my former thanks, I wish to thank the following for material and permission to use it: Miss Lucy Shoe, Miss Lucy Talcott and the

PREFACE

American School of Classical Studies at Athens (12, 16, 30, 31); M. Georges Daux and the French School at Athens (28); Miss Alison Frantz (31, 36, 38, 41); Mr. G. P. Stevens (35); Deutscher Kunstverlag, Munich (60); Paul Geuthner, Paris (62); Mr. John Pollard (67); the Metropolitan Museum of Art, New York (77); Dr. H. Schleif (58, 77). Pl. 28 was drawn by Mr. T. E. Jones and Mr. I. ap Thomas of Bangor.

I should like to express my gratitude for help and advice to Professor Homer Thompson and Professor Eugene Vanderpool (on the Athenian agora), Professor Richard Stilwell (Corinth), and M. Georges Daux and M. Pierre Amandry (Delphi); and to acknowledge the great benefit derived from a period spent as a visiting member of the Institute for Advanced Study at Princeton, and from study in the agora at Athens made possible by a generous grant from the American Philosophical Society. I am grateful also to the Press Board of the University of Wales for giving me a grant to meet the cost of having a new plan of Delphi made, and to Messrs. Swain & Co. for producing the new blocks.

In returning to this task after twenty years, I wish to pay grateful tribute to the memory of two men whose kindness meant much to a young scholar— John Penoyre, who as Librarian, first showed me the great resources of the Hellenic Society, and W. H. D. Rouse.

R. E. W.

May, 1955.

x

LIST OF ILLUSTRATIONS WITH SOURCES

Frontispiece. Modern Sparta and Mount Taygetus (photo, Hellenic Society).

1. Central and Southern Greece.
2. Attica and Megaris.
3. Argolis.
4. Laconia.
5. Messenia.
6. Elis.
7. Achaia.
8. Arcadia.
9. Phocis and Boeotia.
10. Athens and Peiraeus (after W. Judeich, *Topographie von Athen*, Fig. 13).
11. Ancient Athens (after Judeich, *Topographie*, Plan 1).
12. Agora, Athens (restored) (plan by J. Travlos, to appear in *Hesperia*).
13. Propylaea, Athens (restored) (after J. E. Harrison, *Ancient Athens*, Fig. 5).
14. Acropolis of Athens (E. Curtius, *Die Stadtgeschichte von Athen*, Pl. V).
15. Erechtheum, Athens (G. P. Stevens and J. M. Paton, *The Erechtheum*, Pl. I).
16. Corinth, Central Area, about A.D. 200 (restored) (*Corinth*, I. iii, Fig. 1).
17. Argive Heraeum (restored) (C. Waldstein, *The Argive Heraeum*, Vol. I, Pl. V).
18. Sanctuary of Epidaurus (Baedeker's *Greece*).
19. Theatre, Epidaurus (restored) (W. Dörpfeld and E. Reisch, *Das griechische Theater*, Fig. 50).

LIST OF ILLUSTRATIONS WITH SOURCES

20. Temple of Zeus, Olympia (restored) (after *Die Funde von Olympia*, Pl. xxxii).

21. Temple of Hera, Olympia (restored) (after *Die Funde von Olympia*, Pl. xxxiv).

22. Olympia in Roman times (after *Olympia, die Ergebnisse, Karten und Pläne*, IV).

23. (a) Hippodrome, Olympia (after A. Hirt, *Baukunst bei den Alten*, pl. xx, 8).
    (b) Temple of Apollo, Bassae (J. Durm, *Die Baukunst der Griechen*, Fig. 391).

24. Megalopolis (after E. A. Gardner and others, *Excavations of Megalopolis*, Plan I).

25. Sanctuary of the Mistress, Lycosura (after Πρακτικὰ τῆς Ἀρχαιολογικῆς Ἑταιρίας, 1896, Pl. X).

26. Temple of Athena Alea, Tegea (restored) (C. Dugas, *Le Sanctuaire d'Aléa Athéna à Tégée*, Pl. ix–x).

27. Delphi (after Baedeker's *Greece*).

28. Sanctuary of Apollo, Delphi (restored) (after plans in P. de la Coste-Messelière, *Au Musée de Delphes*, and J. Bousquet, *Le Trésor de Cyrène*).

29. Cape Sunium (photo, J. van der Woude).

30. West Side of Agora of Athens (model by C. Mammelis and J. Travlos).

31. Athens, View to East from Hill of Nymphs (photo, Miss Alison Frantz).

32. Temple of Olympian Zeus, Athens (photo, Neue Photographische Gesellschaft, Berlin).

33. S.-E. foot of Acropolis, Athens (photo, German Archaeological Institute, Athens).

34. Acropolis from South-West, Athens (photo, Deutscher Kunstverlag, Berlin).

35. Model of Acropolis of Athens, by G. P. Stevens.

36. Central Doorway of Propylaea, Athens (photo, Miss Alison Frantz).

37. East Front of Propylaea, Athens (photo, Kunstgeschichtl. Seminar, Marburg).

38. Erechtheum, Athens, from roof of Parthenon (photo, Miss Alison Frantz).

39. Gravestones, Athens (photo, Alinari).

xii

40. Grave of Athenians, Marathon (photo, R. E. W.).
41. Aegosthena, East Wall (photo, Miss Alison Frantz).
42. Spring of Peirene, Corinth (photo, R. E. W.).
43. Temple of Apollo, Corinth (photo, Kunstgeschichtl. Seminar, Marburg).
44. Acrocorinthus (photo, Hellenic Society).
45. Temple of Zeus, Nemea (photo, R. E. W.).
46. Grave Circle, Mycenae (photo, Hellenic Society).
47. Treasury of Atreus, Mycenae (photo, Hellenic Society).
48. Cyclopean Masonry, Tiryns (photo, German Archaeological Institute, Athens).
49. Foundations of Tholos, Epidaurus (photo, Hellenic Society).
50. Theatre, Epidaurus (photo, German Archaeological Institute, Athens).
51. Temple of Aphaea, Aegina (photo, Kunstgeschichtl. Seminar, Marburg).
52. Temple of Menelaus, Therapne (photo, Hellenic Society).
53. Arcadian Gate, Messene (photo, German Archaeological Institute).
54. Site of Olympia, from North-West (photo, Alinari).
55. Temple of Zeus, Olympia (photo, Kunstgeschichtl. Seminar, Marburg).
56. Temple of Hera, Olympia (photo, German Archaeological Institute, Athens).
57. (a) Head of Hera (photo, Hellenic Society).
    (b) Head of Hermes (photo, Kunstgeschichtl. Seminar, Marburg).
58. Olympia, Model by H. Schleif.
59. Entrance to Race-course, Olympia (photo, R. E. W.).
60. Bronze head of boxer from Olympia (Hege and Rodenwaldt, *Olympia*, Pl. 93).
61. Relief from Mantineia (photo, German Archaeological Institute, Athens).
62. Heads from Tegea (Dugas, *Sanctuaire d'Aléa Athéna à Tégée*, Pl. XCIX and CII).
63. (a) Valley of River Styx (photo, Hellenic Society).
    (b) Valley of Stymphalus (photo, S. C. Atchley, Esq.).

LIST OF ILLUSTRATIONS WITH SOURCES

64. Theatre and Thersilium, Megalopolis (photo, German Archaeological Institute, Athens).
65. Temple of the Mistress, Lycosura (photo, Kunstgeschichtl. Seminar, Marburg).
66. (a) Artemis, Lycosura (photo, Kunstgeschichtl. Seminar, Marburg).
    (b) Demeter, Lycosura (photo, Kunstgeschichtl. Seminar, Marburg).
67. Temple of Apollo, Bassae (photo, Mr. J. R. T. Pollard).
68. Temple of Apollo, Bassae, interior (photo, Kunstgeschichtl. Seminar, Marburg).
69. Treasury of Minyas, Orchomenus (photo, Hellenic Society).
70. Grave of Thebans, Chaeroneia (photo, German Archaeological Institute, Athens).
71. View Eastward from Delphi (photo, Kunstgeschichtl. Seminar, Marburg).
72. Site of Delphi (photo, German Archaeological Institute, Athens).
73. Marmaria, Delphi (photo, German Archaeological Institute, Athens).
74. Castalia, Delphi (photo, Alinari).
75. Portico of Athenians, Delphi (photo, Hellenic Society).
76. Omphalos, Delphi (photo, R. E. W.).
77. Delphi, Sanctuary of Apollo (model by H. Schleif).
78. Theatre, Delphi (photo, Hellenic Society).
79. Race-course, Delphi (photo, J. van der Woude).
80. Starting-line, Race-course, Delphi (photo, Hellenic Society).
81. Wall, Tithorea (photo, Hellenic Society).
82, 83, 84. Coin Plates (Hellenic Society).
85. (a) and (b) Pediments of Temple of Zeus, Olympia, restored) (*Jahrbuch d. deutsch. arch. Inst.*, 1889, Pl. 8, 9, and 1888, Pl. 5, 6).
    (c) Chest of Cypselus (restored) (*Journal of Hellenic Studies*, XIV, Pl. I).

LIST OF PASSAGES
ILLUSTRATED

	PLATE
I.	2
I. i. § 1	29
I. i. § 1–ii. § 3	10
I. ii. § 1–xxix. § 1	11, 31
I. iii. § 1–xviii. § 1	12
I. iii. § 1–I. xiv. § 6	30
I. xviii. § 6–§ 8	32
I. xx. § 3–xxviii. § 4	14, 34, 35
I. xx. § 3–xxi. § 3	33
I. xxii. § 4–xxiii. § 8	13, 36, 37
I. xxvi. § 5–xxvii. § 3	15, 38
I. xxix. § 2	39
I. xxxii. § 3	40
I. xliv. § 4–5	41
II.	3
II. ii. § 6–iv. § 5	16
II. iii. § 2, 3	42
II. iii. § 6	43
II. iv. § 6–v. § 4	44
II. xv. § 2, 3	45
II. xvi. § 5–§ 7	46, 47
II. xvii	17
II. xxv. § 8	48
II. xxvii.	18
II. xxvii. § 3	49
II. xxvii. § 5	19, 50
II. xxx. § 3	51
III. xi. § 1–xviii. § 5,	Frontispiece
III. xix. § 9	52
IV. xxxi. § 5, xxxiii. § 3	53

	PLATE
V. x. § 1–VI. xxi. § 2	22, 54, 58
	22, 54
V. x. § 2–xii. § 8	20, 55
V. x. § 5–§ 8	85 (a) and (b)
V. xvi. § 1–xx. § 5	21, 56
V. xvii. § 1, § 3	57
V. xvii. § 5–xix. § 10	85 (c)
VI. iv. § 5	60
VI. xx. § 8	59
VI. xx. § 10–§ 14	23 (a)
VII. ix. § 1	61
VIII. xvii. § 6–xviii. § 6	63 (a)
VIII. xxii.	63 (b)
VIII. xxx. § 2–xxxii. § 5	24, 64
VIII. xxxvii. § 1–§ 7	25, 65
VIII. xxxvii. § 3, § 4	66
VIII. xli. § 7–§ 9	23 (b), 67, 68
VIII. xlv. § 4–xlvii. § 3	26
VIII. xlv. § 6–7	62
IX. xxxviii. § 2	69
IX. xl. § 10	70
X. viii. § 6–xxxii. § 1	27, 71, 72
X. viii. § 6	73
X. viii. § 9, § 10	74
X. ix. § 1–xxxii. § 1	28, 77
X. xi. § 6	75
X. xvi. § 3	76
X. xxxii. § 1	78, 79, 80
X. xxxii. § 8–§ 11	81

SELECT BIBLIOGRAPHY

This list may be supplemented by use of the detailed bibliographies in Dinsmoor and Robertson (see " General " section below).

ATHENS.

Judeich, W. : *Topographie von Athen.* Munich, 1931.

Harrison, Jane E. : *Mythology and Monuments of Ancient Athens.* London, 1890.

Hill, Ida T. : *The Ancient City of Athens.* London, 1953.

Pickard-Cambridge, A. W. : *The Theatre of Dionysus in Athens.* Oxford, 1946.

Raubitschek, A. E., and Jeffrey, L. : *Dedications from the Athenian Acropolis.* Cambridge, Mass., 1949.

Stevens, G. P., and Paton, J. M. : *The Erechtheum.* Cambridge, Mass., 1927.

Hesperia, from Vol. II, 1933, onwards, gives reports of the work of the American School in the agora ; note especially VI, 1937, pp. 1 ff., for the west side, and Suppl. IV, 1940, for the Tholos, etc., both by H. A. Thompson ; and Vol. XVII, 1949, pp. 128 ff., for E. Vanderpool on the route of Pausanias. A brief guide (*The Athenian Agora*, Athens, 1954) is now available.

CORINTH.

Corinth : Results of Excavations Conducted by the American School at Athens, 1929–   ; especially Vol. I, Pt. I, 1932, Pt. II, 1941, Pt. III, 1951, and Pt. IV, 1954, which deal with Topography and Architecture.

Ancient Corinth, a Guide to the Excavations (fifth edition). Athens, 1951.

SELECT BIBLIOGRAPHY

MYCENAE.

    Wace, A. J. B.: *Mycenae.* Princeton, 1949. (Further investigations are in progress, and preliminary reports have appeared in the archaeological journals, e.g., *Journal of Hellenic Studies*, LXXI, 1951, pp. 239, 254; LXXII, p. 97; LXXIII, pp. 114, 131.)

ARGOS, HERAEUM.

    Waldstein, C.: *The Argive Heraeum.* Boston, 1902. (See further P. Amandry in *Hesperia*, XXI, 1952, pp. 222 ff.)

EPIDAURUS

    Defrasse, A., and Lechat, H.: *Epidaure.* Paris, 1895.
    P. Kavvadias: *The Shrine of Asklepios at Epidauros.* Athens, 1900.
    Robert, F.: *Epidaure.* 1935.

OLYMPIA.

    Curtius, E., Adler, F., and others: *Olympia : Die Ergebnisse der vom Deutschen Reich veranstalteten Ausgrabungen.* Berlin, 1890–97.
    Gardiner, E. N.: *Olympia, its History and Remains.* Oxford, 1925.
    Rodenwaldt, G., and Hege, W.: *Olympia.* London, 1936.
    For more recent work on the stadium, etc., see reports in *Jahrbuch des deutsch. arch. Inst.*, LII, LIII, LVI, and *Olympische Forschungen*, I, Berlin, 1944.

MEGALOPOLIS

    Gardner, E. A., and others: *Excavations at Megalopolis.* London, 1892.

TEGEA

    Dugas, C., and others: *Le Sanctuaire d'Aléa Athéna à Tégée au IVᵉ siècle.* Paris, 1924.

SELECT BIBLIOGRAPHY

DELPHI

    Homolle, T., and others : *Les Fouilles de Delphes.*
       Paris, 1902– .

    Bourget, E. : *Les Ruines de Delphes.* Paris, 1914.

    Pomtow, H., and Schober, F. : *Delphoi*, in Pauly-
       Wissowa, *Real-Encyclopädie*, Suppl. IV and V,
       1924 and 1931.

    Poulsen, F. : *Delphi.* London, 1920.

    Daux, G. : *Pausanias à Delphes.* Paris, 1936.

GENERAL

    Frazer, J. G. : *Pausanias.* London, 1898.

    Robert, C. : *Pausanias als Schriftsteller.* 1909.

    Lawrence, A. W. : *Classical Sculpture.* London,
       1929.

    Richter, G. M. A. : *Sculpture and Sculptors of the
       Greeks* (second edition). 1950.

    Dinsmoor, W. B. : *The Architecture of Ancient Greece*
       (third edition), London and New York, 1950.

    Robertson, D. S. : *A Handbook of Greek and Roman
       Architecture* (second edition). Cambridge, 1945.

PLATE 1

CENTRAL AND SOUTHERN
GREECE
Scales
0 50 100   200   300
Greek Stadia
0 5 10   20   30   40
English Miles

PLATE 2

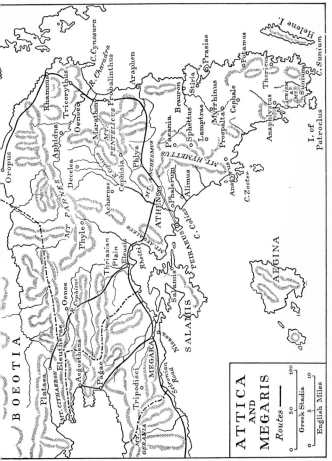

ATTICA
AND
MEGARIS

Routes ——

Greek Stadia
0   50   100

English Miles
0   5   10

PLATE 5

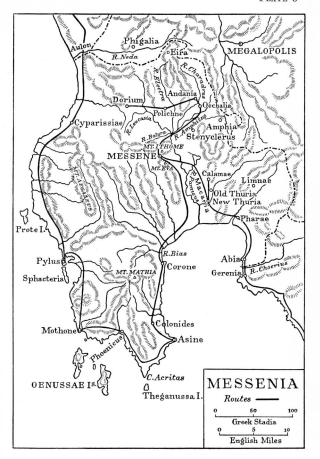

Phigalia
Aulon
R. Neda
Eira
MEGALOPOLIS
R. Electra
R. Charadrus
Dorium
Andania
Oechalia
Polichne
Cyparissiae
R. Leucasia
Amphia
R. Balyra
R. Amphitus
Stenyclerus
MT. ITHOME
MESSENE
MT. EVA
Calamae
Limnae
MT. AEGALEUS
R. Pamisus
R. Macaria
Old Thuria
New Thuria
Prote I.
Pharae
R. Bias
Abia
Pylus
Corone
Gerenia
R. Choerius
Sphacteria
MT. MATHIA
Mothone
Colonides
Asine
Phoenicus
OENUSSAE I^s.
C. Acritas
Theganussa I.

MESSENIA
Routes ———

0	50	100

Greek Stadia

0	5	10

English Miles

PLATE 6

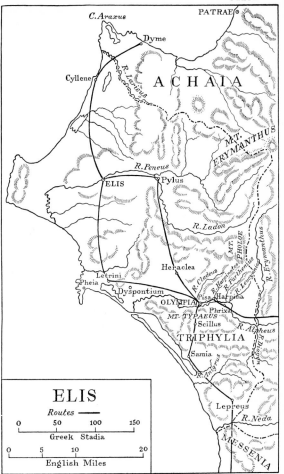

C. Araxus

PATRAE ⊙

Dyme

Cyllene

R. Larissus

A C H A I A

MT. ERYMANTHUS

R. Peneus

ELIS   Pylus

R. Ladon

Heraclea

R. Cladeus
R. Harpinates
R. Parthenius
R. Leucanias
MT. PHOLOE
R. Erymanthus

Letrini
Pheia
Dyspontium

Pisa Harpina

OLYMPIA   Phrixa
MT. TYPAEUS   Scillus   R. Alpheus

TRIPHYLIA

Samia

R. Anigrus

R. Diagon

Lepreus
R. Neda

MESSENIA

ELIS

Routes ——

0	50	100	150

Greek Stadia

0	5	10	20

English Miles

11

PLATE 7

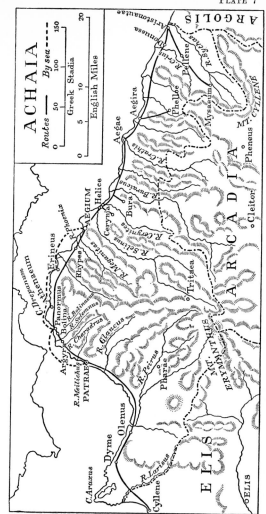

ACHAIA

Routes —— By sea – – –

0   50   100   150
Greek Stadia

0   5   10   20
English Miles

PLATE 8

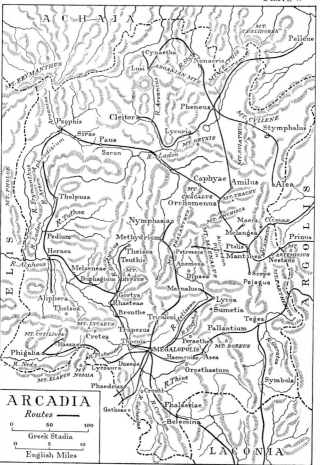

ARCADIA

Routes ———

0   50   100
Greek Stadia

0   10
English Miles

PLATE 9

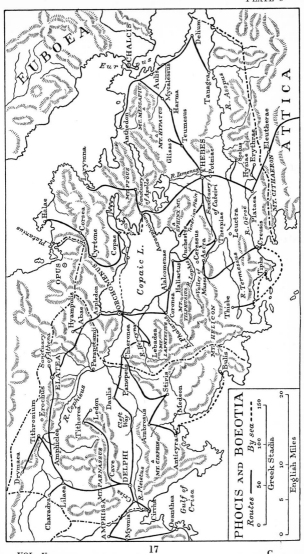

PHOCIS AND BOEOTIA

Routes ---- By sea -·-·-

Greek Stadia.

0   50   100   150

English Miles

0   5   10   20

10. ATHENS AND PEIRAEUS. (I. i. § 1–ii. § 3.)

Peiraeus occupied a rocky peninsula about five miles south-west of Athens. Its three natural harbours (I. i. § 2) were known as Cantharus on the west (Pausanias' "largest harbour"), Zea in the middle, and Munychia (I. i. § 4) on the east. (At least that is the usual view; Professor E. A. Gardner in *Ancient Athens* contends that Pausanias' "three harbours" were all parts of the great harbour, and that his "Munychia" was what is labelled "Zea" in our plan.) The line of the walls, begun in 493 B.C. under Themistocles, can be traced, though most of the existing fragments belong to the rebuilding of 393 B.C. In Pausanias' time the town had long been unwalled.

Around Munychia and Zea are many traces of the docks (I. i. § 2). Inscriptions record that Munychia originally had 82, Zea 196 and Cantharus 94. The ships rested upon long stone bases sloping down to the water, separated from one another by rows of columns which supported the roof.

Munychia and Zea were bases for the war fleet of Athens, Cantharus served for purposes of peaceful trade. On its eastern side are a few remains of a line of porticoes; the "long portico" (I. i. § 3)—a warehouse for grain—stood at the north-east corner, near the maritime market-place; the other market-place probably occupied the depression west of the hill Munychia. The site of the grave of Themistocles is possibly marked by a square rock-cutting (I. i. § 2). Other remains in Peiraeus, scanty at best, throw little light on Pausanias' description, and the sites of other monuments mentioned by him are very uncertain.

Eastward from Peiraeus stretches the bay of Phalerum, with the pre-Themistoclean harbour of Athens (I. i. § 4). It is disputed whether the village Phalerum stood near a hill opposite the middle of the bay, or near the headland which encloses the bay on the east. If the second and more usual view is correct, Cape Colias (I. i. § 5) will not be this headland but one about three miles to the south-east.

Pausanias first approached Athens from Phalerum (I. ii. § 1); afterwards he took the more usual approach—the road from Peiraeus (I. ii. § 2) leading to the Dipylum (see Pl. 12), a more convenient starting-place for his tour of Athens. On his right would be the remains of the two long walls, running parallel at a distance of 550 feet from one another. These walls were first built towards the middle of the fifth century, not under Themistocles as stated in I. ii. § 2. Their line can still be traced; but the position of the third (Phaleric) wall is quite uncertain, since there are no undoubted remains and the position of Phalerum is disputed.

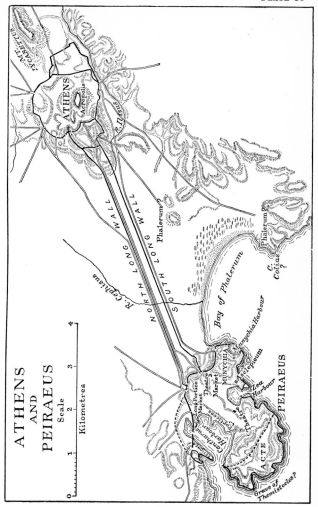

PLATE 10

ATHENS
AND
PEIRAEUS

Scale

Kilometres

0 1 2 3 4

11. ANCIENT ATHENS. (I. ii. § 1–xxix. § 1.)

In describing Athens Pausanias follows a line which is fairly easily traced. Entering no doubt by the Dipylum on the north-west, he reaches the market-place and lingers there for a long time (I. ii. § 4–xviii. § 1) before continuing his route to the Prytaneum on the northern side of the Acropolis. The Prytaneum is his starting-point for two excursions—firstly to the Olympieum and the southern and eastern suburbs (I. xviii. § 2–xix. § 6), and secondly to the Acropolis by way of its eastern end and southern foot (I. xx. § 1–xxviii. § 4). Lastly, he climbs the Hill of Ares (I. xxviii. § 5) and leaves the city, for the Academy, at the point where he entered (I. xxix. § 2). There are only two important digressions (topographical—the historical digressions are, of course, numerous and cumbersome); one contains a list of the works of Hadrian at Athens (I. xviii. § 9), the other an account of the Athenian lawcourts.

Immediately after entering the Dipylum or Double Gate, Pausanias would find the Pompeium, the "building for the preparation of processions " (I. ii. § 4) on his right. It was a Hadrianic restoration of a fourth-century building destroyed, like many others, by Sulla; rectangular and divided by two rows of columns; substantial foundations still survive. Near by on the south-west was the Sacred Gate, with the Sacred Road which Pausanias traversed at a later stage of his wanderings (I. xxxvi. § 3). From the Dipylum a street called the "Dromus " led south-eastwards to the market-place; its course can be traced, thanks to the survival of the foundations and steps (identified by an inscription) of Eubulides' offering (I. ii. § 5), about 150 m. south-east of the Dipylum.

(For the Agora see Pl. 12.)

Pausanias now skirts the northern foot of the Acropolis. The enclosure of Aglaurus, Cecrops' daughter, who threw herself down at this point (I. xviii. § 2), was probably immediately under the wall, a little to the west of the Erechtheum; here, below a section of the wall into which architectural fragments are built, is a wide grotto (56 in Pl. 14) with votive niches possibly connected with the cult. A little further east—the exact site is uncertain—was the Prytaneum (I. xviii. § 3), the Town-Hall of Athens; here was the common hearth of the city where a perpetual fire burned and Hestia was worshipped; and here too foreign ambassadors and citizens distinguished for public services were frugally entertained.

I. xviii. § 4–xix. § 6 describes the south-eastern part of the city and suburbs. The bed of the river Ilisus would naturally be

thought of as " the lower part of the city " (I. xviii. § 4) by one coming down from the slopes of the Acropolis.

The great temple of Olympian Zeus (I. xviii. § 6–§ 8) (see Pl. 32) dominated this quarter of the city; as indeed it still does though only fifteen columns still stand, while another lies prostrate but almost entire. Originally the colonnade was double along the sides and triple at the ends, with twenty columns by eight in the outer row (counting the corner columns twice, as always). The temple measured 135 feet by 354 feet; its columns are 57 feet high and of grand Corinthian style. Hadrian's work was merely to put the finishing touches upon a scheme which proceeded spasmodically for many centuries under the auspices of several famous rulers. The Peisistratid family planned the temple in the sixth century B.C.—as a Doric building, however; the Corinthian order had not yet been invented—and the work was carried forward under Antiochus Epiphanes in the second century B.C. The buttressed enclosing wall (668 m. long—roughly Pausanias' four stades) is probably Hadrianic.

Pausanias pauses here for a moment to make a brief list of several buildings which can be conveniently grouped together although they do not follow one another topographically. The first of the two groups of a hundred pillars (I. xviii. § 9) probably belonged to the large square building east of the portico of Attalus and north of the Roman market-place.

Pausanias next appears to emerge into the suburbs. The Gardens (I. xix. § 2) were perhaps immediately outside the walls south of the Olympieum. Cynosarges too (I. xix. § 3), formerly assumed to have been out east, is now placed with better reason in the southern suburbs, though whether certain alleged remains excavated by the British School at Athens in 1896 really belong to it is very doubtful. Like the Lyceum in the eastern suburbs, to which Pausanias next proceeds (I. xix. § 3), and the Academy, three-quarters of a mile north-west from the Dipylum, it was an extensive precinct where a hero (in this case Heracles) was worshipped; with a gymnasium attached, where a school of philosophy arose; here the Cynics gathered, as the Peripatetics at the Lyceum and the followers of Plato at the Academy.

The district Agrae (I. xix. § 6) lay along the left bank of the Ilisus, in the neighbourhood of the stadium (I. xix. § 6). The form of the latter is accurately described by Pausanias and is characteristic of the Greek stadium. It should be remembered that the Greeks raced up and down a straight course, not round a circular track, as do modern runners. The stadium was normally a rectangle about 220 yards long, enclosed along the sides and at one end (occasionally both) by an embankment for the spectators. Usually advantage was taken as far as

21

possible of a natural depression in the ground. At Athens, little artificial embanking was needed except towards the south-east. Originally constructed in the fourth century B.C., the Athenian stadium was provided with marble seats, accommodating 50,000 spectators, by Herodes Atticus, though he was very far from using up the Pentelic quarries in the process.

This point is the limit of Pausanias' excursion to the south-east, and he now makes a fresh start from the Prytaneum (I. xx. § 1). Remains of several of the " shrines," actually monuments of choregic victories, mark the line of the road called Tripods, and one—the monument erected by Lysicrates in 335–4 B.C.—stands complete, except for the tripod which once surmounted the floral ornament upon its roof. It is a small round Corinthian temple of Pentelic marble, 6 m. high and 2 m. in diameter, with the spaces between its columns filled by marble slabs, upon a quadrangular base 4 m. high.

The street of Tripods brought Pausanias to the theatre (the discovery of the base of a choregic monument near the theatre proves that the street was prolonged so far), and so he continued along the southern foot of the Acropolis to its western end (for the Acropolis and the buildings to the south see Pls. 13, 14, 15).

Leaving at the same point he naturally crossed over to the Areopagus, the Hill of Ares, a rock rising to 377 feet, joined to the Acropolis by a saddle (I. xxviii. § 5–xxix. § 1). There are no identifiable remains here, merely numerous rock-cuttings. The sanctuary of the August Goddesses was probably on the north-eastern side, and the court may have sat near this point. The mention of this famous court induces Pausanias to digress for the same purpose as at I. xviii. 9—to list together a group of similar places.

Pausanius says nothing of the city-wall of Athens; this in spite of repeated reconstruction still followed in most of its course the line which it took under Themistocles' direction in the fifth century B.C.; but on the east it had been extended considerably in the reign of Hadrian. This newly-formed quarter of the city apparently did not interest Pausanias.

A conspicuous ancient monument which he might have been expected to notice is the Pnyx, the meeting-place of the Athenian general assembly, on the slope of a hill west of the Areopagus and the Acropolis. It consisted of a large semicircular terrace supported by a massive retaining wall; upon this the audience stood and the orators faced them upon a rock-hewn platform projecting from a scarp cut vertically in the rock. For the history of the Pnyx see *Hesperia*, I, pp. 90 ff.

(For graves outside city see Pl. 39.)

Pausanias seems to regard the name " Cerameicus " (I. iii. § 1) as synonymous with " Agora." In earlier authors the word when used alone generally means the " Outer " Cerameicus—the district outside the city-walls on the north-west—the Agora being part of the " Inner " Cerameicus.

The American excavation of the area is now almost complete. Many monuments have been identified with certainty or great probability, and the route of Pausanias is mainly clear. He entered at the north-west, and first examined the west side. Here stood many of the older shrines and public buildings, dating back to the fifth and fourth centuries, when they replaced the still older monuments of the archaic agora, destroyed by the Persians. The portico of Zeus, the temple of Apollo, and the Metroon, Council-House and Tholos are described in the notes on Pl. 30.

From the Tholos, Pausanias appears to turn back northward along the eastern side of the same street. The long base surrounded by a fence is so very appropriate to the *eponymoi* that we must assume he is making a slight error when he says that they stand " farther up "; he is in fact descending again (I. v. § 1). A series of statues now leads him on to the shrine of Ares (I. viii. § 4), whose temple almost certainly stood on a foundation discovered near the middle of the agora. Clear architectural evidence shows that it was transferred, in Augustan times, from an unknown site elsewhere. Its original date was shortly after the middle of the fifth century, and in design and style it was very like the temple of Hephaestus above. At about the same time as the removal, the Odeum (I. viii. § 6) was built, and the original open character of the square was thus radically changed. The Odeum was a large theatre, with an external colonnaded gallery. The mysterious figures of giants, known long before the recent excavations, are now shown to have belonged to an elaborate façade given to the building when it was reconstructed in Pausanias' own time. The statues of Harmodius and Aristogiton (I. viii. § 5) probably stood near the processional " Panathenaic Street " in front of the Odeum; a fragment of an inscribed base has been found.

The fact that Pausanias places Enneacrunos (I. xiv. § 1, after further long historical digressions) at this point, while others place it to the south-east of the city, has given rise to much dispute. A fountain-house has now been found to the south-east of the agora

("S.E. Fountain") in a position which suits Pausanias well enough. Though difficulties remain, one can now feel fairly sure that Pausanias saw here a fountain which he at least took to be Enneacrunos. Perhaps some duplication of the name explains the discrepancy.

Pausanias continues along the Panathenaic Way until he reaches the Eleusinium (I. xiv. § 3), whose site, long disputed, has now been fixed, by a wealth of epigraphical evidence and minor finds, to the south-east of the agora (off this plan) below the north-west slope of the Acropolis. Unfortunately, it passes out of the area of excavation, and we cannot say just what monuments it contained. Presumably Pausanias' two temples (I. xiv. § 1) were attached to it; the foundations of one temple have been found.

Next Pausanias visits the Market Hill (Kolonos Agoraios) before making a new approach to the agora from the north and finally leaving it in a south-easterly direction. On top of the hill is the temple of Hephaestus ("Theseum"; I. xiv. § 6; see Pl. 30); on its north slope are the remains of a small building, partly cut off by the railway, which was probably the temple of Heavenly Aphrodite (I. xiv. § 7). The Painted Portico (I. xv), probably built about 460 B.C. and later used by Zeno and the "Stoics," must have been on the north side, beyond the region of excavation; but fragments which are thought to belong to it have been found, and show traces of iron pins by which the boards on which the pictures were painted were attached to the walls. The altar of Mercy (I. xvii. § 1) may have been a name given in later times to the altar of the Twelve Gods, a famous place of asylum; the shrine of the Twelve has been found on the northern edge of the excavation.

The gymnasium of Ptolemy (Philadelphus, 285–246 B.C., or Philometor, 181–145 B.C.; I. xvii. § 2) must have been to the east of the agora; the sanctuary of Theseus (I. xvii. 2–6) and the sanctuary of the Dioscuri (I. xviii. § 1) further south—we know that the last was close under the Acropolis.

Pausanias was not interested in commercial buildings. He says nothing of the vast stoas which transformed the Hellenistic agora—the great market-hall on the east donated by Attalus II of Pergamum (159–138 B.C.) and the contemporary group of colonnades which seem to have formed a separate market on the south; nor of the "Roman Market," the large colonnaded court, of Augustan date, some distance east of the agora. Nor does he mention the library dedicated by the philosopher Pantaenus to Athena and Trajan.

13. Propylaea, Athens (restored). (I. xxii. § 4–xxiii. § 8.)

The Propylaea (I. xxii. § 4) consist of an elaboration of a simple form of gateway common in ancient Greece—a columnar porch on either side of the gateway proper. The earlier Propylaea (built early in the fifth century) were of this simple type; their plan can be traced, and is shown by a dotted line in the illustration (Old Propylaea).

The later entrance was part of the great building schemes carried out under Pericles, and built between 436 and 432 B.C. Pentelic marble is the material used. Doric porches nearly sixty feet wide, each with six columns, face east (Pl. 37) and west on either side of a great central gateway; through this the road up to the Acropolis passes, and on either side of it are two smaller doorways for foot-passengers. The outer porch, the western, is nearly three times as deep as the eastern, and at a lower level; five steps lead up from it to the doorways; and within it the road-way is flanked on either side by three Ionic columns, which helped to carry the marble ceiling (painted blue with golden stars) so much admired by Pausanias (I. xxii. § 4).

The building with pictures (I. xxii. § 6), sometimes called the Pinakotheke (Pl. 36), was a smallish wing on the north-west, with a porch, facing south, of three Doric columns. The walls show no trace of frescoes—probably the pictures described by Pausanias were painted on detachable boards or set up on easels. Facing this on the south is another wing which has a similar façade but is much less deep and is open on the west to give free access to the bastion on which the temple of Victory stands. The plan of the Propylaea was much curtailed in execution, to save expense and to avoid encroaching on earlier shrines and incurring the wrath of the deities who were to be its neighbours. Otherwise the south-western wing would have been as large as the north-western, though no doubt still open on the west; and extensive wings in the form of porticoes facing eastward would have been built on the east, in the position shown by dotted lines in the plan (North-East Hall and South-East Hall). Otherwise the south-western wing would have been as large as the north-western; and large halls, probably to serve as store-rooms, would have been built on the east, in the position shown by the dotted lines. More recent investigation shows that it is unlikely that the eastern front of these two east wings, and the western front of the south-west wing, were in the form of colonnades as indicated in our plan.

Pausanias ignored the chariot-group erected to honour Augustus' great minister Agrippa, which stood upon a marble pedestal still conspicuous on the left of the approach to the Propylaea.

Instead, he turned to the lofty bastion on the right, where stands the temple of Wingless Victory, who was really Athena in the character of Victory (II. xxii. § 4). This is a simple little temple with a prostyle porch of four monolithic Ionic columns at each end; 5·38 m. by 8·27 m.; built a few years later than the Propylaea. Pausanias mentions the ancient wooden image incidentally in V. xxvi. § 6. The bastion upon which the temple stands dominates the approach to the Acropolis on the right. Its parapet was adorned on the outer side (where they would be difficult to see and apparently did not attract Pausanias' attention) with beautiful figures of Victory in relief. Aegeus (I. xxii. § 4) had his shrine probably at the foot of the bastion to the right. Pausanias does not mention the shrine of Hecate here; but in II. xxx. § 2 he speaks of a statue of Hecate by Alcamenes near the temple of Wingless Victory. The shrine probably abutted the south wing of the Propylaea.

A number of interesting statues stood near by. The " sons of Xenophon " (I. xxii. § 4) (actually Xenophon was merely one of several dedicators who put up the statues c. 450 B.C., as inscriptions show) stood upon two little projecting platforms in which the steps in front of the wings of the Propylaea terminate. Many others no doubt stood in front of the western porch and lining the road through the Propylaea. A fragment of the base of Calamis' Aphrodite (I. xxiii. § 2) turned up in the agora excavations some distance to the north-west. The base of the Diitrephes (I. xxiii. § 3), naming Cresilas as the sculptor, was found west of the Parthenon (not *in situ*).

Athena in the character of Health (I. xxiii. § 4) had her precinct at the south-eastern corner of the Propylaea; its extent is uncertain; abutting the corner column of the eastern porch is the semicircular base of the statue seen by Pausanias (it is just visible in Pl. 37, at the foot of the furthest column). The inscription says that the Athenians dedicated it to Health Athena, and Pyrrhus, an Athenian, made it (possibly he did so after the great plague of 429 B.C.). In front of it is the foundation of an altar which was erected later, and a little to the east is a platform with the remains of an older altar.

To enter the sanctuary of Brauronian Artemis (I. xxiii. § 8) from this point, Pausanias would ascend a stairway on his right leading to a higher terrace bounded on this side by a rock-cutting which formerly carried a wall.

Finally, near this point is one of the most important extant sections of the old " Pelasgian " wall (I. xxviii. § 3) (see Pl. 14). It abuts the south-west wing of the Propylaea, the corner of which is actually bevelled to accommodate it. It was of great thickness, as the thick black lines in the plan indicate, and of " Cyclopean " construction (see Pl. 48).

30

PLATE 13

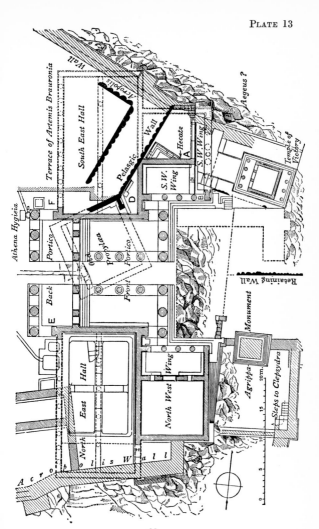

31

14. ACROPOLIS OF ATHENS (I. xx. § 3–xxviii. § 4).

The " road called Tripods " (I. xx. § 1) led Pausanias round the eastern end of the Acropolis to its southern slopes and to the sanctuary of Dionysus (I. xx. § 3) (see Pl. 33). A small piece of the foundations of the older of Pausanias' "two temples" abuts the stage buildings. Remains of the later, which was built at the end of the fifth century and contained Alcamenes' statue, stand a little farther south (44 in plan). The theatre was in origin a mere appendage of the sanctuary, and the dramatic performances a part of the worship of Dionysus.

Foundations of a square building with rows of interior columns (like those of the *telesterion* at Eleusis) have been found, encroaching on the theatre on the east. This was an Odeum built in 442 B.C. under Pericles' direction, and used for musical contests, rehearsals of plays, and more general purposes. Probably it is the " structure which is said to be a copy of Xerxes' tent "; though it is difficult to see from the plan in what the resemblance lay— possibly it was in the form of the roof (I. xx. § 4).

The present remains of the theatre (I. xxi. § 1) (42 in plan) belong to the building as it was seen by Pausanias with one important exception—the stage-front (for a general account of the Greek theatre see Pl. 19, the theatre at Epidaurus). The auditorium in its permanent stone form, 90 m. deep, with rows of limestone benches divided by two horizontal passages, was built in the fourth century B.C. The orchestra (diameter about 18 m.), originally a circle of mere hardened earth, had been richly paved in the first century A.D. The sculptured stage-front dedicated by Phaedrus was built at an uncertain date after Pausanias' time; its mutilated state is due to a still later reconstruction, when the figures were plastered over with cement. The theatre held up to 17,000 spectators.

(For the cave above the theatre—45 in plan—mentioned in I. xxi. § 3 see Pl. 33.)

The sanctuary of Asclepius (I. xxi. § 4) extends westward from the theatre. It has features which recall the great sanctuary of the god at Epidaurus (Pl. 18), especially a long portico (47) which was used for dream oracles and cures. In front of this stood the small temple, to the west the priests' quarters; and in the rock behind is a grotto (48) containing the spring seen by Pausanias.

Pausanias does not mention the great portico (51), stretching westward from the theatre to the Odeum, which was associated with the name of Eumenes II of Pergamum (second century B.C.). The Odeum (52) (see Pl. 34) with which Herodes Atticus commemorated his wife who died in 160 A.D. was apparently not yet

in existence when Pausanias toured Athens, but it was built in time to receive passing mention in VII. xx. § 6. It is a theatre of Roman type—the auditorium is a mere semicircle, and the stage buildings are not detached from it.

The Acropolis itself, helped out by artificial terracing on the south, forms a plateau about 900 feet east to west by 500 feet north to south. The main approach has always been on the west (see I. xxii. § 4), where the slope is gentlest, but there are narrow stairways on the north (30, 38). Pausanias has something to say of the walls (I. xxii. § 4, xxviii. § 3). The old Pelasgian fortification, built of Cyclopean masonry (see Pl. 48), a relic of the time when the Acropolis was a Mycenean fortress, cannot have been so conspicuous as he seems to imply. It was destroyed at the fall of the Peisistratids or after the Persian invasion. Sections of it are still extant on the southern side, near the south wing of the Propylaea, at the south-west corner of the Parthenon, and near the modern museum at the extreme east (at points marked 12). On the north it is quite obliterated by the fifth-century wall which follows the same course; on the south the long straight stretches built by Cimon to form a retaining wall for the terracing extend farther outward. A medieval facing hides most of the large square blocks of the fifth-century masonry. (For the Propylaea, 6, see Pl. 13.)

The present gateway to the Acropolis, the Beulé gate (1), named after the man who investigated it in 1853, was not constructed until after Pausanias' time.

Brauronian Artemis (I. xxiii. § 7) possessed a spacious precinct (13) on a terrace to the right inside the Propylaea, enclosed on the north by a rock-cutting, on the west by the Pelasgian wall, on the south by the Acropolis wall, and on the east by a still higher terrace. There seems to have been no temple, but on east and south were porticoes.

On his way from the Propylaea to the Parthenon, Pausanias comments, as usual, only on a judicious selection of the monuments. Fragments of several of the bases have been found (see A. Raubitschek, *Dedications from the Athenian Acropolis*, p. 459), including the wooden horse (I. xxiii. § 8), Epicharinus (I. xxiii. § 9), and Conon and Timotheus (I. xxiv. § 3). An extant group may be the Procne and Itys, dedicated, and probably made, by Alcamenes (I. xxiv. § 3). A fixed point is provided by an inscription cut in the rock (24) which marks the place of the image of Earth (I. xxiv. § 3). The shrine of Ergane probably stood near, but the defective state of the text leaves it uncertain whether the temple mentioned belonged to this precinct.

Pausanias entered the Parthenon from the east. The temple is a great Doric building, with Ionic columns in the western

33

chamber; of Pentelic marble; 30·86 m. by 69·51 m.; with eight columns by seventeen. It was built between the years 447 B.C. and 432 B.C. Pausanias ignores it architecturally, though he could appreciate fine architecture (as at Bassae and Tegea) and concentrates on the great cult statue which stood upon a base (22) in the eastern chamber surrounded on three sides by a narrow colonnade (I. xxiv. § 5–7).

Ignoring the little round temple of Rome and Augustus (26) east of the Parthenon, Pausanias continued to the south-east corner of the Acropolis, where the Acropolis Museum (20) is now unobtrusively placed. The group mentioned in I. xxv. § 2, dedicated by Attalus I towards 200 B.C., stood just above the theatre, into which one of the figures once fell. Thence Pausanias crossed to the eastern end of the north side, where, at the foot of the rock, an archaic figure has been found which may be Endoeus' Athena (I. xxvi. § 4).

(For the Erechtheum, 31, see Pl. 15.)

The last series of monuments described (I. xxvii. § 4–I. xxviii. § 2) probably stood along an ancient road, cut in the rock, which led from the direction of the Erechtheum to the north-east corner of the Propylaea. South of this road, about thirty yards east of the Propylaea, are two quadrangular spaces, partly cut in the rock. The northern of these (40) is probably the place of the bronze Athena of Pheidias (I. xxviii. § 2). A little to the south of it, and not far north of the processional way, is the other (41), on which probably stood (in Pausanias' time, if not in Herodotus') the bronze chariot dedicated after a victory over the Boeotians and Chalcidians in 507 B.C. (I. xxviii. § 2; Herodotus V. 77).

A rock-cut stair leads down from the north-west corner of the Propylaea to Clepsydra (53), which is the fountain seen by Pausanias (I. xxviii. § 4); it lies in a deep rectangular basin, originally accessible by stairs; after serious collapses of the roof in Roman times, the water was drawn from above by a shaft, built over by a little chapel.

A series of caves cutting into the Acropolis rock extend eastward from Clepsydra (for that of Aglaurus see Pl. 11). One is immediately above the fountain but difficult of access and apparently containing no cult. Pausanias' sanctuary of Apollo was in a cave a little to the east, on the spot marked 54 in the plan, "beneath the Long Rocks," as it was called. In it are votive niches and other traces. To the east are other caves, unidentified. The site of the shrine of Pan (I. xxviii. § 4) is uncertain.

(See further Pls. 34, 35.)

15. ERECHTHEUM, ATHENS (restored). (I. xxvi. § 5–xxvii. § 3.)

The Erechtheum was a building of unique and complicated plan. The main part of the building was an Ionic temple, divided into an eastern and a western section; but there was also a large porch at the western end of the north side, and a small one at the same end of the south. The floor levels too were complicated—the eastern section and the south porch were ten feet higher than the rest of the building. The design was complicated and distorted to accommodate the various cult spots on and around the site. The temple was built in the last two decades of the fifth century B.C.; but in the fourth century and again in Roman times it was much damaged and repaired.

It is very difficult to bring Pausanias' account into relation with the remains, since it is impossible to recognise in his description any of the features which are now conspicuous—he says nothing, for instance, of the six female figures which supported the roof of the south porch; and though the exterior is fairly well preserved, the interior arrangement, about which Pausanias says a good deal, is almost obliterated.

American archaeologists have made a very thorough investigation of the building, and it is perhaps safest to adopt their conclusions. If the old temple (see Pl. 38) no longer existed, Pausanias entered by the great north porch of the Erechtheum and first described the western section. On architectural evidence this is thought to have been divided by a north–south wall into two parts, the eastern of which was again divided into a northern and a southern room (A, B). When Pausanias says that the building is double (I. xxvi. § 5) he refers not to the division of the whole Erechtheum, but more probably to the main division of the western half, which he is describing when he uses the words; the suggestion that he is distinguishing the crypts from the ground floor is hardly likely.

How the altar of Poseidon-Erechtheus, the salt spring and the other sacred spots (I. xxvi. § 5) were distributed in these western rooms is problematical; later cisterns have largely obliterated the evidence. In a crypt under the north porch, with holes in floor and ceiling above, are marks in the rock which one is tempted to attribute to Poseidon's trident; but it is also possible that the altar of Zeus the Most High, " before the (northern) entrance," stood here, and that the spot was struck by a thunderbolt.

There is less doubt about the eastern half of the Erechtheum, which was very probably the shrine of Athena Polias, containing the ancient image of the goddess and Callimachus' golden lamp (I. xxvi. § 6–xxvii. § 2). There is no evidence for direct connection with the western part and Pausanias probably entered afresh from the east.

The shrine of Pandrosus (I. xxvii. § 2) extended westward from the Erechtheum. The sacred olive (I. xxvii. § 2) probably grew towards the eastern end of it; where the temple was is quite uncertain. A recently discovered precinct of Eros and Aphrodite, at the foot of the Acropolis a little to the east of the Erechtheum, is shown by its investigator to be the shrine of Aphrodite to which the maidens mentioned in I. xxvii. § 3 descended (see *Hesperia*, I. p. 31); there must have been two shrines of " Aphrodite in the Gardens" at Athens (cf. I. xix. § 2). Foundations to the north-west of the Erechtheum (36 in Pl. 14) have been associated with the house of the maidens; an underground stair actually leads from this point to the foot of the Acropolis rock, though not directly to the shrine of Aphrodite, which is farther east. The *arrhephoroi* may possibly be represented in the Caryatids who support the south porch of the Erechtheum. Special adjustments were made in the structure of the main building at its south-west corner to accommodate a shrine of Cecrops.

(See also Pl. 38.)

16. Corinth, Central Area. (II. ii. § 6–iv. § 5.)

Pausanias approaches Corinth from the east, from one of the harbours, Cenchreae. The city lay two miles inland from the coast of the gulf and the other harbour Lechaeum (II. ii. § 3), comprising an extensive area on broad terraces at the northern foot of the Acrocorinthus.

The American excavations of central Corinth are now almost complete, and the plan can be reconstructed. Unfortunately, Pausanias' highly selective method and the vagueness of his topography make it difficult to trace his route and to identify monuments. He draws a distinction between what is ancient and what belongs to the new city (II. ii. § 6); there was a great break in the history of Corinth between its sack by Mummius in 146 B.C. and its refounding by Julius Caesar. New Corinth took shape in the two centuries after 44 B.C. Some ancient monuments were obliterated, some survived or rose again in a new form.

The agora extended south and west from the spring of Peirene, and south of the low hill on which the temple of Apollo stands. In pre-Roman times it was simpler and more open, though its southern limit was defined, from the fourth century B.C., by the huge South Stoa, with shops and taverns behind. In the Roman reconstruction it was almost surrounded with colonnades, shops and basilicas; and by the row of "Central Shops" it was organized into two distinct terraces, a lower on the north and a higher on the south. A "Senate-House" and various public offices were built into the rear of the restored South Stoa. Characteristically, Pausanias says nothing of all this, but singles out for mention the shrines and the ancient fountains.

The site of the shrine of Artemis (II. ii. § 6) is quite uncertain; the images of Dionysus have very tentatively been placed in the apsidal building at the west end of the Central Shops. Pausanias next appears to turn to the shrines which stood on a terrace on the west side, and these have been identified with greater probability. An inscription shows that temple F was dedicated to Venus, but it was probably Pausanias' temple of Fortune (II. ii. § 8), Aphrodite being regarded as the Tyche of the city. G will then be the Pantheon. H and J were built in the reign of Commodus, after Pausanias, and are conjecturally assigned to Poseidon and Heracles; but under J are remains of Pausanias' fountain of Poseidon. The "Babbius Monument" was an elaborate little

circular shrine with Corinthian columns. What stood in it one cannot say—the Aphrodite would be appropriate. D was probably the temple of Hermes, K is uncertain. The large peripteral temple E, to the west, is problematical too; like Pausanias' temple of Octavia (II. iii. § 1) it is " above the agora," but there is evidence that its date is too late for this identification. The Capitolium has been suggested, but only by straining the sense of Pausanias' words can one say that the temple is " above the theatre " (II. iv. § 5).

The gateway (II. iii. § 2) which gave access to the colonnaded street leading to Lechaeum was a triumphal arch, repeatedly remodelled. Pausanias would find the famous fountain of Peirene on his right (Pl. 42). Its basic elements, the long reservoirs driven into the rock to the south, and the draw-basins in front of them, go back to archaic times. In the Roman city it was given an increasingly elaborate façade and forecourt; the great domed apses were added by Herodes Atticus in Pausanias' time The colonnaded court adjoining on the north is the enclosure of Apollo (II. iii. § 3), and still farther north are possible remains of the baths of Eurycles (II. iii. § 5).

The road to Sicyon (II. iii. § 6) leaves the agora at the north-west. There is nothing in Pausanias which seems to correspond to temple C in its colonnaded court; it may be the temple of Hera Acraea, which was probably near Glauce. To the temple of Apollo (II. iii. § 6), " on the right of the road," are usually assigned the impressive archaic columns which still stand on the hill (Pl. 43). The Well of Glauce is another archaic rock-cut fountain, with cisterns and draw-basins hewn out of a cubical mass, and a pillared façade; it retained much more of its primitive character than Peirene. To the north-west of the fountain was the Odeum, a theatre of Roman type built towards the end of the first century A.D., with seats supported on concrete vaults; a little farther to the north was the great theatre itself (II. iv. § 5). The two buildings were joined by a colonnaded court so as to form a single complex; only the south-eastern part can be seen in the plan.

Still further in this direction, on the northern edge of the city, Pausanias saw the spring of Lerna and the shrine of Asclepius (II. iv. § 5). These have been excavated; it appears that the fourth-century temple of Asclepius, the successor of a simpler shrine possibly dedicated to Apollo, stood in a colonnaded court-yard. The rock-cut cisterns of Lerna are on the south side of an adjoining court in a hollow to the west. The shrine was closely associated with the spring, and both, probably, with the gymnasium (II. iv. § 5), whose site may be marked by a few column bases to the south.

(For the Acrocorinthus see Pl. 44.)

17. ARGIVE HERAEUM (restored). (II. xvii.)

The Heraeum, the national sanctuary of the Argives, lay nearly three miles south of Mycenae (Pausanias considerably under-estimated the distance, which is about 25 stades instead of his 15 (II. xvii. § 1)), upon a rocky terraced hill facing south-east towards Argos, at the foot of Mount Euboea, which rises behind the site to a height of 1744 feet. Acraea is probably a mountain east of Euboea, and Prosymna the low ground below the site (II. xvii. § 2).

On either side is the bed of a stream; the Water of Freedom (II. xvii. § 1) probably flowed along that which skirts the sanctuary on the west, but the Asterion, sometimes identified with the small stream immediately to the east, is more likely to be a river some distance away on that side.

Pausanias gives most of his attention to the later temple of Hera built to the plans of the architect Eupolemus (II. xvii. § 3–§ 6) (V in the plan), a Doric structure of limestone with details in marble, with two rows of inner columns dividing the cella. A great monumental stairway led to the terrace upon which it stood—the second of three terraces into which the hillside is divided. Only the foundations of the temple (39·6 m. by 20 m.) remain in place, and nothing is left of Polycleitus' famous statue of Hera or even its base, but many beautiful fragments survive of the sculptures " carved above the pillars " (II. xvii. § 3), *i.e.* in the metopes and gables.

The older temple (II. xvii. § 7) (I in the plan) occupied the third and highest terrace, which was supported by a wall of huge blocks of Cyclopean masonry (see Pl. 48). All that remains of it is a fragment of the southern side, and a small section of a pave-ment of irregular slabs which no doubt once surrounded the building. Fire destroyed this temple in 423 B.C.—Pausanias probably saw little more of it than is visible now—and its successor was built a few years later.

It is to Pausanias' credit as an archaeologist that he mentions the scanty remains. It is characteristic too of his interest in things religious and antique rather than secular and more recent that while he does so he ignores the other buildings of the sanctuary. Yet these were numerous and varied, as at other great national shrines. The deficiency of his account makes it difficult to name the purpose of the buildings excavated. At Olympia, on the other

hand, he mentions most of the corresponding buildings, though even there only incidentally in connection with altars and statues.

The large hall to the east of the temple, with rows of interior columns (IV in the plan), is rather like the Telesterium or hall of mysteries at Eleusis, and possibly served the same purpose. Building VII was possibly a kind of Prytaneum, containing dining-halls, and the great colonnaded court X may have been a gymnasium or a palaestra—the shrine would no doubt have facilities for athletic practice. The complex building IX was certainly a bath of Roman type and date, and contained an atrium and rooms heated by hypocausts.

PLATE 17

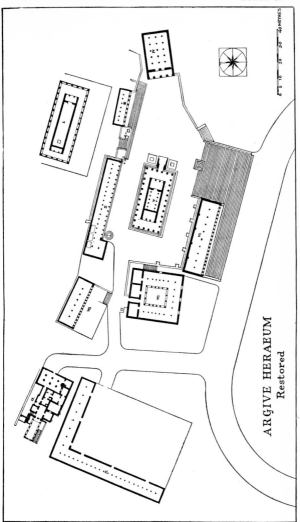

ARGIVE HERAEUM
Restored

18. Sanctuary of Asclepius, Epidaurus. (II. xxvii.)

This sanctuary lies about six miles south-west of the ancient town of Epidaurus, in an open valley. It must have included a considerable area, for the theatre, which is a quarter of a mile to the south-east of the temple, was still "within the sanctuary" (ἱερόν) (II. xxvii. § 5); not, however, within the immediate "enclosure" (περίβολος) of the temple.

Pausanias began his tour at the temple of Asclepius (II. xxvii. § 2), a smallish Doric building, of the early fourth century B.C. Only the foundations and sculptural fragments survive. "The place where the suppliants of the god sleep" (II. xxvii. § 2), expecting him to reveal to them a cure, was a long Ionic portico north of the temple, with two storeys in the western part, the upper on a level with the single storey of the eastern. The Tholos (II. xxvii. § 3) is still "worth seeing" for its remarkable plan (Pl. 49) and the fineness of its workmanship—it was built in the fourth century B.C.

Like other great sanctuaries, Epidaurus possessed many subsidiary shrines, besides that of the god held in chief honour. South-east of the temple is a small Doric building dedicated to Artemis (II. xxvii. § 5). The "small cella" may be the temple of Themis (II. xxvii. § 5), and the building numbered 2 the "sanctuary of the gods called Bountiful" (II. xxvii. § 6).

Pausanias says that the form of the race-course was typical (II. xxvii. § 5). (For the Greek stadium in general, see Pl. 11, Ancient Athens.) At Epidaurus, as elsewhere, some advantage was gained from a natural depression. The course was first laid out in the fifth century B.C., and stone seats were added later. The end was square, not round as at Athens and Delphi. Round the course ran a stone gutter to supply drinking-water, and at either end was a starting-line (see Pl. 81).

The baths of Antoninus (II. xxvii. § 6) are the complicated structure north of the temple. South-east of the temple of Artemis is a square court thought to be the portico of Cotys (II. xxvii. § 6) and probably a wrestling-ground. Further south is a gymnasium in the court of which an Odeum was later built.

So Epidaurus possessed almost as great a variety of buildings as Olympia. Besides the shrines, there were facilities for both dramatic and athletic shows. Accommodation too was provided for priests and for visitors; the latter were housed in the "Catagogium," a large building with four square courts, not mentioned by Pausanias (see Pl. 50). The peculiar nature of the buildings upon the site was determined by the character of the sanctuary as a popular resort for miraculous cures and dream oracles.

48

PLATE 18

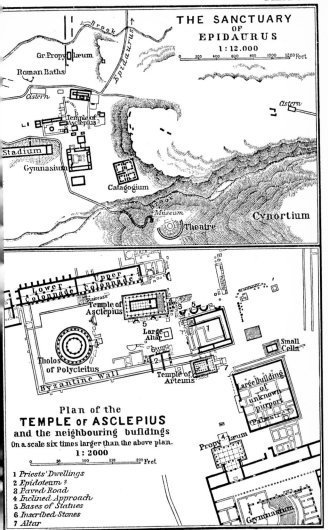

THE SANCTUARY
OF
EPIDAURUS
1 : 12.000

Brook

Epidaurus

Gr. Propylæum

Roman Baths

Cistern

Temple of Asclepius

Cistern

Stadium

Gymnasium

Catagogium

Cynortium

Museum

Theatre

Upper Colonnade

Lower Colonnade

Staircase

Temple of Asclepius

Large Altar

Tholos of Polycleitus

Byzantine Wall

Temple of Artemis

Small Cella

Large building of unknown purport

Propylæum

Gymnasium

Plan of the
TEMPLE OF ASCLEPIUS
and the neighbouring buildings
On a scale six times larger than the above plan.
1 : 2000

1 Priests' Dwellings
2 Epidoteum ?
3 Paved Road
4 Inclined Approach
5 Bases of Statues
6 Inscribed Stones
7 Altar

[From Baedeker's Greece.

19. THEATRE, EPIDAURUS (restored). (II. xxvii. § 5.)

It is fortunate that this theatre, which Pausanias considered the finest of all he saw, is very well preserved and provides the best example from which to study the nature of the Greek theatre. This, it should be remembered, was in its origin simply a convenient hill-side sloping down to a flat dancing-place; its fully developed form consisted of three parts—the semi-circular auditorium; a flat circular space (*orchestra*); and the stage-building (*skene*) with a raised platform (*proskenion*) in front; when this platform first appeared and whether it was used as a regular stage are matters of endless dispute.

The theatre at Epidaurus was built mainly in the second half of the fourth century B.C.; but the *skene* was remodelled and the *proskenion* added in Hellenistic times. Only the foundations of these parts remain. The orchestra was a circle of beaten earth 19·5 m. in diameter. A passage (*parodos*), with a Corinthian doorway of Hellenistic date, led into it from either side. There are fifty-five rows of limestone seats—mere benches, as usual in Greek theatres, except for the lowest row and the rows immediately above and below the horizontal gangway, which have carved backs.

It is hardly necessary to go into subtle details of measurement, as some have done, to appreciate the beauty seen by Pausanias in this theatre. It is due to some extent to certain features which had at the same time the practical purpose of affording a better view. The upper part of the auditorium has a slightly steeper slope than the lower; and the seats are not entirely concentric with the circle of the orchestra—their extreme ends follow a slightly wider curve (Pl. 50).

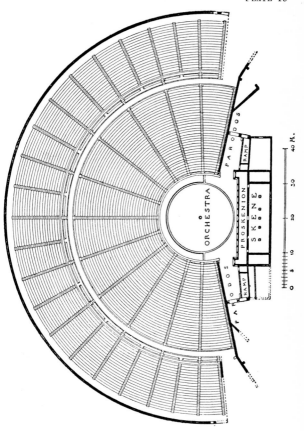

PLATE 19

PARODOS

RAMP

PROSKENION

SKENE

ORCHESTRA

PARODOS

RAMP

40 M.

30

20

10

0 5

51

20. TEMPLE OF ZEUS, OLYMPIA (restored). (V. x. § 2–xii. § 8.)

The temple of Zeus was a great Doric building measuring 27·66 m. by 64·12 m. (unless otherwise stated, dimensions of temples are invariably taken along the uppermost of the three steps). The dimensions given by Pausanias (V. x. § 3) are roughly correct if assumed to be in Roman feet of ·296 m. and to include the ramp at the eastern end. The chief material (V. x. § 2) is a local shell conglomerate, originally coated with stucco. The outer columns number six on the ends and thirteen along the sides.

The cella besides its main room had both a front and rear chamber, and it was in metopes over the entrance to these that the labours of Heracles (V. x. § 9) were carved. Between the antae and columns of the front chamber are three thresholds, with sockets for the hinges on which stood the bronze doors (V. x. § 10) in three pairs.

The interior pillars (V. x. § 10), in two storeys, divided off two narrow aisles, and in the upper part of these no doubt were the porticoes or galleries which gave a nearer view of the image. Possible remains of the stairways exist at the eastern corners.

Beyond the second pair of interior columns, access to the central nave was prevented by barriers, except for a narrow passage at the western end behind the image. It has sometimes been thought that these were the screens (V. xi. § 4, 5) upon which the paintings of Panaenus appeared, but it is much more probable that in V. xi. § 4 Pausanias is referring to panels between the legs of the god's throne.

The base of the great statue occupied almost a third of the nave. The *square* pavement of black Eleusinian limestone in front of it (V. xi. § 10) had a rim of Pentelic, not Parian marble; which was probably purely ornamental—it can hardly have served the curious purpose mentioned by Pausanias.

The temple was probably built between 468 and 456 B.C.; but it seems that the statue was not made till some years later, and the interior arrangement generally, which is closely parallel to that of the Parthenon, may be later too (Pl. 55).

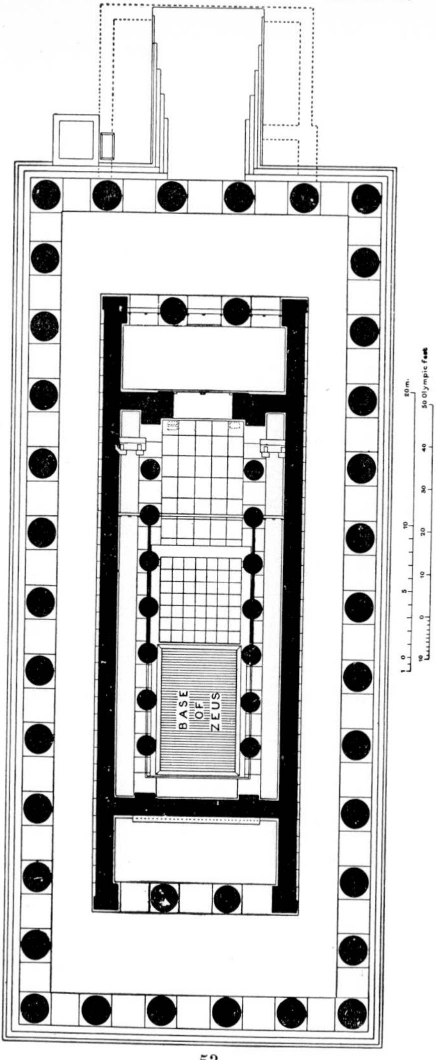

PLATE 20

BASE
OF
ZEUS

21. TEMPLE OF HERA, OLYMPIA (restored). (V. xvi. § 1–xx. § 5.)

The tradition recorded by Pausanias would make this temple date from about 1100 B.C.; but a Doric building of such well-developed plan would have been impossible so early, and the date usually assigned to it now is the end of the seventh century B.C., though it had precursors.

The dimensions of the temple are 18·75 m. by 50·01 m.; Pausanias' measurement of the length (V. xvi. § 1) is slightly short—the breadth given in the text is a restoration. There were altogether sixteen columns along each side and six at each end, varying remarkably in style, from the archaic type with flat capitals to the normal later type. This, and Pausanias' statement that one of the pillars in the rear-chamber was of oak (V. xvi. § 1), suggest that originally the whole colonnade was of wood, and was gradually replaced in stone.

The cella walls were built in the lower parts of limestone and in the upper of sun-dried brick. The long limestone base which supported the statues of Zeus and Hera (V. xvii. § 1) (Pl. 57) still stands at the western end. Other statues, including Praxiteles' Hermes (V. xvii. § 3) (Pl. 57), stood between the interior columns along either side of the cella; the chest of Cypselus (V. xvii. § 5) is known to have occupied the rear-chamber (Pl. 56).

PLATE 21

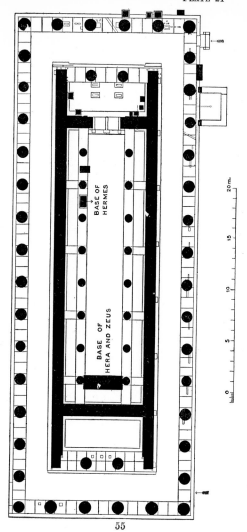

BASE OF HERMES

BASE OF HERA AND ZEUS

20m.

15

10

5

0

22. OLYMPIA IN ROMAN TIMES. (V. x. § 1–VI. xxi. § 2.)

The sanctuary of Zeus covered a large and ill-defined area (see Pl. 54), but the sacred enclosure or Altis (V. x. § 1) was a comparatively small space, enclosed by walls on the south and west, and by the " Echo " Portico (V. xxi. § 17) and by Mount Cronius.

Pausanias explored the site thoroughly; the only noteworthy building he does not mention is the semi-circular exedra, containing water-tanks, built by Herodes Atticus; while of the buildings he mentions, remains of almost all have been found, though seldom standing higher than the lower parts of the walls; exceptions are the altar of Zeus (V. xiii. § 8), the pillar of Oenomaus (V. xx. § 6) and the Hippodameium (VI. xx. § 7). The topographical thread running through the description is almost obliterated by lengthy digressions.

Pausanias begins with the temple (V. x. § 1–xii. § 8) (Pl. 20) (contrast Book X). Then follows the Pelopium (V. xiii. § 1–§ 7) (see Pl. 55), an irregular enclosure farther north. Pausanias' account of the position of the great altar of Zeus (V. xiii. § 8–xiv. § 3—by "in front " he means to the east) is accepted as correct now that certain curved foundations east of the Pelopium are assigned not to it but to prehistoric houses.

Here follows a list of the other altars (V. xiv. § 4–xv. § 12). Several have been found but none identified. The monthly sacrificial procession (V. xiv. § 4, § 10, xv. § 10) must have taken a very leisurely and erratic course. A number of interesting buildings with altars in or near are mentioned incidentally in this digression :—

V. xv. § 1, the workshop of Pheidias, outside the Altis on the west, later converted into a church.

V. xv. § 2, the Leonidaeum, a complex building surrounding a court, used as a " Catagogium " (see Pl. 18) or hostel.

V. xv. § 4, the Front Seats (Proedria) variously identified with a long platform in front of the Echo Portico, and one wing of the Council-House; more probably the South Portico (recent investigation has shown that this was of unusual design, with its middle section projecting forwards).

V. xv. § 6, the hippodrome (see below).

V. xv. § 8, the Theëcoleon, on the west, the quarters of certain priests, built around two courts—its growth has been aptly compared with that of an Oxford or Cambridge college. The building noticed by Pausanias near it is no doubt the " Heroüm," so called because of dedications to an unnamed hero found in its circular chamber.

V. xv. § 8, § 9, § 12, the Town-Hall (Prytaneum) at the north-west corner of the Altis; one of the oldest foundations at Olympia,

like most of the buildings it was elaborated and rebuilt in Roman times. Here the officials dined and entertained. There were dining-halls and kitchens around colonnaded courts.

V. xv. § 8, the gymnasium (see below).

At V. xvi. § 1 Pausanias returns from his digression to describe the buildings in the northern part of the Altis—the temple of Hera (V. xvi. § 1–xx. § 5) (Pl. 21); the pillar of Oenomaus (V. xx. § 6–§ 8); the Metroüm, in which some of the statues of Roman emperors (V. xx. § 9) have actually been found; and the Philippeum (V. xx. § 9, 10), a circular Ionic building.

Pausanias now takes a different line. V. xxi.–VI. xviii. contains the " description of the statues and votive offerings " proposed in V. xxi. § 1. V. xxi. § 1–xxvii. § 12 deals with the " offerings " (firstly the images of Zeus, then others, including Paeonius' Victory, which stood some 30 m. east of the south-east corner of the temple, V. xxvi. § 1); VI. i. § 1–xviii. § 7 with statues of victors and others. The author's classification is artificial— the statues of victors would be offerings no less than the others.

Pausanias takes his cue from the " Zanes " (V. xxi. § 2–§ 18), which he would naturally notice before mounting the treasury terrace, as he ultimately did (VI. xix.). The bases of the Zanes still stand at the north-east corner (see Pl. 59). The Painted or Echo Portico, mentioned in connection with them (V. xxi. § 17), was a Doric building, on the east side of the Altis, erected (or re-erected) in the age of Philip and Alexander, when there was great building activity here. The Council-House (V. xxiii. § 1, xxiv. § 1, 9), seat of the Elean council which controlled the festival, was the triple building on the south. It had two long wings ending in apses; the northern—the oldest part of the building, dating from the sixth century—was probably the Council-Chamber proper; but the south wing seems to be a rebuilding of an even more primitive predecessor, with sides slightly curved.

With the help of numerous extant bases it is possible to follow roughly the course taken by Pausanias in going the round of the statues (VI. i.–xviii.). He first describes a group south of the Heraeum, and others between the Heraeum and the eastern end of the temple of Zeus (VI. i. § 3–iii. § 13). Opposite this end of the temple—the main front—statues were naturally particularly numerous (VI. iii. § 13–xiv. § 13). Others stood on the south (VI. xiv. § 13–xvi. § 5) or opposite the west (VI. xvi. § 5–§ 9). Pausanias' route up to this point is the ἔφοδος of which he speaks in VI. xvii. § 1. The remaining group must have stood between the temple and the Pelopium—" to the right " probably means round the right-hand side of the latter.

At VI. xix. § 1 Pausanias returns abruptly to the north-east corner and the treasury terrace. Of the treasuries mentioned, the

Sicyonian and Megarian, from which fragments of the sculpture (VI. xix. § 13) have been recovered, are identified by inscriptions (I and XI in plan). About others there is some dispute owing to a defect in the text at VI. xix. § 8; while the building marked VIII in the plan, sometimes called the Treasury of Cyrene, is too small and may have been the altar of Earth (V. xiv. § 10). E. N. Gardiner (*Olympia*, p. 222) identifies the foundations on the terrace thus—I. Siconian treasury, II. Syracusan (Pausanias' "Carthaginian"), III. (possibly) Samian, IV. Epidamnian, V. Byzantine, VI. Sybarite, VII. Cyrenaean, VIII. altar of Earth, IX. Selinuntine treasury, X. Metapontine, XI. Megarian, XII. Geloan.

(For nature of treasuries see Pl. 28.)

The slopes of Mount Cronius, thickly wooded and steep (VI. xx. § 1–§ 6), rise behind the terrace; there is now no trace of the monuments which stood there. Pausanias next visits the Hippodameium (VI. xx. § 7) before entering the stadium; there can be little doubt that this sanctuary stood in the north-eastern corner of the Altis, especially since in V. xxii. § 2 it is mentioned immediately after certain statues near the entrance of the stadium.

The difficulty is that it is said to be "by the processional entrance," and in V. xv. § 2 this unquestionably means the gate at the south-western corner; it is simplest to assume that either Pausanias is using the expression very loosely in VI. xx. § 7, meaning the gate of the stadium, or κρυπτή ("hidden") should be read for πομπική ("processional").

The rest of the description is devoted chiefly to the athletic buildings, in which contests were actually held, or facilities for practice offered to the athletes (the contests in boxing and wrestling took place in the open space in front of the great altar).

(For stadium see Pl. 59.)

No trace of the hippodrome has been found—perhaps the floods of the Alpheius have quite obliterated it (VI. xx. § 10–xxi. § 2). No doubt it lay to the south-east of the stadium; it was over 600 m. long (Pl. 23 (*a*)).

To the west of the Altis were the gymnasium (VI. xxi. § 2) and the wrestling-ground (palaestra) (Pausanias' "smaller enclosure," VI. xxi. § 2). The gymnasium had a colonnade on the south and a covered running-track on the east; the west side has been washed away by the Cladeus. The adjoining Palaestra was more compact and regular, and contained a variety of rooms for the athletes' use.

The handsome buildings for the convenience of athletes and visitors were mainly Hellenistic additions. In the fifth and early fourth centuries the architecture of Olympia was much simpler, with little beyond the shrines and the old Prytaneum and Council-House.

23. (a) HIPPODROME, OLYMPIA. (VI. xx. § 10–§ 14.)

This plan is based upon and explains Pausanias' elaborate description of the starting arrangements of the hippodrome (race-course) at Olympia.

There are no actual remains—the course has probably suffered severely from the erratic movements of the Alpheius.

The arrangement by which the two lines of stalls resembled in shape the prow of a ship is obvious, but it is disputable whether the " prow " extended across the whole of the hippodrome, from end to end of the portico of Agnaptus, or across one half of it only. A separate cord was apparently stretched across each stall; the cords of the outermost stalls, nearest the portico, were loosed first, and the chariots from these stalls advanced until they were level with the second pair; then these two were released.

It is difficult to see what purpose this elaborate scheme served, since ultimately all the chariots had to come into line in the ordinary way. Possibly the object was merely spectacular; though possibly confusion before the start was avoided by thus keeping the competitors well apart.

Besides the temporary altar which was used in giving the signal for the start, other altars too stood permanently near the starting-place, and are described by Pausanias in his list (V. xv. § 5).

(b) TEMPLE OF APOLLO, BASSAE (restored).
(VIII. xli. § 7–§ 9.)

This temple attracted Pausanias' particular interest and admiration. It is a Doric building, measuring 14·63 m. by 38·29 m., with six columns at each end and fifteen along each side; and it stands upon a terrace about 3700 feet high on the southern side of Mount Cotilius, about four miles from Phigalia.

On architectural grounds it is now dated about 450 B.C.; whereas Pausanias, perhaps because of a misunderstanding of the title of the god, seems to assign it to a date early in the Peloponnesian War. The sculpture and some architectural details, however, do not appear to have been completed until towards 420 B.C.

The material which Pausanias admired is the local limestone. Several unusual features of plan, construction and decoration

make the building peculiarly interesting even now. It faces north, and is an exception to the almost invariable rule of an east to west orientation of Greek temples. The cella has an unusually deep fore-temple, and a side door (as have the temples at Lycosura and Tegea, Pl. 25 and Pl. 26) at the southern end of its eastern side. All three orders of architecture were represented— Doric by the outer colonnade; Ionic by columns with very unorthodox capitals and curious bases, attached by short walls to the walls of the cella; and Corinthian by the single column in the middle of the cella and probably also by those on either side of it, *i.e.* the southernmost pair of columns engaged in the walls; this is the earliest known use of the Corinthian order. Round the interior, over the engaged columns, ran a sculptured frieze, representing battles of Lapiths and Centaurs, and Greeks and Amazons. The position of this frieze suggests that the cella was open to the sky; Dinsmoor, however, finds architectural evidence to the contrary, and also to show that the statue stood in the main room, in front of the central column, not as formerly thought opposite the door of the smaller room cut off by the screen of Corinthian columns. Besides the frieze there were metopes as at Olympia above the inner porches, and possibly also pedimental groups.

It seems remarkable that Ictinus the architect should have reserved his unorthodox ideas for a remote corner of Arcadia; it is perhaps to be regretted that they were not applied more widely in Doric architecture (Pl. 67 and Pl. 68).

PLATE 23

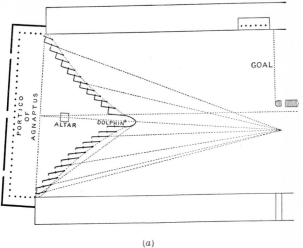

(a)

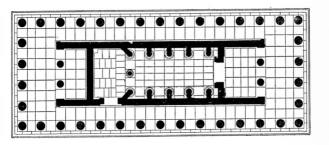

(b)

63

24. MEGALOPOLIS (VIII. xxx. § 2–xxxii. § 5).

The walls of Megalopolis extended about two miles north to south by one mile east to west; Pausanias confines his attention to the central part. On the north bank of the river was the agora, regular in plan and almost completely enclosed by buildings. The northern side was formed by the portico named in honour of Philip II. of Macedon (VIII. xxx. § 6)—a long Doric building with projecting wings—and a smaller building which may have contained Pausanias' " offices " (VIII. xxx. § 6). On the east a long foundation marks the position of the portico called " Myropolis." The river has washed away the southern part of the market-place, destroying the portico of Aristander (VIII. xxx. § 10), but leaving most of the massive foundations of the sanctuary of Zeus; the pillars (VIII. xxx. § 10) ran in two rows around a small square court, except where the temple broke their continuity on the west. The sanctuary of the great Goddesses (VIII. xxxi. § 1–§ 7) and the gymnasium (VIII. xxxi. § 8) must have completed the western side of the agora. The buildings of the agora are difficult to date and the remains are probably largely Hellenistic. To the north the ground rises to form an undulating plateau; but the hills (VIII. xxx. § 9) cannot be safely identified.

Apart from the theatre and the Thersilium the topography of the southern bank of the river is uncertain. The theatre (VIII. xxxii. § 1) was built in the slope of the rising ground—little artificial embanking was needed. Pausanias is right in calling it the largest in Greece; the auditorium was 145 m. in diameter and held about 20,000 spectators. The spring (VIII. xxxii. § 1) still trickles down between the seats into a gutter which runs round the orchestra; another spring, above the auditorium to the west, may be that of Dionysus (VIII. xxxii. § 3). The theatre was built about the middle of the fourth century B.C., but it was not provided with a permanent stage until at any rate two centuries later. The approach to the orchestra from the west is filled by a long building used for housing stage properties. The theatre and the Thersilium were very closely connected—the same structure, a long Doric portico, served as stage-building and as entrance to the Thersilium. The Council-Chamber itself measured 65 m. from east to west by 53 m. from north to south. Its most interesting feature was the arrangement of the columns which supported the roof. These were placed where a series of rectangles cut lines radiating from the point where speakers stood—a flat space a little south of the central point, to which the floor sloped from east, north and west. The Thersilium was built not many years after the founding of Megalopolis (371 B.C.) (Pl. 64).

PLATE 24

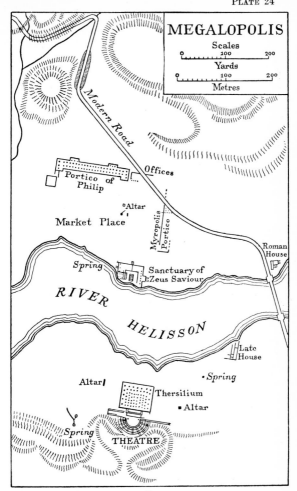

MEGALOPOLIS

Scales

0 — 100 — 200
Yards

0 — 100 — 200
Metres

Modern Road

Offices

Portico of Philip

Altar

Market Place

Myropolis Portico

Roman House

Spring

Sanctuary of Zeus Saviour

RIVER

HELISSON

Late House

Altar

Spring

Thersilium

Altar

Spring

THEATRE

25. SANCTUARY OF THE MISTRESS, LYCOSURA.
(VIII. xxxvii. § 1–§ 7.)

This sanctuary occupies a terrace on the northern side of a ridge projecting eastwards from a rocky hill upon which stand the walls of Lycosura (VIII. xxxviii. § 1). The remains correspond in every point with Pausanias' description. The entrance (VIII. xxxvii. § 1) is on the east, near a point where now stand the ruins of a Byzantine church. Along the whole of the northern side stretch the foundations of the Doric portico seen by Pausanias on his right (VIII. xxxvii. § 1), connected by cross-walls with a buttressed boundary-wall. In front of it are scanty remains of the altars of Demeter (on the east), the Mistress, and the Great Mother (on the west). The temple itself (Pl. 65) was a smallish building with a porch of marble Doric columns facing east, built probably early in the second century B.C. The lower part of the walls was of native limestone, the upper of brick. The great base (VIII. xxxvii. § 3) (Pl. 66) occupies the whole of the back of the cella, and in front of it the floor is decorated with a mosaic.

Pausanias no doubt left the building by a small door in the southern wall which opens out on to a staircase leading up the hillside (VIII. xxxvii. § 7).

PLATE 25

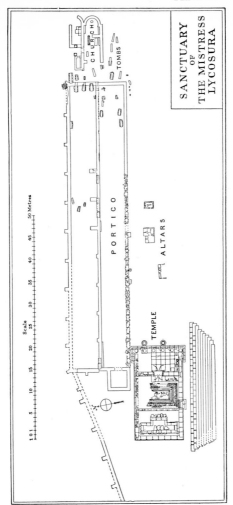

SANCTUARY
OF
THE MISTRESS
LYCOSURA

CHURCH

TOMBS

PORTICO

ALTARS

TEMPLE

Scale

1 0 1   5   10   15   20   25   30   35   40   45   50 Metres

26. Temple of Athena Alea, Tegea (restored).
(VIII. xlv. § 4–xlvii. § 3.)

The old sanctuary of Athena was destroyed by fire (VIII. xlv. § 4) in 395 B.C., and Scopas built the new temple towards the middle of the fourth century. Pausanias exaggerates its size (VIII. xlv. § 5)—actually it is only 19·16 m. by 47·52 m., far smaller than the temple of Zeus at Olympia; its style deserves his praise, however, both for the beauty of the material (marble from Doliana south-east of Tegea), and the fineness of its workmanship. Pausanias' first κόσμος (VIII. xlv. § 5) is the outer colonnade—the columns of the front and back chamber too are Doric; the Corinthian columns were engaged in the cella wells; the Ionic probably stood somewhere *outside* the temple—the original text (ἐκτός) and not the emendation (ἐντός) seems to be correct—for there is no place for Ionic columns in the cella (two rows of foundations running east and west along it are Byzantine). The cella had a side door on the north—an unusual feature which occurs, curiously, in two other Arcadian temples too—at Lycosura (VIII. xxxvii. § 1–§ 7, Pl. 25) and at Bassae (VIII. xli. § 7–§ 9, Pl. 23 (*b*)).

Remains of the temple are scanty, but include precious fragments of the sculptures from the gables (VIII. xlv. § 6, 7). There were also sculptured metopes over the inner porches as at Olympia and Bassae.

PLATE 26

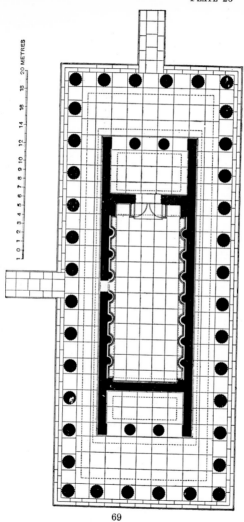

27. DELPHI. (X. viii. § 6–xxxii. § 1.)

Delphi lies at a height of over 1800 feet, on the lower southern slopes of Parnassus. Behind it rise towering cliffs, cleft deeply at this point by a ravine, forming the two great rocks known as the Phaedriadae (Pl. 72). To the south the ground falls away steeply again to the valley of the Pleistus (X. viii. § 8). Even within the city itself the ground slopes considerably (X. ix. § 1), so that constant terracing was necessary. There was no continuous circuit of walls, though on the ridge to the west are remains of fortifications built in 355 B.C. by the Phocian leader Philomelus.

Pausanias approached from the east (Pl. 71) and first reached the terrace now called Marmaria, where remains of his "row of temples" (X. viii. § 6) have been found. The easternmost—the older temple of Athena—was destroyed by the falling rocks which were a constant menace at Delphi. Next to it were two small buildings of the "treasury" type (Pl. 73). The beautifully constructed Doric tholos a little further east probably does not correspond to any of the buildings mentioned by Pausanias. The temple of Athena Pronoia, a Doric limestone building of the fourth century B.C., ended the row on the west.

In the gymnasium (X. viii. § 8) facilities were provided for athletes training for the Pythian games. The remains occupy two terraces; on the upper were porticoes intended for running exercise, on the lower a wrestling-ground and a bathing establishment with a circular swimming pool.

The water of Castalia (X. viii. § 9, 10) (Pl. 74) issues at the foot of the eastern side of the ravine.

Pausanias entered the precinct of Apollo at its south-eastern corner, and left it at the north-west to ascend to the race-course (X. xxxii. § 1). Here the twelve tiers of seats built in the hill-side on the north are well preserved, but little is left of the six tiers which were raised artificially on the south (Pl. 79 and Pl. 80). Pausanias' statement that the reconstruction due to Herodes Atticus was in marble is incorrect.

PLATE 27

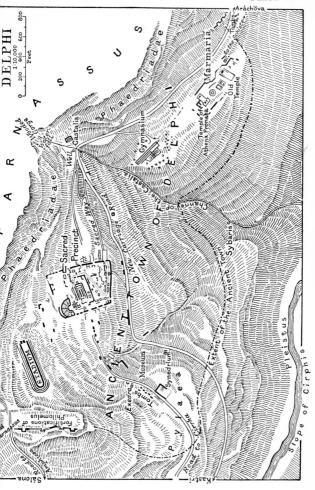

DELPHI

1:110,000

0 200 400 600 800
Feet

[After Baedeker's *Greece*.

28. DELPHI, SANCTUARY OF APOLLO (restored).
(X. ix. § 1–xxxii. § 1.)

The sacred enclosure at Delphi is bounded by walls which measure about 125 m. on the south and 190 m. on the east; on the east and west these are pierced by several openings which provide the passages mentioned in X. ix. § 1. Pausanias entered by the main gate at the south end of the east wall, and gradually ascended the Sacred Way (the paving is later than his time but is included in the plan to indicate the course of the way) and then climbed still higher to explore the northern part of the enclosure. (At Olympia, by contrast, he made the temple of Zeus his starting-point.) His general route is clear, and so is the general topography of the site; but because of his highly selective method and the slightness of the indications which he gives of the relation of one monument to another, and also because of the scantiness and confusion of the remains, the identification of many of the monuments is highly uncertain. The accompanying plan is schematic and simplified, and open to question in details. The dates of some monuments are much disputed too. As usual, Pausanias mentions little or nothing of late Hellenistic or Roman date, though there were many monuments of these periods at Delphi.

An important and interesting series of monuments, mostly commemorating victories of Greek over Greek, lined the first few yards of the Sacred Way. An Athenian or Lacedaemonian must have traversed this part of the road with curiously mixed feelings. On the right immediately inside the entrance still stands the pedestal of the Corcyraean bull (X. ix. § 3). Inscriptions on a long base just beyond it show that what Pausanias calls Tegeate offerings (from Lacedaemonian spoils; X. ix. § 5) were, in fact, dedicated by the Arcadians as a whole. Here, and on the large structure immediately behind, containing the Lacedaemonian offerings after the battle of Aegospotami in 405 B.C., can still be read many of the names recorded by Pausanias (X. ix. § 7–§ 10). The statues of Argive heroes (X. x. § 5) occupied a semicircular foundation, as inscriptions show; no doubt the Epigoni (X. x. § 4) confronted them in the similar structure on the south. The other monuments mentioned by Pausanias in this section (X. x. § 1–§ 8) must have stood on the southern side of the road too, though the remains are here scantier and not so easily identifiable. The great variety of form shown by these victory monuments is remarkable.

At Delphi, as at Olympia, " treasuries " were numerous; they did not, however, stand in a regular line as at Olympia, but were scattered about the lower part of the enclosure. These treasuries were small temples dedicated by individual states in the great Pan-Hellenic sanctuaries, and associated primarily with the name

of the state in question—that of the god could be taken for granted. They would be used by official visitors from the cities which had erected them; and they would contain sacrificial vessels and offerings of citizens—hence the name " treasuries."

At Delphi in many cases there can be little certainty or agreement in identifying the treasuries mentioned by Pausanias with actual remains. The labels attached in the plan are not all free from doubt. The Sicyonian (X. xi. § 1), first on his list, is naturally thought to be the first which one reaches in ascending the Sacred Way; the metopes found on the site, older than the building itself, are now generally thought to have belonged to a curious archaic predecessor rather than to another treasury. The unusually rich sculptural decoration of the Siphnian treasury (X. xi. § 2; formerly called Cnidian, now securely identified) is explained by the mineral wealth of the island. Round the first bend of the Way stands the treasury of Athens (X. xi. § 5), the identity of which has never been in doubt, though dates assigned to it, in the late sixth or early fifth century, vary greatly. It has been fully rebuilt, mainly from ancient material, through the enthusiasm of the modern Athenians.

After rounding the bend, Pausanias would have upon his left the great terrace wall of beautifully constructed polygonal masonry, which was built in the sixth century at the time of the Alcmaeonid rebuilding of the temple of Apollo. The monuments described in X. xi. § 6–xiii. § 3 stood underneath the wall; at its eastern end it formed the back wall of the Ionic portico (Pl. 75) built by the Athenians probably soon after the battle of Salamis (480 B.C.), certainly not as late as Phormio (X. xi. § 6). The rock of the Sibyl (X. xii. § 1) is probably the most prominent of a group which stands a few yards west of the portico. Pausanias does not mention the Council-House in which the Delphic senate met, or the sphinx (still extant) dedicated on a lofty column by the Naxians about 565–560 B.C. Many monuments stood on the opposite side of the road too (X. xiii. § 4, 5) flanking the *Halos*, a broad flat space with seats around, where processions mustered and sacred dramas were performed.

As at Olympia, monuments were very densely grouped opposite the eastern end of the temple. The visitor on arriving here might notice with approval that memorials of victories of Greeks over barbarians were now more prominent. Here stood the Plataean tripod (X. xiii. § 9); its substructure—quadrangular, surmounted by two round blocks—is still in place. The supporting column, consisting not of a single serpent but of three intertwined, was taken by Constantine to Constantinople, and is still there. The statue of Apollo commemorating the naval victory at Salamis may have stood just north of the tripod (X. xiv. § 6). On the opposite side of the road is the tower-like pedestal of the Great

Altar of Apollo (X. xiv. § 7), the chief altar of Delphi, dedicated as its inscription shows by the Chians, possibly after the battle of Mycale (479 B.C.). The colossal statue of Apollo Sitalcas was probably supported by the large square foundation west of two black limestone bases upon which stood tripods erected by the tyrants of Syracuse after victories over the Carthaginians, about 480–465 B.C. Near these bases was found the omphalos (X. xvi. § 3) (Pl. 76) and recently the site of the bronze palm of the Eurymedon has been fixed here too (X. xv. § 5). Scanty remains indicate that in X. xvi. § 5–xix. § 3 Pausanias is making his way along the upper terrace south of the temple to the western end. Inscribed fragments of the Liparaean offerings (X. xvi. § 7) have been found, and remains of the Aetolian dedication (X. xvii. § 7).

The temple at Delphi (X. xix. § 3–xxiv. § 5) suffered many vicissitudes. The building seen by Pausanias replaced that built by an Athenian family, the Alcmaeonidae, late in the sixth century B.C., which had itself several predecessors, even if the fantastic list given in Chapter v is not to be taken seriously. The later building was begun in 367 B.C., and officially opened in 305, though the work dragged on into the third century. It was a large Doric building of limestone. Remains are so scanty (Pl. 77) that the interior arrangement is very doubtful. There was a front and rear porch, besides the large main room in which stood the objects mentioned in X. xxiv. § 4, 5; the arrangement of the inner sanctum, the *adyton* (X. xxiv. § 5), like the procedure of the oracle, is highly conjectural. There were probably inner colonnades; some of the outer columns on the east have recently been re-erected.

On leaving the temple Pausanias turns to the left (*i.e.* north) to reach the sanctuary of Neoptolemus (I. xxiv. § 6). The only building which answers to his description of its position is a quadrangular enclosure immediately east of the structure where the excavators found copies of Lysippus' statue of Agias and statues of other Thessalian worthies ("Daochus").

The water of Cassotis (X. xxiv. § 7) still trickles down from a point east of the theatre. Above it on a terrace at the top of the enclosure are the foundations of the Cnidian *Lesche* (X. xxv. § 1), a club-room where men met for discussion and conversation; possibly the painting of Odysseus' visit to the underworld occupied the west wall and the western parts of the north and south walls, and the sack of Troy was similarly disposed in the eastern part of the building.

The thirty-three rows of seats of the theatre (X. xxxii. § 1) are unusually well preserved; the theatre seats about 5000 and has, in fact, been used for dramatic performances in modern times (Pl. 78).

74

PLATE 28

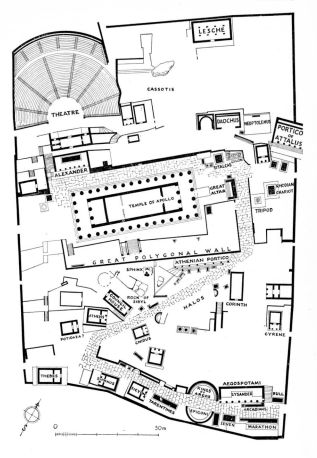

LESCHE

CASSOTIS

THEATRE

DAOCHUS

NEOPTOLEMUS

PORTICO OF ATTALUS

ALEXANDER

SITALCAS

GELON

GREAT ALTAR

RHODIAN CHARIOT

TEMPLE OF APOLLO

TRIPOD

GREAT POLYGONAL WALL

ATHENIAN PORTICO

SPHINX

ROCK OF SIBYL

COUNCIL HOUSE

HALOS

CORINTH

ATHENS

POTIDAEA?

CNIDUS

CYRENE

THEBES

SIPHNUS

SICYON

TARENTINES

KINGS OF ARGOS

EPIGONI

AEGOSPOTAMI

LYSANDER

BULL

ARCADIANS

SEVEN

MARATHON

0   50m

75

29. Cape Sunium. (I. i. § 1.)

The Doric columns which crown the rocky peninsula of Sunium (200 feet high) are now proved by inscriptions to have belonged not to the temple of Athena (I. i. § 1), but that of Poseidon. Yet they are " on the peak of the promontory," while the scantier remains of the temple of Athena stand on lower ground to the north; possibly Pausanias confused the two buildings.

The island of Patroclus (I. i. § 1) three miles west of Sunium appears in the background of the photograph.

Built shortly after the middle of the fifth century, the temple of Poseidon may have been the work of the same architect as the temple of Hephaestus at Athens (see Pl. 30); it is similar in size and has affinities in design. Its columns numbered six by thirteen.

PLATE 29

30. WEST SIDE OF AGORA OF ATHENS (I. iii. § 1–v. § 1, xiv. § 6).
MODEL BY C. MAMMELIS AND J. TRAVLOS (see Pl. 12).

Though little in the agora stands above foundation level, study
of the surviving fragments of superstructure makes an accurate
restoration possible.

The *stoa* at the north end was a sophisticated form of the simple
open colonnade, with projecting wings. Built in the latter part
of the fifth century, it was no doubt the portico associated with
Zeus, God of Freedom, containing Euphranor's pictures (I. iii. § 3);
but it was probably also the Royal Portico (I. iii. § 1). At first
Pausanias appears to speak of two buildings, but a closer examination of his words makes it at least doubtful whether he has moved
on. The northern end of the agora is beyond the excavations
and an element of doubt must remain; but the line of the road
from the Dipylon is known, and it is difficult to find room for a
second *stoa*. Between the wings stood bases which probably
carried the statues seen by Pausanias; the Hadrian has been
found, and so have fragments of the group of Hemera and
Cephalus from the roof.

South of the *stoa* stood the temple of Apollo (I. iii. § 4), a
fourth-century building replacing a small apsidal temple destroyed
by the Persians. Farther south again, the sanctuary of the
Mother, the Metroon (I. iii. § 5), originally a simple shrine, was
rebuilt in the second century B.C. with a long colonnade in front
of a series of rooms, some of which contained the city's archives.

Behind the Metroon was the Council-House of the Five Hundred,
restored as a small covered theatre; built late in the fifth century,
it replaced an archaic Council-House of which remains lie under
the south part of the Metroon. The circular foundations of the
Tholos (I. v. § 1), office of the Presidents of Council, were un-
mistakable. The Tholos was first built soon after the Persian
Wars, and retained its essential form, though repeatedly
reconstructed.

The well-preserved temple on the Market-Hill to the west,
" above the Cerameicus and the Royal Portico," is now reasonably
identified as the temple of Hephaestus (I. xiv. 6), though still
popularly called " Theseum "; traces of bronze-working nearby
confirm the identification. It was built soon after the middle of
the fifth century, and was a Doric structure of Pentelic marble
(13·72 m. by 31·77, with six columns by thirteen). Recent
investigation has revealed that it had an interior colonnade.

PLATE 30

31. ATHENS, VIEW TO EAST FROM HILL OF NYMPHS
(see Pl. 11).

In the centre are the agora excavations (see Pl. 12). To the left is the " Theseum," on the Market Hill; to the right, in front of the Acropolis, is the Areopagus. The pointed hill in the background is Lycabettus, north-east of the ancient city; Hymettus (I. xxxii. § 1, 2) rises in the distance to the right.

PLATE 31

32. TEMPLE OF OLYMPIAN ZEUS, ATHENS (I. xviii. § 6–§ 8), FROM NORTH-WEST (see Pl. 11).

Fifteen columns of the temple of Zeus still stand, and one more lies prostrate. From this point of view Hymettus (I. xxxii. § 1) forms a background to them, and on the left the reconstructed race-course (I. xix. § 6) is partly visible, behind the hill Ardettus.

PLATE 32

83

33.   S.E. FOOT OF ACROPOLIS, ATHENS (I. xx. § 3–xxi. § 3)
(see Pl. 14).

In the immediate foreground are the scanty remains—part of
the northern side—of the older temple of Dionysus (I. xx. § 3)
abutting the foundations of the stage buildings, which stand to a
height of several courses.   Behind, the slope of the auditorium
leads up to the Acropolis wall and the cave (I. xxi. § 3) now used
as a chapel.   In front of the cave once stood a choregic monument
in the form of a Doric porch, erected by Thrasyllus in 319 B.C.
The tripod seen by Pausanias no doubt surmounted this monument,
and the Corinthian columns higher up the slope must have carried
choregic tripods too.

PLATE 33

34. ACROPOLIS FROM SOUTH-WEST, ATHENS. (I. xxii. § 4–xxviii. § 4) (see Pl. 14).

On the left are the Propylaea (I. xxii. § 4–xxiii. § 6) and towards the right the Parthenon (I. xxiv. § 5–§ 7) with the Erechtheum (I. xxvi. § 5–xxvii. § 2) between. In front of the Propylaea is the Odeum of Herodes, with the Portico of Eumenes extending eastward from it. The long row of arches buttressed a terrace wall, and was originally concealed by the back wall of the stoa itself. Behind, Mt. Anchesmus (I. xxxii. § 2) rises on the left, and Lycabettus on the extreme right.

PLATE 34

87

35. Model of Acropolis of Athens (see Pl. 14).

This model was designed by Mr. G. P. Stevens, in accordance with his researches into the topography of the Acropolis (see *Hesperia*, V, p. 443; XV, pp. 1 and 73; and Suppl. III). It is here seen as from the north-west, with the monument of Agrippa in the foreground; and it shows the Acropolis as it appeared in the first century A.D.

Before the time of Pausanias the zig-zag ramp and the terraces on the approach to the Propylaea had been replaced by a broad flight of steps. The awkward combination of roofs in the Propylaea, which would be largely concealed from the ground, is obvious in the photo of the model.

Stevens finds reason to believe that behind the great bronze Athena of Pheidias rose a high terrace wall of Mycenean origin, which made a separate forecourt of the western part of the Acropolis; at the south-east corner was a small propylon (seen just below the Parthenon) which led into the court immediately west of the Parthenon. The large building on the south side of the Acropolis, seen behind the stoas of the shrine of Artemis Brauronia, is the *chalkotheke*, a store-house, not mentioned by Pausanias.

The building in front of the Erechtheum is what may have been the dwelling of the *arrhephoroi* (I. xxvii. § 3); the enclosure behind it is the shrine of Zeus Polieus (I. xxiv. § 4). Beyond the Parthenon is the small round Ionic temple of Rome and Augustus, not mentioned by Pausanias.

PLATE 35

36. Central Doorway of Propylaea, Athens
(I. xxii. § 4) (see Pl. 13).

Between two Ionic columns of the deep outer porch can be seen the façade of the north-west wing, Pausanias' " building with pictures " (I. xxii. § 6).

PLATE 36

37. East Front of Propylaea, Athens (I. xxii. § 4–xxiii. § 6) (see Pl. 13).

The semicircular base of the statue of Athena surnamed Health (I. xxiii. § 4) can just be distinguished at the foot of the furthest column.

PLATE 37

38. ERECHTHEUM, ATHENS (I. xxvi. § 5–xxvii. § 2), FROM ROOF OF PARTHENON (see Pl. 15).

In the shadow to the left (west) of the Erechtheum is the olive tree planted some years ago on the presumed site of the sacred olive of Athena.

A little in front and to the right of the Caryatid porch are the two column bases which belong to the Mycenean palace.

The plan of the archaic (Peisistratid) temple of Athena is clearly revealed by its foundations, south of the Erechtheum. The outer row carried the colonnade. The interior structure had a porch at each end; behind the porch on the east was a large room with two interior rows of columns; on the west were two inner chambers behind a single broad room, as in the Erechtheum. There has been much debate on the question to what extent the temple was restored after being destroyed in the Persian Wars, and whether it still stood after the building of the Erechtheum. Some have even believed that it was seen by Pausanias and has to be taken into account in his description; this would involve a drastic redistribution of the monuments he mentions. Dinsmoor suggests that only the western end of the inner structure was restored, and was used for a century as a treasury. It is in fact very improbable that Pausanias saw anything of the building, or that the highly complex topographical problems in which the pre-Parthenon temples of the Acropolis are involved concern him in any way.

PLATE 38

95

39. Gravestones, Athens (I. xxix. § 2) (see Pl. 11).

The chief cemetery of Athens lay outside the Dipylum and the Sacred Gate. The most conspicuous groups of extant gravestones are not amongst those seen by Pausanias along the road to the Academy, but line a street which branches to the left from the Sacred Way and joins the road to Peiraeus. They consist of a number of family groups, each marked off from the rest by having a distinct common foundation. Two such groups appear in the photograph.

PLATE 39

[Photo, Alinari.

40. Grave of Athenians, Marathon. (I. xxxii. § 3.)

The mound erected over the Athenians who fell in 490 B.C. stands towards the southern end of the plain of Marathon. Bones, fragments of vases and other objects found in it prove its identity. It is towards 40 feet high and measures 200 yards round the base, and was originally surmounted by commemorative slabs in marble. The vegetation here seen growing on the top has more recently been cleared away, and the mound tidied up.

PLATE 40

99

41. AEGOSTHENA, EAST WALL (I. xliv. § 4–5).

Aegosthena, in the Megarid at the head of the Corinthian Gulf (Pl. 2), possesses one of the finest extant fortification walls, comparable with the wall of Messene which Pausanias so much admired (Pl. 53). In the best preserved section, on the east, there are four massive square towers projecting from a curtain wall 12 feet thick, which is built of regular square blocks facing a rubble core. The south-eastern tower is of great height, with windows in the top storey, and apparently served as a watch-tower.

The wall is tentatively dated to the early fourth century (R. Scranton, *Greek Walls*, Harvard U.P., 1941); but walls are notoriously hard to date.

PLATE 41

42. SPRING OF PEIRENE, CORINTH (II. iii. § 2, 3) (see Pl. 16).

Pausanias' "chambers like caves" appear through the arches of the main (southern) façade, and in front on the left is the "open-air well." The line of Corinthian columns was not added until Byzantine times.

PLATE 42

103

43. TEMPLE OF APOLLO, CORINTH (II. iii. § 6), FROM WEST
(see Pl. 16).

These seven Doric monoliths of limestone have long been the most conspicuous feature of the site; originally there were six columns at each end and fifteen along each side of the temple. The massive shafts and flattish capitals place the date of the building about the middle of the sixth century B.C.

PLATE 43

44. ACROCORINTHUS. (II. iv. § 6–v. § 4.)

The Acrocorinthus, grandest of all Greek citadels, rises to the south of the site of Corinth (notice the columns of the temple of Apollo in the middle distance). It is approached from the west, the least precipitous side. It reaches its highest point (1880 feet) towards the east, and here stood the temple of Aphrodite (II. v. § 1), of which the foundations have been explored. Extensive medieval walls, containing a few ancient fragments, encircle the summit.

A little below the site of the temple, and to the west, is the fountain of upper Peirene, in a vaulted underground chamber. There is no truth in the belief, mentioned by Pausanias (II. v. § 1), that water flowed from this spring to the other Peirene below.

PLATE 44

107

45. TEMPLE OF ZEUS, NEMEA. (II. xv. § 2, 3.)

Nemea lies in a fertile valley amongst barren hills. Pausanias' Mount Apesas is the table-mountain, visible in the photograph, which rises on the north-east to a height of 2700 feet.

Of the three standing columns of the temple, the two on the left in the photograph belonged to the front chamber of the cella, the other (34 feet high) to the eastern end of the outer colonnades (originally six by twelve). The temple is an example of fourth-century Doric; its columns are unusually slender. There were interior columns of the Corinthian order; the temple had affinities with both Bassae (Pl. 23b) and Tegea (Pl. 26).

PLATE 45

46. Grave Circle, Mycenae (II. xvi. § 5–§ 7).

In this photograph the grave circle is in the foreground, with the great outer wall of the fortress behind it and the Lion Gate (II. xvi. § 5) on the extreme right in the background; over the gate can be seen the back of the triangular slab upon which the lions were carved.

It is hardly likely that Pausanias actually saw the grave circle; possibly the slabs which stood over the graves were visible; possibly it was only tradition which associated this spot with the remains of Agamemnon and the rest (II. xvi. § 6, 7).

Actually the six rectangular rubble-lined pits found within the grave circle were tombs of a dynasty of the sixteenth century B.C.; but they were carefully preserved in later ages; and when the present fortress was built—in the fourteenth century, Mycenae's greatest days—the huge Cyclopean wall was made to bulge at this point (on the west) to include them; the ground was levelled and a double circle (26·5 m. in diameter) of stone slabs, with others laid horizontally upon them, was erected to keep the ancient cemetery intact.

In recent years Mycenae has been yielding a fresh crop of treasures, mainly in the lower town. A little to the west of the citadel part of another grave circle has been excavated. It was partly destroyed when one of the great tholos tombs (the "Tomb of Clytemnestra") was built. The enclosing wall, of about the same diameter as the one inside the citadel, was not so carefully built. Within it were a number of shaft graves, surmounted by *stelai*, one of which was actually found *in situ*—the *stelai* may have been seen by Pausanias. These graves are of similar date to the other group, or somewhat earlier. It may well be that what Pausanias took to be the graves of Clytemnestra and Aegisthus (II. xvi. § 7) were at this spot; of course the attribution was not correct—both groups of shaft graves are much earlier than the Trojan War.

Pausanias' fountain of Persea (II. xvi. 6) is now identified with certain Hellenistic remains near this same point, rather than as formerly with a spring some distance to the east of the citadel.

PLATE 46

47. TREASURY OF ATREUS, MYCENAE. (II. xvi. § 6.)

Pausanias' " underground chambers of Atreus and his children " were actually tombs of the later dynasty which succeeded the occupants of the shaft graves. Nine of these " bee-hive " tombs have been found outside the walls at Mycenae, showing a steady development culminating in the so-called " treasury of Atreus "; which was contemporary with the great wall of Mycenae (*i.e.* fourteenth century)—its regular ashlar masonry is very like certain sections of the wall, especially the parts adjoining the Lion Gate. A long approach leads through the hillside from the east to a great door 2·7 m. wide, at the bottom, and 5·4 m. high, with a huge lintel and a relieving triangle above. The bee-hive chamber, from which a smaller square room opens on the north, is 14·5 m. in diameter and 13·2 m. in height, and still stands intact, unlike the similar structure at Orchomenus which Pausanias so admired (IX. xxxviii. § 2, Pl. 69).

Wace dates all the most splendid architecture of Mycenae, *i.e.* the " treasury of Atreus," the Lion Gate and the Cyclopean walls, to " L.H. IIIA late " (*Mycenae*, p. 134), *i.e.* after the middle of the fourteenth century; but both absolute and relative dating of the monuments of Mycenae has been the subject of much dispute.

PLATE 47

48. CYCLOPEAN MASONRY, TIRYNS. (II. xxv. § 8.)

The photograph shows a section of masonry—roughly contemporary with the great walls of Mycenae (fourteenth century B.C.)—which illustrates both the aptness and the deficiency of Pausanias' description. The large and small stones are there; but the former are not unworked but roughly hewn, and approximate to horizontal courses; and the latter are not the only filling —clay mortar too was used and at this point is still visible. The large blocks are often eight feet or more in length by three or four feet in height and breadth; they are of limestone, some grey and some reddish.

PLATE 48

115

49. FOUNDATIONS OF THOLOS, EPIDAURUS (II. xxvii. § 3) (see Pl. 18).

Six concentric rings of masonry formed the foundation of this building. The inner three were joined by cross-walls and broken by openings so as to form a curious maze, the purpose of which is obscure—possibly it was used for the performance of mystic rites The outer three rings carried a Doric colonnade, a solid wall, and a Corinthian colonnade respectively; the inner three a rich marble pavement. The diameter of the whole was 21·82 m.

PLATE 49

117

50. Theatre, Epidaurus (II. xxvii. § 5) (see Pl. 19).

In the background are the remains of the Sanctuary of Asclepius; the extensive foundations to the right of the modern buildings belong to the " Catagogium."

The light entrance gateway across the western *parodos* has been reconstructed since this photo was taken.

PLATE 50

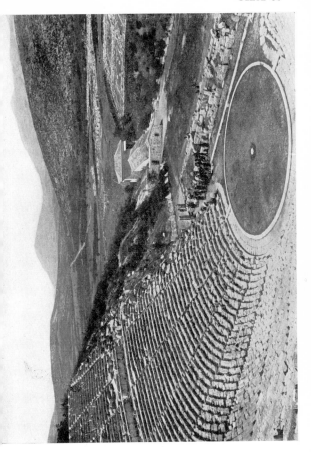

51. Temple of Aphaea, Aegina (II. xxx. § 3), from South-East.

This temple, long famous on account of its position and good preservation, was once said to be that of Zeus Panhellenius (II. xxx. § 4) or of Athena, but inscriptions prove that actually it is Pausanias' temple of Aphaea, an obscure local goddess associated with Artemis.

It is a limestone Doric building of moderate size, with columns originally numbering six on the ends and twelve along the sides. In the foreground in Pl. 51 are the foundations of a portal leading to the walled terrace on which the temple stood. The temple was built early in the fifth century B.C., to replace a smaller and simpler building without a colonnade. Pausanias does not mention the notable pedimental groups of battles before Troy.

PLATE 51

52. THERAPNE, TEMPLE OF MENELAUS. (III. xix. § 9.) See also frontispiece, MODERN SPARTA AND MOUNT TAYGETUS.
(III. xi. § 1–xviii. § 5, xx. § 3, 4.)

Modern Sparta occupies the southern part of the ancient site which lies on the right bank of the River Eurotas. Identifiable points—as the shrine of Artemis (III. xvi. § 7) in the river-bed and the acropolis, to the north, with the theatre (III. xiv. § 1 and the shrine of Athena of the Bronze House (III. xvii. § 2)— are too few to determine the topography of Pausanias' account.

The foothills of Taygetus rise abruptly about three miles to the west, and behind them the highest peaks of the great range tower to nearly 8000 feet. Pausanias' Taletum (III. xx. § 4) is probably the highest point of all, towards the left in the photograph.

The heights of Therapne (about 700 feet) face Mount Taygetus on the opposite bank of the Eurotas. The remains of the temple of Menelaus—foundations only—stand upon a platform supported by a wall of massive blocks.

PLATE 52

123

53. ARCADIAN GATE, MESSENE. (IV. xxxi. § 5, xxxiii. § 3.)

The wall of Messene, the strongest seen by Pausanias, is also the finest extant in Greece; it was built when Greek military architecture had reached its highest development—in the fourth century B.C.

The Arcadian Gate belongs to the best preserved section—on the north, where the wall ascends the north-western slope of Mount Ithome (IV. xxxi. § 4). It consists of an outer gateway, flanked by towers, and an inner, with a circular court over 60 feet in diameter between; the whole built of beautifully constructed masonry in blocks up to $5\frac{1}{2}$ feet long. The Herm seen by Pausanias (IV. xxxiii. § 3) probably stood in the niche visible to the left in the photograph. Higher up the slope is the best preserved of the towers noticed by Pausanias, joined to the Gate by a curtain wall 9 feet thick.

As usual in the best Greek masonry, no binding material is used. What is most remarkable is that in this part of the wall (though not elsewhere) there is no rubble core; nor as in the walls of Mantinea, were the upper parts of unburnt brick—solid ashlar masonry was used throughout.

PLATE 53

54. SITE OF OLYMPIA, FROM NORTH-WEST (V. vii. § 1, x. § 1)
(see Pl. 22).

Mount Cronius (VI. xx. § 1–§ 6) is on the left, and below it in the foreground is the bed of the Cladeus (V. vii. § 1, VI. xxi. § 3). The sanctuary lies below the hill and to the south of it, towards the river Alpheius (V. vii. § 1), which can be seen in the middle distance. The general aspect of the site is strikingly different from the setting of the second great national sanctuary of Greece —Delphi (contrast Pl. 71 and Pl. 72).

PLATE 54

[Photo, Alinari.

55. TEMPLE OF ZEUS, OLYMPIA (V. x. § 2, xiii. § 1) (see Pl. 20 and Pl. 22).

The north-western corner of the temple is on the extreme right. In the foreground on the left are foundations belonging to the Pelopium (V. xiii. § 1).

PLATE 55

56. TEMPLE OF HERA, OLYMPIA (V. xvi. § 1–xx. § 5) FROM NORTH-EAST (see Pl. 21 and Pl. 22).

PLATE 56

131

57. (a) HEAD OF HERA (V. xvii. § 1).

The limestone head, twice life size, found to the West of the Heraeum at Olympia belonged very probably to the image of Hera seen by Pausanias in the temple. The high crown is appropriate to Hera; and the primitive style agrees with Pausanias' remarks—the eyes are large and triangular, the mouth is a simple curve, and the whole face is flattish. The statue was probably made about 600 B.C.

(b) HEAD OF HERMES. (V. xvii. § 3.)

Pausanias distinguishes between the older and newer dedications in the Heraeum (V. xvii. § 3) and the contrast between the archaic Hera and the refined features and technical perfection of Praxiteles' Hermes is extreme; it is enhanced by the difference of material—the Hermes is of beautiful Parian marble—and the wonderful preservation of the later statue, due to its having been covered by clay from the disintegrating walls. The Hera represents the first rude beginnings of Greek sculpture, the Hermes its highest technical development in the middle of the fourth century B.C.

PLATE 57

(b)

(a)

133

58. OLYMPIA, MODEL BY H. SCHLEIF.

The sanctuary is seen as from the north-east, over the top of Mount Cronius. The monuments can readily be identified with the help of Pl. 22.

PLATE 58

59. ENTRANCE TO RACE-COURSE, OLYMPIA (VI. xx. § 8)
(see Pl. 22).

The vaulted passage is Pausanias' "Hidden Entrance" (VI. xx. § 8). On the left are two of the bases which supported the Zanes (V. xxi. § 2–§ 18). Standing in this position the statues would serve as a timely warning against breach of the rules to competitors about to enter the race-course.

This end of the stadium, the western, was originally left open. In the next phase there was an embankment with an unroofed cutting through it; the vault was not built till late Hellenistic times. The stadium has been the subject of much recent investigation and its history has been traced. It was never provided with stone seating though the embankments were repeatedly remodelled. The race-course was surrounded by a low stone barrier, within which ran a stone gutter opening into basins; the starting-lines at each end were of the same type as at Delphi (Pl. 80). On the south side a stand for the judges was built.

PLATE 59

60.   Bronze Head of Boxer from Olympia (VI. iv. § 5 ?)

Of the numerous athlete statues listed by Pausanias, a number of bases are extant, but remains of the actual figures are very slight. This fine bronze head of an old boxer, now in the National Museum at Athens, has been conjecturally identified as belonging to the statue of the veteran Satyrus, a late work of the fourth-century Athenian sculptor Silanion, who made a portrait of Plato. It is more realistic and individualised than earlier athlete statues.

PLATE 60

139

61. Relief from Mantineia (VIII. ix. § 1).

Three marble slabs, found at Mantineia and now placed in the Museum at Athens, belonged without doubt to the pedestal seen by Pausanias. He merely speaks of " Muses together with Marsyas playing the flute." Actually on one slab are represented Apollo seated with his lyre, Marsyas with his flute, and between them, a Phrygian slave armed with the knife with which Marsyas was to be flayed. On each of the other slabs is a graceful group of three Muses; probably there was once a fourth slab on which the remaining three were carved.

PLATE 61

141

62. HEADS FROM TEGEA (VIII. xlv. § 6–7) (see Pl. 26).

Among the fragments of the pedimental sculptures discovered in the temple of Athena are a number of striking heads of heroes. The one at the bottom on the left may be identified as Heracles by the lion-skin head-dress. These heads, though very battered, reflect in such features as the deeply sunken eyes the passion and intensity characteristic of Scopas. Pausanias merely names Scopas as the architect, but it is a natural assumption that he was responsible for the sculpture too.

PLATE 62

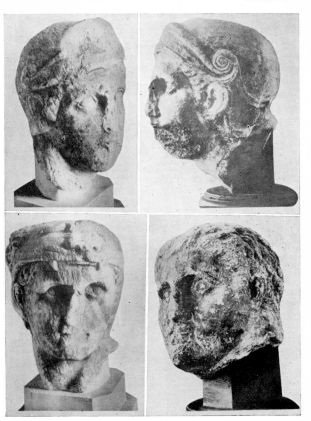

63. (*a*) VALLEY OF RIVER STYX. (VIII. xvii. § 6–xviii. § 6.)

Pl. 63 shows two examples of Arcadian scenery, very different but each typical in its own way.

The Styx, rising high up on the north-eastern side of the Aroanian Mountains and falling over a tremendous precipice (VIII. xvii. § 6), flows north-eastwards down a deep rocky glen to join the valley of the Crathis (VIII. xviii. § 4).

(*b*) VALLEY OF STYMPHALUS. (VIII. xxii.)

At Stymphalus as elsewhere in Arcadia the streams find difficulty in escaping from the mountain walls which enclose the valley; an underground chasm on the south provides a precarious exit. Consequently a mere of varying size forms in the valley (VIII. xxii. § 3).

The city of Stymphalus stood upon a ridge to the north, seen upon the left in the photograph.

PLATE 63

(a)

(b)

145

64. THEATRE AND THERSILIUM, MEGALOPOLIS (VIII. xxxii. § 1)
(see Pl. 24).

Facing the seats of the theatre are the steps of the porch of the Thersilium, with the great hall itself behind; the bases of its numerous interior columns stand in rows; beyond is the broad gravelly bed of the Helisson (VIII. xxx. § 2).

PLATE 64

65. TEMPLE OF THE MISTRESS, LYCOSURA (VIII. xxxvii. § 1–§ 7)
(see Pl. 25).

From the ridge to the south which Pausanias ascended after leaving the sanctuary (VIII. xxxvii. § 8) the plan of the temple is clearly seen, with the great base at the western end.

Across the valley to the north rise the foothills of Mount Lycaeus; when he describes the mountain as being to the left (xxxviii. 2), Pausanias imagines himself looking out eastward from the front of the temple.

PLATE 65

149

66. (*a*) ARTEMIS, LYCOSURA. (VIII. xxxvii. § 3, 4.)

(*b*) DEMETER, LYCOSURA.

Of the surviving fragments of Damophon's group, the best preserved, the heads of Demeter, Artemis and Anytus, and an elaborately carved fragment of drapery, are in the museum at Athens and are well known; but in the small museum on the site are considerable fragments of the rest of the figures, including the torsos of Demeter and Artemis illustrated here (the heads are restored).

The group was of marble, in several pieces, not one only, as Pausanias imagined. Demeter was seated on the right of the Mistress; Artemis, running forward with uplifted torch, flanked the group on the spectator's left, balanced by the bearded Titan Anytus on the right. These subsidiary figures were on a smaller scale, but still colossal.

The date at which Damophon worked is now generally placed early in the second century B.C.

PLATE 66

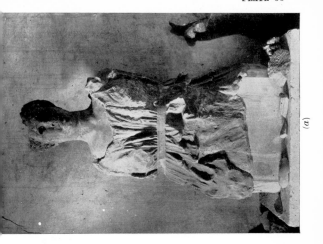

(a)

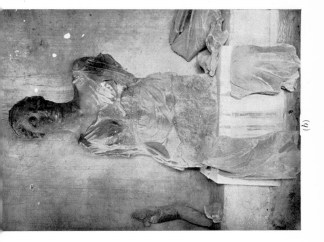

(b)

67.   Temple of Apollo, Bassae (VIII. xli. § 7–§ 9), from North-West (see Pl. 23 (*b*)).

PLATE 67

153

68.   TEMPLE OF APOLLO, BASSAE, INTERIOR, FROM SOUTH (see
Pl. 23 (*b*)).

Notice in the foreground the base of the free-standing Corinthian
column.

PLATE 68

155

69. Treasury of Minyas, Orchomenus. (IX. xxxviii. § 2.)

This building, which is, in fact, a tomb rather than a treasury, is very similar in style and design to the " treasury of Atreus" at Mycenae, with an approach cut through the hillside, a large circular domed chamber, and a smaller square inner chamber. In size too it is only slightly less than the " treasury of Atreus"— the diameter of the main room is about 14 m. But in point of preservation it is now far inferior. Much of the gateway still stands, tapering slightly towards the top, where it is crowned by a huge lintel, but only about eight courses of the wall of the circular chamber remain.

PLATE 69

70. GRAVE OF THEBANS, CHAERONEIA. (IX. xl. § 10.)

The grave of the Thebans who fell at the battle of Chaeroneia in 338 B.C. stands a little to the east of the city. The great marble lion measures 18 feet high; its fragments were restored and set upon a new pedestal in 1904. The actual grave consisted of a quadrangular enclosure sunk in the ground.

PLATE 70

159

71. VIEW EASTWARD FROM DELPHI (X. viii. § 6) (see Pl. 27).

The valley of the river Pleistus (X. viii. § 8) is on the right.
In the middle distance on the left Marmaria (see Pl. 73) is seen,
and behind it stretches the modern road from the east which
follows roughly the same line as that by which Pausanias
approached.

PLATE 71

72. SITE OF DELPHI (X. viii. § 6–xxxii. § 1) (see Pl. 27).

The remains of the sanctuary of Apollo are on the left.   Behind
rise the two great cliffs, 800 feet high, divided by the ravine from
the foot of which Castalia (see Pl. 74) flows.

PLATE 72

73. MARMARIA, DELPHI (X. viii. § 6) (see Pl. 27).

The two small temples seen by Pausanias are in the foreground. Beyond the round building are the remains of the temple of Athena. The slope of Mt. Cirphis rises away to the left, beyond the valley of the Pleistus. A section of the colonnade of the round building has now been re-erected. The purpose of this fine building of the early fourth century is quite uncertain. The " temple " nearer to it is generally identified as the treasury of Massilia.

PLATE 73

74. CASTALIA, DELPHI (X. viii. § 9, 10) (see Pl. 27).

In early times the spring received monumental treatment. The face of the rock is cut flat and contains several votive niches. The water, issuing at the foot on the right, enters first a deep narrow reservoir, the front of which is now largely broken away, then a wide open basin 10 m. by 3 m.

PLATE 74

[Photo, Alinari.

75. PORTICO OF ATHENIANS, DELPHI (X. xi. § 6) (see Pl. 28).

PLATE 75

76. OMPHALOS, DELPHI (X. xvi. § 3) (see Pl. 28).

The omphalos seen by Pausanias has been found outside the eastern end of the temple.   It is of marble, decorated with garlands of wool in relief.

Probably this was not the actual cult object, but a showy replica displayed for visitors to see.   The true omphalos stood in the innermost shrine.   In the ruins of the temple was found the small plain hemisphere of limestone seen in the photo on top of the marble replica; this was thought to be the sacred omphalos itself, but a recent careful examination (*Bulletin de Correspondence Hellénique*, LXXV, pp. 210–223) has shown that in fact it is an ancient block re-worked into its present shape in modern times to form the cupola of a small shrine.   The crude inscription, once interpreted as being E (a sacred symbol at Delphi) and ΓΑΣ "of earth," proves to be part of the name of one Papaloukas.

PLATE 76

77. DELPHI, SANCTUARY OF APOLLO, MODEL BY
H. SCHLEIF (See Pl. 28).

PLATE 77

78. THEATRE, DELPHI (X. xxxii. § 1) (see Pl. 28).

PLATE 78

175

79. RACE-COURSE, DELPHI (X. xxxii. § 1) (see Pl. 27).

PLATE 79.

80. Starting-line, Race-course, Delphi.

The line is formed of a row of marble slabs, sunk into the earth, divided into sections by holes in which posts were once set. Between these are pairs of grooves in which the runners placed their feet.

The race-courses at Epidaurus (Pl. 18) and Olympia (Pl. 22) had similar starting-lines.

Behind can be seen the seats on the north side and one of the stairways leading up to them.

PLATE 80

81. WALL, TITHOREA. (X. xxxii. § 8–§ 11.)

The walls of Tithorea provide a third example of Greek fortification at its best (for others see Pl. 41 and Pl. 53). They stand upon the north-eastern slopes of Parnassus. Large sections are preserved on the northern and western sides. They are built of fine ashlar masonry, almost perfectly regular, with massive square towers. The best preserved of these—seen in the photograph—stands to a height of almost 30 feet.

PLATE 81

181

82. Coins illustrating Pausanias.

1. Coin of Athens, bronze, reverse (British Museum Catalogue of Coins, Athens 801).

Eirene in long chiton; in right hand sceptre, on left arm infant Plutus, with cornucopia; copy of Cephisodotus' group (I. viii. § 2).

2. Coin of Cyzicus, electrum, obverse (B.M.C. Cyzicus 75).

Harmodius and Aristogeiton, charging to right; Aristogeiton with sword in right hand, chlamys on left arm; Harmodius with right hand upraised, holding sword; copy of group (I. viii. § 5). Beneath, tunny.

3. Coin of Athens, bronze, reverse (B.M.C. Athens 754).

Zeus, on throne, naked to waist; sceptre in left hand, figure of Victory on right; probably a copy of statue in Olympieum (I. xviii. § 6).

4. Coin of Athens, bronze, reverse (B.M.C. Athens 807).

Theatre; above, wall of Acropolis; above, in centre, Parthenon; to left, Propylaea, to right, Erechtheum.

5. Coin of Athens, bronze, reverse (B.M.C. Athens 707).

Olive tree entwined by snake; owl in branches; to left, Poseidon, trident in raised right hand; to right, Athena, with shield and spear in left hand (I. xxiv. § 5).

6. Coin of Athens, bronze, reverse (in Fitzwilliam Museum, Cambridge).

On left, Athena standing looking back towards Marsyas; Marsyas' right hand raised in attitude of surprise; possibly copy of Myron's group (I. xxiv. § 1).

7. Coin of Athens, bronze, reverse (B.M.C. Athens 691).

Athena standing; on right hand, Victory; in left, spear and shield; snake at feet; copy of Athena in Parthenon (I. xxiv. § 5–7).

8. Coin of Athens, bronze, reverse (B.M.C. Athens 678).

Athena standing; spear in right hand, shield on left arm, aegis on breast; probably copy of Pheidias' bronze Athena (I. xxviii. § 2).

9. Coin of Athens, bronze, reverse (B.M.C. Athens 803).

Acropolis; on left, Parthenon; on right Propylaea; between, Athena Promachus (I. xxviii. § 2); below, cave with Pan seated (I. xxviii. § 4).

10. Coin of Paphos, Cyprus, silver, reverse (B.M.C. Paphos 45).

Female figure wearing long chiton, and peplos fastened on shoulder with griffin's head fibula; in left hand branch, in right phiale; probably copy of Nemesis of Rhamnus (I. xxxiii. § 3).

11. Coin of Megara, bronze, reverse (B.M.C. Megara 43).

Artemis in short chiton, running to right; torch in each hand; copy of Artemis Saviour (I. xl. § 2).

12. Coin of Megara, bronze, reverse (B.M.C. Megara 50).

Asclepius, on left, half-draped; staff entwined with serpent in left hand; looking towards Health, who holds out right hand to him; probably copy of Bryaxis' group (I. xl. § 6).

PLATE 82

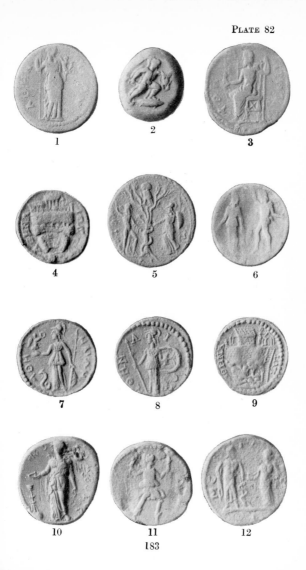

83. COINS.

1. Coin of Corinth, bronze, reverse (B.M.C. Corinth 624).
Round temple; inside, Palaemon on dolphin; on either side, trees; temple of Palaemon (II. ii. § 1).

2. Coin of Corinth bronze, reverse (B.M.C. Corinth 691).
Lioness standing over prostrate ram, on Doric capital; tomb of Lais (II. ii. § 4).

3. Coin of Corinth, bronze, reverse (B.M.C. Corinth 696).
Aphrodite, naked to waist, holding shield; on right, Eros; probably representing statue of Aphrodite on Acrocorinthus (II. v. § 1).

4. Coin of Corinth, bronze, reverse (B.M.C. Corinth 608).
Hermes seated on rock; right hand on head of ram; copy of statue mentioned in II. iii. § 4.

5. Coin of Corinth, bronze, reverse (B.M.C. Corinth 616).
Acrocorinthus; temple on top; at foot buildings and trees (II. iv. § 6–v. § 4).

6. Coin of Sicyon, bronze, reverse (B.M.C. Sicyon 245).
Tomb (small temple) on basis between two terminal figures and two cypresses (see II. vii. § 2).

7. Coin of Argos, silver, obverse (B.M.C. Argos 33).
Head of Hera, of fine style, wearing flowered crown; type probably influenced by Polycleitus' Hera (II. xvii. § 4).

8. Coin of Epidaurus, silver, reverse (B.M.C. Epidaurus 156).
Asclepius seated, with dog and snake; probably copy of Thrasymedes' statue (II. xxvii. § 2).

9. Coin of Argos, bronze, reverse (B.M.C. Argos 151).
Leto, with right hand raised to shoulder, left hand extended over small figure of Chloris; copy of Praxiteles' group (II. xxi. § 9).

PLATE 83

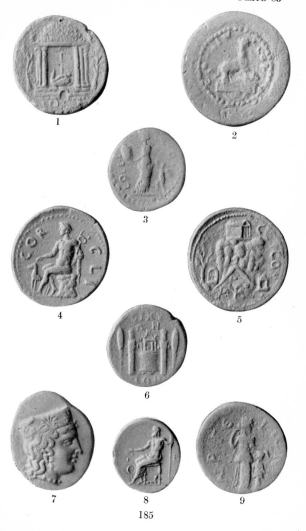

1

2

3

4

5

6

7

8

9

185

84. Coins.

1. Coin of Sparta, bronze, reverse (B.M.C. Laconia 87).

Athena, with helmet, spear and shield; lower part of body arranged in bands; copy of Athena of the Bronze House (III. xvii. § 2).

2. Coin of Sparta, silver, reverse (B.M.C. Laconia 1).

Apollo, in long chiton, with helmet, spear and bow; beside him, goat; probably copy of Apollo of Amyclae (III. xix. § 1).

3. Coin of Sparta, bronze, reverse (B.M.C. Laconia 80).

Apollo, similar to above but without chiton and on basis; later and probably more faithful copy of Apollo of Amyclae.

4. Coin of Messene, silver, reverse (B.M.C. Messenia 11).

Zeus striding to right; in right hand, thunderbolt; on left wrist, eagle; free copy of Zeus Ithomatas (IV. xxxiii. § 2).

5. Coin of Elis, bronze, obverse (in Paris).

Head of Zeus, crowned with laurel wreath; copy of Pheidias' Zeus (V. xi.).

6. Coin of Elis, bronze, reverse (in Florence).

Zeus seated on throne; in left hand, sceptre; on right hand, figure of Victory; copy of Pheidias' Zeus.

7. Coin of Patrae, bronze, reverse (B.M.C. Patrae 34).

Priestess in chariot drawn by two stags; representation of rite described in VII. xviii. § 12.

8. Coin of Patrae, bronze, reverse (B.M.C. Patrae 38).

Artemis, in short chiton with right breast bare; chlamys over left arm; right hand on hip, in left hand bow; to left, dog; to right, pedestal; copy of Artemis Laphria (VII. xviii. § 8).

9. Coin of Delphi, bronze, reverse (B.M.C. Delphi 33).

Temple with six columns at side; in entry, statue of Apollo, resting left elbow on pillar, right arm advanced; at feet omphalos or altar; conventional representation of temple of Apollo (X. xix.; see Pl. 28).

(Representations of statues are common on Greek coins, particularly in the Roman Imperial period, and most especially in the age of Hadrian and the Antonine emperors, Pausanias' own time. It is to this age that most of the coins shown here belong. Earlier coins—Pl. 82. 2, 83. 7, 84. 2, 4—give freer and less faithful representations.)

PLATE 84

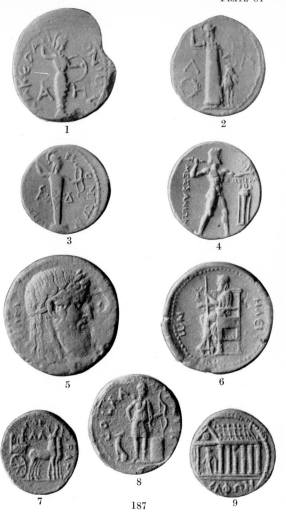

1   2

3   4

5   6

7   8   9

187

85 (*a*) and (*b*). PEDIMENTS OF TEMPLE OF ZEUS, OLYMPIA (restored). (V. x. § 5–§ 8.)

These restorations are by G. Treu (*Jahrbuch d. deutsch. arch. Inst.*, 1889, Pl. 8, 9, and 1888, Pl. 5, 6). Other attempts at arranging the fragments and filling in the gaps vary in many details, but this is perhaps the most reliable version.

Pausanias mentions every figure in the eastern pediment. Oenomaus and his wife were " on the right " of the central figure Zeus from the spectator's point of view; Pelops and his bride balanced them on the left. Next on either side was a chariot with three attendants. Oenomaus' attendants, apart from his charioteer, were an interesting old man and a girl, not two men as Pausanias says. The two river gods reclined in the extreme corners.

The description of the western pediment breaks off abruptly in the middle. The calm majestic figure in the centre must be a god, no doubt Apollo, not Peirithous as Pausanias says. Peirithous would be taking a hand in the fight. He probably stood upon Apollo's right, Theseus on his left, each attacking a Centaur who is carrying off a woman. On either side of this central composition was a Lapith struggling with a Centaur, followed by groups of three—a woman, a Centaur and a Lapith, and finally, in each of the corners, an old woman and a young woman reclining. Pausanias becomes rather vague before breaking off altogether. When he says " One Centaur has seized a maid, another a boy," it is difficult to see to which groups he refers.

Few believe Pausanias' statement that the pedimental sculptures were made by Paeonius and Alcamenes. They must have been made some years before the middle of the fifth century; and on other evidence the work of the two artists is placed much later in the century. Recently, however, C. H. Morgan has argued convincingly that Pausanias is, after all, correct (*Hesperia*, XXI, pp. 295 ff.).

(*c*) CHEST OF CYPSELUS (restored). (V. xvii. § 5–xix. § 10.)

Several restorations of the chest have been attempted, based upon Pausanias' description and on the treatment of similar subjects on vases. The best and most probably correct, illustrated here, is by H. Stuart Jones (*Journal of Hellenic Studies*, XIV, 1894, Pl. 1).

The chest was probably a work of Corinthian art, produced early in the sixth century B.C. The figures were inlaid. It is not certain how the five bands mentioned by Pausanias were arranged; most probably they were entirely on the front of the chest, or possibly they extended round the ends too. Pausanias begins at the bottom, and describes the first, third and fifth rows from right to left, and the second and fourth from left to right. The figures in the second and fourth rows seem to have been divided into smaller and more distinct groups than in the rest. The first row is described in chap. xvii. § 6–§ 11; the second in xviii. § 1–§ 5; the third in xviii. § 6–§ 8; the fourth in xix. § 1–§ 6; the fifth in xix. § 7–§ 9.

GENERAL INDEX

GENERAL INDEX

ABAE, IV. xxxii. § 5, X. iii. § 2, X. xxxv. § 1–4

Abantes, V. xxii. § 3, 4, VII. ii. § 4, iv. § 9

Abantidas, tyrant of Sicyon, II. viii. § 2

Abantis, in Epirus, V. xxii. § 3, 4

Abaris, Hyperborean, III. xiii. § 2

Abas, son of Lynceus, II. xii. § 2, xvi. § 2, xxv. § 5, III. xiii. § 8, X. xxxv. § 1

—— son of Melampus, I. xliii. § 5

Abasa, VI. xxvi. § 9

Abdera, VI. v. § 4, xiv. § 12

Abia, IV. xxx. § 1

Abrupolis, king of Sapaeans, VII. x. § 6

Abydus, III. ix. § 12

Acacallis, nymph, X. xvi. § 5

—— daughter of Minos, VIII. liii. § 4

Acacesium, VIII. iii. § 2, xxvii. § 4, xxxvi. § 10

Acacus, son of Lycaon, VIII. iii. § 2, xxxvi. § 10

Academy, I. xxix. § 2, 4, xxx. § 1, 3

Acamas, son of Theseus, I. v. § 2, X. x. § 1, xxvi. § 2

Acanthus, Lacedaemonian victor, V. viii. § 6

Acarnania, I. xxv. § 4, xxviii. § 3, III. x. § 2, IV. xxv. § 1–10, V. xxvi. § 1, VI. ii. § 1, VII. xviii. § 9, xxi. § 2, VIII. xxiv. § 9, IX. xxxi. § 5, X. xvi. § 6

Acastus, I. xviii. § 1, III. xviii. § 16, V. xvii. § 10, VI. xx. § 19

Acê, VIII. xxxiv. § 2

Acesidas, V. xiv. § 7

Acesis, II. xi. § 7

Acestium, daughter of Xenocles, I. xxxvii. § 1

Achaeus, son of Xuthus, II. vi. § 5, VII. i. § 2, 3, 6

Achaia, spring, IV. xxxiii. § 7

—— description VII, history VII. i. § 1–8, vi. § 1–xvii. § 4

Acharnae, I. xxxi. § 6

Achelous, river in Aetolia, I. xxxiv. § 3, xli. § 2, II. ii. § 3, III. xviii. § 16, IV. xxxiv. § 1, V. i. § 8, VI. xix. § 12, VIII. xxiv. § 9, 11, xxxviii. § 10, IX. xxxiv. § 3, X. viii. § 9

—— river in Arcadia, VIII. xxxviii. § 9, 10

Acheron, river, I. xvii. § 5, V. xiv. § 2, X. xxviii. § 1, 4

Acherusia, lake, I. xvii. § 5, II. xxxv. § 10

Achichorius, Gaul, X. xix. § 7, xx. § 10, 12, 13, xxiii. § 12

Achilleius, harbour, III. xxv. § 4

Achilles, I. iv. § 4, xi. § 1, xii. § 1, xiii. § 9, xxii. § 6, xxxiii. § 8, xxxvii. § 3
II. v. § 5, xxiii. § 6
III. iii. § 8, iv. § 7, xviii. § 12, xix. § 8, xxiv. § 10, 11, xxv. § 1, xxvi. § 7
IV. vi. § 3, xvii. § 4, xxviii. § 7, xxx. § 1
V. xi. § 6, xix. § 1, 9, xxii. § 2
VI. xi. § 5
VIII. xvi. § 3, xlv. § 7
IX. xxix. § 7, xxxi. § 5, xxxviii. § 8
X. vii. § 1, xiv. § 4, xvi. § 4, xxiv. § 4, xxv. § 10, xxvi. § 4, xxvii. § 2, xxix. § 10

—— cult, II. i. § 8, III. xix. § 11, xx. § 8, xxiv. § 5, VI. xxiii. § 3, xxiv. § 1

—— representations, X. xiii. § 5, xxx. § 3.

Achladaeus, Corinthian general, IV. xix. § 2

Acidas, river, V. v. § 8

Acorns, eaten, VIII. i. § 6

Acraea, II. xvii. § 1, 2

GENERAL INDEX

Acraephnium, IX. xxiii. § 5

Acratus, I. ii. § 5

Acriae, III. xxi. § 7, xxii. § 4–6, VI. xxi. § 10

Acrisius, II. xvi. § 1–3, xxiii. § 7, xxv. § 7, III. xiii. § 8, X. v. § 11

Acritas, cape, IV. xxxiv. § 12

Acrochersites, VI. iv. § 1

Acrocorinthus, II. i. § 6, iv. § 6, v. § 1, 4, VII. vii. § 6, viii. § 3.

Acropolis of Athens, I. xxi. § 4–xxviii. § 3

Acrotatus, son of Areus, III. vi. § 6
—— son of Cleomenes, I. xiii. § 5, III. vi. § 11, 13, xxx. § 7

Actaea, Attica called, I. ii. § 6

Actaeon, I. xliv. § 5, IX. ii. § 3, 4, xxxviii. § 5, X. xvii. § 3, xxx. § 5, xxxi. § 3

Actaeus, king of Attica, I. ii. § 6, v. § 3, xiv. § 7

Actium, v. xxiii. § 3, VII. xviii. § 8, VIII. viii. § 12, X. viii. § 3

Actor, son of Phorbas, and sons, II. xv. § 1, III. xviii. § 15, v. i. § 10–ii. § 1, iii. § 3, VI. xx. § 16, VIII. xiv. § 9

Acusilaus, of Miletus, II. xvi. § 4
—— Rhodian victor, VI. vii. § 1–3

Adeimantus, Athenian general, IV. xvii. § 3, X. ix. § 11

Admetus, III. xviii. § 16, V. xvii. § 9, 10

Adonis, II. xx. § 6, VI. xxiv. § 7, IX. xvi. § 4, xxix. § 8, xli. § 2, 3

Adrasteia, X. xxxvii. § 8
—— spring, II. xv. § 3

Adrastus, Lydian, VII. vi. § 6
—— son of Polyneices, II. xx. § 5
—— son of Talaus, I. xxx. § 4, xxxix. § 2, xliii. § 1, xliv. § 4, II. vi. § 6, xi. § 1, 2, vx. § 5, xxiii. § 2, III. xviii. § 12, VII. xvii. § 7, VIII. xxv. § 8–10, IX. ix. § 2, v. § 12, ix. § 2, 3, xviii. § 1, xix. § 2, X. x. § 3, xxv. § 7

Adriatic Sea, V. xxv. § 3, VIII. liv. § 3

Adristas, VIII. iv. § 1

Aeacides, father of Pyrrhus, I. ix. § 7, xi. § 1, 3, 4

Aeacus, I. xiii. § 3, 9, xxxix. § 6, xliv. § 9, II. xxix. § 2–xxx. § 5

Aechmagoras, son of Heracles, VIII. xii. § 3

Aechmeas, Parapotamian victor, X. xxxiii. § 8

Aedos, I. xvii. § 1, III. xxx. § 10

Aegae, VII. vi. § 1, xxv. § 12, VIII. xv. § 9

Aegean Sea, I. i. § 1, II. xxii. § 1, v. xxi. § 10, VIII. xiv. § 12, IX. xi. § 5

Aegeira, VI. iii. § 6, VII. vi. § 1, xxvi. § 1–14, xxvii. § 11, VIII. xv. § 5, 8

Aegeus, son of Oeolycus, III. xv. § 8, IV. vii. § 8
—— son of Pandion, I. v. § 2, 4, xiv. § 7, xix. § 3, xxii. § 4, xxvii. § 8, xxxix. § 4, II. iii. § 8, xxxii. § 7, IV. ii. § 6, VIII. xxiii. § 3, X. x. § 1, xxix. § 10, xxxv. § 8

Aegiae, III. xxi. § 5–7

Aegialea, II. v. § 6, vi. § 2, vii. § 7

Aegialeus, son of Adrastus, I. xliii. § 1, xliv. § 4, II. xviii. § 4, xx. § 5, xxx. § 10, IX. v. § 13, xix. § 2, X. x. § 4

Aegialus, II. v. § 6, vi. § 5, v. i. § 1, VII. i. § 1–4

Aegila, IV. xvii. § 1

Aegimius, II. xxviii. § 6, VII. xvii. § 6

Aegina, daughter of Asopus, II. v. § 1, 2, xxix. § 2, v. xxii. § 6, X. xiii. § 6
—— island, I. xxix. § 5, 7, xxxv. § 2, II. xxix. § 2–xxx. § 5, xxxviii. § 5, III. iv. § 2, VIII. v. § 8

Aeginetan style (sculpture), I. xli. § 5, II. xxx. § 1, v. xxv. § 13, VII. v. § 5, VIII. xliii. § 11, X. xvii. § 12, xxxvi. § 5

Aeginetes, son of Derites, VII. xviii. § 5
—— son of Pompus, VIII. v. § 8–10

Aegisthus, I. xxii. § 6, II. xvi. § 6, xviii. § 2, 6, grave II. xvi. § 7

Aegium, II. ix. § 4, III. xii. § 7, xxi. § 1, VI. iii. § 12, 13, VII. vi. § 1, vii. § 2, xxii. § 10–xxiv. § 5, xxv. § 4, X. xxiii. § 14

Aegospotami, III. viii. § 6, xi. § 5, xvii. § 4, IV. xvii. § 3, xxvi. § 2, v. iii. § 15, ix. xxxii, § 7, 9, offerings from spoils III. xviii. § 8, X. ix. § 7–11

Aegosthena, I. xliv. § 4, 5

Aegyptus, son of Belus, II. xxiv. § 2, VII. xxi. § 13
—— river, IX. xl. § 6

Aeneas, I. xi. § 7, II. xxi. § 1, xxiii. § 5, III. xxii. § 11, v. xxii. § 2, VII. xix. § 7, VIII. xii. § 8, X. xvii. § 6, xxvi. § 1

GENERAL INDEX

Aenesidemus, of Leontini, V. xxii. § 7

Aenetus, Laconian victor, III. xviii. § 7

Aenianians, X. viii. § 2, 3, xxii. § 8–10

Aeolians, I. xxxv. § 4, III. ii. § 1, v. xxiv. § 6, VII. v. § 1, VIII. xii. § 9, dialect IX. xxii. § 3

Aeolus, IV. ii. § 5, V. viii. § 2, VI. xxi. § 11, xxii. § 2, IX. xx. § 1, xl. § 5, X. xi. § 3, xxxviii. § 4

Aepytus, son of Cresphontes, IV. iii. § 6–9, ix. § 4–10, v. § 1, x. § 5, xxvii. § 6, VIII. v. § 7

—— son of Elatus, VIII. iv. § 4, 7, xvi. § 2, 3

—— son of Hippothous, VIII. v. § 4–6, x. § 3

—— founder of Priene, VII. ii. § 10

Aeropus, VIII. v. § 1, xliv. § 8

Aeschines, Elean victor, VI. xiv. § 13

Aeschylus, I. ii. § 3, xiv. § 5, xxi. § 2 xxviii. § 6, II. xiii. § 6, xx. § 5, xxvi. § 4, VIII. vi. § 6, xxxvii. § 6, IX. xxii. § 7, X. iv. § 7

Aesimides, archon, I. iii. § 3, IV. v. § 10

Aesymnetes, VII. xx. § 1, 2, xxi. § 6

Aesymnus, Megarian, I. xliii. § 3

Aesypus, Elean victor, VI. ii. § 8

Aetha, mare of Agamemnon, V. viii. § 3

Aethidas, Messenian hero, IV. xxxii. § 2

Aethiopians, I. xxxiii. § 3–5, xlii. § 2–5, II. v. § 3, V. vii. § 4, xii. § 1, 3, VI. xxvi. § 2, 9, VIII. xxxviii. § 6, IX. xxi. § 2, 6, X. xxxi. § 7

Aethlius, king of Elis, v. i. § 3, viii. § 2

Aethra, wife of Phalanthus, X. x. § 8

—— mother of Theseus, I. xli. § 4, II. xxxi. § 9, xxxiii. § 1, V. xix. § 3, X. xxv. § 7, 8

Aetius, II. xxx. § 8, 9, xxxi. § 10

Aetna, III. xxiii. § 9, X. xxviii. § 4

Aetolians, I. iv. § 4, xxv. § 4, xxvi. § 3, xxxvi. § 5, II. viii. § 4, III. x. § 2, IV. xxv. § 3, v. i. § 3, 8, iii. § 7, iv. § 2, vi. § 1, xv. § 12, xviii. § 6, VI. xiv. § 11, xv. § 2, xvi. § 1, 2, xxiii. § 8, VII. vii. § 6–8, viii. § 3, ix. § 6, xi. § 3, xviii. § 6–9, xx. § 6, xxi. § 2, VIII. xxiv. § 11, xlix. § 7, 1. § 10, X. xv. § 2, xvi. § 4, 6, xix. § 4, xx. § 4, xxii. § 2–13, xxiii. § 12, xxxi. § 3, xxxviii. § 4

Aetolus, son of Endymion, v. i. § 4, 8, iii. § 6

Aetolus, son of Oxylus, V. iv. § 4

Agamedes and Trophonius, VIII. x. § 2, IX. xi. § 1, xxxvii. § 4–7, xxxix. § 6, X. v. § 13

Agamemnon, I. ii. § 3, iv. § 6, xxxiii. § 8, xliii. § 1, II. iv. § 2, v. § 4, vi. § 7, xii. § 5, xviii. § 2, xxii. § 6, xxvi. § 10, III. ix. § 3, 4, xix. § 6, xxii. § 10, xxvi. § 7, IV. xxx. § 1, xxxvi. § 6, v. xix. § 4, xxiv. § 11, xxv. § 9, VII. v. § 11, xxiv. § 2, VIII. i. § 3, xxviii. § 4, IX. xvii. § 3, xix. § 7, xxxviii. § 8, xli. § i, X. xxv. § 8, xxvi. § 8, xxix. § 10, xxx. § 3, tomb II. xvi. § 6, sceptre worshipped IX. xl. § 11

Agametor, Mantinean victor, VI. ix. § 9

Aganippe, IX. xxix. § 5

Agapenor, king of Arcadia, VIII. v. § 2–4, x. § 3, x. § 10, liii. § 7

Agasisthenes, Spartan, VII. xii. § 7

Agathocles, archon, X. ii. § 3

—— son of Lysimachus, I. ix. § 6, x. § 3

—— of Syracuse, VI. xii. § 2

Agdistis, mountain, I. iv. § 5

—— deity, VII. xvii. § 10–12

Agelaus, Tegean victor, V. vii. § 7

Ageles, Chian victor, VI. xv. § 2

Agelus, son of Poseidon, VII. iv. § 8

Agemachus, Cyzicene victor, VI. xiii. § 7

Agenor, Theban victor, VI. vi. § 2

Agesarchus, Tritaean victor, VI. xii. § 2

Agesicles, Spartan, III. vii. § 6

Agesilas, victor, of Lusi, VIII. xviii. § 8

Agesilaus, son of Archidamus, III. viii. § 1–x. § 3, IV. xvii. § 5, VI. iv. § 9, VIII. vi. § 2, IX. xiii. § 2, xiv. § 5

—— son of Doryssus, III. ii. § 4, IV. iv. § 2

Agesipolis, son of Cleombrotus, I. xiii. § 4, III. vi. § 2

—— son of Pausanias, III. v. § 7–vi. § 1, VIII. viii. § 7–9, IX. xiv. § 4

Agiadae, III. ii. § 1, vii. § 1, xiv. § 2

Agiadas, Elean victor, VI. x. § 9

Agias, seer, III. xi. § 5, X. ix. § 7

Agis, son of Archidamus, III. v. § 2, viii. § 1–10, IV. iv. § 8, VI. ii. § 3, VII. x. § 2

—— son of Eudamidas, II. viii. § 5, III. x. § 5, VI. ii. § 4, VII. vii. § 3,

GENERAL INDEX

VIII. viii. § 11, x. § 5–8, xxvii. § 13, 14, xxxvi. § 6

Aglaurus, I. ii. § 6, xviii. § 2, xxxviii. § 3

Aglaus, of Psophis, VIII. xxiv. § 13

Agnaptus, portico, V. xv. § 6, VI. xx. § 10, 13

Agorius, descendant of Orestes, V. iv. § 3

Agrae, I. xix. § 6

Agrigentines, V. xxv. § 5, 7

Agrolas, I. xxviii. § 3

Ajax, son of Oileus, I. xv. § 1, III. xix. § 12, 13, v. xi. § 6, xix. § 5, X. xxvi. § 3, xxxi. § 1–3

—— son of Telamon, I. v. § 2, xxviii. § 11, xlii. § 4, II. xxix. § 4, III. xix. § 13, V. xix. § 2, xxii. § 2, X. xiv. § 2, xxxi. § 1, worship I. xxxv. § 2–5

Alagonia, III. xxi. § 7, xxvi. § 11

Alalcomenae, IX. iii. § 4, xxxiii. § 5–7, xxxiv. § 1

Alalcomenia, spring, VIII. xii. § 7

Alcaenetus, Leprean victor, VI. vii. § 8, 9

Alcaeus, VII. xx. § 4, X. viii. § 10

Alcamenes, Spartan, III. ii. § 7, iii. § 1, IV. iv. § 4, v. § 9

—— Achaean, VII. xv. § 8, 10

Alcander, III. xviii. § 2

Alcathous, son of Pelops, I. xli. § 3–xliii. § 5

Alcetas, king of Epirus, I. xi. § 1–5

Alcetus, victor, of Cleitor, VI. ix. § 2

Alcibiadas, Lacedaemonian, VII. ix. § 2–4

Alcibiades, I. xxii. § 6, xxix. § 13, III. xvii. § 4, IX. xxxii. § 6, victory in chariot-race I. xxii. § 7, statue VI. iii. § 15

Alcimedon, VIII. xii. § 2

Alcimus, III. xv. § 1

Alcinous, I. ii. § 3, III. xxiv. § 11, v. xix. § 9, VIII. xlviii. § 3, 6

Alcippe, daughter of Ares, I. xxi. § 4

Alcis, daughter of Antipoenus, IX. xvii. § 1

Alcmaeon, son of Amphiaraus, I. xxxiv. § 3, II. i. § 8, xx. § 5, V. xvii. § 7, VI. xvii. § 6, 8, VIII. xxiv. § 7–10, X. x. § 4

Alcman, I. xli. § 4, III. xv. § 2, 3. xviii. § 6, xxvi. § 2

Alcmena, V. xvii. § 8, xviii. § 3, IX.

xi. § 1, 3, xvi. § 7, altar I. xix. § 3, tomb I. xli. § 1

Alcon, shrine of, III. xiv. § 7

Alcyone, daughter of Atlas, II. xxx. § 8, III. xviii. § 10, IX. xxii. § 5

Alcyonian Lake, II. xxxvii. § 5, 6

Alea, VIII. xxiii. § 1, xxvii. § 3

Aleaea, games, VIII. xlvii. § 4

Ales, river, VII. v. § 10, VIII. xxviii. § 3

Alesiae, III. xx. § 2

Alesius, Mount, VIII. x. § 1, 2

Aletes, II. iv. § 3, 4, V. viii. § 8

Aleuadae, III. vii. § 9, VII. x. § 2

Aleus, king of Arcadia, V. v. § 5, VIII. iv. § 4–10, xxiii. § 1, xlv. § 1, 4, xlviii. § 7, liii. § 10

Alexander the Great, I. iv. § 1, vi. § 2, 3, vii. § 1, ix. § 5, 8, xi. § 1, xii. § 3, xxv. § 3, 5, xxxvii. § 5, II. i. § 5, xxxiii. § 5, IV. xiv. § 8, xxvii. § 10, xxxv. § 4, V. xxi. § 9, VI. iv. § 8, xviii. § 2, 3, 6, VII. iii. § 9, v. § 1, vi. § 9, x. § 3, 10, xvii. § 2, xxvii. § 7, VIII. vii. § 7, xviii. § 6, xxviii. § 1, xxxii. § 1, lii. § 5, IX. vi. § 5, vii. § 1, 2, x. § 1, xxiii. § 5, 6, xxv. § 10, xl. § 9, statues I. ix. § 4, V. xx. § 10, xxv. § 1, VI. xi. § 1

—— son of above, I. vi. § 3, IX. vii. § 1

—— son of Cassander, I. x. § 1, xxxvi. § 6, IX. vii. § 3

—— son of Cleopatra, I. ix. § 1–3

—— son of Lysimachus, I. x. § 4, 5

—— son of Priam, I. xiii. § 9, III. xii. § 6, xviii. § 12, V. xix. § 5, xxii. § 2, X. xxxiii. § 2, made sanctuary of Aphrodite III. xxii. § 1, 2

—— tyrant of Pherae, VI. v. § 2, IX. xv. § 1

—— poet, II. xxii. § 7

Alexandra, III. xix. § 6, xxvi. § 5

Alexandria, in Egypt, I. ix. § 2, xviii. § 4, II. ix. § 3, V. xxi. § 9–13, 18, VI. xxiii. § 6, VIII. xxxiii. § 3

—— in Troad, X. xii. § 4, 5, xiv. § 4

Alexanor, II. xi. § 5–7, xxiii. § 4

Alexiarus, IX. xxv. § 7

Alexibius, Heraean victor, VI. xvii. § 4

Alexinicus, Elean victor, VI. xvii. § 7

Alimus, I. xxxi. § 1

Aliphera, VIII. iii. § 4, xxvi. § 5, 6. xxvii. § 7

GENERAL INDEX

Alitherses, VII. iv. § 1, X. x. § 3

Almus, son of Sisyphus, II. iv. § 3, IX. xxxiv. § 10, xxxvi. § 1, xxxvii. § 1

Alœus, II. iii. § 10, IX. xxii. § 6, xxix. § 1, 2

Alope, I. v. § 2, xiv. § 3, xxxix. § 3

Alopecus, III. xvi. § 9

Alphesiboea, VIII. xxiv. § 8

Alpheius, Lacedaemonian, III. xii. § 9

Alpheius, river, III. viii. § 4, V. vi. § 7, vii. § 1–5, x. § 7, xiii. § 11, xiv. § 3, 6, xxiv. § 7, VI. xxi. § 4, 5, xxii. § 6, 9, VIII. xiv. § 12, xx. § 3, xxiv. § 4, xxix. § 5, xxx. § 1, xxxiv. § 5, xxxv. § 1, 3, xxxvi. § 9, xxxviii. § 9, xliv. § 3, liv. § 1–3, X. xxv. § 3

Altars, of Olympia, V. xiii. § 8—xv. § 12, of ashes V. xiii. § 8, V. xiv. § 8, xv. § 9, IX. xi. § 7, of unbaked brick VI. xx. § 11, of unshaped stones VII. xxii. § 5, of wood IX. iii. § 6, of silver II. xvii. § 6, tomb of Aeacus II. xxix. § 8

Althepus, II. xxx. § 5–7, xxxii. § 8

Altis, V. x. § 1

Alyattes, V. x. § 3, X. xvi. § 1

Alyssus, spring, VIII. xix. § 3

Amalthaea, IV. xxx. § 6, VI. xix. § 6, xxv. § 4, VII. xxvi. § 8

Amarynceus, V. i. § 10, iii. § 4

Amarysia, I. xxxi. § 5

Amazons, I. ii. § 1, xv. § 2, xvii. § 2, xxv. § 2, xli. § 7, II. xxxi. § 4, xxxii. § 9, III. xxv. § 3, IV. xxxi. § 8, V. x. § 9, xi. § 4, 7, xxv. § 11, VII. ii. § 7, 8

Amber, V. xii. § 7, IX. xli. § 5

Ambracia, V. xxiii. § 2, 3, VI. iii. § 7, X. ix. § 10, xi. § 6, xviii. § 4

Ambrosus, IV. xxxi. § 5, IX. xiii. § 3, X. iii. § 2, xxxvi. § 1–5

Aminius, river, VIII. xxix. § 5

Ammon, III. xviii. § 3, xxi. § 8, IV. xiv. § 8, xxiii. § 10, V. xv. § 11, VI. viii. § 3, VIII. xi. § 11, xxxii. § 1, IX. xvi. § 1, X. xiii. § 5

Ampheia, IV. v. § 9–vii. § 3, 10, ix. § 3

Amphiaraus, I. xxxiv. § 1–5, II. xiii. § 7, xxxvii. § 5, III. xii. § 5, xviii. § 2, V. xvii. § 7–9, VII. xvii. § 7, IX. viii. § 3, xviii. § 1, xix. § 4, cult I. viii. § 2, xxxiv. § 1–5, II. xxiii. § 2, III. xii. § 5, VIII. ii. § 4, xlv. § 7, X. x. § 3

Amphicleia, X. iii. § 2, xxxiii. § 9–xxxiv. § 1

Amphiclus, VII. iv. § 9

Amphictyon, son of Deucalion, I. ii. § 5, 6, xxxi. § 3, X. viii. § 1, 2

Amphictyones, II. ix. § 6, VI. iv. § 3, xiv. § 10, VII. x. § 10, xxiv. § 4, VIII. xviii. § 8, X. ii. § 1, 4, iii. § 3, v. § 13, vii. § 3–6, viii. § 1–5, xv. § 1, 7, xix. § 1, 2, xxxiii. § 8, 9, xxxvii. § 6, 8

Amphilochus, son of Amphiaraus, II. xviii. § 4, 5, xx. § 5, V. xvii. § 7, X. x. § 4, cult I. xxxiv. § 3, III. xv. § 8

Amphimachus, Elean, V. iii. § 3, 4

Amphion, II. vi. § 4, xxi. § 9, VI. xx. § 18, IX. v. § 6–9, viii. § 4, xvi. § 7, xvii. § 2–7, xxv. § 3, grave IX. xvii. § 4, X. xxxii. § 11

Amphipolis, I. x. § 2, xxix. § 13

Amphissa, II. viii. § 4, III. iii. § 9, VII. xiv. § 7, X. xxii. § 12, xxxviii. § 4–9

Amphitrite, I. xvii. § 3, II. i. § 7, 8, III. xvii. § 3, xix. § 3, V. xi. § 8, xxvi. § 2

Amphitryon, I. xxxvii. § 6, V. xviii. § 3, VIII. xiv. § 2, xv. § 6, IX. x. § 4, xi. § 1, 2, xvii. § 3, xix. § 3, grave I. xli. § 1

Amphitus, river, IV. xxxiii. § 3

Amphoterus, son of Alcmaeon, VIII. xxiv. § 9

Ampyx, son of Pelias, V. xvii. § 10, VII. xviii. § 5

Amyclae, II. xvi. § 4, 6, III. i. § 3, 6, x. § 1, 8, xii. § 9, xvi. § 2, xviii. § 6–xix. § 6, xx. § 6, IV. xviii. § 3, V. xi. § 4

Amyclas, Spartan, III. i. § 3, VII. xviii. § 5, X. ix. § 5

Amymone, daughter of Danaus, II. xxxvii. § 1, xxxviii. § 2, IV. xxxv. § 2

—— river, II. xxxvii. § 1, 4, V. xvii. § 11

Amyntas, Ephesian victor, VI. iv. § 5

—— father of Philip of Macedon, I. vi. § 8, statue V. xx. § 10

Amythaon, son of Cretheus, V. viii. § 2

Anacharsis, I. xxii. § 8

Anaclethris, rock, I. xliii. § 2

Anacreon, I. ii. § 3, xxv. § 1

Anactorium, V. xxiii. § 2, 3

Anactorum, building, II. xiv. § 4

GENERAL INDEX

Anaea, VII. iv. § 3
Anagyrus, I. xxxi. § 1
Anaphlystus, II. xxx. § 9
Anauchidas, Elean victor, V. xxvii. § 12, VI. xiv. § 11, xvi. § 1
Anax, son of Earth, I. xxxv. § 6, VII. ii. § 5
Anaxagoras, king of Argos, II. xviii. § 4, xxx. § 10
Anaxander, king of Sparta, III. iii. § 4, 5, xiv. § 4, IV. xv. § 3, xvi. § 2, 3, 8, xxii. § 5, 6
—— Laconian victor, VI. i. § 7
Anaxandra, III. xvi. § 6
Anaxandrides, III. iii. § 5, 9, 10
Anaxibia, II. xxix. § 4
Anaxicrates, archon, X. xxiii. § 14
Anaxidamus, III. vii. § 6, IV. xv. § 3
Anaxilas, IV. xxiii. § 6, 8, 9, V. xxvi. § 4
Anaximenes, VI. xviii. § 2–6
Anaxis, II. xxii. § 5, III. xviii. § 13
Ancaeus, son of Lycurgus, VIII. iv. § 10, xlv. § 2, 7
—— son of Poseidon, VII. iv. § 1
Anchesmus, Mount, I. xxxii. § 2
Anchises, VIII. xii. § 8, 9
Anchisiae, VIII. xii. § 9, xiii. § 1
Ancyra, I. iv. § 5
Andania, IV. i. § 2, 8, 9, ii. § 6, iii. § 7, 10, xiv. § 7, xvii. § 10, xxvi. § 6, 8, xxvii. § 1, 3, xxxiii. § 6
Andraemon, son of Codrus, V. iii. § 7, VII. iii. § 5, X. xxxviii. § 5
Andreus, IX. xxxiv. § 6, 9, 10, X. xiii. § 4
Andrians, VI. xxvi. § 2, X. xiii. § 4
Androcles, son of Phintas, IV. iv. § 4, v. § 6, 7, xiv. § 3, xv. § 7
—— descendant of above, IV. xvi. § 2, xvii. § 9
Androclus, son of Codrus, VII. ii. § 8, iv. § 2
Androdamas, II. vi. § 6, vii. § 6, xii. § 6
Androgeos, I. i. § 2, 4, xxvii. § 10
Andromache, II. xi. § 1, II. xxiii. § 6, X. xxv. § 9, 10, cult I. xi. § 2
Andropompus, II. xviii. § 8, IX. v. § 16.
Androsthenes, Maenalian victor, VI. vi. § 1
Androtion, VI. vii. § 6, 7, X. viii. § 1
Anemosa, VIII. xxxv. § 9
Anigraea, road, II. xxxviii. § 4

Anigrus, river, V. v. § 3, 7–9, 11, vi. § 1–4
Anochus, Tarentine victor, VI. xiv. § 11
Anonus, spring, III. xx. § 7
Antaeus, IX. xi. § 6
Antagoras, Rhodian poet, I. ii. § 3
Antalcidas, IX. i. § 4, xiii. § 2.
Antander, Messenian, IV. vii. § 4, 8, x. § 5
Antenor, X. xxvi. § 7, 8, xxvii. § 3, 4
Anteros, I. xxx. § 1, VI. xxiii. § 5
Anthas, king of Troezen, II. xxx. § 8, IX. xxii. § 5
Anthedon, VI. x. § 1, IX. xxii. § 5, 6, xxvi. § 2
Antheia, in Achaia, VII. xviii. § 3–xix. § 1
—— in Messenia, IV. xxxi. § 1
—— in Troezenia, II. xxx. § 8
Anthemocritus, herald, I. xxxvi. § 3, 4
Anthium, well, I. xxxix. § 1
Anthracia, VIII. xxxi. § 4, xlvii. § 3
Anticleia, IV. xxx. § 3, X. xxix. § 8
Anticyra, VII. vii. § 9, X. i. § 2, iii. § 1, xxxvi. § 5–xxxvii. § 3
Antigone, IX. xxv. § 2
Antigonus, father of Demetrius, I. vi. § 4–8, viii. § 1, ix. § 7, x. § 1, xii. § 3, xvi. § 1, xxv. § 6, 8, VI. xi. § 1, xvi. § 2, X. x. § 2
—— Doson, II. viii. § 4, 6, ix. § 2. 3, VI. xvi. § 3, VII. vii. § 3–5, vi.i. § 3, VIII. viii. § 11, xlix. § 5–7
—— Gonatas, I. i. § 1, ii. § 3, vii. § 3, ix. § 8, x. § 2, xiii. § 1–3, 7, 9, xvi. § 2, xxx. § 4, II. xxxiv. § 1, III. vi. § 4–6, v. v. § 1, VI. vv. § 7, X. xx. § 5
Antilochus, III. xix. § 13, xxiv. § 11, IV. xxxi. § 11, X. xxx. § 3
Antimachus, poet, VIII. xxv. § 4, 9, IX. xxxv. § 5
Antinoe, VIII. viii. § 4, 5, ix. § 5, xi. § 3
Antinous, VIII. ix. § 7, 8, x. § 1
Antioch, VIII. xxix. § 3
Antiochus, son of Heracles, I. v. § 2, X. x. § 1
—— Athenian sailor, III. xvii. § 4, IX. xxxii. § 6
—— Epiphanes V. xii. § 4
—— historian, X. xi. § 3
—— Leprean victor, VI. iii. § 9
—— Phocian general, X. xx. § 3

GENERAL INDEX

Antiochus, king of Messenia, IV. iv. § 4, v. § 8
—— son of Seleucus, I. vii. § 3, xvi. § 2, X. xii. § 10, xx. § 5
—— the Great, I. viii. § 5, v. xii. § 4, VII. viii. § 3, ix. § 7, VIII. li. § 4
Antiope, Amazon, I. ii. § 1, xli. § 7
—— daughter of Nycteus, I. xxxviii. § 9, II. vi. § 1–4, x. § 4, xvii. § 4, 6, xxv. § 3, X. xxxii. § 10
Antipater, father of Cassander, I. iv. § 1, vi. § 8, viii. § 3, xi. § 3, xiii. § 6, xxv. § 3, 6, III. x. § 5, v. iv. § 9, VI. iv. § 7, 8, VII. x. § 4, VIII. vi. § 2, X. iii. § 4
—— son of Cassander, IX. vii. § 3
—— Milesian victor, VI. ii. § 6
Antiphemus, VIII. xlvi. § 2
Antiphilus, architect, VI. xix. § 7
Antipoenus, daughters of, IX. xvii. § 1
Antitheus, archon, VII. xvi. § 10
Antoninus Pius, II. xxvii. § 6, 7 (?), VIII. xliii. § 1–6
—— second, VIII. xliii. § 6
Antony, IV. xxxi. § 1, VIII. viii. § 12, xlvi. § 1
Anyte, poetess, X. xxxviii. § 13
Anytus, VIII. xxxvii. § 5, 6
Aoede, muse, IX. xxix. § 2
Aones, IX. v. § 1, 2
Aornum, IX. xxx. § 6
Aous, river, IV. xxxiv. § 3
Aperopia, II. xxxiv. § 9
Apesas, Mount, II. xv. § 3
Aphaia, II. xxx. § 3
Aphareus, king of Messenia, III. i. § 4, xi. § 11, XIV. § 7, IV. ii. § 4–7, iii. § 1, 7, xxvii. § 6, xxxi. § 11, V. v. § 6
Apheidas, VIII. iv. § 2–8, xliv. § 8, xlv. § 1, X. ix. § 5, 6
Apheta, street, III. xii. § 1, 5, 8
Aphetaeus, III. xiii. § 6
Aphidna, I. xvii. § 5, xli. § 3, 4, II. xxii. § 6, III. xvii. § 2, xviii. § 4, 5
Aphrodisias, city, III. xxii. § 11, VIII. xii. § 8
—— well, I. xxvi. § 5
Aphrodisium, forest, VIII. xxv. § 1
—— place, VIII. xliv. § 2
Aphrodite :
myths, I. iii. § 1, II. i. § 8, iv. § 6, v. xi. § 8, xviii. § 3, 5, xix. § 5, VII. xxiii. § 2, IX. v. § 2, xxvii. § 2, xxxi. § 2, X. xxvi. § 1, xxx. § 1, 2

Aphrodite :
cult and images, I. i. § 3, 5, viii. § 4, xiv. § 7, xix. § 2, xxii. § 3, xxiii. § 2, xxvii. § 3, xxxiv. § 3, xxxvii. § 7, xl. § 6, xliii. § 6, xliv. § 9
II. ii. § 3, 4, 8, v. § 1, x. § 5, xi. § 8, xix. § 6, xx. § 8, xxiii. § 8, xxv. § 1, xxvii. § 5, xxix. § 1, 6, xxxii. § 3, 6, 7, xxxiv. § 11, 12, xxxvii. § 2, xxxviii. § 1
III. xii. § 11, xiii. § 9, xv. § 10, 11, xvii. § 5, xviii. § 1, 8, xix. § 4, xxii. § 1, 2, xxiii. § 1, 10, xxv. § 9
IV. xiv. § 2, xxx. § 5, xxxi. § 6
v. xiii. § 7, xv. § 3, 6, xvii. § 3, xxvi. § 2
VI. xx. § 6, xxiv. § 7, xxv. § 1. xxvi. § 5
VII. xx. § 9, xxi. § 10, 11, 14, xxiv. § 2
VIII. v. § 2, vi. § 5, ix. § 6, xii. § 9, xiii. § 2, xxiv. § 6, xxviii. § 6, xxxi. § 5, 6, xxxii. § 2, xxxvii. § 12, xli. § 10, xlviii. § 1, liii. § 7
IX. xvi. § 3, 4, xxii. § 1, xl. § 3, xli. § 2
X. xxxviii. § 9, 12
—— titles : Acraea, I. i. § 3, II. xxxii. § 6
Alliance, VIII. ix. § 6
Apostrophia, IX. xvi. § 3, 4
Areia, III. xvii. § 5
Armed, II. v. § 1, III. xv. § 10, xxiii. § 1
Beside the Amyclaean, III. xviii. § 8
Bringer of Victory, II. xix. § 6
Cnidian, I. i. § 3
Colias, I. i. § 5
Deviser, VIII. xxxi. § 6
Doritis, I. i. § 3
Epistrophia, I. xl. § 6
Erycine, VIII. xxiv. § 6
Euploia, I. i. § 3
Heavenly, I. xiv. § 7, xix. § 2, II. xxiii. § 8, III. xxiii. § 1, VI. xx. § 6, xxv. § 1, VIII. xxxii. § 2, IX. xvi. § 3, 4
Hera, III. xiii. § 9
In Brick, VIII. xlviii. § 1
In the Gardens, I. xix. § 2, xxvii. § 3
Limenia, II. xxxiv. § 11
Melaenis, II. ii. § 4, VIII. vi. § 5
IX. xxvii. § 5

Aphrodite:
    titles: Migonitis, III. xxii. § 1, 2
    Morpho, III. xv. § 10, 11
    Nymphaea, II. xxxii. § 7
    Olympia, III. xii. § 11, xiii. § 2
    Pandemus, I. xxii. § 3, VI. xxv. § 1,
    VIII. xxxii. § 2, IX. xvi. § 3, 4
    Paphia, VIII. xxiv. § 6, xliii. § 7
    Pontia, II. xxxiv. § 11
    Praxis, I. xliii. § 6
Aphytis, III. xviii. § 3
Apia, Peloponnesus called, II. v. § 7
Apis, god, I. xviii. § 4, VII. xxii. § 4
—— son of Jason, v. i. § 8
—— son of Telchis, II. v. § 6, 7
Apobathmi, II. xxxviii. § 4
Apollo, myths, I. xiii. § 9, xxi.
  § 3, xxx. § 3, xxxviii. § 4, xlii. § 2, 6,
  xliii. § 7
    II. v. § 8, vi. § 7, vii. § 7, xxi.
  § 9, xxii. § 9, xxvi. § 2, 4, 6, xxx.
  § 3, xxxiii. § 2, xxxv. § 2
    III. i. § 6, x. § 5, xiii. § 4, xvi. § 1,
  xviii. § 15, xix. § 5, xxi. § 8, IV. ii.
  § 2, xxxiv. § 11
    v. vii. § 10, xi. § 2, xiv. § 8, xviii.
  § 2, 4, vi. ii. § 5
    VII. iv. § 1, xx. § 4, xxiii. § 4
    VIII. xx. § 4, xxiv. § 10, xxv. § 4,
  xxxi. § 3, xxxvii. § 1
    IX. x. § 2–6, xx. § 1, xxii. § 6,
  xxvi. § 1, xxix. § 6, xxx. § 1, xxxiii.
  § 2, xl. § 4–6
    X. v. § 6, vi. § 3, 6, vii. § 2, xi.
  § 1, xiii. § 7, xvi. § 5, xvii. § 3,
  xxvii. § 2, xxxi. § 3, xxxviii. § 4
  —— cult, I. xix. § 1, 3, xxi. § 7,
  xxviii. § 4, xxxi. § 1, 2, 4, xxxii.
  § 1, 2, xxxiv. § 3, 4, xxxvii. § 6, 7,
  xli. § 3, 6, xlii. § 5, xliii. § 7, 8, xliv.
  § 2, 10
    II. iii. § 6, v. § 4, 5, vii. § 8, ix. § 7,
  x. § 2, xi. § 1, xiii. § 7, 8, xix. § 3, 4,
  xxiv. § 1, 2, 5, xxvii. § 6, 7, xxx.
  § 1, xxxi. § 6. xxxii. § 2, xxxiv. § 6,
  xxxv. § 2, xxxvii. § 2, 3, 5
    III. x. § 1, x¹. § 9, xii. § 8, xiii.
  § 5, xiv. § 6, xvi. § 2, xviii. § 9,
  xix. § 6, xxii. § 7, xxiii. § 2, xxv. § 3
    IV. iv. § 1, xxiv. § 2, xxvii. § 6,
  xxxi. § 1, xxxii. § 5, xxxiv. § 7,
  11, xxxvi. § 7
    V. iv. § 6, vii. § 3, xiv. § 8, xv.
  § 4, 7, xxi. § 5, xxvii. § 1
    VI. iii. § 8, xxiv. § 6

Apollo, cult, VII. ii. § 6, iii. § 1, 2, v.
  § 3, 4, 10, xx. § 3–7, xxi. § 11, 13,
  xxiii. § 8, xxiv. § 1, xxvi. § 6, xxvii.
  § 4
    VIII. v. § 4, viii. § 12, xv. § 5–8,
  xxiv. § 5, xxv. § 11, xxix. § 4,
  xxxii. § 2, xxxiv. § 5, xxxviii. § 2, 8,
  xxxix. § 4, xl. § 5, xli. § 7–10, xlvi.
  § 3, xlviii. § 3, liii. § 3, 6–8, liv. § 5
    IX. ii. § 1, x. § 2, 4, xi. § 7, xii. § 1,
  xiv. § 2, xxii. § 1, xxiii. § 3, 6,
  xxiv. § 4, xxxvii. § 5, xxxviii.
  § 3–5, xxxix. § 4, 5
    X. i. § 4–xix. § 4, xxii. § 12–xxiv.
  § 1, 4–7, xxvii. § 6, xxxii. § 6,
  xxxiii. § 4, 12, xxxv. § 1, xxxvii.
  § 8
  —— representations, I. iii. § 4, 5,
  viii. § 4, xvi. § 3, xxiv. § 8, xxxvii.
  § 6, xlii. § 5, xliv. § 2, 9, 10, II. ii.
  § 8, iii. § 3, 6, x. § 5, xiii. § 7, xix. § 3,
  4, xxiv. § 1, 2, 5, xxxvii. § 6, xxx. § 1,
  xxxi. § 6, xxxii. § 5, xxxv. § 2, xxxvi.
  § 3, III. x. § 8, xi. § 9, xix. § 3, 5,
  xxi. § 8, xxii. § 7, xxiii. § 3, xxiv.
  § 1, 8, xxv. § 10, xxvi. § 5, 7, IV.
  xxxi. § 10, xxxiii. § 4, xxxiv. § 7,
  V. xi. § 8, xvii. § 3, xx. § 2, VI. xix.
  § 6, xxiv. § 6, VII. xx. § 3, xxi. § 11,
  xxvi. § 6, xxvii. § 4, VIII. ix. § 1,
  xxx. § 3, 4, xxxi. § 3, 5, 7, xxxii. § 2,
  4, 5, xxxvii. § 1, 12, xli. § 9,
  xlii. § 7, liii. § 1–3, 6, IX. ix. § 2,
  xvii. § 2, xxiv. § 4, xxx. § 1, xxxv.
  § 3, X. v. § 9–13, ix. § 5, 7, x. § 1,
  xiii. § 4–7, xv. § 2, xvi. § 6, 7, xviii.
  § 4, 7, xix. § 4, xxiv. § 1, 3–7, xxxiii.
  § 4, 12, xxxvii. § 8
  —— titles : Acesius, VI. xxiv. § 6
    Acritas, III. xii. § 8
    Actius, VIII. viii. § 12
    Agraeus, I. xli. § 3, 6
    Agyieus, I. xxxi. § 6, II. xix. § 8,
  VIII. xxxii. § 4, liii. § 1–3, 6
    Alexicacus, I. iii. § 4, VI. xxiv.
  § 6, VIII. xli. § 8, 9
    Amazonius, III. xxv. § 3
    Amyclaeus, III. x. § 8, xvi. § 2,
  xviii. § 8–xix. § 6, IV. xix. § 2
    Archegetes, I. xlii. § 5
    Argeotas, III. xxxiv. § 7
    Boedromius, IX. xvii. § 2
    at Branchidae, I. xvi. § 3, VII.
  v. § 4, VIII. xlvi. § 3, IX. x. § 2
    Carinus, I. xliv. § 2

Apollo, titles: Carneius, II. x. § 2,
  xi. § 2, III. xiii. § 4–6, xiv. § 6, xxi.
  § 8, xxiv. § 8, xxv. § 10, xxvi. § 5,
  7, IV. xxxi. § 1, xxxiii. § 4
    Carnias, III. xxi. § 8
    Cereatas, VIII. xxxiv. § 5
    Clarius, II. ii. § 8
    Corynthus, IV. xxxiv. § 7
    Decatepho us, I. xlii. § 5
    Deiradiotes, II. xxiv. § 1, 2
    Delius, IX. xl. § 4
    Delphinius, I. xix. § 1
    at Didyma, II. x. § 5, VII. ii. § 6
    Dionysodotus, I. xxxi. § 4
    Egyptian, II. xxvii. § 6
    Elean, VIII. xlvi. § 3
    Epibaterius, II. xxxii. § 2
    Epicurius, VIII. xxx. § 4, xxxviii.
  § 8, xli. § 7–10
    Hecatus, X. xii. § 6
    Horius, II. xxxv. § 2
    Ismenius, II. x. § 5, IV. xxvii. § 6,
  xxxii. § 5, IX. x. § 2, 4, 5
    Latous, I. xliv. § 10
    Lycius, I. xix. § 3, II. ix. § 7, x. xix.
  § 3, 4, VIII. xl. § 5, xlvi. § 3
    Malcates, II. xxvii. § 7, III. xii. § 8
    Moiragetes, X. xxiv. § 4
    Musegetes, I. ii. § 5
    Oncaeatas, VIII. xxv. § 11
    Oncaeus, VIII. xxv. § 9
    Paeon, I. xxxiv. § 3
    Parnopius, I. xxiv. § 8
    Parrhasius, VIII. xxxviii. § 2, 8
    Patrous, I. iii. § 4
    Platanistius, II. xxxiv. § 6
    Proopsius, I. xxxii. § 2
    Prostaterius, I. xliv. § 2
    Ptous, IV. xxxii. § 5, IX. xxiii. § 6
    Pythaeus, II. xxxv. § 2, xxxvi.
  § 5, III. x. § 8, xi. § 9
    Pythius, I. xix. § 1, xlii. § 5, II.
  xxxi. § 6, 8, V. xv. § 4, VIII. xv.
  § 5, 6, 8, xxxviii. § 8, liv. § 5
    Sitalcas, X. xv. § 2
    Smintheus, X. xii. § 5, 6
    Spelaites, X. xxxii. § 5
    Spodius, IX. xi. § 7, xii. § 1
    Thearius, II. xxxi. § 6
    Theoxenius, VII. xxvii. § 4
    Thermius, V. xv. § 7
    Thyrxeus, VII. xxi. § 13
Apollodorus, general, I. xxix. § 10
—— tyrant, IV. v. § 4
Apollonia, V. xxii. § 3, 4

Apollonius, boxer, V. xxi. § 12–14
—— of Rhodes, II. xii. § 6, VIII. iv. § 3
Apollophanes, II. xxvi. § 7
Appius, VII. ix. § 3–6
Apples, I. xxxiii. § 3, II. x. § 5, V. xix.
  § 6
Aptera, in Crete, IV. xx. § 8, X. v.
  § 10
Arabia, VIII. xxii. § 4, 6, IX. xxi. § 5,
  xxviii. § 3, 4
Arachnaeus, Mount, II. xxv. § 10
Araenum, III. xxiv. § 10
Araethyrea, II. xii. § 5, 6
Arantia, Phlius called, II. xii. § 4, 5.
  xiv. § 4
Aratus, of Sicyon, II. vii. § 5, viii. § 1–
  ix. § 6, x. § 3, IV. xiv. § 8, xxix. § 9,
  VI. xii. § 5, 6, xix. § 6, VII. vii. § 3,
  viii. § 3, VIII. viii. § 11, x. § 6, 7,
  xxvii. § 12, 1. § 4, lii. § 5
—— of Soli, poet, I. ii. § 3
Araxus, Cape, VI. xxvi. § 10
Arba, VII. xvii. § 6
Arcadia, description, VIII.
Arcadians, history, III. xi. § 7, IV.
  xxix. § 7, VI. xii. § 8, VII. xv. § 5,
  VIII. i. § 4–vi. § 3, viii. § 12, xxvii.
  § 3–7, X. xx. § 1, in Elis IV. vi. § 2,
  viii. § 3, xx. § 4, 6, xxii. § 3
—— customs, IV. xi. § 3, VIII. i. § 6,
  xlii. § 6, xlviii. § 6, liii. § 9
Arcas, VIII. iv. § 1–8, ix. § 4, xxii. § 1,
  xxxvi. § 8, xxxvii. § 11, liii. § 6, 9,
  X. ix. § 5, grave VIII. ix. § 3
Arcesilaus, Arcadian, VIII. x. § 10
—— Boeotian, IX. xxxix. § 3
—— Lacedaemonian victor, VI. ii. § 2
—— Pitanaean, VIII. xlix. § 2
Archander, II. vi. § 5, VII. i. § 6
Archedamus, Elean victor, VI. i. § 3
Archelaus, son of Agesilaus, III. ii.
  § 5, 6
—— general of Mithridates, I. xx § 5
—— king of Macedon, I. ii. § 2
Archemoros, VIII. xlviii. § 2 (*see also*
  Opheltes)
Archias, son of Aristaechmus, II.
  xxvi. § 8
—— of Corinth, V. vii. § 3
—— of Thurii, I. viii. § 3
Archidameia, priestess, IV. xvii. § 1
Archidamus, son of Agesilaus, III. x.
  § 3–5, VI. iv. § 9, xv. § 7
—— son of Anaxidamus, III. vii. § 6
—— son of Zeuxidamus, ravage

Attica, I. xxix. § 6, III. vii. § 10–viii. § 1, xv. § 1, IX. i. § 7

Archidamus, Elean victor, VI. xvii. § 5

—— son of Theopompus, III. vii. § 5, 6, IV. xv. § 3

Archilochus, VII. x. § 6, X. xxviii. § 3, xxxi. § 12

Archimedes, archon, IV. xxiv. § 5

Archippus, Mytilenaean victor, VI. xv. § 1

Archiroe, VIII. xxxi. § 4

Architeles, II. vi. § 5, VII. i. § 6

Ardalus, son of Hephaestus, II. xxxi. § 3

Areion, horse, VIII. xxv. § 7–10

Areithous, VIII. iv. § 10, xi. § 4

Areius, king of Teuthrania, I. xi. § 2

Arene, IV. i. § 3, ii. § 4–6, iii. § 7, V. vi. § 2, 3

—— spring, V. v. § 6

Areopagus, I. xxiv. § 2, xxviii. § 5, 6, xxix. § 1, 15, IV. v. § 2, VII. xxv. § 1, 2, VIII. xxxiv. § 4

Ares, myths, I. xxi. § 4, xxviii. § 5, II. xiii. § 3, v. i. § 6, vii. § 10, xviii. § 5, xxii. § 6, VI. xix. § 12, VII. xxii. § 8, VIII. xliv. § 7, IX. xxxvi. § 1, 3, xxxvii. § 7

—— cult, I. viii. § 4, II. xxv. § 1, xxxii. § 9, III. xix. § 7, xxii. § 6, 7, v. xv. § 6, VII. xxii. § 9, VIII. xxxii. § 3, xxxvii. § 12, xliv. § 7, IX. x. § 5

—— representations, I. viii. § 4, II. xxv. § 1, III. xix. § 7, V. xviii. § 5, xx. § 3, VI. xix. § 12, VII. xxii. § 10, VIII. xlviii. § 4

—— titles : Aphneius, VIII. xliv. § 7
   Gynaecothoenus, VIII. xlviii. § 4
   Horse-god, V. xv. § 6
   Theritas, III. xix. § 8

Aresthenas, II. xxvi. § 5

Arethusa, V. vii. § 2, 3, VII. xxiii. § 2, xxiv. § 3, VIII. liv. § 3

Areus, son of Acrotatus, I. xiii. § 5, III. vi. § 2, 4, 6, VI. xii. § 5, xv. § 9

—— distinguished Lacedaemonian, VII. ix. § 2–4

Argeathae, VIII. xxiii. § 8

Argeus, II. xxviii. § 6, V. xviii. § 10

Arginusae, VI. vii. § 7

Argives, history, I. xxix. § 7–9, II. xv. § 4, xvi. § 5, xviii. § 4 ff., xxxviii. § 5, III. vii. § 5, xi. § 7, IV. v. § 2, xi. § 1, xxix. § 7, V. xii. § 8, VIII. xl.

§ 3, IX. ix. § 4, xiv. § 4, xxxiii. § 1, X. x. § 4, ancient power VII. xvii. § 1, dialect II. xxxvii. § 3

Argo, I. xviii. § 1, II. xii. § 6, IV. xxxiv. § 7, V. xvii. § 9, VII. iv. § 4, xxiv. § 14, IX. xxxii. § 4

Argolis, II.

Argos, II. iv. § 2, viii. § 6, xviii. § 4, xix. § 3–xxiv. § 4, III. v. § 8, VII. xvii. § 1

Argus, II. xvi. § 1, xx. § 8, xxv. § 8, xxvi. § 2, xxxix. § 4, III. iv. § 1, 5, 6, grave II. xxii. § 5

Argyra, VII. xviii. § 6, xxiii. § 1, 2, 4

Ariadne, I. iii. § 1, xx. § 3, xxii. § 5, II. xxiii. § 8, V. xix. § 1, IX. xl. § 3, 4, X. xxix. § 3, 4

Aricia, II. xxvii. § 4

Aridaeus, king of Macedon, I. vi. § 2, 3, x. § 1, xi. § 3, 4, xxv. § 3, 6, VIII. vii. § 7

Arimaspi, I. xxiv. § 6, xxxi. § 2

Arimnestus, king of Etruria, V. xii. § 5

—— Plataean, IX. iv. § 2

Arion, poet, III. xxv. § 7, IX. xxx. § 2

Aris, river, IV. xxxi. § 2

Aristaenus, of Megalopolis, VIII. li. § 4

Aristaeus, VIII. ii. § 4, X. xvii. § 3–5, xxx. § 5

Aristander, portico of, VIII. xxx. § 10

Aristarchus, guide at Olympia, V. xx. § 4, 5

Aristeas, poet, I. xxiv. § 6, v. viii. § 9

—— victor, of Stratonicea, V. xxi. § 10

Aristeides, Athenian, VIII. lii. § 2

—— Elean victor, VI. xvi. § 4, 5

Aristera, island, II. xxxiv. § 8

Aristeus, Argive victor, VI. ix. § 3

Aristias, dramatist, II. xiii. § 6

Aristion, Athenian, I. xx. § 5, 7

—— Epidaurian victor, VI. xiii. § 6

Aristocrates, son of Aechmis, VIII. v. § 5–13, xiii. § 5

—— son of Hicetas, IV. xvii. § 2–7, xxii. § 1–7, VIII. v. § 13

Aristodama, II. x. § 3, IV. xiv. § 7

Aristodemus, son of Aristomachus, II. iv. § 4, xviii. § 7, xix. § 1, III. i. § 5, 6, ii. § 1, vii. § 1, xvi. § 6, IV. iii. § 3–5, 8, v. § 1

—— Elean victor, VI. iii. § 4

—— Lacedaemonian, III. v. § 7

—— Messenian, IV. vi. § 2, 4, ix. § 6–

GENERAL INDEX

xiii. § 5, xxiii. § 6, xxvi. § 4, VIII.
v. § 10

Aristodemus, tyrant of Megalopolis,
VIII. xxvii. § 11, 12, xxx. § 7, xxxii.
§ 4, xxxv. § 5, xxxvi. § 5

Aristogeiton, I. viii. § 5, xxiii. § 2,
xxix. § 15

Aristomachus, son of Cleoedaeus, II.
vii. § 6, xviii. § 7, V. iii. § 5, iv. § 1,
VIII. v. § 6, X. xxxviii. § 10

—— tyrant of Argos, II. viii. § 6

Aristomelidas, VIII. xlvii. § 6

Aristomenes, Messenian, IV. vi. § 3–5,
xiv. § 7–xxiv. § 3, xxvi. § 8, xxxii.
§ 3–6, VI. vii. § 3, VIII. lii. § 1, IX.
xxxix. § 14, cult IV. xiv. § 7, xxvii.
§ 6

—— Rhodian victor, V. xxi. § 10

Ariston, king of Sparta, III. iv. § 4, vii.
§ 7, viii. § 7

Aristonautae, II. xii. § 2, VII. xxvi.
§ 14

Aristophanes, V. v. § 3

Aristophon, Athenian victor, VI. xiii.
§ 11

Aristotimus, tyrant of Elis, V. v. § 1,
VI. xiv. § 11

Aristotle, VI. iv. § 8

Arne, Chaeroneia called, IX. xl. § 5

—— fountain, VIII. viii. § 1

Aroanian Mountains, VIII. xviii. § 7

Aroanius, rivers, VIII. xiv. § 3, xv. § 6,
xix. § 4, xxi. § 1, 2, xxiv. § 3

Aroe, VII. xviii. § 2–6, xix. § 1, 8,
xxi. § 13

Arrephori, I. xxvii. § 3

Arrhachion, Phigaleian victor, VIII.
xl. § 1, 2

Arrhiphon, critic, II. xxxvii. § 3

Arrows, poisoned, II. xxxvii. § 4

Arsen, river, VIII. xxv. § 1

Arsinoe, daughter of Leucippus, II.
xxvi. § 7, III. xii. § 8, xxvi. § 4,
IV. iii. § 2, xxxi. § 6, 12

—— wife of Lysimachus, I. x. § 3

—— wife of Ptolemy II, I. vii. § 3,
viii. § 6, IX. xxxi. § 1

—— spring, IV. xxxi. § 6

Artaphernes, horses of, I. xxxii. § 7

Artaxerxes, son of Dareius, I. iii. § 2,
III. ix. § 1–7, IX. xv. § 5

—— son of Xerxes, I. viii. § 2, VI. v. § 7

Artemidorus, victor, of Tralles, VI.
xiv. 2

Artemis, myths, I. xxi. § 3, xxiii. § 7,

xli. § 3, II. iii. § 2, vii. § 7, xxi. § 9,
xxvi. § 6, III. ix. § 3, xviii. § 4, 15,
VIII. iii. § 6, xxvii. § 17, xxxi. § 2,
xxxvii. § 6, xli. § 4–6, liii. § 1, IX.
ii. § 3, xix. § 1, 7, X. xi. § 1, xxx. § 1,
xxxv. § 7

Artemis, cult, I. i. § 4, xix. § 6, xxiii.
§ 7, xxix. § 2, xxxi. § 1, 4, 5, xxxvi.
§ 1, xxxviii. § 6, xli. § 6, xliii. § 1

II. vii. § 6, x. § 7, xxi. § 1, xxiv.
§ 5, xxv. § 3, 6, xxvii. § 4, 5, xxviii.
§ 2, xxix. § 1, xxx. § 1, 3, 7, xxxi.
§ 1, 4, 5, xxxii. § 10, xxxv. § 1

III. ii. § 6, x. § 7, xii. § 8, xiv. § 2, 6,
xiv. § 7–xvii. § 1, xx. § 7, 9, xxii.
§ 8, 12, xxiii. § 10, xxiv. § 8, 9, xxv.
§ 3, 4, xxvi. § 11

IV. iv. § 2, xvi. § 9, xxx. § 5,
xxxi. § 3, 7, 8, xxxiv. § 6, xxxv. § 8

v. vi. § 5, xii. § 3, 4, xiv. § 5,
6, xv. § 4–8, xix. § 2, 5

VI. ii. § 15, 16, xxii. § 1, 8–11,
xxiii. § 8

VII. ii. § 6, 7, v. § 4, vi. § 6, xviii.
§ 8–xix. § 8, xx. § 1, 2, 7–9, xxii.
§ 11, xxiv. § 1, xxvi. § 3, 5, 11,
xxvii. § 4

VIII. v. § 11, vi. § 6, xii. § 5, xiii.
§ 1, 2, xiv. § 5, xv. § 5, 8, 9, xviii.
§ 8, xxii. § 7–9, xxiii. § 1–7, xxviii.
§ 6, xxxii. § 4, xxxv. § 5, 7, 8, xxxvi.
§ 7, xxxvii. § 1, xxxix. § 5, xliv. § 2,
xlvii. § 6, liii. § 3, 11

IX. xvii. § 1

X. xii. § 2, xix. § 3, xxvi. § 6,
xxxiii. § 4, xxxv. § 7, xxxvi. § 5,
xxxvii. § 1, 3, 8, xxxviii. § 6, 9, 12

—— representations, I. xxiii. § 7,
xxvi. § 4, xxix. § 2, xxxiii. § 1, xl.
§ 2, 3, xliv. § 2, 4

II. ii. § 3, 6, iii. § 5, ix. § 6, x. § 2,
xiii. § 5, xix. § 7, xxii. § 2, xxiii. § 5,
xxiv. § 5, xxix. § 1, xxx. § 1, xxxi. § 1

III. x. § 7, xi. § 9, xvi. § 7, xviii.
§ 8, 9, xix. § 4

IV. xiii. § 1, xiv. § 2, xxxi. § 10

v. xi. § 2, 8, xvii. § 3, xix. § 5,
xx. § 2, xxvi. § 2

VI. xxii. § 8

VII. xviii. § 8, xxiv. § 1, xxvi. § 4,
xxvii. § 4

VIII. vi. § 6, ix. § 1, xiii. § 2, xxii.
§ 7, xxxi. § 1, xxxvi. § 7, xxxvii.
§ 1, 4, xxxix. § 5, xliv. § 2, xlvi.
§ 3, liii. § 11

GENERAL INDEX

Artemis, representations. IX. xvii.
§ 1, xix. § 6, xx. § 1, xxii. § 1, xxiv.
§ 4
   X. ix. § 7, 8, xiii. § 4, 7, xv. § 2,
xvi. § 6, xix. § 3, xxxiii. § 4, xxxv.
§ 4, xxxvi. § 5, xxxvii. § 1, 3, 8,
xxxviii. § 9
—— titles : Aeginaea, III. xiv. § 2
   Aetole, X. xxxviii. § 12
   Agoraea, V. xv. § 4
   Agrotera, I. xix. § 6, xli. § 3, 6,
v. xv. § 8, VII. xxvi. § 3, 11, VIII.
xxxii. § 4
   Alpheiaea, VI. xxii. § 8–10
   Amarysia, I. xxxi. § 4
   Anaiitis, III. xvi. § 8
   Ariste, I. xxix. § 2
   Astrateia, III. xxv. § 3
   Brauronia, I. xxiii. § 7, xxxiii. § 1,
VIII. xlvi. § 3
   Calliste, I. xxix. § 2, VIII. xxxv. § 8
   Caryatis, III. x. § 7
   Cedreatis, VIII. xiii. § 2
   Cnacalesia, VIII. xxiii. § 3, 4
   Cnaceatis, VIII. liii. § 11
   Cnagia, III. xviii. § 4
   Coccoca, V. xv. § 7
   Colaenis, I. xxxi. § 4, 5
   Conduleatis, VIII. xxiii. § 6
   Cordaca, VI. xxii. § 1
   Coryphaea, II. xxviii. § 2
   Daphnaea, III. xxiv. § 8
   Dereatis, III. xx. § 7
   Dictynna, III. xxiv. § 9
   Dictynnaea, X. xxxvi. § 5
   Elaphiaea, VI. xxii. § 10, 11
   Ephesia, II. ii. § 6, IV. xxxi.
§ 8, V. vi. § 5, xii. § 4, xix. § 2, VI.
iii. § 15, 16, VII. ii. § 6, 7, v. § 4,
VIII. xiii. § 1, xxiii. § 1, xxx. § 6,
X. xxvi. § 6, xxxviii. § 6
   Eucleia, IX. xvii. § 1, 2
   Eurippa, VIII. xiv. § 5
   Eurynome, VIII. xli. § 4, 5
   Hemerasia, VIII. xviii. § 8
   Hiereia, VIII. xliv. § 2
   Hymn a, VIII. v. § 11, xiii. § 1
   Iphigeneia, II. xxxv. § 1
   Issoria, III. xiv. § 2, xxv. § 4
   Laphria, IV. xxxi. § 7, VII. xviii.
§ 8–xix. § 1, xx. § 2
      Leader III. xiv. § 6, VIII. xxxvii.
§ 1, xlvii. § 6
   Leucophryene, I. xxvi. § 4, III.
xviii. § 9

Artemis, titles : Limnaea, II. vii. § 6,
III. xiv. § 2
   Limnatis, III. xxiii. § 10, IV. iv. § 2,
xxxi. § 3, VII. xx. § 7–9, VIII. liii. § 11
   Lyceia, II. xxxi. § 4, 5
   Lycoatis, VIII. xxxvi. § 7
   Lygodesma, III. xvi. § 11
   Munychia, I. i. § 4
   Mysia, III. xx. § 9
   Orthia, II. xxiv. § 5, III. xvi. § 7,
9, 11, xvii. § 1, VIII. xxiii. § 1
   Paedotrophus, IV. xxxiv. § 6
   Patroa, II. ix. § 6
   Peitho, II. xxi. § 1
   Persian, VII. vi. § 6
   Pheraea, II. x. § 7, xxiii. § 5
   Philomeirax, VI. xxiii. § 8
   Phosphorus, IV. xxxi. § 10
   Propylaea, I. xxxviii. § 6
   Protothronie, X. xxxviii. § 6
   Pyronia, VIII. xv. § 9
   Saronia, II. xxxii. § 10
   Saronis, II. xxx. § 7
   Saviour, I. xl. § 2, 3, xliv. § 4,
II. xxxi. § 1, III. xxii. § 12, VII.
xxvii. § 3, VIII. xxx. § 10, xxxix. § 5
   Sciatis, VIII. xxv. § 5
   Selasphorus, I. xxxi. § 4
   Strangled, VIII. xxiii. § 6, 7
   Stymphalia, VIII. xxii. § 7–9
   Tauric, I. xxiii. § 7, III. xvi. § 8
   Triclaria, VII. xix. § 1–8, xx. § 1,
xxii. § 11
Artemisia, III. xi. § 3
Artemisium, I. xiv. § 5, III. xvi. § 6,
X. xiv. § 5
Artemisius, Mount, II. xxv. § 3, VIII.
vi. § 6, vii. § 1
Artontes, son of Mardonius, IX. ii. § 2
Asamon, Elean victor, VI. xvi. § 5
Ascalaphus, IX. xxxvii. § 7
Ascalon, Aphrodite at, I. xiv. § 7
Asclepius, myths, I. xxiii. § 4, II. x.
§ 2, xxvi. § 4, 7, 10, xxix. § 1, III.
xx. § 5, xxvi. § 9, IV. iii. § 2, xiv.
§ 8, xxx. § 3, xxxi. § 12, VIII. xxv.
§ 11
—— cult, I. xxi. § 4, xxii. § 1
II. ii. § 3, iv. § 5, xi. § 8, xiii. § 5,
xxi. § 1, xxiii. § 2, 4, xxvi. § 1–
xxvii. § 6, xxviii. § 1, xxix. § 1,
xxx. § 1, xxxvi. § 1
   III. iii. § 8, xiv. § 2, 7, xix. § 7,
xxi. § 2, 8, xxii. § 9, 10, 13, xxiii.
§ 7, 11, xxiv. § 5, 8, xxvi. § 10

GENERAL INDEX

Asclepius, cult, IV. xxx. § 1, xxxi.
§ 10, xxxiv. § 6, xxxvi. § 7
v. vii. § 1, xiii. § 3
VI. xxi. § 4, xxvi. § 5
VII. v. § 9, xxi. § 14, xxiii. § 7, 8,
xxvi. § 7, xxvii. § 11
VIII. ix. § 1, xxi. § 3, xxv. § 1, 3,
11, xxvi. § 6, xxviii. § 1, xxxii. § 4, 5,
liv. § 5
IX. xxxix. § 3, 4
X. xxxii. § 12, xxxiv. § 6, xxxviii.
§ 13
—— representations, I. xxi. § 4, xl.
§ 6, II. iv. § 5, x. § 3, xi. § 8, xiii. § 5,
xxiii. § 4, xxix. § 1, xxx. § 1, xxxii.
§ 4, III. xxi. § 8, xxiii. § 10, xxiv.
§ 2, xxvi. § 4, IV. xxxi. § 10, xxxiv.
§ 6, xxxvi. § 7, V. xi. § 11, xx. § 3,
xxvi. § 2, VII. xx. § 9, xxiii. § 7,
xxvi. § 7, xxvii. § 11, VIII. xxviii.
§ 1, xxxi. § 1, xxxii. § 4, xlvii. § 1,
X. iv. § 4, xxxii. § 12, xxxiv. § 6
—— titles : Agnitas, III. xiv. § 7
Archagetas, X. xxxii. § 12
Aulonius, IV. xxxvi. § 7
Boy, VIII. xxv. § 11, xxxii. § 5
Causius, VIII. xxv. § 1
Cotyleus, III. xix. § 7
Demaenetus, VI. xxi. § 4
Gortynius, II. xi. § 8
Philolaus, III. xxii. § 9

Ascra, IX. xxix. § 1, 2, xxxviii. § 4
Asea, VIII. iii. § 4, xxvii. § 3, xliv. § 3,
liv. § 2
Asia, mountain, III. xxiv. § 6
Asinarus, VII. xvi. § 5
Asine, II. xxviii. § 2, xxxvi. § 4, 5, III.
vii. § 4, IV. viii. § 3, xiv. § 3, xv. § 8,
xxiv. § 4, xxvii. § 8, xxxiv. § 9–12
Asius, poet, II. vi. § 4, 5, xxix. § 4,
IV. ii. § 1, V. xvii. § 8, VII. iv. § 1, 2,
VIII. i. § 4, IX. xxiii. § 6
Asopia, II. i. § 1, iii. § 10
Asopus, king, IX. i. § 2, iii. § 1
—— city, III. xxi. § 7, xxii. § 9, 10
—— river in Boeotia, II. v. § 2, vi. § 1, 4,
v. xiv. § 3, IX. i. § 1, iv. § 4, viii.
§ 1, xx. § 1, xxvi. § 6
—— river in Sicyonia, I. xxxv. § 2, II.
v. § 1–3, vii. § 1, 9, xi. § 4, 5, xii. § 4,
6, xv. § 1, 3, xxix. § 2, V. xxii. § 6
Asphodicus, IX. xviii. § 6
Aspledon, IX. xxxviii. § 9, xxxix. § 1
Ass, II. xxxviii. § 3, X. xviii. § 4,
xxix. § 1

Assus, VI. iv. § 9
Assyrians, I. xiv. § 7, V. xii. § 4, VIII.
xxxiii. § 2
Asteius, archon, VII. xxv. § 4, IX. i. § 8
Asterion, river, II. xv. § 5, xvii. § 1, 2
—— Argonaut, V. xvii. § 9
—— son of Minos, II. x xxi. § 1
Asterius, I. xxxv. § 6, VII. ii. § 5
Astrabacus, III. xvi. § 6, 9
Astyages, v. x. § 3
Astyanax, Arcadian, VIII. xxxviii. § 5
—— son of Hector, X. xxv. § 9
Astycrateia, I. xliii. § 5
Astylus, victor, of Croton, VI. xiii. § 1
Astypalaea, VI. ix. § 6, VII. iv. § 1
Astyra, springs, IV. xxxv. § 10
Atalanta, III. xxiv. § 2, V. xix § 2,
VIII. xxxv. § 10, xlv. § 2, 5, 6
Atarneus, IV. xxxv. § 10, VII. ii. § 11
Athamantian plain, IX. xxiv. § 1, 3
Athamas, son of Aeolus, I. xliv. § 7,
VII. iii. § 6, IX. xxiii. § 6, xxxiv. § 1,
xxxiv. § 5–8
Athena, myths, I. xiv. § 6, xviii. § 2,
xxiv. § 1–7, II. xxx. § 6, III. xvii. § 3,
xviii. § 13, xix. § 5, V. xvii. § 11, VI.
xix. § 12, xxv. § 2, VIII. xviii. § 3,
xxvi. § 6, xxviii. § 5, xxxi. § 2, IX.
xi. § 2, xxxiii. § 5–7, X. xxx. § 1
—— cult, I. i. § 1–4, v. § 3, xiii. § 2, 3,
xxvi. § 2, 6, xxviii. § 3, 6, xxviii. § 5,
xxx. § 2, 4, xxxi. § 1, 4, 6, xxxvi.
§ 4, xxxvii. § 2, xli. § 6, xlii. § 4
II. iv. § 5, v. § 6, vi. § 3, xi. § 1, 7,
xii. § 1, xv. § 1, xviii. § 4, 7, xxi. § 3, 6,
xxiii. § 5, xxiv. § 2, xxv. § 10, xxx.
§ 6, xxxi. § 6, xxxii. § 5, xxxiii. § 1,
xxxiv. § 8, xxxvi. § 8, xxxviii. § 2
III. iii. § 8, v. § 6, vii. § 10, ix.
§ 13, xi. § 9, xii. § 4, xiii. § 6, xv.
§ 6, xvii. § 2–7, xviii. § 2, xxi. § 9,
xxii. § 9, 10, xxiii. § 10, xxiv. § 7,
xxv. § 10, xxvi. § 5
IV. xv. § 5, xxx. § 5, xxxv. § 8,
xxxvi. § 2, 7
V. iii. § 2, xiv. § 5, 9, xv. § 6,
xvi. § 7
VI. ix. § 7, xxi. § 6, xxvi. § 3
VII. v. § 4, xvii. § 5, 9, xx. § 2, 9,
xxii. § 8–10, xxiii. § 9, xxv. § 3,
xxvi. § 3, 4, xxvii. § 2
VIII. iv. § 8, v. § 3, ix. § 6, xiv.
§ 4, xxi. § 4, xxiii. § 1, xxxi. § 9,
xxxvi. § 5, 8, xxxvii. § 12, xliv. § 2, 4,
xlv. § 4–xlvii. § 5

GENERAL INDEX

Athena, cult, IX. iv. § 1, xii. § 2, xix. § 1, xxxiii. § 5, xxxiv. § 1–5
  X. i. § 10, iv. § 9, v. § 11, viii. § 6, xxii. § 1, xxxii. § 10, xxxiv. § 6–8, **xxxviii.** § 5

—— representations, I. i. § 3, ii. § 5, viii. § 4, xiv. § 6, xv. § 3, xvii. § 2, xxii. § 6, xxiii. § 4, xxiv. § 6, xxv. § 7, xxvi. § 4, 6–xxvii. § 6, xxviii. § 2, xxxii. § 2, xxxvii. § 6, xlii. § 4
  II. iii. § 1, iv. § 5, xv. § 1, xxii. § 2, 9, xxiii. § 5, xxv. § 10, xxix. § 1, xxxii. § 5, xxxv. § 8
  III. xi. § 11, xii. § 4, 5, xvii. § 2, xviii. § 11, xix. § 4, 5, xx. § 8, xxi. § 9, xxiv. § 5, xxvi. § 5
  IV. xxxiv. § 6, xxxv. § 8
  v. xi. § 8, 10, xiv. § 5, xvii. § 2, xix. § 5, 12, xxvi. § 6
  VI. xix. § 12, xxvi. § 3
  VII. v. § 5, 9, xviii. § 9, xx. § 3, 5, xxii. § 9, 10, xxiv. § 2, xxvi. § 4, xxvii. § 2
  VIII. ix. § 3, 6, xxi. § 4, xxvi. § 6, 7, xxviii. § 6, xxxi. § 7, xxxii. § 4, xxxvii. § 12, xliv. § 2, xlv. § 4–xlvii. § 5
  IX. iv. § 1, x. § 2, xi. § 6, xii. § 2, xvii. § 3, xxvi. § 8, xxxiii. § 5, xxxiv. § 1, xl. § 3
  X. iv. § 9, viii. § 6, x. § 1, xiii. § 7, xv. § 2, xviii. § 1, xxvi. § 3, xxxii. § 10, xxxiv. § 6–8, xxxviii. § 5, 7

—— titles : Aeantis, I. xlii. § 4
  Aethyia, I. v. § 3, xli. § 6
  Agoraea, III. xi. § 9
  Alea, II. xvii. § 4, III. v. § 6, vii. § 10, xix. § 7, VIII. iv. § 8, v. § 3, ix. § 6, xxiii. § 1, xlv. § 4–xlvii. § 4
  Anemotis, IV. xxxv. § 3, 8
  Apaturia, II. xxxiii. § 1
  Areia, I. xxviii. § 5, IX. iv. § 1
  Asia, III. xxiv. § 7
  Axiopoenus, III. xv. § 6
  Celeutheia, III. xii. § 4
  Chalinitis, II. iv. § 1, 5
  Cissaea, II. xxix. § 1
  Contriver, VIII. xxxvi. § 5
  Coria, VIII. xxi. § 4
  Coryphasia, IV. xxxvi. § 2
  Counsellor, III. xiii. § 6
  Cranaea, X. xxxiv. § 7
  Cydonia, VI. xxi. § 6

Athena, titles, Cyparissia, III. xxii. § 9, IV. xxxvi. § 7
  Ergane, I. xxiv. § 3, III. xvii. § 4, v. xiv. § 5, VI. xxvi. § 3, VIII. xxxii. § 4, IX. xxvi. § 8
  Health, I. xxiii. § 4, xxxi. § 6
  Hippolaitis, III. xxv. § 9
  Horse goddess, I. xxx. § 4, xxxi. § 6, V. xv. § 6, VIII. xlvii. § 1
  Itonia, I. xiii. § 2, III. ix. § 13, IX. xxxiv. § 1–5, X. i. § 10
  Larisaea, VII. xvii. § 5
  Leitis, v. xiv. § 5
  Lemnia, I. xxviii. § 2
  Maiden, I. xxiv. § 5–7, v. xi. § 10, X. xxxiv. § 8
  Mother, v. iii. § 2
  Narcaea, V. xvi. § 7
  Of Bronze House, III. xvii. § 2–7, IV. xv. § 5, X. v. § 11
  Onca, IX. xii. § 2
  Ophthalmitis, III. xviii. § 2
  Oxyderces, II. xxiv. § 2
  Paeonia, I. ii. § 5, xxxiv. § 3
  Panachais, VII. xx. § 2
  Pania, II. xxii. § 8
  Pareia, III. xx. § 8
  Polias, I. xxvi. § 6–xxvii. § 4, II. xxx. § 6, VII. v. § 9, VIII. xxxi. § 9
  Poliatas, VIII. xlvii. § 5
  Poliuchus, III. xvii. § 2
  Promachorma, II. xxxiv. § 8
  Pronaus, IX. x. § 2
  Pronoia, X. viii. § 6, 7
  Sais, IX. xii. § 2
  Saitis, II. xxxvi. § 8, xxxvii. § 2
  Salpinx, II. xxi. § 3
  Saviour, VIII. xliv. § 4
  Sciras, I. i. § 4, xxxvi. § 4
  Sthenias, II. xxx. § 6, xxxii. § 5
  Sunias, I. i. § 1
  Telchinia, IX. xix. § 1
  Tithrone, I. xxxi. § 4
  Trachinis, X. xxii. § 1
  Trichonia, IX. xx. § 1
  Tritonia, VIII. xiv. **§ 4**
  Victory, I. xlii. § 4
  Xenia, III. xi. § 11
  Zosteria, IX. xvii. § 3
Athenaeum, VIII. xliv. § 2
Athenaeus, Ephesian victor, VI. iv. § 1
Athene, village, II. xxxviii. § 6
Athenians, character, I. viii. § 4, xiv. § 2, xvii. § 1, xxiv. § 3, xxviii. § 6,

GENERAL INDEX

II. xiv. § 4, IV. xxxv. § 5, VIII. x.
§ 9, history *passim*
Athens, in Boeotia, IX. xxiv. § 2
—— in Attica, I. ii. § 1–xxix. § 1,
III. iv. § 2, vi. § 4, vii. § 8, ix. § 2,
IV. v. § 10, X. viii. § 5
Atherion, VII. xx. § 7
Athletes, training and rules, I. xliv.
§ 1, V. xxi. § 2–18, xxiv. § 9, VI.
vii. § 10
Athmoneis, I. xiv. § 7, xxxi. § 4
Atlas, I. xxxiii. § 5, 6, II. xxx. § 8,
III. xviii. § 10, IV. xxxiii. § 6, V. x.
§ 6, 9, xi. § 5, xviii. § 4, VI. xix. § 8,
VIII. xii. § 7, xliii. § 3, IX. xx. § 6,
xxii. § 5
Atreus, II. xvi. § 6, xviii. § 1, IX. xl.
§ 11
Attaginus, Theban, VII. x. § 2
Attalus, king of Pergamus, I. v. § 5,
vi. § 1, viii. § 1, xxv. § 2, xxxvi. § 5,
VII. viii. § 9, xvi. § 1, 8, IX. xxxv.
§ 6, X. xv. § 3
Attalus II, VII. viii. § 9, xvi. § 1
Atthis, daughter of Cranaus, I. ii.
§ 6
Attica, I. i. § 1–xxxix. § 3, islands I.
xxxv. § 1–xxxvi. § 2, mountains I.
xxxii. § 1, 2, rivers I. xix. § 5,
books about VI. vii. § 6, X. viii. § 1,
xv. § 5
Attis, I. iv. § 5, VII. xvii. § 9–11, xx.
§ 3
Auge, VIII. iv. § 8, 9, xlvii. § 2, 4,
xlviii. § 7, X. xxviii. § 8
Augeas, II. xv. § 1, v. i. § 9–ii. § 1, iii.
§ 1, 3, viii. § 3, VI. xx. § 16, VIII.
xiv. § 9, cult V. iv. § 2
August goddesses, I. xxviii. § 6, xxxi.
§ 4, II. xi. § 4, VII. xxv. § 2
Augustus, II. iii. § 1, xvii. § 3, III. xxi.
§ 6, xxvi. § 7, IV. i. § 1, xxx. § 2,
xxxi. § 1, V. xii. § 7, xxiii. § 3, VII.
xvii. § 5, xviii. § 7–9, xxii. § 1, 6,
VIII. viii. § 12, xlvi. § 1, 2, 4, X.
viii. § 3, xxxviii. § 4, 9, cult III. xi.
§ 4, 5
Aulis, III. ix. § 3, 10, VIII. xxviii.
§ 4, 5, IX. xix. § 6–8, X. xxvi. § 3
Aulon, Arcadian, III. xii. § 9
—— in Messenia, IV. xxxvi. § 7
Aura, mare, VI. xiii. § 9
Autesion, III. i. § 7, xv. § 6, IV. iii. § 4,
IX. v. § 15
Autolaus, VIII. iv. § 2, 6, xxv. § 11

Autolycus, son of Daedalion, VIII. iv.
§ 6, X. viii. § 8
—— pancratiast, I. xviii. § 3, IX.
xxxii. § 8
Autonoe, I. xliv. § 5, X. xvii. § 4
Autosthenes, archon, IV. xxiii. § 4
Auxesia, II. xxx. § 4, xxxii. § 2
Auxo, IX. xxxv. § 2
Averters of evil, II. xi. § 1
Axe, tried for murder, I. xxiv. § 4,
xxviii. § 10, dedicated X. xiv. § 1,
of Peisander III. iii. § 8, of Tenedos
X. xiv. § 1–4
Axius, river, V. i. § 5
Azan, son of Arcas, V. i. § 8, VIII. iv.
§ 2–7, X. ix. § 5

BABYLON, I. x. § 4, xvi. § 1, II. xi. § 6,
IV. xxiii. § 10, VIII. xxxiii. § 3, walls
I. xvi. § 3, IV. xxxi. § 5
Bacchanals, II. ii. § 7, vii. § 5, xx. § 4,
xxii. § 1
Bacchidae, II. i. § 1, iv. § 4, V. xvii. § 5
Bacis, IV. xxvii. § 4, IX. xvii. § 5, 6,
X. xii. § 11, xiv. § 6, xxxii. § 8, 9, 11
Back chambers, v. x. § 9, xiii. § 1,
xv. § 3, xvi. § 1
Bady, v. iii. § 2
Baetis, river, IV. xix. **§ 3**
Bagrae, II. xxvi. § 9
Balari, X. xvii. § 9
Balyra, river, **IV.** xxxiii. § 3
Baphyras, river, IX. xxx. § 8
Barley, in cult, I. xxxvii. § 6, xli.
§ 9, III. xxiii. § 8, VI. xx. § 2, IX.
xxxix. § 11
Barsina, IX. vii. § 2
Basilae, VI. xx. § 1
Basilis, VIII. xxix. § 5
Basket, in cult, VIII. xxv. § 7, xxxvii.
§ 4
Bassae, VIII. xxx. § 4, xli. § 7
Bathos, VIII. xxix. § 1, 5
Bathyllus, spring, VIII. xxxi. § 9
Baton, charioteer, II. xxiii. § 2, V.
xvii. § 8, X. x. § 3
Batrachium, I. xxviii. § 8
Battus, III. xiv. § 3, X. xv. § 6, 7
Baucis, Troezenian victor, VI. viii. § 4
Beacon festival, II. xxv. § 4
Beans, I. xxxvii. § 4, VIII. xv. § 3
Bears, I. xxxii. § 1, III. xx. § 4, IV. xi.
§ 3, VII. xviii. § 12, VIII. iii. § 7, xvii.
§ 3, xxiii. § 9, X. xxxi. § 10

GENERAL INDEX

Beautiful Crown, nymphs and olive of, V. xv. § 3, 6, 10

Bees, I. xxxii. § 1, IX. xxiii. § 2, xl. § 2, X. v. § 9

Bel, I. xvi. § 3, IV. xxiii. § 10, VIII. xxxiii. § 3

Belemina, III. xxi. § 3, VIII. xxxv. § 3, 4

Belistiche, Macedonian victor, V. viii. § 11

Bellerophontes, II. i. § 9, ii. § 3–5, iii. § 5, iv. § 1–3, vii. § 2, xxxi. § 9, III. xviii. § 13, IX. xxxi. § 3

Belus, IV. xxiii. § 10, VII. xxi. § 13

Berenice, wife of Ptolemy I, I. vi. § 8, vii. § 1

—— daughter of Ptolemy Philometor, I. ix. § 3

Bias, son of Amythaon, II. vi. § 6, xviii. § 4, xxi. § 2, IV. xxxiv. § 4, xxxvi. § 3

—— of Priene, X. xxiv. § 1

—— river, IV. xxxiv. § 4

Biblis, VII. v. § 10, xxiv. § 5

Bidaeans, III. xi. § 2, xii. § 4

Birds, omens from I. xxxiv. § 4, X. vi. § 1, sacrificed II. xi. § 7, IV. xxxi. § 9, VII. xviii. § 12

Biris, III. xix. § 3

Birthplace, place in Argolis, II. xxxii. § 9, VIII. vii. § 2

Bison, X. xviii. § 1–3

Bithynia, V. xii. § 7, VIII. ix. § 7

Bithynium, VIII. ix. § 7

Biton, II. ix. § 5, xix. § 5, xx. § 3

Black robes, II. iii. § 7, IV. xiv. § 4

Blackbirds, VIII. xvii. § 3, IX. xxii. § 4

Blood, in ritual, II. xxiv. § 1, III. xvi. § 10, VII. xxv. § 13, X. iv. § 10

Blooming Nymphs, V. xv. § 6

Boars, I. xxxii. § 1, III. xiv. § 10, xx. § 4, V. vi. § 6, VII. xxvi. § 10, VIII. xvii. § 3, xxiii. § 9, IX. xxiii. § 7

—— in myth, I. xxvii. § 9, III. xviii. § 16, V. x. § 9, xliii. § 6, II. vii. § 9, VIII. xxiv. § 5, Calydonian I. xxvii. § 6, 9, xliii. § 6, II. vii. § 9, III. xviii. § 15, VIII. iv. § 10, xlv. § 2, 6, xlvi. § 7, xlvii. § 2

—— in ritual, IV. xv. § 8, V. xxiv. § 9–11, VII. xviii. § 12, VIII. xxxviii. § 8, X. xviii. § 6

Boar's tomb, IV. xv. § 7, 8, xix. § 3

Boat race II. xxxv. § 1

Boeae, I. xxvii. § 5, III. xxi. § 7, xxii. § 11, 13, xxiii. § 1, 2, 4, 6, 10

Boeo, poetess, X. v. § 7

Boeotarchs, IX. xiii. § 6, 7, xiv. § 5, X. xx. § 3

Boeotia, IX.

Boeotians, history, I. xxv. § 4, xxviii. § 2, xxix. § 11, VII. xvi. § 9, IX. i. § 1, xxiii. § 7, xxxiv. § 1, X. viii. § 4, xx. § 3

Boeotus, IX. i. § 1

Boleoi, II. xxxvi. § 3

Bolgius, Gaul, X. xix. § 7

Bolina, VII. xviii. § 6, xxiii. § 4

Bolinaeus, river, VII. xxiii. § 4

Bones of heroes and great men, I. i. § 2, xvii. § 6, xxviii. § 7, xxxv. § 5, 8, II. x. § 2, xxi. § 4, xxii. § 2, 9, III. iii. § 6, 7, xi. § 10, xiv. § 1, xxvi. § 10, IV. xxxii. § 3, V. xiii. § 4–6, VI. xx. § 7, xxii. § 1, VII. i. § 8, VIII. ix. § 3, xxxii. § 5, xxxvi. § 8, liv. § 4, IX. xviii. § 5, xxix. § 8, xxx. § 9, 11, xxxviii. § 3, X. xii. § 8, xxxvi. § 10

Booneta, III. xii. § 1, 3, xv. § 10

Boreas, I. xix. § 5, xxii. § 7, xxxviii. § 2, V. vii. § 7, xvii. § 11, xix. § 1, VIII. xxvii. § 14, xxxvi. § 6, X. xvii. § 11

Boreius, Mount, VIII. xliv. § 4

Borysthenes, river, VIII. xxviii. § 2

Bountiful Gods, II. xxvii. § 6

—— spirit, III. xvii. § 9

Bow, Cretan I. xxiii. § 4, IV. viii. § 3, 12, Scythian X. xxxi. § 8, of Philoctetes I. xxii. § 6

Boxing, at Olympia, V. vii. § 7, 9, gloves V. xxi. § 14, VIII. xl. § 3

Boys, in ritual, II. xxxv. § 5, VII. xix. § 4, xxiv. § 4, VIII. xli. § 3, xlvii. § 3, X. xxxiv. § 8, xxxviii. § 7

Branchidae, I. xvi. § 3, V. vii. § 5, VII. v. § 4, xlvi. § 3, IX. x. § 2

Brasiae, III. xxi. § 7, xxiv. § 3–5

Brasidas, III. xiv. § 1

Brauron, I. xxiii. § 7, xxxiii. § 1, III. xvi. § 7, 8, VIII. xlvi. § 3

Brennus, Gaul, X. viii. § 2, xix. § 7–xx. § 10, xxii. § 2–xxiii. § 12

Brenthe, VIII. xxviii. § 7

Brentheates, river, V. vii. § 1, VIII. xxviii. § 7

Briareos, II. i. § 6, iv. § 6

Brick, burnt I. xlii. § 5, II. xviii. § 3, V. xx. § 10, unburnt II. xxvii. § 6,

GENERAL INDEX

v. v. § 6, VI. xx. § 11, VIII. viii. § 7, X. iv. § 4, xxxv. § 10

Brimias, Elean victor, VI. xvi. § 5

Briseis, V. xxiv. § 11, X. xxv. § 4

Britain, I. xxxiii. § 4, VIII. xliii. § 4

Britomartis, II. xxx. § 4, III. xiv. § 2, VIII. ii. § 4, IX. xl. § 3

Bronze, casting III. xvii. § 6, VIII. xiv. § 7, 8, IX. xii. § 4, xli. § 1, X. xxxviii. § 6, weapons III. iii. § 6, 8, Corinthian II. iii. § 3, Tartessian VI. xix. § 2

Broteas, II. xxii. § 3, III. xxii. § 4

Bryas, Argive general, II. xx. § 2

Bryseae, III. xx. § 3, 4

Bucephala, cape, II. xxxiv. § 8

Bulis, X. xxxvii. § 2, 3

Bull, Aethiopian V. xii. § 1, IX. xxi. § 2, Paeonian IX. xxi. § 2, X. xiii. § 1–3

—— in myth, I. xxvii. § 9, 10, II. xix. § 4, 7, III. xviii. § 11, 16, V. xx. § 9

—— in ritual, I. xxiv. § 2, II. xi. § 7, IV. xxxii. § 3, VII. xxii. § 11, xxv. § 13, VIII. xix. § 2, IX. iii. § 8, xii. § 1, X. ix. § 3, 4

Bunus, son of Hermes, II. iii. § 10, iv. § 7

Buphagium, VIII. xxvi. § 8

Buphagus, of Pheneus, VIII. xiv. § 9

—— son of Iapetus, VIII. xxvii. § 17

—— river, V. vii. § 1, VIII. xxvi. § 8, xxvii. § 17, xxviii. § 1

Buporthmus, Mount, II. xxxiv. § 8

Bura, VII. vi. § 1, xxv. § 8–10

Buskins, worn by gods, VIII. xxxi. § 4

Bustrophedon writing, V. xvii. § 6

Butas, Milesian victor, VI. xvii. § 3

Butes, I. xxvi. § 5

Bycelus, Sicyonian victor, VI. xiii. § 7

Byzantines, III. xvii. § 7, 8, IV. xxxi. § 5, VI. xv. § 7, xix. § 9

Byzes, Naxian, V. x. § 3

Caanthus, IX. x. § 5, 6

Cabeiri, I. iv. § 6, IV. i. § 7, IX. xxii. § 5, xxv. § 5–10, X. xxxviii. § 7

Cachales, river, X. xxxii. § 11

Cadmea, I. iii. § 4, II. v. § 2, vi. § 4, III. xvii. § 1, IX. i. § 4, v. § 2, 6, vii. § 6

Cadmean victory, IX. ix. § 3

Cadmus, I. xliv. § 5, III. i. § 8, xxiv. § 3, IX. v. § 1–6, x. § 1, xii. § 1–4, xvi. § 3, 5, xix. § 4, xxvi. § 3, 4, X. xxxv. § 5, shrine III. xv. § 8

Caecinus, river, VI. vi. § 4

Caenepolis, III. xxi. § 7, xxv. § 9

Caeneus, V. x. § 8, X. xxix. § 10

Caesar, II. i. § 2, iii. § 1, V. i. § 2, temple III. xi. § 3, 4

Caicus, river, I. x. § 4, V. xiii. § 8, xxiv. § 6, VII. xvi. § 1, VIII. iv. § 9, xlv. § 7, IX. v. § 14, xviii. § 4, X. xxv. § 10

Caius, emperor, IX. xxvii. § 3

Cakes, sacrificial, I. xxvi. § 5, xxxviii. § 6, VI. xx. § 2, VIII. ii. § 3, IX. xxxix. § 11, xl. § 12, X. viii. § 10

Calades, lawgiver, I. viii. § 4.

Calamae, IV. xxxi. § 3

Calathium, mountain, III. xxvi. § 11

Calauria, I. viii. § 3, II. xxxiii. § 2, 5, X. v. § 6

Calchas, I. xliii. § 1, VII. iii. § 7, IX. xix. § 6

Caletor, X. xiv. § 2

Calliae, VIII. xxvii. § 4, 7

Callias, Athenian victor, V. ix. § 3, VI. vi. § 1

—— peacemaker, I. viii. § 2, xxiii. § 2, xxvi. § 4

—— son of Lysimachides, X. xviii. § 1

Callichorum, well, I. xxxviii. § 6

Callicrates, Achaean, VII. x. § 5–xii. § 8

—— Magnesian victor, VI. xvii. § 3

Callimachus, general, I. xv. § 3

Calliope, IX. xxx. § 4

Callipateira, V. vi. § 7, 8, VI. vii. § 2

Callipolis, I. xlii. § 6, xliii. § 5

Callippus, general, I. iii. § 5, iv. § 2, X. xx. § 5

—— historian, IX. xxix. § 2, xxxviii. § 10

—— Athenian athlete, V. xxi. § 5

Callirhoe, daughter of Achelous, VIII. xxiv. § 9, 10

—— in Calydon, VII. xxi. § 1–5

Callisto, I. xxv. § 1, VIII. iii. § 6, 7, xxxv. § 8, X. ix. § 5, 6, xxxi. § 10

Callistratus, VII. xvi. § 4–6

Calliteles, Laconian victor, VI. xvi. § 6

Callium, sack of, X. xxii. § 3–7

Callon, Elean victor, VI. xii. § 6

Calm, image of, II. i. § 9

Calos, I. xxi. § 4, xxvi. § 4

Calydon, III. x. § 2, IV. xxxi. § 7, V. i. § 3, VII. xxi. § 1, 5, xviii. § 8, 9. See also Boars

Cambaules, Gaul, IX. xix. § 5, 6

Cambyses, I. xxviii. § 11, xlii. **§ 3**

Camels, IX. xxi. § 2

Canathus, spring, II. xxxviii. § 2

Capaneus, II. xviii. § 5, IX. viii. **§ 7,** X. x. § 3

Caphereus, II. xxiii. § 1, IV. xxxvi. § 6

Caphyae, VIII. xiii. § 4, 6, xxiii. § 2–8, xxxvi. § 4

Cappadocians, III. xvi. § 8

Caprus, Elean victor, v. xxi. § 10, VI. xv. § 4, 5, 10, xvi. § 1

Capua, v. xii. § 3

Car, king of Megara, I. xxxix. § 6, xl. § 6, xliv. § 6

Caranus, IX. xl. § 8, 9

Carcinus, poet, X. xxxviii. § 11

Cardamyle, III. xxvi. § 7

Caria, acropolis of Megara, I. xl. § 6

—— in Asia, II. v. § 3, vii. § 1, VIII. xxix. § 11, xliii. § 4

Carians, VII. ii. § 5, 10, iii. § 1–7, iv. § 9

Carian tongue, IX. xxiii. § 6

Carmanor, II. vii. § 7, xxx. § 3, X. vii. § 2, xvi. § 5

Carnasian grove, IV. xxxiii. § 4

Carnasium, IV. ii. § 2, xxxiii. § 4, 5, VIII. xxxv. § 1

Carneus, II. xiii. § 3–5

Carnion, river, VIII. xxxiv. § 5

Carnus, seer, III. xiii. § 4

Carpo, IX. xxxv. § 2

Carthage, Carthaginians, I. xii. § 5, II. i. § 2, V. xxv. § 6, VI. xii. § 3, xix. § 10, VIII. xxx. § 8, xliii. § 4, X. viii. § 6, viii. § 9, treasury VI. xix. § 7

Caryae, in Laconia, III. x. § 7, IV. xvi. § 9

—— in Arcadia, VIII. xiii. § 6, xiv. § 1

Carystians, I. xxv. § 4, xxxii. § 3, VI. x. § 3, X. xvi. § 6

Cassander, I. iv. § 1, vi. § 4, 7, x. § 1, xi. § 4, 5, xv. § 1, xxv. § 6, xxvi. § 3, xxix. § 7, xxxv. § 2, IV. xxvii. § 10, V. xxiii. § 3, VII. vii. § 9, VIII. vii. § 2, 7, IX. iii. § 6, vii. § 1, 2, 4, x. xviii. § 7, xxxiv. § 2, 3

Cassandra, I. xv. § 2, II. xvi. § 6, 7, III. xix. § 6, xxvi. § 5, V. xi. § 6, xix. § 5, VII. xix. § 7, X. xxvi. § 3, xxvii. § 1

Cassotis, spring, X. xxiv. § 7, xxv. § 1

Castalia, spring, X. viii. § 9

Castor, III. ii. § 8, xxi. § 9, xxiv. § 7, v. viii. § 4, VIII. xlv. § 7, cult III. xiii. § 1, VIII. ii. § 4

Catalogue of Women, poem, I. xliii. § 1, III. xxiv. § 10

Catana, V. xxiii. § 6, VII. xvi. § 5, X. xxviii. § 4

Caucon, IV. i. § 5–9, ii. § 6, xxvi. § 8, xxvii. § 6, v. v. § 5

Caulonia, VI. iii. § 11, 12

Caunus, I. iii. § 5, VI. vii. § 6

Caus, VIII. xxv. § 1

Cecrops, son of Erechtheus, I. v. § 3, xxvii. § 1, VII. i. § 2, VIII. ii. § 2, 3, X. x. § 1

—— son of Pandion, I. ii. § 6, v. § 3, xxxi. § 5, IX. xxxiii. § 1

Cedar-wood, III. xv. § 11, V. xvii. § 5, VI. xix. § 8, 12, VIII. xvii. § 2, IX. x. § 2

Ceisus, son of Temenus, II. xix. § 1, 2, xxvi. § 2, xxviii. § 3

Celadus, river, VIII. xxxviii. § 9

Celaeno, X. vi. § 3

Celbidas, VII. xxii. § 8

Celeae, II. xii. § 4, xiv. § 1, 4

Celenderis, II. ix. § 9

Celery, crowns of, VIII. xlviii. § 2

Celeus, I. xiv. § 2, xxxviii. § 2, 3, xxxix. § 1, II. xiv. § 2, 3

Celts, I. iv. § 1, 2, ix. § 5, xiii. § 2, xxxiii. § 4, xxxv. § 5, V. xii. § 1, xiv. § 3, VIII. i. § 1, IX. xxi. § 3, X. iii. § 4, xv. § 2, xix. § 5–xxiii. § 14. *Cf.* Gauls

Cenchreae, in Argolis, II. xxiv. § 7

—— port of Corinth, II. i. § 5, ii. § 3, VII. vi. § 7

Centaurs, I. xvii. § 2, xxviii. § 2, III. xviii. § 10, 16, v. v. § 10, x. § 8, xix. § 7, 9

Ceos, V. xxiii. § 2

Cephalae, I. xxxi. § 1

Cephallenia, I. xxxvii. § 6, IV. xx. § 8, VI. xv. § 7, X. vii. § 7

Cephalus, I. iii. § 1, xxxvii. § 6, III. xviii. § 12, X. xxix. § 6

Cepheus, IV. xxxv. § 9, VIII. iv. § 8, xxiii. § 3, xlvii. § 5

Cephisades, IX. xxxiv. § 9

Cephisian Lake, IX. xiii. § 3, xxiv. § 1, 2, xxxiv. § 5, xxxviii. § 6, 7

Cephisodorus, I. xxxvi. § 5, VIII. ix. § 10

Cephisus, river, in Argolis, II. xv. § 5, xx. § 6, 7

—— in Attica, I. xxxiv. § 3, xxxvii. § 3, 4, xxxviii. § 5

GENERAL INDEX

Cephisus, in Boeotia, IX. xxiv. § 1, xxxiv. § 9, xxxviii. § 7, 8, X. iv. § 7, vi. § 4, viii. § 10, xxxiii. § 1-xxxiv. § 1

Cerameicus, I. ii. § 4, iii. § 1, xiv. § 6, VIII. ix. § 8

Cerausius, Mount, VIII. xli. § 3

Cerberus, II. xxxi. § 2, xxxv. § 10, III. xviii. § 13, xxv. § 5, 6, V. xxvi. § 7, VIII. xviii. § 3, IX. xxxiv. § 5

Cercyon, son of Agamedes, VIII. v. § 4, xlv. § 7

—— son of Poseidon, I. v. § 2, xiv. § 3, xxxix. § 3

Cerdo, tomb of, II. xxi. § 1

Ceressus, IX. xiv. § 2-4

Cerycius, Mount, IX. xx. § 3

Ceryneia, VII. vi. § 1, xxv. § 5-8

Cerynes, II. xxviii. § 3, 5

Ceryx, I. xxxviii. § 3

Cestrinus, I. xi. § 1, 2, II. xxiii. § 6

Ceyx, I. xxxvii. § 6

Chabrias, I. xxix. § 3, IX. xv. § 4

Chaereas, Sicyonian victor, VI. iii. § 1, 2

—— Theban general, IX. xiii. § 3

Chaeron, victor, of Pellene, VII. xxvii. § 7

—— son of Apollo, IX. xl. § 5

Chaeronea, I. xli. § 8, IX. xl. § 5-xli. § 7, lion of IX. xl. § 10, battles of I. xviii. § 8, xxv. § 3, xxix. § 13, IV. xxviii. § 2, V. iv. § 9, xx. § 10, VI. iv. § 7, VII. vi. § 5, xv. § 6, 9, VIII. vi. § 2, xxvii. § 10, IX. i. § 8, vi. § 5, xxix. § 8, xl. § 7, 10, X. iii. § 3, 4

Chalcis, in Euboea, I. xxviii. § 2, V. xxiii. § 2, VI. xiii. § 8, VII. vii. § 6, IX. xii. § 6, xviii. § 1, xix. § 3, xxxi. § 3

—— at Erythrae, VII. v. § 12

Chalcodon, VIII. xv. § 6, 7, IX. xvii. § 3, xix. § 3

Chaldaeans, I. xvi. § 3, IV. xxxii. § 4

Chamynus, VI. xxi. § 1

Chaon, Mount, II. xxiv. § 6

Chaos, IX. xxvii. § 2

Characoma, III. xxi. § 2

Charadra, X. iii. § 2, xxxiii. § 6

Charadrus, rivers, II. xxv. § 2, IV. xxxiii. § 5, VII. xxii. § 11, xxiii. § 1, X. xxxiii. § 6

Charillus, king of Sparta, II. xxxvi. § 4, III. ii. § 5, vii. § 3, IV. iv. § 4, VIII. v. § 9, xlviii. § 4

Charinus, Elean victor, VI. xv. § 2

Chariot, place called, I. xxxiv. § 2, IX. xix. § 4, 8

—— dedicated, I. xxviii. § 2, VI. i. § 6, iv. § 10, ix. § 4, x. § 6, xii. § 1, 6, xvi. § 6, 9, xviii. § 1

—— races, v. viii. § 7, 10, 11, VI. xx. § 10-15

Charisia, VIII. iii. § 4, xxvii. § 3, xxxv. § 5

Charmidas, III. ii. § 7

Charmides, Elean victor, VI. vii. § 1

Charmus, I. xxx. § 1

Charon, ferryman, X. xxviii. § 1-4

—— historian, X. xxviii. § 1

Chasms, VIII. xiv. § 1, xxii. § 3, 8, 9, xxiii. § 2, xliv. § 4, liv. § 2

Chastiser, stone, IX. xi. § 2, 7

Cheese, eaten by athletes, VI. vii. § 10

Cheimarrhus, river, II. xxxvi. § 7

Cheimerium, spring, VIII. vii. § 2

Cheimon, Argive victor, VI. ix. § 3

Chelone, cape, I. ii. § 4

Chelydorea, mountain, VIII. xvii. § 5

Chersias, IX. xxxviii. § 9, 10

Chilon, sage, III. xvi. § 4, X. xxiv. § 1

—— Achaean victor, VI. iv. § 6-8, VII. vi. § 5

Chimaera, II. xxvii. § 2, III. xviii. § 13, xxv. § 6

Chionis, Lacedaemonian victor, III. xiv. § 3, IV. xxiii. § 4, 10, VI. xiii. § 2-5, VIII. xxxix. § 3

Chios, I. xxix. § 11, IV. xxxv. § 10, VII. iv. § 1, 8-10

Chiron, III. xviii. § 12, V. v. § 10, xix. § 9, IX. xxxi. § 5

Chloris, II. xxi. § 9, V. xvi. § 4, IX. xxxvi. § 8, X. xxv. § 9

Choerilus, dramatist, I. xiv. § 3

—— Elean victor, VI. xvii. § 5

Choerius, IV. i. § 1, xxx. § 1

Chorea, maenad, II. xx. § 4

Chorus, place in Sparta, III. xi. § 9

Chronius, VIII. xlvii. § 6

Chrysaoris, V. xxi. § 10

Chryse, island, VIII. xxxiii. § 4

—— daughter of Almus, IX. xxxvi. § 1

Chryseis, II. xvii. § 7, III. v. § 6

Chrysippus, son of Pelops, VI. xx. § 7

—— of Soli, I. xvii. § 2, xxix. § 15

Chrysothemis, Cretan victor, X. vii. § 2

Chthonia, festival, II. xxxv. § 5-8

GENERAL INDEX

Cillas, charioteer, v. x. § 7

Cimon, I. xvii. § 6, xxviii. § 3, xxix. § 8, 13–15, II. xxix. § 4, III. iii. § 7, IV. xxiv. § 6, VIII. viii. § 9, lii. § 3

Cinadus, III. xxii. § 10

Cinaethon, Laconian poet, III. iii. § 9, xviii. § 6, IV. ii. § 1, VIII. liii. § 5

Cinnabar, VIII. xxxix. § 6

Circe, v. xix. § 7

Cirrha, II. ix. § 6, VII. xix. § 7, X. i. § 2, viii. § 8, xxxvii. § 5

Cissa, spring, VIII. xii. § 4

Cithaeron, king of Plataea, IX. i. § 2, iii. § 1, 2

—— Mount, I. xxxviii. § 8, xli. § 3, 6, II. ii. § 7, IX. i. § 2, ii. § 1, 4, iii. § 9, xiii. § 7

Cladeus, V. vii. § 1, x. § 7, xv. § 7, VI. xx. § 6, xxi. § 3

Claea, III. xxvi. § 11

Clarus, VII. iii. § 1–4, v. § 3, 4, X. xii. § 5

Claudius, emperor, IX. xxvii. § 3

Clay, statues of, I. ii. § 5, VII. xxii. § 9

Clazomenae, VI. xvii. § 2, VII. iii. § 8, 9, v. § 11

Clearetus, then victor, VI. xvi. § 9

Cledones, IX. xi. § 7

Cleft Road, IX. ii. § 4, X. v. § 3, 4, xxxv. § 8

Cleinias, II. viii. § 2, x. § 7

Cleinomachus, Elean victor, VI. xv. § 1

Cleisthenes, Athenian, I. v. § 1, xxix. § 6

—— tyrant of Sicyon, II. viii. § 1, ix. § 6, X. vii. § 6, xxxvii. § 6

Cleitodemus, author, X. xv. § 5

Cleitomachus, Theban victor, VI. xv. § 3–5

Cleitor, V. xxiii. § 7, VIII. iv. § 4, 5, xix. § 4, xxi. § 1–4, xxiii. § 9

Cleo, priestess, III. xiv. § 4

Cleobis, II. xx. § 3

Cleoboea, X. xxviii. § 3

Cleobulus, X. xxiv. § 1

Cleodaeus, II. vii. § 6, III. xv. § 10

Cleogenes, Elean victor, VI. i. § 4

Cleolas of Phlius, V. xxii. § 1

Cleombrotus, son of Anaxandrides, III. iii. § 9

—— son of Pausanias, I. xiii. § 4, III. v. § 7, vi. § 1, IX. iii. § 3–10

—— son-in-law of Leonidas, III. vi. § 7

Cleomedes, of Astypalaea, victor, VI. ix. § 6–8

Cleomenes, satrap of Egypt, I. vi. § 3

—— I, son of Anaxandrides, king of Sparta, II. xx. § 8, III. iii. § 9–iv. § 7, vii. § 8

—— II, son of Cleombrotus, I. xiii. § 4, III. vi. § 2, xxiv. § 1 (wrongly called son of Agesipolis)

—— III, son of Leonidas II, II. ix. § 1–3, III. vi. § 9, vii. § 1, x. § 7, IV. xxix. § 7, 9, 10, VII. vii. § 3, 4, VIII. viii. § 11, xxvii. § 15, 16, xxviii. § 7, xlix. § 4–6

Cleon, Athenian, I. xxix. § 13

—— Magnesian, X. iv. § 6

—— tyrant of Sicyon, II. viii. § 1

Cleonae, I. xxix. § 7, II. xv. § 1, 2, VII. iii. § 9, xxv. § 6, X. xi. § 5

Cleonice, III. xvii. § 8, 9

Cleonnis, Messenian general, IV. vii. § 4, 8, viii. § 11, x. § 5, 6, xi. § 3, xiii. § 5

Cleonymus, I. xiii. § 4, 5, III. vi. § 2, 3, 7, xxiv. § 1, IV. xxviii. § 3

Cleopatra, wife of Meleager, IV. ii. § 7

—— daughter of Philip, I. vi. § 3

—— mother of Ptolemy Philometor, I. ix. § 1–3

—— niece of Attalus, VIII. vii. § 7

Cleopus, son of Codrus, VII. iii. § 10

Cleosthenes, Epidamnian victor, V. xxiii. § 5, VI. x. § 6–8

Clepsydra, spring, IV. xxxi. § 6, xxxiii. § 1

Cleson, I. xxxix. § 6, xlii. § 7

Cleta, Grace, III. xviii. § 6, IX. xxxv. § 1

Clymene, mother of Homer, X. xxiv. § 2

—— daughter of Minyas, X. xxix. § 6, 7

—— saviour of Perseus, II. xviii. § 1

Clymenus, deity, II. xxxv. § 9, 10

—— son of Cardys, v. viii. § 1, xiv. § 8, VI. xxi. § 6

—— son of Phoroneus, II. xxxv. § 4

—— son of Presbon, IX. xxxvii. § 1

Clytemnestra, II. xviii. § 2, xxii. § 3, 6, xxxi. § 4, III. xix. § 6, VIII. xxxiv. § 1, 4, grave II. xvi. § 7

Clytidae, VI. xvii. § 6

Clytius, son of Alcmaeon, VI. xvii. § 6

Cnacadium, mountain, III. xxiv. § 6, 8

Cnacalus, mountain, VIII. xxiii. § 4

212

GENERAL INDEX

Cnacias, horse, VI. x. § 7

Cnageus, III. xviii. § 4, 5

Cnidos, I. i. § 3, ii. § 2, II. i. § 5, V. xxiv. § 7, VIII. xxx. § 2, X. xi. § 1, 3, xxxii. § 1, treasury X. xi. § 5, lounge X. xxv. § 1

Cnossus, I. xviii. § 5, xxvii. § 10, III. ii. § 4, xii. § 11, V. x. § 9, VI. iv. § 11, VIII. liii. § 8, IX. xl. § 3

Cock, II. xxxiv. § 2, V. xxv. § 9, VI. xxvi. § 3, IX. xxii. § 4

Codrus, I. xix. § 5, xxxix. § 4, VII. ii. § 1, 3, iii. § 10, xxv. § 2, VIII. lii. § 1, IX. xxxvii. § 8, X. x. § 1

Coeranus, I. xliii. § 5

Coeus, IV. xxxiii. § 6

Colaenus, I. xxxi. § 4, 5, IV. xxxiv. § 8

Colchis, I. xviii. § 1, xxiv. § 2, II. iii. § 10, III. xix. § 7, 8, xxiv. § 7, IX. xxxiv. § 8

Colias, cape, I. i. § 5

Colona, in Sparta, III. xiii. § 7

Colonides, IV. xxxiv. § 8, 12

Colonies, statues at Athens, I. xviii. § 6

Colontas, II. xxxv. § 4

Colophon, I. ix. § 7, III. xiv. § 9, VI. xvii. § 4, VII. iii. § 1–9, v. § 1, 4, 10, VIII. xxviii. § 3, IX. xxxii. § 6, xxxiii. § 2, X. xii. § 5

Colossi, I. xliii. § 6, xlii. § 3, II. xxxv. § 3, IX. xi. § 6

Colyergia, cape, II. xxxiv. § 8

Comaetho, priestess, VII. xix. § 2–5

Combutis, Gaul, X. xxii. § 3

Cometes, son of Thestius, VIII. xlv. § 6

—— son of Disamenus, VII. vi. § 2

Comon, Messenian, IV. xxvi. § 2, 3

Condylea, VIII. xxiii. § 6, 7

Conon, I. i. § 3, ii. § 2, iii. § 2, xxiv. § 3, xxix. § 15, III. ix. § 2, VI. iii. § 6, vii. § 6, VIII. lii. § 4, grave I. xxix. § 15, statues I. iii. § 2, xxiv. § 3, VI. iii. § 16

Contest, statue of, V. xx. § 3, xxvi. § 3

Copae, IX. xxiv. § 1

Copaic Lake, see Cephisian

Corcyra, daughter of Asopus, II. v. § 2, v. xxii. § 6

—— island, I. xi. § 6, xii. § 1, II. iii. § 9, v. § 2, V. xxii. § 1, xxvii. § 4, xxvii. § 9, VI. xxiv. § 4, xxv. § 1, X. ix. § 3, 4

Cordax, VI. xxii. § 1

Coresus, priest, VII. xxi. § 1–5

Coresus at Ephesus, V. xxiv. § 8, VII. ii. § 7

Corinna, IX. xx. § 1, xxii. § 3

Corinth, description II. ii. § 4–v. § 4, history II. i. § 1, 2, ii. § 2, iii. § 1, 10, 11, iv. § 2, 3, 4, viii. § 4, xx. § 1, IV. xi. § 1, xv. § 8, xix. § 1–3, v. i. § 2, xxiv. § 1, xxv. § 1, VII. viii. § 1, 3, xvi. § 7, 8, X. xx. § 1, battle of I. xxix. § 11, IX. vi. § 4, ports II. ii. § 3, treasury X. xiii. § 5, 6

Corinthian bronze, II. iii. § 3

—— order in architecture, VIII. xlv. § 5

—— war, III. ix. § 12, IV. xvii. § 5

Corinthus, II. i. § 1, iii. § 10

Corn, in ritual VIII. xx. § 1, first sown I. xiv. § 2, VII. xviii. § 2, VIII. iv. § 1

Coroebus, Argive, I. xliii. § 7–xliv. § 1

—— Elean victor, v. viii. § 6, VIII. xxvi. § 3, 4

—— son of Mygdon, X. xxvii. § 1

Coronea, in Boeotia, IV. xxxiv. § 5, IX. xxxiv. § 1, 3, 4, 5, battle III. ix. § 13, IX. vi. § 4

—— in Messenia, IV. xxxiv. § 4–6

Coronis, II. xi. § 7, xii. § 1, xxvi. § 4, 6, 7, IV. iii. § 2

Corsea, IX. xxiv. § 5

Corsica, X. xvii. § 8, 9

Corybantes, III. xxiv. § 5, VIII. xxxvii. § 6

Corybas, VI. xxv. § 6

Corycian cave, X. vi. § 3, xxxii. § 2, 7

Corycus, mountain, X. xii. § 7

Corynetes, VIII. xi. § 4

Coryphasium, cape, IV. xxxvi. § 1

Coryphe, mountain, VII. v. § 9

Coryphum, mountain, II. xxviii. § 2

Cos, I. ii. § 4, III. iv. § 9, 10, xxiii. § 6, VI. xiv. § 12, xvii. § 2, VIII. xliii. § 4

Cosmeterium, at Sicyon, II. vii. § 5

Costobocs, X. xxxiv. § 5

Cotilius, Mount, VIII. xli. § 7, 10

Cotys, portico of, II. xxvii. § 6

Couches, sacred, II. xvii. § 3, V. xx. § 1, VIII. xlvii. § 2, X. xxxii. § 12

Council chambers, I. iii. § 5, v. § 1, xlii. § 4, xliii. § 1, II. ix. § 6, III. xi. § 2, V. xxiii. § 1, xxiv. § 1, 9, VI. xxiii. § 7, VIII. xxx. § 9, xxxii. § 1, X. xxxv. § 6

Cows, in myth, I. xxxv. § 7, III. xvi. § 4, xviii. § 13, IV. xxxvi. § 2, 3, V.

213

GENERAL INDEX

i. § 9, x. § 9, xix. § 1, VII. xx. § 4,
IX. xii. § 1, xix. § 4, xxxi. § 10, in
cult II. xxxv. § 6, v. xvi. § 3, IX.
iii. § 8, X. xxxv. § 7. *See also* Ox
Cranae, island, III. xxii. § 1
Cranaus, I. ii. § 6, xxxi. § 3
Cranes, I. xii. § 4, xl. § 1
Craneum, II. ii. § 4
Cranius, III. xx. § 9
Crannon, v. viii. § 8, X. iii. § 4
Crataemenes, Samian, IV. xxiii. § 7
Crathis, mountain and river, in
Arcadia, VII. xxv. § 11, VIII. xv.
§ 8, 9, xviii. § 4
Cratinus, victor, of Aegeira, VI. iii. § 6
Cratisthenes, victor, of Cyrene, VI.
xviii. § 1
Crauxidas, victor, of Crannon, v. viii.
§ 8
Creon, I. xxxix. § 2, IX. v. § 13, x. § 3,
xxv. § 1, X. xxv. § 6
Creophylus, poet, IV. ii. § 3
Cresius, Mount, VIII. xliv. § 7
Cresphontes, II. xviii. § 7, xix. § 1,
III. i. § 5, IV. iii. § 3–8, v. § 1, xvi.
§ 1, xxvii. § 6, xxx. § 1, xxxi. § 11,
v. iii. § 6, VIII. v. § 6, xxix. § 5
Crete, legends I. xvii. § 3, 6, xxi. § 4,
xxvii. § 9, III. ii. § 4, VIII. xxxviii.
§ 2, history I, xxxvi. § 5, xxxix. § 6,
xli. § 5, xliv. § 3, III. iii. § 7, VII. ii.
§ 5, iii. § 1, bowmen I. xxiii. § 4,
xxix. § 6, IV. viii. § 3, 12, IV. xix.
§ 4, VII. xvi. § 1
Cretea, VIII. xxxviii. § 2
Creugas, boxer, of Epidamnus, II.
xx. § 1, VIII. xl. § 3–5
Creusa, daughter of Erechtheus, I.
xxviii. § 4
—— wife of Aeneas, X. xxvi. § 1
Creusis, IX. xxxii. § 1, 2
Criannius, Elean victor, VI. xvii. § 1
Crisa, X. xxxvii. § 5
Crison, victor, of Himera, v. xxiii. § 4
Crisus, son of Phocus, II. xxix. § 4
—— Tegean, VIII. xlviii. § 1
Critodamus, Cleitorian victor, VI. viii.
§ 5
Critolaus, II. i. § 2, VII. xiv. § 4–xv.
§ 8
Crius, river, VII. xxvii. § 11
—— Euboean, X. vi. § 6
—— seer, III. xiii. § 3, 4
—— Titan, VII. xxvii. § 11
Croceae, II. iii. § 5, III. xxi. § 4

Crocodiles, I. xxxiii. § 6, II. xxviii.
§ 1, IV. xxxiv. § 3
Crocon, Eleusinian, I. xxxviii. § 2
—— Eretrian victor, VI. xiv. § 4
Croesus, III. ii. § 3, IV. v. § 3, VIII.
xxiv. § 13, dedications III. x. § 8,
X. viii. § 7
Cromi, VIII. iii. § 4, xxvii. § 4, xxxiv.
§ 6
Cromyon, I. xxvii. § 9, II. i. § 3
Cronius, Mount, v. xxi. § 2, VI. xix.
§ 1, xx. § 1
Cronus, myths v. vii. § 6, 10, VII.
xxiii. § 4, VIII. ii. § 2, viii. § 2,
xxi. § 3, swallows stone VIII. xxxvi.
§ 3, IX. ii. § 7, xli. § 6, X. xxiv.
§ 6
—— cult, I. xviii. § 7, v. vii. § 6, VI.
xx. § 1, IX. xxxix. § 5
—— images, IX. ii. § 7, xxxix. § 4
Croton, III. iii. § 1, xix. § 11, 12, VI.
xiii. § 1, xix. § 6, VII. xxv. § 11,
athletes VI. ix. § 5, xiii. § 1, xiv.
§ 5–8, X. v. § 13, vii. § 4, ix. § 2
Crotopus, king of Argos, I. xliii. § 7,
II. xvi. § 1, xix. § 8, xxiii. § 7
Crows, IV. xxxiv. § 5, 6, IX. iii. § 4,
xxxviii. § 3, X. xv. § 5, island of
VIII. xxv. § 12
Cruni, spring, VIII. xxxv. § 8
Cteatus, II. xv. § 1, v. iii. § 3, 4,
VI. xx. § 16
Ctesias, IX. xxi. § 4
Ctesippus, II. xix. § 1, III. xvi. § 6
Cuckoo, Mount, II. xxxv. § 1
Cumae, VII. iii. § 10, xxii. § 8, VIII.
xxiv. § 5, X. xii. § 8
Curetes, III. xxv. § 2, IV. xxxi. § 9,
xxxiii. § 1, v. vii. § 6, viii. § 1, xiv.
§ 7, 9, VIII. ii. § 2, xxiv. § 9, xxxvii.
§ 6, X. xxxi. § 3, xxxviii. § 7
Cyamites, I. xxxvii. § 4
Cyannippus, king of Argos, II. xviii.
§ 4, 5, xxx. § 10
Cyathus, II. xiii. § 8
Cychreus, I. xxxv. § 2, xxxvi. § 1
Cyclopes, II. xvi. § 5, xxv. § 7, xxxv. § 8,
VII. xxv. § 6, VIII. xxix. § 2, X. xxii.
§ 7, altar II. ii. § 1
Cycnus, opponent of Heracles, I.
xxvii. § 6, III. xviii. § 10
—— turned into swan, I. xxx. § 3
—— king of Colonae, X. xiv. § 1–3
Cydias, X. xxi. § 5
Cydon, VIII. liii. § 4

GENERAL INDEX

Cydonia, VI. xxi. § 6, VIII. liii. § 4, X. ii. § 7

Cylarabis, gymnasium, II. xxii. § 8, 9

Cyllene, Mount, VIII. iv. § 4, 6, xv. § 4, xvii. § 1, 4
—— port, IV. xxiii. § 1, 3, 5, VI. xxvi. § 4, 5, VIII. v. § 8, liv. § 3

Cylon, Argive, III. ix. § 8
—— Athenian, I. xxviii. § 1, xl. § 1, VII. xxv. § 3
—— Elean tyrannicide, V. v. § 1, VI. xiv. § 11

Cynaethae, V. xxii. § 1, VIII. xix. § 1, 3

Cynisca, III. viii. § 1, 2, xv. § 1, V. xii. § 5, VI. i. § 6

Cyniscus, Mantinean victor, VI. iv. § 11

Cynortas, III. i. § 3, xiii. § 1

Cynortium, mountain, II. xxvii. § 7

Cynosarges, I. xix. § 3

Cynuria, III. ii. § 2, 3

Cynus, port, X. i. § 2

Cyparissiae, IV. xxxvi. § 7, VIII. i. § 1

Cyparissus, X. xxxvi. § 5

Cyphanta, III. xxiv. § 2, 3

Cypresses, II. ii. § 4, xi. § 6, xiii. § 3, xv. § 2, xxiv. § 5, IV. xxxiii. § 4, VIII. xxiv. § 7, xli. § 4, X. xxxviii. § 9, wood used for statues VI. xviii. § 7, VIII. xvii. § 2

Cypria, poem, III. xvi. § 1, IV. ii. § 7, X. xxvi. § 1, 4, xxxi. § 2

Cyprus, I. vi. § 6, 8, ix. § 1, xxix. § 13, II. xxix. § 4, III. xi. § 5, VI. ii. § 5, IX. xix. § 1, X. xxiv. § 3

Cypselus, king of Arcadia, IV. iii. § 6, 8, VIII. v. § 6, 13, xxix. § 5
—— tyrant of Corinth, I. xxiii. § 1, II. iv. § 4, xxviii. § 8, V. ii. § 3, xviii. § 7, X. xxiv. § 1, chest V. xvii. § 5 ff.

Cyrene, mother of Aristaeus, X. xvii. § 3
—— city, I. vi. § 5, 8, vii. § 1, 2, II. xxvi. § 9, III. xiv. § 3, xvi. § 2, VI. viii. § 3, xii. § 2, 7, xiii. § 7, xviii. § 1, xix. § 10, X. ii. § 3, iii. § 1, xiii. § 5, 6, xv. § 6, 7

Cyrtone, IX. xxiv. § 4

Cyrus, elder, VIII. xliii. § 6
—— younger, III. ix. § 1, V. vi. § 5, IX. xv. § 5, xxxii. § 7
—— sanctuary of Asclepius, VII. xxvii. § 11

Cythera, I. xiv. § 7, xxvii. § 5, II. ii. § 8, III. xxiii. § 1

Cytherus, VI. xxii. § 7

Cyzicus, IV. xxxv. § 8, VIII. xlvi. § 4

DACTYLS, Idaean, V. vii. § 6, 9, viii. § 1, xiv. § 7, VIII. xxxi. § 3, IX. xix. § 5, xxvii. § 8

Daedala, festival, IX. iii. § 2–8

Daedalus, I. xxi. § 4, xxvi. § 4, xxvii. § 1, II. iv. § 5, xv. § 1, III. xvii. § 6, V. xxv. § 13, VII. iv. § 4–7, VIII. xvi. § 3, xxxv. § 2, xlvi. § 2, liii. § 8, IX. iii. § 2, xi. § 4, 5, xxxix. § 8, xl. § 3, 4, X. xvii. § 4

Daetus, I. xxxvii. § 6

Daiphantes, Phocian, X. i. § 8, 10

Damagetus, king of Ialysus, IV. xxiv. § 2, 3

Damagetus, Rhodian victor, VI. vii. § 1–3

Damarchus, Parrhasian victor, VI. viii. § 2

Damaretus, Heraean victor, V. viii. § 10, VI. x. § 4, 5, VIII. xxvi. § 2, X. vii. § 7
—— Messenian victor, VI. xiv. § 11

Damarmenus, V. xiii. § 5, 6

Damasias, V. iv. § 3, VII. vi. § 2

Damasichthon, son of Codrus, VII. iii. § 3
—— son of Opheltes, IX. v. § 16

Damasistratus, X. v. § 2

Dameon, VII. xx. § 16

Damia, II. xxx. § 4, xxxii. § 2

Damis, Messenian, IV. x. § 5, 6, xi. § 2, xiii. § 5

Damiscus, Messenian victor, VI. ii. § 10, 11

Damithales, VIII. xv. § 4

Damocritus, Cleitorian victor, VI. viii. § 5
—— Achaean general, VII. xiii. § 1–5

Damon, Athenian, VII. ii. § 4, iii. § 10
—— victor, of Thurii, IV. xxvii. § 9, VI. v. § 3, VII. xxv. § 4, VIII. xxvii. § 8

Damonicus, V. xxi. § 16

Damophon, king of Pisa, VI. xxii. § 3, 4
—— king of Corinth, II. iv. § 3
—— tyrant of Pisa, V. xvi. § 5

Damoxenidas, Maenalian victor, VI. vi. § 3

GENERAL INDEX

Damoxenus, Syracusan boxer, VIII. xl. § 3, 4

Danai, VII. i. § 7, VIII. xxv. § 9

Danaus, II. xvi. § 1, xix. § 3–7, xx. § 6, 7, xxv. § 4, xxxvii. § 1, 2, xxxviii. § 4, III. xii. § 2, xxii. § 11, IV. xxx. § 2, xxxv. § 2, VII. i. § 6, xxi. § 13, xxii. § 5, X. x. § 5, xxxv. § 1

Dances, III. x. § 7, xi. § 9, xviii. § 14, IV. xvi. § 9, VIII. xvi. § 3, IX. xl. § 3, X. iv. § 3

Daphne, VIII. xx. § 1–4, X. vii. § 8

Daphnis, X. v. § 5

Dardanus, II. xix. § 6

Darius I, III. iv. § 2, vii. § 8, ix. § 6, xii. § 7, VII. x. § 1, VIII. xlvi. § 3, X. xxxiii. § 2

—— II, VI. v. § 7

—— III, I. xxv. § 5, VI. xvii. § 5, IX. xl. § 9

Dasea, VIII. iii. § 2, 3, xxvii. § 4, xxxvi. § 9

Dasmon, Corinthian victor, IV. xiii. § 7

Datis, X. xi. § 5, xxviii. § 6

Daulis, I. iii. § 1, III. xviii. § 12, V. xix. § 1, xxxv. § 8

Day, I. iii. § 1, III. xviii. § 12, V. xix. § 1, xxii. § 2

Dead Sea, V. vii. § 4, 5

Death, III. xviii. § 1, V. xviii. § 1

Decelea, I. xxix. § 5, III. viii. § 6

Deer, III. xx. § 4, V. vi. § 6, VII. xxvi. § 10, VIII. x. § 10, xvii. § 4, xxii. § 9, in myth II. xxx. § 7, V. x. § 9, VIII. xlviii. § 7, IX. xix. § 6, in cult I. xxxiii. § 3, VII. xviii. § 12, VIII. X. § 10, xviii. § 12, X. xxxii. § 16

Degmenus, Elean archer, v. iv. § 2

Deianeira, I. xxxii. § 6, II. xxiii. § 5, VI. xix. § 2

Deidamia, IV. xxxv. § 3

Deinicha, III. x. § 3

Deinocrates, IV. xxix. § 11, VIII. li. § 7, 8

Deinolochus, Elean victor, VI. i. § 4, 5

Deinome, X. xxvi. § 2

Deinomenes, father of Hiero, V. xxvii. § 1, VI. xii. § 1

—— son of Hiero, VI. xii. § 1, VIII. xli. § 8, 9

—— assassin, VI. xii. § 4

Deinosthenes, Lacedaemonian victor, VI. xvi. § 8

Deiphobus, v. xxii. § 2

Deiphontes, II. xix. § 1, xxvi. § 1, 2, xxviii. § 3–6, xxix. § 5, VII. iv. § 2

Deiras, in Argos, II. xxiv. § 1, xxv. § 1, 4

Delium, I. xxix. § 13, III. vi. § 1, IX. vi. § 3, xx. § 1

Delos, I. xxix. § 1, II. v. § 3, xxxii. § 5, III. xxiii. § 3–5, IV. xxvii. § 9, xxxiii. § 2, xxxvi. § 6, VIII. xxi. § 3, xxiii. § 5, xxxiii. § 2, xxxiv. § 6, xxxv. § 3, X. xxviii. § 6, legends I. xviii. § 5, xix. § 6, v. vii. § 8, VIII. xlviii. § 3, cults I. xviii. § 5, xxix. § 1, xxxi. § 2, II. xxvii. § 1, IV. iv. § 1, xxxii. § 2, V. vii. § 8, xix. § 10, VIII. xxxiii. § 2, IX. xii. § 6, xl. § 3

Delphi, description X. v. § 5–xxxii. § 1, development of oracle II. xxxiii. § 2, X. v. § 5–8, history I. iv. § 4, ix. § 3, II. xxxiii. § 2, III. iv. § 3, x. § 3, 4, IV. xxxiv. § 11, VII. xxiv. § 4, IX. xxxvi. § 2, X. ii. § 2, vii. § 1, xxiii. § 1–10

Delphus, X. vi. § 4, xxxii. § 2

Delta, in Argos, II. xxi. § 1

—— in Egypt, VI. xxvi. § 9

Demades, VII. x. § 4

Demaenetus, VI. xxi. § 4

Demaratus, III. iv. § 3, vi. § 8, vii. § 7, 8, viii. § 7, IV. xv. § 3

Demeter, myths, I. xiii. § 8, xiv. § 1–3, xxxvii. § 2, 4, xxxix. § 1, xliii. § 2, II. v. § 8, xviii. § 3, xxxv. § 4, VIII. xv. § 3, 4, xxv. § 2–7, xxxvii. § 6, xlii. § 1–7

—— cult. I. i. § 4, ii. § 4, 5, xiii. § 8, xiv. § 1, xxii. § 3, xxxi. § 1, 4, xxxvii. § 2, 4, xxxviii. § 1, 3, xxxix. § 5, xl. § 6, xlii. § 6, xliv. § 3 II. iv. § 7, xi. § 2, 3, xiii. § 5, xviii. § 3, xxi. § 4, xxxii. § 1, xxxii. § 8, xxxiv. § 6, 12, xxxv. § 4–10, xxxvi. § 3 III. xiv. § 5, xx. § 5, 7, xxi. § 8, xxv. § 9 IV. xvii. § 1, xxxi. § 9 v. v. § 6 VI. xx. § 9, xxi. § 1, xxiii. § 3 VII. xxi. § 11, xxiv. § 3, xxv. § 9, xxvii. § 9 VIII. viii. § 1, ix. § 2, x. § 1, xxi. § 3, xxv. § 2–7, xxix. § 5, xxxi. § 1–5, xxxv. § 7, xxxvi. § 6, xxxvii. § 2, xlii. § 1–7, 11, xliv. § 5, liii. § 7, liv. § 5

GENERAL INDEX

Demeter, cult, IX. iv. § 3, vi. § 5, viii.
§ 1, xvi. § 5, xix. § 5, 6, xxii. § 5,
xxiv. § 1, 2, xxv. § 5, xxvii. § 8,
xxxix. § 4

     X. xxviii. § 3, xxxiii. § 12, xxxv.
§ 2, 9, 10

—— hymns, I. xxii. § 7, II. xiv. § 4,
IV. i. § 5, xxx. § 4

—— mysteries, I. xxxvii. § 4, II. xii.
§ 5, xiv. § 1–3, xxxiv. § 10, xxxv.
§ 8, xxxvi. § 7, VIII. xv. § 1, 3, 4,
IX. xxv. § 6, X. xxviii. § 3

—— representations, I. ii. § 4, xxxvii.
§ 6, II. xi. § 3, xiii. § 5, xviii. § 3,
xxxvi. § 3, xxxvii. § 1, III. xix. § 4,
IV. xiv. § 2, V. xvii. § 3, VI. xx'. § 2,
VII. xxi. § 11, xxv. § 9, VIII. v. § 8,
xxv. § 2–7, xxxi. § 5, xxxv. § 2,
xxxvii. § 2–6, IX. iv. § 4, xvi. § 5,
xix. § 5, xxii. § 5, xxxix. § 5, X.
xxxiii. § 12, xxxv. § 10

—— titles, Anesidora, I. xxxi. § 4
     Black, VIII. v. § 8, xlii. § 1–7, 11
     Cabeiraea, IX. xxv. § 5
     Chamyne, VI. xx. § 9, xxi. § 1, 2
     Chloe, I. xxii. § 3
     Chthonia, II. xxxv. § 5–10, III.
xiv. § 5
     Cidaria, VIII. xv. § 3
     in Corythenses, VIII. liv. § 5
     Deo, VIII. xlii. § 6
     Eleusinian, II. xiv. § 1, III.
xx. § 5, VIII. xv. § 1, 3, xxv. § 2, 3,
xxix. § 5, IX. iv. § 3
     Eulius, VIII. xxi. § 3
     Europe, IX. xxxix. § 4, 5
     Fruit-bringer, VIII. liii. § 7
     Fury, VIII. xxv. § 4–6, 11
     Lawgiver, I. xxxi. § 1, xlii. § 6,
II. xxxii. § 8, IX. vi. § 5, xvi. § 5, X.
xxxiii. § 12
     Lernaea, II. xxxvi. § 7
     Lusia, VIII. xxv. § 6, 7
     Malophorus, I. xliv. § 3
     in Marsh, VIII. xxxvi. § 6
     Mycalessia, IX. xix. § 5, 6, xxvii.
§ 8
     Mysia, II. xviii. § 3, VII. xxvii. § 9
     Panachaea, VII. xxiv. § 3
     Pelasgis, II. xxii. § 1
     Prostasia, II. xi. § 3
     Prosymne, II. xxxvii. § 1
     Stiritis, X. xxxv. § 9
     Thermasia, II. xxxiv. § 6, **12**
     Thesmia, VIII. xv. § 4

Demetrius, son of Antigonus, I. vi.
§ 5, 6, x. § 1, 2, xi. § 6, xii. § 3,
xiii. § 6, xvi. § 1, xxv. § 6–8, xxxvi.
§ 6, II. vii. § 1, VI. xvi. § 2, VII. viii.
§ 5, IX. vii. § 3, xxxix. § 12, X. xii.
§ 10, statues VI. x. § 7, xvi. § 3,
X. x. § 2

—— son of Phanostratus, I. xxv. § 6

—— son of Philip, II. ix. § 5, IV.
xxix. § 1–3, xxxii. § 2

Demo, Sibyl, IX. xii. § 8, 9
Democles, archon, X. xxiii. § 14
Democrates, victor, of Tenedos, VI.
xvii. § 1
Demodocus, I. ii. § 3, III. xviii. § 11
Demonassa, III. xv. § 8, V. xvii. § 7,
IX. v. § 15
Demophon, I. xxviii. § 8, X. xxv. § 7, 8
Demos, statue of, I. i. § 3, iii. § 3, 5,
III. xi. § 10
Demosthenes, general, I. xiii. § 5,
xxiii. § 3, xxix. § 12, 13
—— orator, I. viii. § 2–4, II. xxxiii.
§ 3–5
Demylus, trainer, VI. x. § 1, **2**
Deo, VIII. xlii. § 6
Derae, IV. xv. § 4, 7
Dereum, III. xx. § 7
Desire, statue of, I. xliii. § 6
Deucalion, I. xviii. § 7, 8, xl. § 1,
v. i. § 3, viii. § 1, X. vi. § 2, viii. § 1,
xxxviii. § 1
Dexamenus, v. iii. § 3, VII. xviii. § 1,
xix. § 9
Diaeus, of Megalopolis, VII. xii. § 3–9,
xiii. § 5–7, xiv. § 1, 4, xv. § 7–xvi.
§ 6
Diagon, river, VI. xxi. § 4
Diagoras, Rhodian victor, IV. xxiv.
§ 3, VI. vi. § 2, **v**ii, § 1–4, 7
Diallus, Smyrnaean victor, VI. xiii.
§ 6
Dicaearchia, spring, IV. xxxv. § 12,
VIII. vii. § 3
Dice, II. xx. § 3, VI. xxiv. § 6, VII.
xxv. § 10, X. xxxi. § 1
Dicon, Caulonian victor, VI. iii. § 11, 13
Dictynna, II. xxx. § 3, III. xii. § 8
Dictys, II. xviii. § 1
Didas, Egyptian boxer, V. xxi. § 15
Didyma, II. x. § 5, V. xiii. § 11, VII. ii.
§ 6
Diitrephes, I. xxiii. § 3, 4
Dindymene, VII. xvii. § 9, xx. § 3,
VIII. xlvi. § 4, IX. xxv. § 3

Dine, spring, VIII. vii. § 2

Diocles, son of Ortolichus, IV. i. § 4, xxx. § 2, 3

Diodorus, Sicyonian victor, VII. xvi. § 10

Diogenes, Boeotarch, X. xx. § 3
—— Macedonian, II. viii. § 6
—— of Sinope, II. ii. § 4

Diognetus, victor, of Croton, X. v. § 13

Diomedes, Argive, I. xi. § 7, xxii. § 6, xxviii. § 9, II. xx. § 5, xxiv. § 2, xxv. § 2, xxx. § 10, xxxii. § 1, 2, IV. xxxv. § 1, 8, V. xxii. § 2, X. x. § 4, xxvii. § 1, xxxi. § 2
—— Thracian, III. xviii. § 12, v. x. § 9

Diomenia, VIII. ix. § 9

Dionysiades, III. xiii. § 7

Dionysias, spring, IV. xxxvi. § 7

Dionysius, tyrant of Syracuse, I. ii. § 3, xiii. § 9, VI. ii. § 6

Dionysus, myths, I. ii. § 5, iii. § 1, xx. § 3, xxiii. § 5, II. vi. § 6, xii. § 6, xx. § 4, xxii. § 1, xxiii. § 7, 8, xxxi. § 2, xxxvii. § 5, III. xviii. § 11, xix. § 3, xxiv. § 3, 4, V. xvi. § 7, VII. ii. § 7, xviii. § 4, VIII. xxxvii. § 5, IX. v. § 4, xvii. § 6, xix. § 1, xx. § 4, xxxi. § 2, X. xxix. § 4, 5
—— cult, I. ii. § 5, xx. § 2, xxi. § 1, 2, xxxi. § 4, 6, xxxviii. § 8, xl. § 6, xliii. § 5
  II. vii. § 5, 6, xiii. § 7, xxiii. § 1, 7, 8, xxiv. § 6, xxix. § 1, xxx. § 1, xxxi. § 5, xxxv. § 1, xxxvii. § 6
  III. xiii. § 7, xix. § 6, xx. § 3, xxii. § 2, xxiv. § 4, 6, 8, xxvi. § 11
  IV. xxvii. § 6, xxxi. § 4, xxxiv. § 6, xxxvi. § 7
  V. xiv. § 10, xv. § 4, xix. § 6
  VI. xxi. § 5, xxiv. § 8, xxvi. § 1, 2
  VII. ii. § 11, xix. § 10, xxi. § 1, 3, 6, xxii. § 9, xxv. § 9, xxvi. § 3, 11, xxvii. § 3
  VIII. vi. § 5, xix. § 2, xxiii. § 1, xxvi. § 1, xxxii. § 3, xxxix. § 6, xlvi. § 5, liii. § 7, liv. § 5
  IX. viii. § 1, 2, xvi. § 6, xx. § 4, xxii. § 6, xxiii. § 5, 7, xxiv. § 1, 2, xxx. § 9, xxxviii. § 1
  X. iv. § 3, vi. § 4, xviii. § 6, xxxii. § 7, xxxiii. § 11, xxxvi. § 3
—— representations, I. xiv. § 1, xx. § 2, 3, xxix. § 2, xxxviii. § 8, xliii. § 5

Dionysus, representations, II. ii. § 6, 7, vii. § 5, xi. § 3, 8, xiii. § 7, xxiii. § 1, 2, xxx. § 1, xxxvii. § 1, 2
  III. xi. § 11, xviii. § 11, xx. § 3, xxi. § 8
  IV. xxxiv. § 6
  V. xvii. § 3, xx. § 3, xxvi. § 3
  VI. xix. § 10
  VII. xix. § 6, xxi. § 1, 6, xxiii. § 9, xxv. § 9, xxvi. § 11
  VIII. ix. § 8, xxiii. § 1, xxv. § 3, xxvi. § 1, xxxi. § 4, xxxix. § 6
  IX. xii. § 4, xx. § 4, xxii. § 1, 6, xxiii. § 5, 7, xxvi. § 8, xxx. § 1, xxxi. § 2, xxxii. § 1
  X. xix. § 3, 4, xxxii. § 1, xxxvii. § 3, bearded II. xxx. § 1, V. xix. § 6
—— titles: Acratophorus, VIII. xxxix. § 6
  Aegobolus, IX. viii. § 1, 2
  Antheus, VII. xxi. § 6
  Aroeus, VII. xxi. § 6
  Auxites, VIII. xxvi. § 1
  Bacchius II. ii. § 6, vii. § 6
  Cadmius, IX. xii. § 4
  Calydonian, VII. xxi. § 1–3
  Citizen, VIII. xxvi. § 1
  Colonatas, III. xiii. § 7, 8
  Cresius, II. xxxi. § 7, 8
  Dasyllius, I. xliii. § 5
  Eleuthereus, I. xx. § 3, xxix. § 2
  Flower-god, I. xxxi. § 4
  Ivy, I. xxxi. § 6
  Leucyanites, VI. xxi. § 5
  Lysius, II. ii. § 6, vii. § 6, IX. xv. § 6
  Melanaegis, II. xxxv. § 1
  Mesateus, VII. xxi. § 6
  Mystes, VIII. liv. § 5
  Nyctelius, I. xl. § 6
  Patrous, I. xliii. § 5, 6
  Phalen, X. xix. § 3
  Psilax, III. xix. § 6
  Saotes, II. xxxi. § 5, xxxvii. § 2
  Singer, I. ii. § 5, xxxi. § 6
  Torch, VII. xxvii. § 3

Diophanes, VIII. xxx. § 5, li. § 1

Diophantus, archon, VIII. xlv. § 4

Dioscuri (Castor and Pollux), I. xvii. § 5, xxxi. § 1, xli. § 3–5, II. xxii. § 5, 6, xxxiv. § 10, III. xii. § 5, 8, xiii. § 1, 8, xvi. § 2, xvii. § 3, xviii. § 4, xix. § 7, xx. § 1, xxiv. § 7, xxvi. § 2, 3, IV. iii. § 1, xvi. § 5, 9, xxvi. § 6, xxvii. § 1, 6, xxxi. § 9, v. viii. § 4,

GENERAL INDEX

xix. § 2, VII. xxii. § 5, X. ix. § 8, xxxviii. § 7

Dioscuri (Castor and Pollux), cult, I. xviii. § 1, II. i. § 9, vii. § 5, xxii. § 5, xxxvi. § 6, III. iii. § 1, 6, xiv. § 6, xvi. § 2, xx. § 2, IV. xxvii. § 1–6, V. xv. § 5, VII. xxii. § 5, VIII. ix. § 2, xxi. § 4, X. xxxiii. § 6

—— representations, I. xviii. § 1, xxxiii. § 8, II. i. § 9, vii. § 5, xxii. § 5, xxxi. § 6, xxxvi. § 6, III. xvii. § 3, xxi. § 4, xxiv. § 5, IV. xxxi. § 9, V. xix. § 2, VIII. xxi. § 4, X. ix. § 7

—— titles, Counsellors, III. xiii. § 6

Great gods, I. xxxi. § 1, VIII. xxi. § 4

Lords, II. xxxvi. § 6, X. xxxviii. § 7

Starters, III. xiv. § 7

Dipaea, III. xi. § 7, VI. vii. § 9, VIII. viii. § 6, xxvii. § 3, xxx. § 1, xlv. § 2

Dirce, IX. xvii. § 6, xxv. § 3

Dium, IX. xxx. § 7, 11, X. xiii. § 5

Dius, king of Elis, V. iv. § 1, 2

Divination, II. xiii. § 7, xxxi. § 5, by means of various animals VI. ii. § 5, birds I. xxxiv. § 4, X. vi. § 1, blood of lamb II. xxiv. § 1, bull IV. xxxii. § 3, chance remarks VII. xxii. § 3, crater III. xxiii. § 9, dice VII. xxv. § 10, inwards of victims I. xxxiv. § 4, VI. ii. § 5, IX. xxxix. § 6, water III. xxiii. § 8, VII. xxi. § 12, IX. ii. § 1. *See also* Dreams

Dodona, I. xiii. § 3, xvii. § 5, xxxvi. § 4, VII. xxi. § 2–4, xxv. § 1, VIII. xi. § 12, xxiii. § 5, xxvii. § 6, IX. viii. § 1, xxv. § 4, X. xii. § 10

Dogs, II. xxvi. § 4, xxvii. § 10, IV. xxi. § 1, VIII. xix. § 3, IX. ii. § 4, xix. § 1, X. xxx. § 5, xxxviii. § 1

—— in cult, III. xiv. § 9, IV. xiii. § 1, xxi. § 1, VI. ii. § 4, VII. xxvii. § 10

Dolopians, X. viii. § 2, 3

Dolphins, I. xliv. § 8, II. i. § 3, ii. § 8, III. xxv. § 7, VI. xx. § 10, VIII. xlii. § 4, X. xiii. § 10

Donacon, IX. xxxi. § 7

Donussa, VII. xxvi. § 13

Doom, figure of, V. xix. **§ 6**

Dorcea, spring, III. xv. § 2

Dorceus, III. xv. § 1, 2

Dorians, II. iv. § 3, 4, vi. § 7, xiii. § 1, 2, xxix. § 5, xxx. § 10, xxxiv. § 5, xxxvii. § 3, III. ii. § 6, v. § 8, xiii.

§ 3, xix. § 6, xx. § 6, xxii. § 6, IV. iii. § 3, 6, 9, v. § 3, viii. § 2, xxx. § 1, xxxiv. § 8, V. i. § 1, 2, iii. § 5, 6, iv. § 1, xxv. § 6, VII. i. § 5–9, VIII. v. § 1, xlvi. § 2, ix. xiv. § 3, X. viii. § 2, xxxviii. § 10, cults III. xii. § 9, xiii. § 4, xxvi. § 7

Doric style of architecture, v. x. § 2, xvi. § 1, xx. § 9, VI. xix. § 2, xxiv. § 2, 5, VIII. xliv. § 5

—— tongue, II. xxvii. § 3, xxix. § 5, xxxvii. § 3, III. xxii. § 1, IV. xxvii. § 11, xxxiv. § 8, V. xv. § 12, IX. xxii. § 3

Doridas, king of Corinth, II. iv. § 3

Dorieus, son of Anaxandrides, III. iii. § 9, 10, iv. § 1, 7, xvi. § 4, 5

—— Rhodian victor, VI. vii. § 1, 4–6

Doris, X. viii. § 5, xxxvii. § 2

Dorium, IV. xxxiii. § 7

Dorycleans, I. xl. § 5

Doryssus, III. ii. § 4, IV. iv. § 2

Dotadas, IV. iii. § 10

Doto, II. i. § 8

Draco, VI. xi. § 6, IX. xxxvi. § 8

Dream-god, II. x. § 2

Dreams, I. xiv. § 3, xxx. § 3, xxxviii. § 7, IV. xiii. § 2, xxxvi. § 3–8, xxvii. § 3, xxxiii. § 5, VII. v. § 1–7, xx. § 8, IX. xxiii. § 3, X. ii. § 6, xii. § 5, xxxii. § 13, xxxviii. § 13, cures I. xxxiv. § 5, II. xxvii. § 1, X. xxxiii. § 11, divination I. xxxiv. § 4, 5, xliv. § 5, III. xxvi. § 1, V. xxiii. § 6, X. xxxiii. § 11

Drepanum, cape, VII. xxiii. § 4

Dripping spring, II. vii. § 4

Dromeus, Mantinean victor, VI. xi. § 4

—— Stymphalian victor, VI. vii. § 10

Dropion, X. xiii. § 1

Drunkenness, II. xxvii. § 3, VI. xxiv. § 8

Dryads, VIII. iv. § 2, xxxix. § 2

Drymaea, X. iii. § 2, xxxiii. § 12

Dryopes, IV. viii. § 3, xxxiv. § 9, 11, v. i. § 2

Dyke, VIII. xliv. § 1, 5, 7

Dyme, II. vii. § 4, v. ix. § 1, VII. vi. § 1, vii. § 3, xvii. § 5–xviii. § 1, VIII. i. § 2

Dyrrhachium, VI. x. § 8

Dysaules, I. xiv. § 3, II. xii. § 4, xiv. § 2–4

Dyscinetus, IV. xxvii. **§ 9**

Dyspontium, VI. xxii. § 4

GENERAL INDEX

EAGLES, III. xvii. § 4, IV. xvi. § 7, xviii.
§ 5, V. xi. § 1, VI. xx. § 12, VIII.
xvii. § 3, **xxx.** § 2, xxxi. § 4, xxxviii.
§ 7

Earth, I. ii. § 6, xiv. § 3, xxxv. § 6, 8,
IV. i. § 5, VIII. xxi. § 11, xxii. § 2,
xxv. § 9, xxix. § 4, IX. xxvii. § 2, X.
v. § 6, vi. § 6
—— cult, I. xviii. § 7, xxii. § 3, xxiv.
§ 3, xxxviii. § 6, xxxi. § 4, III. xi.
§ 9, xii. § 8, V. xiv. § 10, VII. xxi.
§ 11, xxv. § 13, VIII. xlviii. § 8, X.
v. § 5, xii. § 10

Ebony, statues of, I. xxxv. § 3, xlii.
§ 5, II. xxii. § 5, VIII. xvii. § 2, liii. § 3

Ececheiria, V. x. § 10, xxvi. § 2

Echecratides, X. xvi. § 8

Echedamia, X. iii. § 2

Echembrotus, Arcadian victor, X. vii.
§ 4, 6

Echemus, I. xli. § 2, xliv. § 10, VIII. v.
§ 1, xlv. § 3, liii. § 10

Echephron, VIII. xxiv. § 2, 6

Echestratus, king of Sparta, III. ii.
§ 2, IV. iv. § 2

Echetlaeus, I. xxxii. § 5

Echetlus, I. xv. § 3

Echidna, III. xviii. § 10, VIII. xviii. § 2

Echinades, islands, IV. xxxiv. § 1, VIII.
i. § 2, xxiv. § 10, xxxviii. § 10

Echion, IX. ii. § 4, v. § 3

Echo, II. xxxv. § 10, V. xxi. § 17

Ectenes, IX. v. § 1

Edonians, I. xxix. § 4, X. xxxiii. § 2

Effort, statue of, I. xvii. § 1

Egypt, II. xl. § 6, X. vii. § 8, xxxii.
§ 18

Eicasius, Colophonian victor, VI.
xvii. § 4

Eilei, II. xxxiv. § 6

Eileithyia, I. xviii. § 5, xliv. § 2,
II. v. § 4, xviii. § 3, xxii. § 6, 7,
xxxv. § 11, III. xiv. § 6, xvii. § 1,
IV. xxxi. § 9, VI. xx. § 2–6, VII.
xxiii. § 5–7, xxv. § 9, xxvii. § 8,
VIII. xxi. § 3, xxxii. § 4, xlviii. § 7, 8,
IX. xxvii. § 2, statues I. xviii. § 5,
xxxv. § 11, IV. xxxi. § 9, VII. xxiii.
§ 5, xxv. § 9, VIII. xxi. § 9, VIII. xlviii. § 7

Eion, VIII. viii. § 9

Eira, Mount, IV. xvii. § 10, xviii.
§ 1, 7, xx. § 5–xxii. § 4, xxiii. § 1, 2,
xxvii. § 9

Eirene, I. viii. § 2, xviii. § 3, VI. ix.
§ 3, IX. xvi. § 2

Elaea, V. xxiv. § 6, IX. v. § 14

Elaius, Mount, VIII. xli. § 7, xlii. § 1, 3

Elaphius, Elean month, V. xiii. § 11,
VI. xx. § 1

Elaphus, river, VIII. xxxvi. § 7

Elatea, I. xx. § 6, xxvi. § 3, VII. xv.
§ 5, VIII. iv. § 4, X. iii. § 2, xviii.
§ 7, xxxiv. § 1–xxxv. § 1

Elatus, II. xxvi. § 6, VIII. iv. § 2, 4, 6,
xlviii. § 8, X. iii. § 5, xxxiv. § 2, 6

Eleans, history, I. xxv. § 4, III. viii.
§ 3–5, IV. xv. § 7, V. i. § 3–v. § 1, vi.
§ 4, xii. § 8, xxiv. § 4, VI. iii. § 3,
xx. § 4, dedications at Olymp a V.
xxiv. § 4, xxvi. § 6, absent from
Isthmian games V. ii. § 2–5, VI.
iii. § 9, xvi. § 2

Electra, daughter of Agamemnon, II.
xvi. § 7, IX. xl. § 12
—— daughter of Ocean, IV. xxx. § 4
—— sister of Cadmus, IX. viii. § 4
—— river, IV. xxxiii. § 6, 7

Electran gate, IX. viii. § 4, 7, xi. § 1

Electryon, II. xxv. § 9, IX. xi. § 1

Eleius, son of Amphimachus, V. iii.
§ 4, 5
—— son of Poseidon, V. i. § 8, 9

Eleon, I. xxix. § 6

Elephants, I. xii. § 3, 4, II. xxi. § 4,
v. xii. § 1–3

Elephenor, I. xvii. § 6, VIII. xv. § 6

Eleusinium, I. xiv. § 3

Eleusis, in Attica, I. v. § 2, xxvi. § 3,
xxxi. § 3, xxxvi. § 4, xxxviii. § 3.
5–7, II. xiv. § 2, VII. § 1–5, IX. ix.
§ 1, sacred road I. xxxvi. § 3–xxxviii.
§ 5, mysteries I. ii. § 5, xxxvii. § 4,
xxxviii. § 3, II. xiv. § 1, V. x. § 1,
VIII. xv. § 1, X. xxxi. § 11
—— in Boeotia, IX. xxiv. § 2

Eleuther, IX. xx. § 1, X. vii. § 3

Eleutherae, I. ii. § 5, xxxviii. § 8, 9,
II. vi. § 3, IX. i. § 1, 6, ii. § 2

Eleutheria, games, IX. ii. § 6

Elis, city, VI. xxiii. § 1–xxvi. § **3**
—— district, V. and VI.
—— statue of, VI. xvi. § **3**

Elpenor, X. xxix. § 8

Elyrus, X. xvi. § 5

Emaution, Arcadian victor, VI. xvii.
§ 4

Emperamus, IV. xx. § 5, 10, xxi. § 1, 12

Emperors, statues, I. xl. § 2, V. xx.
§ 9, VI. xix. § 10, X. viii. § 6, temples
II. viii. § 1, III. xxii. § 9, VI. xxv. § 1

GENERAL INDEX

Enaraephorus, III. xv. § **1**

Enceladus, VIII. xlvii. § **1**

Encheleans, IX. v. § 3

Endeis, II. xxix. § 9, 10

Endymion, V. i. § 3–5, 8, iii. § 6, viii. § 1, 2, VI. xix. § 11, xx. § 9

Enneacrunus, I. xiv. § 1

Enope, III. xxvi. § 8

Enyalius, III. xiv. § 9, xv. § 7, xx. § 2, v. xviii. § 5

Enyo, I. viii. § 4, IV. xxx. § 5

Eoeae, poem, II. ii. § 3, xvi. § 4, xxvi. § 2, IV. ii. § 1, VI. xxi. § 10, IX. xxxi. § 5, xxxvi. § 7, xl. § 5, X. xxxi. § 3

Epaminondas, I. iii. § 4, IV. xxvi. § 6–xxvii. § 8, xxxi. § 10, xxxii. § 1, 6, VII. xvii. § 2, VIII. viii. § 10, xi. § 5–xii. § 1, xxvii. § 2, xlix. § 3, lii. § 4, IX. xii. § 6–xv. § 6, statues IV. xxxi. § 10, xxxii. § 1, IX. xii. § 6, xv. § 6

Epebolus, IV. ix. § 5, 8, x. § 5

—— son of Endymion, V. i. § 4–11

—— son of Panopeus, I. xxiii. § 8, II. xix. § 6, X. xxvi. § 2

Ephesus, I. ix. § 7, III. xvii. § 4, IV. xxxi. § 8, V. xxiv. § 8, VI. iii. § 15, 16, xviii. § 6, VII. ii. § 7–9, iii. § 4, 5, iv. § 2, v. § 4, 10

Ephialtes, Boeotian, IX. xxix. § 1

—— Athenian, I. xxix. § 15

—— Trachinian, I. iv. § 2, III. iv. § 8

Ephors, III. xi. § 2

Ephyraea, II. i. § 1, iii. § 10

Epicaste, IX. v. § 11, xxvi. § 3

Epicharinus, runner, I. xxiii. § **9**

Epicleidas, II. ix. § 1, 3

Epicradius, Mantinean victor, VI. x. § 9

Epidamnus, VI. x. § 7, 8, xix. § 8

Epidauria, festival, II. xxvi. § 8

Epidaurus, I. xxv. § 4, II. i. § 4, viii. § 5, x. § 3, xxiii. § 3, xxvi. § 1–xxix. § 1, xxx. § 4, xxxvi. § 1, III. xxiii. § 6, 7, V. xi. § 11, xxiii. § 2, VII. iv. § 2, IX. vii. § 5, xxiii. § 1, X. xv. § 1, xxxviii. § 13

—— Limera, III. xxi. § 7, xxiii. § 6, 10

Epidelium, III. xxiii. § 2–6

Epidotes, II. xxvii. § 6, III. xvii. § 9

Epigoni, IX. ix. § 4, xix. § 2, xxv. § 7, X. x. § 4, xxv. § 7

Epimeliades, VIII. iv. § **2**

Epimelides, IV. xxxiv. § 5, 6

Epimenides, I. xiv. § 4, II. xxi. § 3, III. xi. § 11, xii. § 11, VIII. xviii. § 2

Epione, II. xxvii. § 5, xxix. § 1

Epiteles, IV. xxvi. § 7, 8

Epitherses, Erythraean victor, VI. xv. § 6

Epochus, son of Lycurgus, VIII. iv. § 10, xlv. § 7

—— brother of Oenoe, I. xxxiii. § 8

Eponymous heroes, I. v. § 2–5, xi. § 1

Epopeus, II. i. § 1, iii. § 10, vi. § 1–5, xi. § 1

Erasinus, river, II. xxiv. § 6, xxxvi. § 6, 7, VIII. xxii. § 3

Erasus, X. ix. § 6

Erato, VIII. iv. § 2, xxxvii. § 11, X. ix. § 5

Erechtheum, I. xxvi. § 5

Erechtheus, I. v. § 2, 3, xxvi. § 5, xxvii. § 4, xxviii. § 4, 10, xxxvi. § 4, xxxviii. § 3, II. vi. § 5, xxv. § 6, VII. i. § 2, IX. xxv. § 6, cult I. xxvi. § 5, statues I. xxvii. § 4, IX. xxx. § 1, X. x. § 1

Erenea, I. xliv. § 5

Eretria, IV. ii. § 3, VII. viii. § 1, x. § 2, IX. xxii. § 2

Erginus, IX. xvii. § 2, xxxvii. § 1–4

Ergoteles, of Himera, victor, VI. iv. § 11

Erichthonius, I. ii. § 6, v. § 3, xiv. § 6, xviii. § 2, xxiv. § 7

Eridanus, river in Athens, I. xix. § 5

—— river in land of Celts, I. iv. § 1, xix. § 5, xxx. § 3, V. xii. § 7, xiv. § 3, VIII. xxv. § 13

Erineus, in Achaia, VII. xxii. § 10

—— in Attica, I. xxxviii. § 5

Eriphyle, I. xxxiv. § 3, II. i. § 8, xxiii. § 2, V. xvii. § 7, 8, VIII. xxiv. § 8, 10, IX. xli. § 2, 3, X. xxix. § 7, 8

Eris, V. xix. § 2, IX. xxxi. § 4

Erochus, X. iii. § 2

Erxicleides, archon, X. v. § **13**

Eryma, VIII. xlvii. § 5

Erymanthus, Mount, I. xxvii. § 9, v. vii. § 1, VIII. xxiv. § 1, 4, 5

—— river, v. vii. § 1, xxvi. § 7, VI. xxi. § 3, 4, VIII. xxiv. § 3, 12, xxv. § 1, xxvi. § 3

Erysichthon, I. ii. § 6, xviii. § 5, xxxi. § 2

Erythrae, in Boeotia, VI. xxi. § 11, IX. ii. § 1

GENERAL INDEX

Erythrace in Ionia, VI. xv. § 6, VII.
iii. § 7, 10, v. § 5–12, IX. xxvii. § 1,
8, X. xii. § 7
Eryx, III. xvi. § 4, 5, IV. xxxvi. § 4,
VIII. xxiv. § 6
Essenes, VIII. xiii. § 1
Eteocles, son of Andreus, IX. xxxiv.
§ 9, 10, xxxv. § 1, 3, xxxvi. § 1,
xxxviii. § 1
—— son of Oedipus, v. xix. § 6, IX.
v. § 12, 13, xviii. § 3, xxv. § 2, X. v.
§ 3
Eteoclus, X. x. § 3
Eteonicus, VI. iii. § 15, IX. xxxii. § 8,
X. ix. § 10
Etis, III. xxii. § 11, VIII. xii. § 8
Euaechme, daughter of Hyllus, IV.
ii. § 1
—— daughter of Megareus, I. xliii. § 4
Euaephnus, IV. iv. § 5–7, v. § 2, 6
Eualcidas, Elean victor, VI. xvi. § 6
Euamerion, II. xi. § 7
Euanoridas, Elean victor, VI. viii. § 1
Euanthes, victor, of Cyzicus, VI. iv.
§ 10
Euboea, mountain, II. xvii. § 1
—— island, I. xxvii. § 5, xxix. § 11,
xxxvi. § 4, v. xxiii. § 4, VIII. i. § 5,
xiv. § 12, IX. xxii. § 3, xix. § 3, xxii.
§ 2
Eubotas, Cyrenian victor, VI. viii. § 3
Eubuleus, I. xiv. § 2
Eubulides, I. ii. § 5, VIII. xiv. § 10
Eubulus, son of Carmanor, II. xxx. § 3
—— son of Spintharus, I. xxix. § 10
Eucles, Rhodian victor, VI. vi. § 2, vii.
§ 2
Euclus, seer, X. xii. § 11, xiv. § 6, xxiv.
§ 3
Eucosmus, III. xvi. § 6
Eudamidas, III. x. § 5
Eudelus, athlete, bribed, v. xxi. § 9
Euergetidas, IV. xxi. § 2, xxiii. § 2, 3
Euergus, v. x. § 3
Euesperitae, IV. xxvi. § 2, 3, 5
Euippus, I. xli. § 3, xliii. § 2
Eumaeus, IX. xli. § 4
Eumantis, IV. xvi. § 1
Eumelus, of Patrae, VII. xviii. § 2, 3
—— of Corinth, II. i. § 1, ii. § 2, iii.
§ 10, IV. iv. § 1, xxxiii. § 2, v. xix.
§ 10
Eumenes, I. v. § 7, viii. § 1
Eumenides, II. xi. § 4, VII. xxv. § 1, 7,
VIII. xxxiv. § 1–3

Eumolpus, I. v. § 2, xxvii. § 4, xxxviii.
§ 2, II. xiv. § 2, 3, VIII. xv. § 1
Eunomus, II. xxxvi. § 4, III. vii. § 2,
IV. iv. § 4
Euoras, III. xx. § 4
Euphaes, king of Messenia, IV. v. § 8,
vii. § 1–x. § 5
Eupheme, IX. xxix. § 5
Euphemus, Carian, I. xxiii. § 5
—— son of Poseidon, v. xvii. § 9
Euphorbus, Eretrian, VII. x. § 2
—— Trojan, II. xvii. § 3
Euphorion, poet, II. xxii. § 7, X. xxvii.
§ 8
Euphrates, II. v. § 4, IV. xxxiv. § 2,
X. xxix. § 4
Euphrosyne, IX. xxxv. § 5
Eupolemus, Elean victor, VI. iii. § 7,
VIII. xlv. § 4
Eupolis, II. vii. § 3
Eupolus, Thessalian, bribes boxers,
v. xxi. § 3, 5, 6
Euripides, I. ii. § 2, xxi. § 1
Euripus, I. xxxviii. § 1, II. xxiv. § 6,
IX. xix. § 6, xxii. § 5
Europa, III. xiii. § 5, v. xxv. § 12,
VII. ii. § 5, iv. § 1, IX. v. § 8, xix.
§ 1, xxxix. § 4
Europs, son of Aegialeus, II. v. § 6
—— son of Phoroneus, II. xxxiv. § 4
Europus, IX. xxiii. § 6
Eurotas, river, III. i. § 1, xiii. § 8,
xviii. § 6, xix. § 7, xxi. § 1, 3, VIII.
xliv. § 3, 4, liv. § 2
Euryalus, son of Mecisteus, II. xx.
§ 5, xxx. § 10, X. x. § 4, xxv. § 6,
xxix. § 1
—— Spartan, IV. xx. § 8
Eurybates, Argive victor, I. xxix.
§ 5
—— herald, X. xxv. § 4, 8
Eurybatus, Lacedaemonian victor,
v. viii. § 7
Eurybiades, III. xvi. § 6
Eurybotus, Athenian victor, II. xxiv.
§ 7
Eurycles, II. iii. § 5, III. xiv. § 6
Euryclides, II. ix. § 4
Eurycrates I, king of Sparta, III. iii.
§ 4, IV. xv. § 3
—— II, III. iii. § 5
Eurydamidas, king of Sparta, II. ix.
§ 1, III. x. § 5
Eurydamus, VI. xvi. § 1, X. xvi. § 4
Eurydice, wife of Aeneas, X. xxvi. § 1

GENERAL INDEX

Eurydice, daughter of Amphiaraus, V. xvii. § 7
—— daughter of Antipater, I. vi. § 8, vii. § 1, ix. § 6
—— daughter of Aridaeus, V. xvii. § 4, xx. § 10
—— daughter of Lacedaemon, III. xiii. § 8
—— wife of Orpheus, IX. xxx. § 6
Euryganea, IX. v. § 11
Euryleon, IV. vii. § 8, viii. § 11
Euryleonis, III. xvii. § 6
Eurylochus, X. xxix. § 1
Eurymedon, charioteer, II. xvi. § 6
—— river, X. xv. § 4
Eurynome, daughter of Ocean, VIII. xli. § 4–6
—— mother of Graces, IX. xxxv. § 5
Eurynomus, X. xxviii. § 7
Eurypon, II. xxxvi. § 4, III. vii. § 1, xii. § 8, IV. iv. § 4
Eurypylus, son of Euaemon, VII. xix. § 1, 6–10, xxi. § 7, IX. xli. § 2, X. xxvii. § 2
—— son of Dexamenus, VII. xix. § 9
—— son of Telephus, III. xxvi. § 9, 10, IX. v. § 15
Eurysaces, I. xxxv. § 2, 3
Eurysthenes, III. i. § 5–9, ii. § 1, vi. § 7, vii. § 1
Eurystheus, I. xxxii. § 6, xliv. § 10, III. vii. § 7, xxv. § 5, IV. xxxiv. § 10, xxxvi. § 3, VIII. xiv. § 2, xviii. § 3, tomb I. xliv. § 10
Euryteae, VII. xviii. § 1
Eurytium, IV. ii. § 3
Eurytion, Centaur, V. x. § 8, VII. xviii. § 1
Eurytus, son of Actor, II. xv. § 1, v. iii. § 3
—— son of Melaneus, III. xviii. § 11, IV. ii. § 3, iii. § 10, xxvii. § 6, xxxiii. § 5
Eutelidas, Lacedaemonian victor, V. ix. § 1, VI. xv. § 8
Euthydemus, II. viii. § 2
Euthymenes, Maenalian victor, VI. viii. § 5
Euthymus, Locrian victor, VI. vi. § 4–vii. § 1, xi. § 4
Eva, village, II. xxxviii. § 6
—— Mount, IV. xxxi. § 4
Evagoras, Elean victor, V. viii. § 10
—— Laconian victor, VI. x. § 8
—— king of Cyprus, I. iii. § 2, II. xxix. § 4

Evander, VIII. xliii. § 2, xliv. § 5
Execestides, Phocian victor, X. vii. § 7

FATES, I. xix. § 2, xl. § 4, II. iv. § 7, xi. § 4, 10, 11, III. xi. § 10, xix. § 4, V. xv. § 5, VII. xxvi. § 8, VIII. xxxvii. § 1, xliii. § 3, IX. xxv. § 4, X. xxiv. § 4, xxxi. § 4
Festival and games: funeral I. xxviii. § 7, xliv. § 8, II. i. § 3, III. xiv. § 1, xviii. § 16, V. i. § 8, viii. § 3, xvii. § 9, VI. xx. § 19, VIII. iv. § 5, IX. ii. § 5, Isthmian I. xliv. § 8, II. i. § 3, 7, Nemean II. xv. § 3, xxiv. § 2, Olympic V. vii. § 6–x. § 1, Pythian X. vii. § 2–8, of Ares III. xxii. § 7, of Artemis I. xxxi. § 5, VIII. xxii. § 8, 9, of Athena I. xxvii. § 3. of Demeter II. xi. § 3, VII. xxvii. § 10, of Dionysus II. xxiv. § 6, VI. xxvi. § 1, VII. xix. § 10, xx. § 1, xiii. § 1, of Eumenides II. xi. § 4, of Heracles IX. xxxii. § 2, of Isis X. xxxi. § 14–18
    Aleaea, VIII. xlvii. § 4
    Athenaea, VIII. ii. § 1
    Beacons, X. xxv. § 4
    Chthonia, II. xxxv. § 5
    Daedala, IX. iii. § 2–8
    Eleutheria, IX. ii. § 6
    Epidauria, II. xxvi. § 8
    Gymnopaediae, III. xi. § 9
    Halotia, VIII. xlvii. § 4
    Heracleia, IX. xxxii. § 2
    Heraea, II. xxiv. § 2, V. xvi. § 2–6
    Hermaea, VIII. xiv. § 10
    Hyacinthia, III. i. § 1, xix. § 3, 4, IV. xix. § 4
    Laphria, VII. xviii. § 11–13
    Lernaea, II. xxxvi. § 7, VIII. xv. § 9
    Lycaea, VIII. ii. § 1, xxxviii. § 5
    Musaea, IX. xxxi. § 3
    Panathenaea, I. xxix. § 1, VIII. ii. § 1
    Saronia, II. xxxii. § 10
    Scieria, VIII. xxiii. § 1
    Stoning, II. xxxii. § 2
    Theoxenia, VII. xxvii. § 4
    Thesmophoria, X. xxxiii. § 12
    Thyia, VI. xxvi. § 1, 2
    of Torches, VII. xxvii. § 3
    Tyrbe, II. xxiv. § 6
Fetters, II. xiii. § 4, VIII. xlvii. § 2,

GENERAL INDEX

statues in III. xv. § 7, VIII. xli. § 6, IX. xxxviii. § 5

Fig-trees, I. xxxvii. § 2, IV. xx. § 2, VI. xviii. § 7

Finger, tomb of, VIII. xxxiv. § 2

Fire in ritual, II. xix. § 5, xxv. § 4, V. xv. § 9, xxvii. § 6, VIII. ix. § 2, xv. § 9, xxxi. § 1, xxxvii. § 11, X. xi. § 4, xxxi. § 4

Fish, I. xxxiii. § 4, xxxviii. § 1, III. xxi. § 5, IV. xxxiv. § 1, VII. xxii. § 4, singing VIII. xxi. § 2

Flamininus, VII. vii. § 9–viii. § 2, 7, VIII. xi. § 11, li. § 1.

Flax, I. xxvi. § 7, V. v. § 2, VI. xxvi. § 6, VII. xxi. § 14.

Flies, V. xiv. § 1, VIII. xxvi. § 7

Flood, I. xviii. § 7, xl. § 1, V. viii. § 1, X. vi. § 2

Flutes, III. xvii. § 5, V. vii. § 10, xvii. § 10, IX. xxx. § 2, in myth I. xxiv. § 1, II. vii. § 9, xxxi. § 3, VIII. ix. § 1, types IV. xxvii. § 7, V. xvii. § 9, IX. xii. § 5, competitions VI. xiv. § 9, X. vii. § 4

Force, sanctuary of, II. iv. § 6

Fore-temple, II. i. § 7, xvii. § 3, V. xii. § 5, VIII. xxxii. § 2, IX. x. § 2, X. viii. § 6, xxiv. § 1

Fort of Athena, VII. xxii. § 10

Fortune, I. xxix. § 11, in myth IV. xxx. § 3–6, VII. xxvi. § 8

—— in cult, I. xliii. § 6, II. ii. § 8, vii. § 5, xx. § 3, xxxv. § 3, IV. xxx. § 3, VI. xxv. § 4, VIII. xxx. § 7, IX. xvi. § 1

—— representations, I. xliii. § 6, II. ii. § 8, vii. § 4, xi. § 8, xxxv. § 3, IV. xxx. § 3, xxxi. § 10, V. xvii. § 3, VI. ii. § 7, xxv. § 4, VII. xxvi. § 8, VIII. xxx. § 7, IX. xvi. § 2, xxvi. § 8

—— titles, Good V. xv. § 6, IX. xxxix. § 5, of the Height II. vii. § 5, Supporter of the City IV. xxx. § 6

Forum, V. xii. § 6, VIII. xlvi. § 4, X. v. § 11

Fountain, see Spring

Fox, IV. xviii. § 6, IX. xix. § 1

Free Laconians, III. xxi. § 6–8, xxvi. § 8

Freedom, water of, II. xvii. § 1

Fruit, in ritual, VII. xviii. § 12, VIII. xxxvii. § 7, IX. xix. § 5

Furies, I. xxviii. § 6, III. xix. § 10, VIII. xxv. § 4, xxxiv. § 4, IX. v. § 15, X. xxx. § 2, xxxi. § 3

GABALA, II. i. § 8

Gadeira, I. xxxv. § 8, X. iv. § 6

Gaeum, V. xiv. § 9, VII. xxv. § 13

Galaco, spring, III. xxiv. § 7

Gallus, Roman, VII. xi. § 1–4

Games, see Festivals

Ganymeda, II. xiii. § 3

Ganymedes, V. xxiv. § 5, xxvi. § 2

Garates, VIII. liv. § 4

Gardens, I. xix. § 2, III. xxiv. § 4, VIII. xlvi. § 5

Gargaphia, spring, IX. iv. § 3

Gaseptum, III. xii. § 8

Gatheae, VIII. xxxiv. § 5

Gauls, I. iii. § 5–iv. § 6, vii. § 2, viii. § 1, xiii. § 2, xvi. § 2, xxv. § 2, VII. vi. § 7, 8, xv. § 3, xviii. § 6, VIII. x. § 9, X. iii. § 4, vii. § 1, viii. § 3, xv. § 2, 3, xvi. § 4, xix. § 1, 4–xxiii. § 14, xx. § 9, xxxii. § 4

—— of Asia, VII. xvii. § 10, X. xxxvi. § 1

Geese, IX. xxxix. § 2, X. xxxii. § 16

Gela, VI. ix. § 4, 5, xix. § 4, VIII. xlvi. § 2, IX. xl. § 4

Gelanor, II. xvi. § 1, xix. § 3, 4

Gelon, son of Deinomenes, V. xxiii. § 6, xxvii. § 1, VI. ix. § 4, 5, 8, xii. § 1, 2, xix. § 7, VIII. xlii. § 8

—— son of Hiero, VI. xii. § 3

—— Phocian, X. i. § 5

Genesium, II. xxxviii. § 4

Genethlium, II. xxxii. § 9, VIII. vii. § 2

Genetyllides, I. i. § 5

Gerania, mountain, I. xl. § 1, xliii. § 8

Gerenia, III. xxi. § 7, xxvi. § 8, 9, 11, IV. i. § 1, iii. § 2, 9

Germans, VIII. xliii. § 6

Geronteium, mountain, VIII. xvi. § 1

Geronthrae, III. ii. § 6, xxi. § 7, xxii. § 6, 8

Geryon, I. xxxv. § 7, 8, III. xvi. § 4, 5, xviii. § 13, IV. xxxvi. § 3, V. x. § 9, xix. § 1, VIII. iii. § 2, X. xvii. § 5

Getae, I. ix. § 6, V. xii. § 6

Giants, I. xxv. § 2, II. xvii. § 3, VI. xix. § 13, VIII. xxix. § 1–3, xxxii. § 5, xxxvi. § 2, xlvii. § 1

Glauce, daughter of Creon, II. iii. § 6

—— nymph, VIII. xlvii. § 3

GENERAL INDEX

Glaucias, of Rhegium, V. xxvii. § 8
—— singer, of Croton, X. vii. § 4
Glaucon, Athenian victor, VI. xvi. § 9
Glaucus, son of Aepytus, IV. iii. § 9
—— son of Anthedon, VI. x. § 1, IX. xxii. § 6, 7, X. iv. § 7
—— son of Antenor, X. xxvii. § 3
—— son of Sisyphus, II. iv. § 3, VI. xx. § 19
—— Carystian victor, VI. x. § 1–3
—— Spartan, II. xviii. § 2, VIII. vii. § 8
—— river, VII. xviii. § 2
Glisas, I. xliv. § 4, IX. v. § 13, viii. § 6, ix. § 4, xix. § 2
Glory, temple of, I. xiv. § 5
Glyceiae, VII. xxvii. § 4
Glyppia, III. xxii. § 8
Gnathon, victor, of Dipaea, VI. vii. § 9
Goats, III. xx. § 4, VII. xxvi. § 2, VIII. xviii. § 16, IX. xiii. § 4, in ritual II. xiii. § 6, xxvi. § 4, xxix. § 6, III. xv. § 9, IV. xxxi. § 9, IX. viii. § 2, X. xi. § 5, xxxii. § 12, 16, images II. xiii. § 6, VI. xxv. § 1, X. xi. § 5, xvi. § 5
Gods, cult of, all together, I. xviii. § 9, II. ii. § 8, xxv. § 6, III. xxii. § 8, IV. xxxii. § 1, V. xiv. § 8, xv. § 1, 10, VIII. xxxvii. § 10
Gold, I. xxiv. § 6, III. xii. § 3, X. xi. § 2, crowns I. xvii. § 3, II. xvii. § 6, shields I. xxv. § 7, v. x. § 4, X. viii. § 7, xix. § 4, statues I. xxix. § 16, II. i. § 8, xvii. § 6, xviii. § 1, v. ii. § 3, xi. § 7, xii. § 4, xix. § 8, VIII. xlvi. § 4, IX. xxxv. § 6, X. v. § 12, xxiv. § 5, tripod X. xiii. § 9, vessels v. x. § 4, xix. § 6
—— and ivory, I. xviii. § 6, xx. § 3, xxiv. § 5, xl. § 4, xlii. § 4, II. i. § 8, vii. § 5, x. § 3, 5, xvii. § 4, 5, xxvii. § 2, V. xi. § 1, xvii. § 3, 4, xx. § 2, 10, VI. xxv. § 1, xxvi. § 3, VII. xviii. § 10, xx. § 2, 9, xxvi. § 4, xxvii. § 2, VIII. xlvi. § 4
—— River of, II. xxxi. § 10
Golgi, VIII. v. § 2
Gonippus, IV. xxvii. § 1, 2
Gonussa, II. iv. § 4, V. xviii. § 7
Good Spirit, IX. xxxix. § 5, 13
Gorgasus, IV. iii. § 10, xxx. § 3
Gorgias, VI. xvii. § 7–9, X. xviii. § 7, xix. § 1

Gorgophone, II. xxi. § 7, III. i. § 4, IV. ii. § 4
Gorgus, son of Aristomenes, IV. xix. § 6, xxi. § 2, 12, xxiii. § 2, 5, 9
—— Elean victor, VI. xv. § 9
—— Messenian victor, VI. xiv. § 11
Gortyn, I. xiv. § 4, II. xv. § 1, VIII. l. § 6, liii. § 4
Gortynius, river, V. vii. § 1, VIII. iv. § 8, xxviii. § 2, 3
Gortys, city, V. vii. § 1, VIII. iv. § 8, xxvii. § 4, 7, xxviii. § 1, 2, 7
—— son of Stymphalus, VIII. iv. § 8
—— son of Tegeates, VIII. liii. § 4
Governors: Lacedaemonian VIII. lii. § 4, IX. vi. § 4, xxxii. § 9, Roman V. xv. § 2, VII. xvii. § 4
Graces, IX. xxxv. § 1–7, cult I. xxxiv. § 10, III. xiv. § 6, xviii. § 6, v. xiv. § 10, VI. xxiv. § 6, 7, VIII. xxxiv. § 3, IX. xxxv. § 1–7, xxxviii. § 1, representations I. xxii. § 8, II. xvii. § 3, 4, III. xviii. § 6–10, VI. xi. § 7, 8, VI. xxiv. § 6, 7, VII. v. § 9, IX. xxxiv. § 1, xxxv. § 1–7, xxxviii. § 1
Graea, IX. xx. § 2
Granianus, Sicyonian victor, II. xi. § 8
Grapes, II. xxxviii. § 3, III. xxii. § 2, VIII. xlii. § 11
Gras, III. ii. § 1
Grasshoppers, VI. vi. § 4
Grave, see Tomb
Great goddesses, IV. i. § 5, 6, 8, ii. § 6, iii. § 10, xiv. § 1, xv. § 7, xvi. § 2, xxvi. § 8, xxvii. § 6, xxxiii. § 5, VIII. xxi. § 4, xxix. § 1, xxxi. § 1–8
Great Mother, III. xii. § 9, VIII. xxxvii. § 2
Griffins, I. xxiv. § 5, 6, VIII. ii. § 7
Grylus, I. iii. § 4, xxii. § 4, VIII. ix. § 5, 10, xi. § 6, IX. xv. § 5
Gryneum, I. xxi. § 7.
Guides, I. xiii. § 8, xxxi. § 5, xxxiv. § 4, xxxv. § 8, xli. § 2, xlii. § 4, II. ix. § 7, xxiii. § 6, xxxi. § 4, IV. xxxiii. § 6, V. vii. § 5, vi. § 7, xv. § 10, xviii. § 6, xx. § 4, xxi. § 8, 9, xxiii. § 6, VII. vi. § 5, IX. iii. § 3
Gyges, IV. xxi. § 5, ix. § 2, IX. xxix. § 4
Gymnasia, I. ii. § 5, xvii. § 2, xviii. § 9, xxix. § 2, 16, xliv. § 2, II. iv. § 5, x. § 1, 7, xxii. § 8, 9, III. xiv. § 6, xxii. § 5, xxiv. § 7, 9, IV. xxxii.

225

GENERAL INDEX

§ 1, v. iv. § 4, xv. § 8, xxi. § 17, VI.
vi. § 3, xxi. § 2, xxiii. § 1–xxiv. § 1,
VII. xxvii. § 5, VIII. ix. § 8, xxxi.
§ 8, xxxix. § 6, IX. xi. § 6, xxii. § 3,
xxiii. § 1, X. viii. § 8, 9, xxxvi. § 9
Gymnopaediae, festival, III. xi. § 9
Gyneus, VIII. xiv. § 2, xviii. § 2
Gypsum, I. xl. § 4, VIII. xxii. § 7, IX.
xxxii. § 1
Gythium, I. xxvii. § 5, III. xxi. § 4–
xxii. § 3, xxiv. § 6, VIII. l. § 8

HADES, I. xvii. § 5, II. v. § 1, xiii. § 3,
xxxi. § 2, xxxvii. § 5, III. xxv.
§ 5, 6, IV. xxxiii. § 7, v. xx. § 3,
VI. xxv. § 3, VIII. xviii. § 3, xxxii.
§ 4, xlviii. § 6, IX. v. § 8, xxiii. § 4,
xxx. § 4, xxxi. § 5, X. xxviii. § 1,
5, 7, cult VI. xxv. § 2
Hadrian, I. v. § 5, xviii. § 6, 9, xx. § 7,
xxxvi. § 3, xlii. § 5, xliv. § 6, II.
iii. § 5, xvii. § 6, VI. xvi. § 4, xix.
§ 9, VIII. viii. § 12, ix. § 7, x. § 2,
xi. § 8, xxii. § 3, X. xxxv. § 4, 6,
statues I. iii. § 2, xviii. § 6, xxiv.
§ 7, v. xii. § 6, VIII. xix. § 1
Haemoniae, VIII. iii. § 3, xliv. § 1, 2
Hagnagora, IV. xxi. § 2, xxiv. § 1
Hagno, VIII. xxxi. § 4, xxxviii. § 3,
xlvii. § 3
Hail, II. xxxiv. § 3
Hair, I. xix. § 1, VIII. xx. § 3, X. xxv.
§ 10, rope VII. v. § 7, dedicated I.
xxxvii. § 3, xliii. § 4, II. iii. § 7,
xi. § 6, xxxii. § 1, VII. xvii. § 8, VIII.
xx. § 3, xxxiv. § 3, xli. § 3
Halae, III. xxiv. § 5
Haliae, II. xxii. § 1
Haliartus, I. xxxii. § 5, III. v. § 3, 5,
IX. xvi. § 6, xviii. § 4, xxxii. § 5–
xxxiii. § 4, xxxiv. § 7, 8, X. xxxv. § 2
Halicarnassus, II. xxx. § 9, xxxii. § 6,
III. xi. § 3, VIII. xvi. § 4
Halice, II. xxxvi. § 1
Halirrhothius, I. xxi. § 4, xxviii. § 5
Halitaea, spring, VII. v. § 10
Haliussa, island, II. xxxiv. § 8
Halls (megara), I. xxxix. § 5, xl. § 6,
III. xxv. § 9, IV. xxxi. § 9, VIII. vi.
§ 5, xxxvii. § 8, IX. viii. § 1
Halotia, games, VIII. xlvii. § 4
Halus, VIII. xxv. § 2
Hannibal, VIII. xi. § 10
Harmodius, I. viii. § 5, xxix. § 15

Harmonia, III. xviii. § 12, IX. v. § 2,
xii. § 3, xvi. § 3, 4, xli. § 2
Harpagus, II. xxxi. § 6, X. viii. § 6
Harpalus, Macedonian, I. xxxvii. § 5,
II. xxxiii. § 3–5
Harpies, III. xviii. § 15, v. xvii. § 11,
X. xxx. § 2
Harpina, v. xxii. § 6, VI. xxi. § 8
Harpleia, III. xx. § 7
Health, I. xxiii. § 4, xxxi. § 6, xxxiv.
§ 3, xl. § 6, II. iv. § 5, xi. § 6, xxiii.
§ 4, xxvii. § 6, III. xxii. § 13, v. xx.
§ 3, xxvi. § 2, VII. xxiii. § 7, 8, VIII.
xxviii. § 1, xxxi. § 1, xxxii. § 4,
xlvii. § 1, IX. xxvi. § 8, xxxix. § 3
Heavenly Goddess, VII. xxvi. § 7, IX.
xxix. § 6
Hebe, I. xix. § 3, II. xii. § 4, xiii. § 3,
xvii. § 5, 6, VIII. ix. § 3
Hebrews, I. v. § 5, IV. xxxv. § 9, v.
v. § 2, vii. § 4, VI. xxiv. § 7, VIII.
xvi. § 4, 5, X. xii. § 9
Hecaerge, I. xliii. § 4, v. vii. § 8
Hecas, seer, IV. xvi. § 1, xxi. § 7, 12
Hecataeus, III. xxv. § 5, IV. ii. § 3,
VIII. iv. § 9, xlvii. § 4
Hecate, I. xliii. § 1, II. xi. § 8, xxii. § 7,
triple image II. xxx. § 2
Hector, king of Chios, VII. iv. § 9
—— son of Priam, III. xviii. § 16, v.
xix. § 2, xxv. § 8, IX. xviii. § 5, X.
iv. § 2, xxxi. § 5
Hecuba, X. xii. § 5, xxvii. § 2
Hegeleos, trumpeter, II. xxi. § 3
Hegesinus, poet, IX. xxix. § 1, 2
Hegias, poet, I. ii. § 1
Helen, I. xxxiii. § 7, 8, xxxv. § 1,
xli. § 5, II. ii. § 3, xii. § 6, xxxii.
§ 7, III. vii. § 7, xii. § 6, xviii. § 15,
xx. § 9, xxii. § 1, xxiv. § 10, III. IV.
xvi. § 9, v. xviii. § 3, xix. § 2, 3,
X. xii. § 2, xxv. § 4–8, cult III. xv.
§ 3, xix. § 9–13, called Dendritis
III. xix. § 10
—— island of, I. xxxv. § 1, VIII. xiv.
§ 12
—— Hebrew woman, VIII. xvi. § 5
Helenus, I. xi. § 1, 2, II. xxiii. § 5, 6,
v. xxii. § 2, X. xxv. § 5
Helicaon, X. xxvi. § 7, 8
Helice, V. iv. § 3, VII. i. § 4, 8, vi. § 1,
vii. § 2, xxiv. § 5, 6, 12–xxv. § 5, 8, 12
Helicon, Mount, IX. xxvi. § 6, xxviii.
§ 1, xxix. § 1, 5, xxx. § 1, xxxi. § 1,
3, 4, 7

226

GENERAL INDEX

Helicon, river, IX. xxx. § 8

Heliodorus Halis, I. xxxvii. § 1

Helisson, city, VIII. iii. § 2, 3, xxvii. § 3, 7, xxx. § 1

—— river in Arcadia, II. xii. § 2, v. vii. § 1, VIII. iii. § 3, xxix. § 5, xxx. § 1, 2, 7, xxxi. § 9, xxxii. § 1, 5, xxxv. § 9, xxxvi. § 5

Helius, *see* Sun

Hellanicus, historian, II. iii. § 8, xvi. § 7

—— Elean, v. v. § 1

—— Leprean victor, VI. vii. § 8

Hellanodicae, *see* Umpires

Hellas, statue of, VI. xvi. § 3

—— in Thessaly, III xx. § 6

Helle, IX. xxxiv. § 5

Hellebore, X. xxxvi. § 7, xxxvii. § 7

Hellen, VII. i. § 2

Hellenium, III. xii. § 6–8

Helos, III. ii. § 7, xx. § 6, 7, xxii. § 3

Helots, I. xxix. § 8, III. ii. § 7, iv. § 1, xi. § 8, xx. § 6, IV. viii. § 2, xi. § 1, xvi. § 6, xxiii. § 1, xxiv. § 5, 6, VIII. li. § 3

Hephaestus, myths I. ii. § 6, xx. § 3, II. i. § 4, xxxi. § 3, III. xvii. § 3, xviii. § 13, 16, v. xi. § 8, xix. § 8, VII. xix. § 6, VIII. xvi. § 3, xli. § 5, liii. § 5, IX. xxix. § 7, xxxv. § 4, xl. § 11, pretended works IX. xli. § 1, 2, 5, X. v. § 12, cult I. xiv. § 6, xxvi. § 5, V. xiv. § 6

Hera, myths, I. xviii. § 5, xx. § 3, xxv. § 1, II. xi. § 2, xiii. § 2, xv. § 5, xvii. § 1–7, xxii. § 4, III. xv. § 9, xvii. § 3, xviii. § 13, 16, v. xix. § 5, VII. iv. § 4, xxv. § 12, VIII. iii. § 6, ix. § 3, xviii. § 2, xxii. § 2, xxxvii. § 5, IX. iii. § 1, 2, xi. § 3, xxv. § 2, X. xxx. § 1

—— cult, I. i. § 5, xviii. § 9 II. iii. § 11, iv. § 7, xi. § 1, xii. § 2, xiii. § 2, 4, xv. § 4, xvii. § 1–7, xxii. § 1, xxiv. § 1, 2, xxv. § 10, xxix. § 1, xxxvi. § 2, xxxviii. § 2, 3 III. xi. § 9, xiii. § 8, xv. § 9 IV. xii. § 6, xxvii. § 6 V. xiii. § 8, xiv. § 8, xv. § 5, 11, xvi. § 1, 2, xvii. § 1, xx. § 5 VI. i. § 3, iii. § 15, 16, xiii. § 1, xxiv. § 10 VII. iv. § 4, v. § 4, xxiii. § 9 VIII. ix. § 3, xxii. § 2, xxiii. § 5, xxvi. § 2, xxxi. § 9

Hera, cult, IX. ii. § 7, iii. § 8, xxxiv. § 3, xxxix. § 5, xl. § 4 X. xxxv. § 2

—— representations, I. i. § 5, II. xiii. § 4, xvii. § 4, III. xviii. § 13, 16, v. xi. § 8, xvii. § 1, xx. § 2, VII. iv. § 4, 7, xx. § 3, xxiii. § 9, VIII. xxxi. § 5, xlvi. § 3, IX. iii. § 7, xxxiv. § 3, xxxix. § 4, X. v. § 2

—— titles : Ammonia, V. xv. § 11
Anthea, II. xxii. § 1
Aphrodite, III. xiii. § 9
Argive, III. xiii. § 8, IV. xxvii. § 6
Bride, IX. ii. § 7, iii. § 1, 2, 8
Bunaea, II. iv. § 7
Girl, Full-grown, and Widow, VIII. xxii. § 2
Goat-eater, III. xv. § 9
of Height, II. xxiv. § 1
Henioche, IX. xxxix. § 5
Horse-goddess, v. xv. § 5
Hypercheiria, III. xiii. § 8
Lacinia, VI. xiii. § 1
Olympian, V. xiv. § 8
Prodromia, II. xi. § 2
Samian, V. xiii. § 8, VII. iv. § 4
Teleia, VIII. xxii. § 2, xxxi. § 9, IX. ii. § 7

Heracleia, in Elis, VI. xxii. § 7

—— on Euxine, V. xxvi. § 7, X. xv. § 1

—— in Thessaly, II. xxiii. § 5, VII. xiv. § 1, xv. § 2, 9, X. xxi. § 1, xxii. § 1, 9, xxiii. § 1, 12

—— festival, II. x. § 1

Heracleidae, I. xli. § 1, 2, xliv. § 10, II. vi. § 7, xii. § 3, xiii. § 1, xviii. § 7, III. i. § 5, xxii. § 11, IV. iii. § 3, 8, viii. § 8, xxxi. § 6, xxxi. § 11, V. iii. § 7, VIII. v. § 7

Heracleides, Alexandrian victor, v. xxi. § 13, 14

Heracleius, river, X. xxxvii. § 3

Heracles, son of Alexander, IX. vii. § 2

—— Egyptian, X. xiii. § 8

—— son of Amphitryo, parentage v. xiii. § 2, xiv. § 1, 9, children I. v. § 2, vi. § 6, xxi. § 3, II. iv. § 3, xix. § 1, III. xvi. § 6, IV. xxx. § 1, VI. xi. § 2, VIII. xii. § 4, xxiv. § 2, IX. xxxi. § 2, X. x. § 1

—— myths I. ii. § 1, xv. § 3, xvii. § 4, xxiv. § 2, xxvii. § 6, 7, xxxii. § 6, xli. § 1, II. xiii. § 8, xxv. § 1, xxviii. § 2, xxxi. § 10, III. x. § 6, xv. § 3, 9, xvi. § 4, xviii. § 6, 10–12, 15, xix.

227

§ 5, 7, xx. § 5, xxi. § 8, IV. viii. § 2, xv. § 8, xxxiv. § 9, 10, xxxvi. § 4, v. ii. § 1, 2, iii. § 1, v. § 4, 10, vii. § 7, 9, viii. § 3, 4, x. § 9, xi. § 6, xiii. § 2, 4, 8, xiv. § 1, 2, xvii. § 9, 11, VI. xix. § 12, xxi. § 3, xxiii. § 1, xxv. § 2, 3, VII. xvii. § 8, xviii. § 1, xix. § 9, VIII. xiv. § 1–3, 9, xv. § 5, 7, xviii. § 3, xix. § 4, xxv. § 10, xxxvi. § 6, xlviii. § 1, IX. x. § 4, xi. § 2, 5, 6, xvii. § 1, 2, xix. § 5, xxiv. § 3, xxv. § 2, 4, xxix. § 9, xxxvii. § 2, xxxviii. § 7, X. iv. § 6, viii. § 9, xxix. § 7

Heracles, particular exploits: Amazons v. x. § 9, xi. § 4, xxv. § 6, VII. ii. § 7, Antaeus IX. xi. § 6, Apollo and tripod III. xxi. § 8, VIII. xxxvii. § 1, X. xiii. § 7, 8, Atlas V. x. § 9, xi. § 5, xviii. § 4, Auge VIII. iv. § 9, xlvii. § 4, X. xxviii. § 8, Augeas II. xv. § 1, v. i. § 9, x. § 9, VI. xx. § 16, VIII. xiv. § 9, IX. xi. § 6, Centaurs III. xviii. § 12, 16, v. v. § 10, xix. § 9, X. xxxviii. § 2, Cretan bull I. xxvii. § 10, v. x. § 9, Eurystheus I. xxiii. § 6, VIII. xiv. § 2, xviii. § 3, Eryman-thian boar v. x. § 9, xxvi. § 7, VIII. xxiv. § 5, Hesperides II. xiii. § 8, VI. xix. § 8, Hippocoon II. xviii. § 7, III. x. § 6, xv. § 5, 6, 9, xix. § 7, VIII. liii. § 9, Hound of Hell II. xxxi. § 2, xxxv. § 10, III. xxiii. § 13, xxv. § 5, VI. xxvi. § 7, IX. xxxiv. § 5, hydra v. x. § 9, xvii. § 11, xxvi. § 7, X. xviii. § 6, Nemean lion III. xviii. § 15, v. x. § 9, xi. § 5, xxv. § 7, xxvi. § 7, VI. v. § 5, Pylus II. xviii. § 7, III. xxvi. § 8, VI. xxv. § 2, Stym-phalian birds v. x. § 9, VIII. xxii. § 4, IX. xi. § 6, Thestius IX. xxvii. § 6, twelve labours I. xix. § 3, xxvii. § 10, III. xvii. § 3, v. x. § 9, xxvi. § 7, IX. xi. § 6

—— cult, I. xv. § 3, xix. § 3, xxx. § 2, xxxi. § 6, xxxii. § 4–6, xxxiv. § 3, II. x. § 1, xi. § 8, xxxii. § 4, III. xv. § 3, xviii. § 11, xix. § 7, IV. viii. § 2, xxiii. § 10, xxx. § 1, xxxii. § 1, v. iv. § 6, viii. § 1, xiii. § 11, xix. § 7, 9, xxv. § 12, VI. xxi. § 3, xxiii. § 3, VII. v. § 5, xxv. § 10, VIII. xvi. § 5, xxxi. § 7, xxxii. § 3, IX. xi. § 4, 6, 7, xxiv. § 3, xxvi. § 1, xxvii. § 6–8, xxxii. § 2, 4, xxxviii. § 6, X. vii. § 6

Heracles, images, I. viii. § 4, xxiv. § 2, xxvii. § 6, II. iii. § 2, iv. § 5, ix. § 8, x. § 1, 7, xi. § 8, xvii. § 6, xxxiv. § 1, III. x. § 6, xiv. § 6, 8, xv. § 3, xvii. § 3, xviii. § 10–16, xix. § 5, xxi. § 8, xxiv. § 6, IV. xxxi. § 10, xxxii. § 1, v. x. § 9, xi. § 6, 8, xxv. § 11, 12, xxvi. § 7, VI. xix. § 12, xxiii. § 5, VII. v. § 5–8, xxiii. § 10, xxiv. § 4, xxv. § 10, xxvi. § 6, VIII. xxxi. § 3, xxxv. § 2, xxxvii. § 1, liii. § 9, IX. xi. § 4, 6, xxv. § 4, xxxii. § 2, xxxiv. § 5, xxxviii. § 6, xl. § 3, X. xiii. § 6, 7, xviii. § 6, xxxii. § 5, floated on raft VII. v. § 5–8, un-wrought stone IX. xxiv. § 3

—— titles : Buraicus, VII. xxv. § 10, xxvi. § 1
   Charops, IX. xxxiv. § 5
   Horse-binder, IX. xxvi. § 1
   Idaean, v. vii. § 6–9, viii. § 1, xiii. § 8, VI. xxi. § 6, xxiii. § 3, VIII. xxxi. § 3, IX. xix. § 5, xxvii. § 8
   Manticlus, IV. xxiii. § 10, xxvi. § 3
   Parastates, v. viii. § 1, xiv. § 7, VI. xxiii. § 3
   Patrous, IV. viii. § 2
   Promachus, IX. xi. § 4
   Rhinocolustes, IX. xxv. § 4
   Spelaites, X. xxxii. § 5
Heraea, III. viii. § 7, 8, v. vii. § 1, VIII. iii. § 4, xxvi. § 1–8
Heralds, I. xxxvi. § 3, III. xii. § 7, v. xxii. § 1, xxvii. § 8
Hercyna, IX. xxxix. § 2–7
Hermaea, games, VIII. xiv. § 10
Hermaeum, VIII. xxxiv. § 6, xxxv. § 2, 3
Hermes, myths, I. xxxviii. § 3, 7, II. iii. § 4, 10, vi. § 6, xix. § 7, xxvi. § 6, III. xviii. § 11, 12, xxvi. § 2, IV. xxx. § 2, v. i. § 7, vii. § 10, xiv. § 8, 9, xix. § 5, VII. xx. § 3, 4, VIII. iv. § 6, xiv. § 10, xvi. § 1, xvii. § 5, xxxii. § 4, 10, xliii. § 2, liii. § 4, IX. v. § 8, xvii. § 2, xx. § 3, xxii. § 1, 2, xxx. § 1, xl. § 11, X. xvii. § 5, xxxii. § 4, 5
—— cult, I. ii. § 5, xxx. § 2, xxxiv. § 3, II. ii. § 8, iii. § 4, IV. i. § 8, v. i. § 7, xiv. § 8, 9, xv. § 5, 11, VII. xx. § 4, xxii. § 2, 4, VIII. xiv. § 10, xvi. § 1, xvii. § 1, xxx. § 6, xxxii. § 2–6, xlvii. § 4, IX. xxii. § 1, xxxiv. § 3

GENERAL INDEX

Hermes, representations, I. xv. § 1, xvii. § 2, xxii. § 8, xxiv. § 3, xxvii. § 1, xxviii. § 6, II. ii. § 8, ix. § 8, xix. § 6, 7, xxxi. § 10, xxxiv. § 1, xxxviii. § 7, III. x. § 6, xi. § 11, xviii. § 11, 12, xix. § 3, xxii. § 13, xxiv. § 7, IV. xxxii. § 1, v. xi. § 8, xvii. § 3, xx. § 2, VIII. xiv. § 10, xvii. § 2, xxxi. § 6, 7, xxxv. § 2, xxxvi. § 10, IX. x. § 2, xvii. § 2, xxiv. § 5, with ram II. iii. § 4, IV. xxxii. § 4, v. xxvii. § 8, IX. xxii. § 1, phallus VI. xxvi. § 5, square or limbless I. xxiv. § 3, II. x. § 7, IV. xxxiii. § 3, VII. xxii. § 2, xxvii. § 1, VIII. xxxi. § 7, xxxii. § 1, xxxiii. § 4, xxxix. § 6, X. xii. § 6
—— titles : Acacesius, VIII. iii. § 2, xxx. § 6, xxxvi. § 10
    Aepytus, VIII. xlvii. § 4
    Agetor, VIII. xxxi. § 7
    Cyllenius, VI. xxvi. § 5, VIII. xvii. § 1, 2
    Dolius, VII. xxvii. § 1
    Epimelius, IX. xxxiv. § 3
    of Games, V. xiv. § 9, xv. § 5
    of Gateway, I. xxii. § 8
    of Market-place, I. xv. § 1, II. ix. § 8, III. xi. § 11, VII. xxii. § 2, IX. xvii. § 2
    Parammon, V. xv. § 11
    Polygius, II. xxxi. § 10
    Promachus, IX. xxii. § 1, 2
    Pronaus, IX. x. § 2
    Spelaites, X. xxxii. § 5
Hermesianax, poet, I. ix. § 7, VII. xvii. § 9, xviii. § 1, VIII. xii. § 1, IX. xxxv. § 5
—— Colophonian victor, VI. xvii. § 4
Hermion, II. xxxiv. § 4–12, xxxv. § 3–10, xxxvi. § 2, III. xiv. § 5, v. xxiii. § 2
Hermione, I. xi. § 1, xxxiii. § 8, II. xviii. § 6, III. i. § 5, xxv. § 1, statue X. xv'. § 4
Hermogenes, Xanthian victor, VI. xiii. § 3
Hermolycus, pancratiast, I. xxiii. § 10
Hermon, pilot, X. ix. § 7, 8
Hermus, river, III. ix. § 6, IV. xxxiv. § 2, V. xiii. § 7, VII. xxvii. § 12, X. iv. § 6
Herodes, I. xix. § 6, II. i. § 7–9, VI. xxi. § 2, VII. xx. § 6, X. xxxii. § 1
Herodotus, Clazomenian victor, VI. xvii. § 2

Herodotus, historian, I. v. § 1, xxxiii. § 5, xliii. § 1, II. xvi. § 1, xx. § 10, xxx. § 4, III. ii. § 3, xxv. § 7, IV. xxxv. § 12, V. xxvi. § 4, X. xx. § 2, xxxii. § 8, 9, xxxiii. § 8, 9, 12
Heroes, cult of, I. i. § 4, xxxii. § 4, xxxiv. § 3, xxxvi. § 1, xliii. § 4, II. x. § 1, xi. § 7, III. iv. § 6, xiii. § 7, IV. xxvii. § 6, v. v. § 2, v. § 12, VI. vi. § 7, ix. § 8, xxi. § 11, VII. xvii. § 8, xix. § 10, xx. § 9, VIII. xiv. § 10, 11, xli. § 1, IX. v. § 14, xviii. § 3, xxix. § 6, xxxviii. § 5, X. iv. § 10, xxiv. § 6, xxxiii. § 6
Herophanes, Troezenian author, II. xxxiv. § 4
Herophile, Sibyl, X. xii. § 1–7
Herse, I. ii. § 6, xviii. § 2
Hesiod, I. ii. § 3, iii. § 1, xxiv. § 7, xxviii. § 6, xliii. § 1, II. vi. § 5, ix. § 5, xxvi. § 7, III. xxiv. § 10, v. xii. § 7, xxvi. § 2, VIII. xviii. § 1, IX. xxvii. § 2, 5, xxx. § 3, xxxi. § 3–6, xxxv. § 5, xxxviii. § 2–4, 10, X. vii. § 3
Hesperides, II. xiii. § 8, X. xi. § 6, xvii. § 2, xviii. § 4, VI. xix. § 8
Hestia, I. xviii. § 3, xxxiv. § 3, II. xxxv. § 1, III. xi. § 11, v. xi. § 8, xiv. § 4, xxvi. § 2
Hetoemocles, Lacedaemonian victor, III. xiii. § 9
Hicetas, son of Aristocrates, IV. xvii. § 2, VIII. v. § 13
Hidden Entrance, VI. xx. § 8
Hiero I, tyrant of Syracuse, I. ii. § 3, V. xxvii. § 1, VI. xii. § 1, 2, xiii. § 1, xv. § 6, VIII. xlii. § 8, 9
—— II, VI. xii. § 2–5, xv. § 6
—— of Priene, VII. ii. § 10
Hierocaesarea, V. xxvii. § 5
Hieronymus, Andrian victor, III. xi. § 6, VI. xiv. § 13
—— historian, of Cardia, I. ix. § 8, xiii. § 9
Hierothesion, IV. xxxii. § 1
Hilaeira, II. xxii. § 5, IV. xxxi. § 12, sanctuary III. xvi. § 1
Hill of Horses, I. xxx. § 4
Himera, III. xix. § 11, 13, VI. iv. § 11, X. xxvi. § 9
Hipparchus, I. viii. § 5, xxiii. § 1, 2, xxix. § 15
Hippasus, II. xiii. § 2

GENERAL INDEX

Hippias, son of Peisistratus, I. xxiii. § 1, 2
—— wise man, V. xxv. § 4
Hippocoon, II. xviii. § 7, III. i. § 4, xiv. § 6, 7, xv. § 1–9, xix. § 7, xxi. § 2, VIII. liii. § 9
Hippocrates, Athenian general, III. vi. § 1, IX. vi. § 3
—— physician, X. ii. § 6
—— Syracusan, VI. xii. § 4
Hippocrene, at Troezen, II. xxxi. § 9
—— in Boeotia, IX. xxxi. § 3
Hippodameia, V. x. § 7, xi. § 6, xiii. § 7, xiv. § 6, xvi. § 4, 6, xvii. § 7, xx. § 1, VI. xx. § 17, 19, xxi. § 7, 9, VIII. xiv. § 10, 11, cult V. xxii. § 2, VI. xx. § 7
Hippolyte, I. xli. § 7
Hippolytus, son of Theseus, I. xxii. § 1, 2, II. xxvii. § 4, xxxi. § 4, xxxii. § 1–10, III. xii. § 9, cult II. xxxii. § 1–4, III. xii. § 8
—— son of Rhopalus, II. vi. § 7
Hippomachus, Elean victor, VI. xii. § 6
Hippomanes, V. xxvii. § 3
Hippomedon, II. xx. § 5, xxxvi. § 8, X. x. § 3
Hippomenes, archon, IV. xiii. § 7
Hippopotamus, IV. xxxiv. § 3, V. xii. § 2, VIII. xlvi. § 4
Hipposthenes, Lacedaemonian victor, III. xiii. § 9, xv. § 7, V. viii. § 3
Hippotas, II. iv. § 3, III. xiii. § 4, IX. xl. § 6
Hippothoon, I. v. § 2, xxxviii. § 4, xxxix. § 3
Hippothous, VIII. v. § 4, x. § 3, xlv. § 7, liii. § 6
Hippus, Elean victor, VI. iii. § 5
Histiaea, VII. iv. § 9, vii. § 9, xxvi. § 4
Histiaeus, X. xxxiii. § 2
Historis, IX. xi. § 3
Hollow Road, II. xxiii. § 1, 3
Homer, life I. ii. § 3, II. xxxiii. § 3, IV. xxxiii. § 7, VII. v. § 12, VIII. xxiv. § 14, IX. xxx. § 3, X. vii. § 3, xxiv. § 3, tomb X. xxiv. § 2, statue V. xxvi. § 2, X. xxiv. § 2
—— poems, I. xii. § 4, xvii. § 5, xxii. § 6, xxviii. § 7, xxxvii. § 3, xxxviii. § 2, II. xiv. § 3, III. v. § 9, IV. xxviii. § 7, xxx. § 4, VII. xxvi. § 13, VIII. iii. § 7, IX. ix. § 5, xxix. § 7, xxx. § 12, xl. § 6, X. xxxvii. § 5

Homer, poems, quoted, I. xii. § 5, xxxviii. § 2
II. iii. § 4, vii. § 1, xii. § 5, xiv. § 3, xvi. § 4, xxi. § 9, xxiv. § 4, xxvi. § 10
III. ii. § 4, xix. § 8, xx. § 6, xxi. § 9
IV. i. § 3, 4, ix. § 2, xxx. § 4, xxxvi. § 5
V. vi. § 2, xxiv. § 11
VI. xxii. § 6, xxv. § 3, xxvi. § 5
VII. i. § 4, xx. § 5, xxi. § 8, xxv. § 12, xxvi. § 13
VIII. iii. § 3, 7, xviii. § 2, 3 xxv. § 8, xxix. § 2
IX. v. § 7, 11, xviii. § 2, xx. § 2, 3, xxix. § 7, xxxvi. § 3, xxxviii. § 7, 8, xli. § 3, 4, 5
X. iv. § 5, xxv. § 1, xxix. § 10, xxxiii. § 7
Homole, mountain, IX. viii. § 6, 7
Honey, I. xxxii. § 1, IX. xxiii. § 2, in ritual I. xviii. § 7, II. xi. § 4, v. xv. § 10, VI. xx. § 2, VIII. xlii. § 11, IX. xxxix. § 11
Hoofs, breastplates made of, I. xxi. § 6
Hoopoe, I. xli. § 9, X. iv. § 8
Horses, breeders of III. viii. § 1, VI. ii. § 1, x. § 8, bronze V. xii. § 5, xxvii. § 2–4, VI. xix. § 4, X. ix. § 12, x. § 1, 3, 6, gilded II. i. § 7, sea II. i. § 9, wooden I. xxiii. § 8, II. xxx. § 4, X. ix. § 12, xxvi. § 2, sacrificed I. xxi. § 6, III. xx. § 4, 9, VIII. vii. § 2
Horse-race at Olympia V. viii. § 8
Horse, tomb of, III. xx. § 9
Human sacrifice, I. v. § 2, xxii. § 6, xliii. § 1, III. xvi. § 10, IV. ix. § 4, VII. xix. § 4, 8, xx. § 1, VIII. ii. § 3, IX. viii. § 2, xxxiii. § 4, xxxiv. § 5, X. xxv. § 10
Hyacinthus, I. xxxv. § 4, II. xxxv. § 5, III. i. § 3, x. § 1, xix. § 3–5
Hyampolis, X. i. § 2–8, iii. § 1, xxxv. § 1, 5–7
Hyanthidas, II. iv.§
Hybla, V. xxiii. § 6
Hybrilides, archon, VI. xi.} 5
Hydarnes, III. iv. § 8, X. xxii. § 8
Hydna, X. xix. § 1, 2
Hydra, II. xxxvii. § 4, V. v. § 9, x. § 9, xvii. § 11, xxvi. § 7
Hydrea, island, II. xxxiv. § 9
Hyettus, IX. xxiv. § 3, xxxvi. § 6–8
Hyllicus, river, II. xxxii. § 7
Hyllus, I. xxxv. § 8, xli. § 2, 3, xliv.

§ 10, III. xv. § 10, IV. ii. § 1, xxx. § 1, V. iii. § 7, VIII. v. § 1, xlv. § 3, liii. § 10

Hymettus, mountain, I. xxxii. § 1, 2

Hypanis, river, IV. xxxv. § 12, VIII. xxviii. § 2

Hypatus, mountain, IX. xix. § 3

Hypenus, Pisan victor, IV. viii. § 6

Hyperboreans, I. iv. § 4, xviii. § 5, III. xiii. § 2, V. vii. § 7, 8, X. v. § 7–9, firstfruits sent to Delos I. xxxi. § 2

Hyperea, II. xxx. § 8, 9

Hypereides, V. xxi. § 5

Hyperenor, IX. v. § 3

Hyperion, I. xliii. § 3

Hypermnestra, mother of Amphiaraus, II. xxi. § 2

—— daughter of Danaus, II. xix. § 6, xx. § 7, xxi. § 1, 2, xxv. § 4, X. x. § 5, xxxv. § 1

Hyperochus, Hyperborean, I. iv. § 4, X. xxiii. § 2

—— historian, X. xii. § 8

Hyperteleatum, III. xxii. § 10

Hypsa, III. xxiv. § 8

Hypsus, city, VIII. iii. § 3, xxxv. § 7

—— mountain, VIII. xxxv. § 7

Hyrieus, IX. xxxvii. § 5

Hyrmina, V. i. § 6, 11

Hyrnetho, II. xix. § 1, xxiii. § 3, xxvi. § 2, xxviii. § 3–7

Hysiae, in Argolis, II. xxiv. § 7, VIII. vi. § 4, xxxi. § 1, liv. § 7

—— in Boeotia, IX. i. § 6, ii. § 1

Hysmon, Elean victor, VI. iii. § 9–11

IACCHUS, I. ii. § 4, xxxvii. § 4

Iamidae, III. xi. § 6, xii. § 8, IV. xvi. § 1, VI. ii. § 4, 5, iv. § 5, VIII. x. § 5

Ianiscus, II. vi. § 6

Iapetus, II. xiv. § 4, VIII. xxvii. § 17

Iaseus, X. xxx. § 4

Iasius, Arcadian victor, V. viii. § 4, VIII. xlviii. § 1

—— son of Eleuther, IX. xx. § 1

Iaso, I. xxxiv. § 3

Iasus, king of Argos, II. xvi. § 1

—— town, VII. xiii. § 7

Iberians, I. xxxiii. § 4, IV. xxxvi. § 3, VI. xix. § 3, VIII. xxxix. § 6, X. xvii. § 5, 9, xxxii. § 19

Ibycus, poet, II. vi. § 5

Icaria, IX. xi. § 5

Icarius, father of Penelope, III. i. § 4, xii. § 1, xx. § 10, 11, VIII. xxxiv. § 4

Icarus, son of Daedalus, IX. xi. § 4, 5

—— victor, of Hyperesia, VI. xv. § 1

Icasius, Colophonian victor, VI. xvii. § 4

Iccus, Epidaurian boxer, VI. ix. § 6

—— Tarentine victor, VI. x. § 5

Ichthyophagi, I. xxxiii. § 4

Ida, Mount, in Crete, v. vii. § 6

—— in Troad, III. xiii. § 5, VI. iv. § 9, VII. iii. § 8, X. xii. § 3, 4

—— nymph, VIII. xlvii. § 3

Idas, Dactyl, v. vii. § 6, xiv. § 7

—— son of Aphareus, III. xiii. § 1, IV. ii. § 6, 7, iii. § 1, V. xviii. § 2

Idomeneus, v. xxv. § 9, 10

Iliad, see Homer

—— Little, III. xxvi. § 9, X. xxvi. § 2

Ilisus, river, I. xix. § 5, 6

Ilium, see Troy

—— Mount, III. xxiv. § 6, 8

Illyrians, I. iv. § 1, IV. xxxv. § 5–7, IX. v. § 3, 13, viii. § 6, X. xix. § 7

Ilus, II. xxii. § 3

Images and statues: in fetters III. xv. § 7, 11, VIII. xli. § 6, IX. xxxviii. § 5, like pillars II. ix. § 6, III. xix. § 2, like pyramid II. ix. § 6, Egyptian I. xlii. § 5, II. xix. § 3, IV. xxxii. § 1, VII. v. § 5, secret II. xiii. § 7, xxxv. § 11, III. xiv. § 4, VII. xxiii. § 9, xxiv. § 3, gilt II. xiii. § 6, v. x. § 4, xvii. § 4, X. xv. § 1, xviii. § 7, painted red II. ii. § 6, VII. xxvi. § 11, VIII. xxxix. § 6, square VIII. xlviii. § 6 (see also Hermes); for materials see amber, bronze, gold, gypsum, iron, ivory, marble, silver, terra-cotta, wood

Immaradus, I. v. § 2, xxvii. § 4, xxxviii. § 3

Immortals, Persians, VI. v. § 7, X. xix. § 11

Inachus, river, I. xxv. § 1, II. xv. § 4, 5, xvi. § 4, xviii. § 3, xxii. § 4, xxv. § 3, III. xviii. § 13, VIII. vi. § 6

Incense, II. xxxv. § 11, v. xv. § 10, VI. xx. § 3, VII. xxi. § 12, xxii. § 3, IX. iii. § 8, xxx. § 1

India, I. xii. § 3, 4, II. xxviii. § 1, III. xii. § 4, IV. xxxii. § 4, V. xii. § 3, VI. xxvi. § 9, VIII. xxix. § 4, IX. xxi. § 2, 4, 5, X. xxix. § 4

Indus, river, IV. xxxiv. § 2, 3

Injustice, V. xviii. § 2

Ino, I. xliv. § 7, 8, II. v. § 3, III. xxiv. § 4, IX. v. § 2, cult I. xlii. § 6, III. xxiii. § 8, xxvi. § 1, IV. xxxiv. § 4, statues II. i. § 9, III. xix. § 3, xxvi. § 4

Inscriptions, I. i. § 7, ii. § 4, xiii. § 2, 3, xix. § 2, xxvi. § 4, xxxvii. § 2
II. vii. § 2, ix. § 8, xvii. § 3, xxvii. § 2, 3, xxxvi. § 1
III. viii. § 2, xiv. § 3
IV. i. § 7–9, xv. § 5, xxii. § 7
V. ii. § 5, iii. § 1, iv. § 6, x. § 2–4, 10, xv. § 2, 11, xvii. § 6, 9, xviii. § 2–4, xix. § 3–10, xx. § 1, 7, 8, xxi. § 4, 6–8, xxii. § 3, 7, xxiii. § 1, 7, xxiv. § 1–3, 7, 8, 11, xxv. § 4, 9, 10, 13, xxvi. § 5, 6, xxvii. § 2, 7, 8, 11, 12
VI. i. § 4, 6, 7, ii. § 6, 9, iii. § 1, 2, 7, 14, iv. § 6–8, 11, v. § 7, vi. § 3, 11, vii. § 9, viii. § 1, 2, ix. § 4, 9, x. § 5, 7, xii. § 7, 8, xiii. § 2, 5–7, 10, xiv. § 10, 11, 12, xv. § 2, 8, xvi. § 2, 4, xvii. § 4, 6, 7, xix. § 4–8, 13–15, xx. § 14
VII. vi. § 6, xvii. § 6, 7, xxi. § 2
VIII. v. § 3, ix. § 6, 9, x. § 10, xi. § 8, xiii. § 3, xiv. § 6, xxvi. § 4, xxx. § 5, xxxi. § 3, xxxvii. § 2, 10, xxxviii. § 5, xl. § 1, xlii. § 9, 10, xlix. § 1, lii. § 6
IX. xi. § 1, xv. § 6, xxxviii. § 4, 10, xl. § 10
X. vii. § 6, x. § 1, xi. § 6, xiii. § 6, xviii. § 1, xxi. § 5, xxiv. § 1, xxv. § 5, xxvii. § 4, xxix. § 1, xxxvi. § 9
—— written boustrophedon V. xvii. § 6, right to left V. xxv. § 9, changed I. iii. § 4, xviii. § 3, II. ix. § 8, xxii. § 3, VIII. ix. § 9, recording treaty V. xii. § 8, xxiii. § 4, distance from Olympia to Sparta VI. xvi. § 8, cures at Epidaurus II. xxvii. § 3, xxxvi. § 1

Io, daughter of Iasus, II. xvi. § 1
—— daughter of Inachus, I. xxv. § 1, III. xviii. § 13

Iocasta, IX. v. § 10

Iodama, priestess, IX. xxxiv. § 2

Iolaidas, Theban victor, X. vii. § 8

Iolaus, I. xxix. § 5, xliv. § 10, V. viii. § 3, 4, xvii. § 11, VII. ii. § 2, VIII. xiv. § 9, xlv. § 6, IX. xl. § 6, cult I. xix. § 3, IX. xxiii. § 1, X. xvii. § 5

Ion, Chian poet, V. xiv. § 9, VII. iv. § 8–10
—— son of Xuthus, I. xxxi. § 3, II. xiv. § 2, VII. i. § 2–5, 9

Ionia, Ionians, I. xxix. § 5, V. i. § 1, v. § 9, vii. § 5, viii. § 7, xxi. § 13, xxiv. § 2, VII. i. § 4–vi. § 1, x. § 1, 2, viii. § 6–xix. § 1, xxiv. § 5, xxvi. § 2, 10, VIII. xii. § 1, xliii. § 1, IX. ii. § 2, xix. § 8, xxxiii. § 2, xxxvii. § 8, X. viii. § 2, xxix. § 2, xxxvi. § 1

Ionic order in architecture, VI. xix. § 2, VIII. xlv. § 5

Ionides, nymphs, VI. xxii. § 7

Iophon, I. xxxiv. § 4

Iops, III. xii. § 5

Ios, island, X. xxiv. § 2

Iphicles, VIII. xiv. § 9, 10

Iphiclus, IV. xxxvi. § 3, V. xvii. § 10, X. xxxi. § 10

Iphicrates, I. xxiv. § 7, III. x. § 1, IX. xiv. § 6, 7

Iphidamas, IV. xxxvi. § 4, V. xix. § 4

Iphigeneia, I. xxxiii. § 1, xliii. § 1, II. xxii. § 7, xxxv. § 1, III. xvi. § 7, VII. xxvi. § 5, IX. xix. § 6

Iphimedea, IX. xxxii. § 6, X. xxviii. § 8

Iphinoe, I. xliii. § 4

Iphitus, son of Eurytus, III. xv. § 3, IV. i. § 4, X. xiii. § 8, xxxvi. § 10
—— Elean, IV. iv. § 5, 6, viii. § 5, ix. § 4, x. § 10, xx. § 1, VIII. xxvi. § 4

Iron, I. xxi. § 5, III. iii. § 5, 6, xii. § 10, X. xvi. § 1, xviii. § 6, xxiv. § 5, chair X. xxiv. § 5, stand for bowl X. xvi. § 1, statues IV. xxxi. § 10, X. xviii. § 6

Isagoras, III. iv. § 2, VI. viii. § 6

Ischepolis, I. xlii. § 6, xliii. § 2

Ischys, II. xxvi. § 6, VIII. iv. § 4

Isis, I. xli. § 3, II. ii. § 3, iv. § 6, xiii. § 7, xxxii. § 6, xxxiv. § 1, 10, III. xxii. § 13, IV. xxxii. § 6, VII. xxv. § 9, xxvi. § 7, X. xxxii. § 13–18, statues II. xiii. § 7, xxxii. § 6, VII. xxvi. § 7, titles II. iv. § 6

Island, artificial VIII. vii. § 3, overwhelmed by waves VIII. xxxiii. § 4

Ismenian nymphs, I. xxxi. § 4

Ismenias, III. ix. § 8, 9

Ismenus, river, IX. x. § 2, 6

Isocrates, I. xviii. § 8

Issedones, I. xxiv. § 6, xxxi. § 2, V. vii. § 9

Ister, river III. xix. § 11, IV. xxxiv.

GENERAL INDEX

§ 2, VIII. xxv. § 13, xxviii. § 2, xxxviii. § 3

Isthmian Games, I. xliv. § 8, II. i. § 3, 7, ii. § 2, xv. § 1, III. x. § 1, v. ii. § 1–5, VI. iii. § 9, xvi. § 2, xx. § 9, VIII. xlviii. § 2

Isthmius, IV. iii. § 8, 10

Isthmus of Corinth, II. i. § 3–ii. § 3, VII. vi. § 7

Italy, I. xi. § 7, xii. § 1, 2, II. xxiii. § 5, xxvii. § 4, III. x. § 5, V. xxv. § 3

Ithaca, III. xx. § 10, VIII. xiv. § 6

Ithomaea, IV. xxxiii. § 2

Ithome, Mount, I. xxix. § 8, III. xi. § 8, IV. i. § 3, iii. § 9, ix. § 1–xxxiii. § 1, VI. iii. § 13, X. xxxviii. § 10

Itonus, V. i. § 4, IX. i. § 1, xxxiv. § 1

Itys, I. xxiv. § 3, xli. § 8

Ivory, I. xii. § 4, xl. § 4, xliii. § 6, III. xxii. § 7, IV. xxxi. § 6, V. xi. § 10, xii. § 3, 7, xvii. § 5, VI. xix. § 10, 11, VII. xxvii. § 2, VIII. xlvi. § 5, IX. xxxiii. § 5. See also Gold

Ivy, I. xxxi. § 6, II. xiii. § 4, VII. xx. § 2, VIII. xxxix. § 6, IX. xxxiii. § 7

JARS by side of Zeus, VIII. xxiv. § 14

Jason, I. xviii. § 1, II. iii. § 8, 9, 11, v. xvii. § 10, xviii. § 3, VIII. iv. § 10, xi. § 2

Jay, VIII. xii. § 3

Jerusalem, VIII. xvi. § 5

Jordan, river, V. vii. § 4

Juba, I. xvii. § 2

Judgment, Place of, II. xx. § 7

Juniper, II. x. § 5, VIII. xvii. § 2

Justice, V. xviii. § 2

KEY, of Hades, V. xx. § 3

Kids, in divination, VI. ii. § 5

Kings, Greece once ruled by IX. i. § 2, of Athens I. iii. § 3, v. § 3, IV. v. § 10, of Argos II. xviii. § 4, xix. § 2. See also Sparta

Kiphos, Messenian word for crown, III. xxvi. § 9

Kites at Olympia, V. xiv. § 1

Kokkos, plant, X. xxxvi. § 1

LABAX, Leprean victor, VI. iii. § 4

Labdacus, king of Thebes, II. vi. § 2, IX. v. § 4, 5

Labotas, king of Sparta, III. ii. § 3, IV. iv. § 2

Labyrinth, I. xxvii. § 10

Lacedaemon, son of Zeus III. i. § 2, xiii. § 8, xviii. § 6, VII. xviii. § 5, IX. xxxv. § 1, shrine III. xx. § 2

—— city. See Sparta

Lacedaemonians, character I. xxviii. § 4, III. v. § 8, viii. § 2, xvii. § 5, IV. viii. § 11, xvii. § 2, VI. ii. § 1, IX. xiii. § 10, 11, history passim. See also Spartans

Lacestades, II. vi. § 7

Lachares, I. xxv. § 7, xxix. § 10, 16

Laciadae, I. xxxvii. § 2

Laconia, II. xxxviii. § 7, III. IV. i. § 1

Laconian dialect, III. xv. § 2

Lacrates, Aetolian general, X. xx. § 4

Ladas, Achaean victor, III. xxi. § 1, X. xxiii. § 14

—— Laconian victor, II. xix. § 7, III. xxi. § 1, VIII. xii. § 5

Ladder, VIII. vi. § 4

Lade, island, I. xxxv. § 6

Ladocea, VIII. xliv. § 1

Ladon, river, V. vii. § 1, VI. xxii. § 5, VIII. xx. § 1, 4, xxi. § 1, xxiii. § 8, xxv. § 1–13, xxvi. § 3, xliii. § 2, X. vii. § 8

Lady of the Lake, III. vii. § 4, VII. xx. § 7

Laestrygones, VIII. xxix. § 2, X. xxii. § 7

Laias, king of Elis, v. iv. § 4, 5

Lais, II. ii. § 4, 5

Laius, IV. viii. § 8, IX. ii. § 4, v. § 5–12, 15, xxvi. § 3, 4, X. v. § 3, 4

Lalichmium, building at Elis, VI. xxiii. § 7.

Lamedon, II. v. § 8, vi. § 3, 5, 6

Lamia, I. i. § 3, viii. § 2, 3, VI. iv. § 7, VII. vi. § 5, x. § 4, 5, X. iii. § 4

Lampis, Lacedaemonian victor, V. viii. § 7

Lampon, III. iv. § 10

Lamps, I. xxvi. § 6, 7, II. xvii. § 1, VII. ii. § 3, xxii. § 2

Lampsacus, VI. xviii. § 2–5, IX. xxxi. § 2

Lamptrae, I. xxxi. § 3

Lampus, Macedonian horse-breeder, VI. iv. § 10

—— Elean athlete, v. ii. § 4

Lancia, spring, III. xxi. § 2

Laodamas, king of Thebes, I. xxxix. § 2, IX. v. § 13, viii. § 6, ix. § 5

Laodice, of Paphos, VIII. v. § 3, liii. § 7

GENERAL INDEX

Laodice, wife of Helicaon, X. xxvi. § 7, 8
Laodocus, X. xxiii. § 2
Laomedon, II. xxiv. § 3, VII. xx. § 4, VIII. xxxvi. § 6
Laonome, VIII. xiv. § 2
Laphaes, Argive tyrant, II. xxi. § 8
Laphria, VII. xviii. § 11–13
Laphystius, Mount, IX. xxxiv. § 5–7
Lapithae, I. xvii. § 2, xxviii. § 2, v. x. § 8
Lapithaeum, III. xx. § 7
Lapithus, v. v. § 8
Larisa, acropolis of Argos, II. xxiv. § 1, 3, xxv. § 4, 10, III. xvii. § 1
—— in Thessaly, II. xvi. § 2, xxiv. § 1, IX. xxx. § 9, 11
Larisus, VI. xxvi. § 10, VII. xvii. § 5, VIII. xlix. § 7
Lark, IV. xxxiv. § 8
Larymna, IX. xxiii. § 7
Larysium, mountain, III. xxii. § 2
Las, hero, III. xxiv. § 10
—— town, III. xxi. § 7, xxiv. § 6
Lastratidas, Elean victor, VI. vi. § 3
Latmus, Mount, V. i. § 5
Laurel, I. xxxi. § 8, VII. xxii. § 5, VIII. xxiii. § 5, xxxix. § 6, xlviii. § 2, IX. x. § 4, xxx. § 3, X. v. § 9, vii. § 8
Laurium, I. i. § 1
Law-courts at Athens, I. xxviii. § 6–xxix. § 1
Leaena, I. xxiii. § 2
Leagrus, I. xxix. § 5
Leandris, III. xiv. § 9
Leaping weights, V. xxvi. § 3, xxvii. § 12, VI. iii. § 10
Lebadea, I. xxxiv. § 2, IV. xvi. § 9, IX. xxxix. § 1–xl. § 3
Lebedus, I. ix. § 7, VII. iii. § 5, v. § 10
Lechaeum, II. i. § 5, ii. § 3, iii. § 2, 4, VII. vi. § 7, VIII. i. § 2, IX. xiv. § 6, xv. § 4, X. xxxvii. § 3
Leda, I. xxxiii. § 7, 8, III. xiii. § 8, xvi. § 1
Ledon, X. ii. § 2, iii. § 2, xxxiii. § 1
Legends discrepant, I. xxxviii. § 7, IV. ii. § 3, VIII. liii. § 5, IX. xvi. § 7
Leis, II. xxx. § 5
Leitus, IX. iv. § 3, xxxix. § 3
Leleges, I. xxxix. § 6, III. i. § 1, IV. i. § 1, xxxvi. § 1, VII. ii. § 8, iv. § 1
Lelex, xxxix. § 6, xlii. § 6, xliv. § 3, III. i. § 1, xii. § 5, xix. § 9, xx. § 2, IV. i. § 1, 5

Lemnos, I. xxii. § 6, xxviii. § 2, VII. ii. § 2, VIII. viii. § 5, xxxiii. § 4
Leocritus, son of Protarchus, I. xxvi. § 2
Leocydes, VIII. x. § 6, 10
Leogorus, king of Samos, VII. iv. § 2, 3
Leon, Ambraciot victor, VI. iii. § 7
—— torchbearer, I. xxxvii. § 1
Leonidaeum, V. xv. § 1–4, VI. xvii. § 1
Leonidas I, son of Anaxandridas, I. xiii. § 5, III. iii. § 9, iv. § 7–9, v. § 1, xii. § 9, xiv. § 1, VII. vi. § 3, VIII. lii. § 2, X. xx. § 2, xxii. § 8
—— II, son of Cleonymus, II. ix. § 1, III. vi. § 7–9, vii. § 1, x. § 7, IV. xxix. § 7, VII. vii. § 3, VIII. xxvii. § 15
—— Naxian, VI. xvi. § 5
—— Rhodian victor, VI. xiii. § 4
Leontichus, VII. v. § 13
Leontini, v. xxii. § 7, VI. xvii. § 7, 9, X. xix. § 1
Leontiscus, victor, of Messene in Sicily, VI. ii. § 10, iv. § 3
Leonymus, Crotonian, III. xix. § 12, 13
Leopard's skin, X. xxvii. § 3, xxxi. § 8
Leos, I. v. § 2, X. x. § 1
Leosthenes, I. i. § 3, xxv. § 5, xxix. § 13, III. vi. § 1, VIII. lii. § 5
Leotychides, son of Agis, III. viii. § 7–10
—— king of Sparta, III. iv. § 3, 4, v. § 6, vii. § 9, 10, IV. xv. § 2, 3, VIII. lii. § 3
Lepreus, III. viii. § 3, 5, IV. xv. § 8, v. v. § 3–6, xxiii. § 2, VI. iii. § 4, 9, xv. § 1
Lerna, city, II. xv. § 5, xxiv. § 2, xxxvi. § 7, xxxvii. § 2
—— spring, II. iv. § 5
Lernaean mysteries, II. xxxvi. § 7, VIII. xv. § 9
Lesbos, I. xxiii. § 1, III. ii. § 1, IV. xxxv. § 10, VIII. xviii. § 5, X. xix. § 3
Lesche. See Lounge
Lescheos, poet, X. xxv. § 5–9, xxvi. § 1, 4, 8, xxvii. § 1, 2
Lessa, II. xxv. § 10, xxvi. § 1
Leto, myths, I. xviii. § 5, xxxi. § 1, II. xxi. § 8–10, III. xiii. § 5, xx. § 5, IV. xxxiii. § 6, VIII. xxxvii. § 6, liii. § 1, IX. v. § 8
—— cult, I. xxxi. § 1, II. xxi. § 8, xxii. § 1, VIII. ix. § 1, IX. xxii. § 1, X. xxxvii. § 8
—— representations, I. xliv. § 2,

234

GENERAL INDEX

II. xxi. § 8, xxii. § 1, xxiv. § 5, III.
xi. § 9, v. xvii. § 3, VIII. ix. § 1,
IX. xx. § 1, x. xi. § 1, xiii. § 7, xix.
§ 4, xxxv. § 4, xxxvii. § 8
Letrini, v. xiv. § 6, VI. xxii. § 8, 10, 11
Leucas, x. xi. § 6
Leucasia, river, IV. xxxiii. § 3
Leucasium, VIII. xxv. § 2
Leucippus, son of Oenomaus, VIII.
xx. § 2–4
—— son of Perieres, III. xii. § 8, xxvi.
§ 4, IV. ii. § 4, iii. § 2, xxxi. § 6, 9, 12,
his daughters I. xviii. § 1, III. xii.
§ 8, xvi. § 1, xvii. § 3, xviii. § 11,
IV. xxxi. § 9, 12
Leucone, VIII. xliv. § 8
Leucophrys, x. xiv. § 1, 3
Leucothea, I. xliii. § 6, xliv. § 8, II. ii.
§ 1, iii. § 4, IV. xxxiv. § 4
Leuctra, in Boeotia, I. iii. § 4, xxix.
§ 11, III. vi. § 1, IV. xxvi. § 3–5,
xxxii. § 4, 5, IX. vi. § 4, xiii. § 3–12,
xiv. § 1, 3, X. xi. § 5
—— in Laconia, III. xxi. § 7, xxvi.
§ 4–7, X. xv. § 6
Leuctrum, VIII. lxxvi. § 4
Leucyanias, river, VI. xxi. § 5
Libations, I. xxvi. § 5, xliii. § 4,
II. xi. § 4, v. ii. § 10–12, VI. xx. § 3,
VIII. ii. § 3, X. iv. § 10, to dead II.
xii. § 3, xxxiii. § 1, III. xviii. § 16,
IV. xiv. § 8
Libethra, IX. xxx. § 9–11
Libethrias, spring, IX. xxxiv. § 4
Libethrius, Mount, IX. xxxiv. § 4
Library of Hadrian, I. xviii. § 9
Libya, Libyans, I. xiv. § 6, xviii. § 9,
xxxiii. § 5, II. xxi. § 6, xxviii. § 1,
v. xv. § 11, xxv. § 5, 6, VI. xviii. § 1,
IX. xxxiii. § 7, X. xvii. § 2–9
—— daughter of Epaphus, I. xliv.
§ 3, IV. xxiii. § 10, X. xv. § 6
Lichas, Lacedaemonian, finds bones
of Orestes, III. iii. § 5, 6
—— Lacedaemonian victor, VI. ii.
§ 1–4
Licymnius, II. xxii. § 8, III. xv. § 4
Lightning, omen, IV. xxi. § 7, sacrifice
to VIII. xxix. § 1
Lilaea, IX. xxiv. § 1, X. iii. § 1, viii.
§ 10, xxxiii. § 3–5
Lilies, I. xxxv. § 4, v. xi. § 1, xxii.
§ 5, IX. xli. § 7
Limnae, III. ii. § 6, IV. xxxi. **§ 3**
Limnaeum, III. xvi. § 7

Linus, son of Amphimarus, II. xix.
§ 8, VIII. xviii. § 1, IX. xxix. § 6–9
—— son of Apollo, I. xliii. § 7, II. xix.
§ 8
—— son of Ismenius, IX. xxix. § 9
Lionesses, I. xxiii. § 2, II. ii. § 4, iii.
§ 9
Lions, VI. v. § 4, IX. xl. § 8, in myth I.
ix. § 5, xli. § 3, 4, 6, v. x. § 9, VI.
v. § 5, figures dedicated VIII. xliv.
§ 3, IX. xvii. § 2, xl. § 10, X. xviii.
§ 6, 7, on gate at Mycenae II. xvi.
§ 5
Liparaeans, X. xi. § 3, 4, xvi. § 7
Lips, wind, III. xxxiv. § 2, 3, VI. xxi.
§ 2
Lizard on statue, VI. ii. § 4
Locri, in Italy, III. iii. § 1, xix. § 12,
VI. vi. § 4, xix. § 6
—— Epicnemidian, II. xxix. § 3, III.
ix. § 9, 10, v. xxii. § 4, VII. xv. § 3,
X. i. § 2, viii. § 2, xiii. § 4, xx. § 2
—— Opuntian, I. xxiii. § 4, V. xix.
§ 5, xxv. § 4, IX. xxiii. § 7, X. xx. § 4
—— Ozolian, II. viii. § 4, IV. xxiv. § 7,
VI. xix. § 5, X. viii. § 5, xxxviii. § 1–13
Locusts, I. xxiv. § 8
Log, worshipped, IX. xii. § 4
Lophis, IX. xxxiii. § 4
Lot's cast for kingdom, IV. iii. § 4
Lounge, III. xiv. § 2, xv. § 8, X. xxv.
§ 1
Love, myths I. xxxiii. § 7, V. xi. § 8,
IX. xxvii. § 1–4, cult I. xxx. § 1,
III. xxvi. § 5, VI. xxiii. § 3, IX. xxvii.
§ 1, xxxi. § 3, representations I. xx.
§ 2, xxxiii. § 7, xliii. § 6, II. v. § 1,
xxvii. § 3, IX. xxxi. § 5, xxiv. § 7,
VII. xxvi. § 8, IX. xxvii. § 1–4
Lusi, VIII. xviii. § 7, 8
Lusius, river, VIII. xxviii. § 2
Lyca, spring, VI. vi. § 11
Lycaea, VIII. xxvii. § 3–5, xxx. § 1
Lycaean games, VIII. ii. § 1, xxxviii. § 5
Lycaeus, Mount, IV. xx. § 2, xxii. § 2,
xxiii. § 2, VIII. ii. § 1, xxvii. § 4,
xxxvi. § 3, xxxviii. § 2–10
Lycaon, I. xxv. § 1, VIII. ii. § 1–6
Lycas, ghost, VI. vi. § 11
Lyceas, poet, I. xiii. § 8, 9, II. xix.
§ 5, xxii. § 2, xxiii. § 8
Lyceum, I. xix. § 3, 4, xxix. § 16
Lycia, I. xix. § 3, II. iv. § 2, vii. § 1,
VII. iii. § 7, VIII. xliii. § 4, IX. xli. § 1,
X. xxvii. § 2

235

GENERAL INDEX

Lycinus, Elean victor, VI. vii. § 9
—— Heraean victor, VI. x. § 9
—— Lacedaemonian victor, VI. ii. § 1, 2
Lyciscus, IV. ix. § 5, 6, x. § 1, xii. § 5, 6
Lycoa, VIII. iii. § 4, xxxvi. § 7
Lycomedes, son of Apollo, III. iv. § 1
—— son of Creon, X. xxv. § 6
—— son of Scyros, I. xvii. § 6, X. xxvi. § 4
Lyconidae, I. xxii. § 7, IV. i. § 5, 7, IX. xxvii. § 2, xxx. § 12
Lycone, Mount, II. xxiv. § 5
Lycorea, IV. xxxiv. § 9, X. xxxvi. § 2
Lycormas, victor, of Larisa, X. vii. § 8
Lycortas, father of Polybius, IV. xxix. § 11, VII. ix. § 4, VIII. xxx. § 8, li. § 5, 6, 8
—— Syracusan, V. xxvii. § 7
Lycosura, VIII. ii. § 1, iv. § 5, x. § 10, xxvii. § 4–6, xxxviii. § 1, 11, xxxix. § 1
Lycuntes, VIII. xxiii. § 8
Lycurgus, Athenian orator, I. viii. § 2, xxix. § 15, 16
—— king of Arcadia, V. v. § 5, VIII. iv. § 8, 10, v. § 12, xlv. § 2
—— father of Opheltes, II. xv. § 3
—— son of Pronax, III. xviii. § 12
—— Spartan lawgiver, III. ii. § 3–5, xiv. § 8, xvi. § 6, 10, xviii. § 2, v. iv. § 5, VII. viii. § 5, VIII. li. § 3, cult III. xvi. § 6
—— Thracian, I. xx. § 3
Lycuria, VIII. xix. § 4, xx. § 1
Lycus, Theban, II. vi. § 2, 3, IX. v. § 5, 6, xvi. § 7, xvii. § 6, xxv. § 3
—— son of Pandion, I. xix. § 3, IV. i. § 4, 6–9, ii. § 6, xix. § 4, xx. § 4, X. xii. § 11
—— horse, VI. xiii. § 10
—— Messenian, II. vii. § 2, 3
—— Thracian, I. xxvii. § 6
Lydia, I. xxxv. § 7, 8, III. ix. § 5, xvi. § 8, xxv. § 7, IV. xxi. § 5, v. i. § 6, xiii. § 7, xxvii. § 5, VII. ii. § 8, vi. § 6, xvii. § 9, 10, IX. xxii. § 4, xxix. § 4, X. xiii. § 5, xvi. § 1
Lydiades, VIII. x. § 6, xxvii. § 12, 15
Lydian music, IX. v. § 7, xii. § 5
Lygdamis, Syracusan victor, V. viii. § 8
Lymax, river, VIII. xli. § 2, 4, 10

Lynceus, son of Aphareus, III. xiii. § 1, xiv. § 7, IV. ii. § 6, 7, iii. § 1
—— Argive, II. xvi. § 1, 2, xix. § 6, xxi. § 1, 2, xxv. § 4, X. x. § 5, xxxv. § 1
Lyrcea, II. xxv. § 4, 5
Lyre, II. xxvii. § 3, III. xii. § 10, xvii. § 5, xviii. § 8, xix. § 7, xxiv. § 1, IV. xxxiii. § 3, v. v. § 5, xiv. § 8, xix. § 1, VIII. xvii. § 5, xxiii. § 9, xxxi. § 3, liv. § 7, IX. v. § 7, 8, viii. § 4, xxx. § 1, 2, 3, X. xxx. § 6, 8
Lysander, son of Aristocritus, III. v. § 1–4, vi. § 7, viii. § 6, 10, ix. § 1, 12, xi. § 5, xvii. § 4, xviii. § 3, v. vi. § 5, VI. iii. § 14, 15, iv. § 1, VII. x. § 3, IX. xxxii. § 5–xxxiii. § 1, X. ix. § 7–11
—— his descendant, III. vi. § 7
Lysandra, wife of Agathocles, I. ix. § 6, x. § 3–5, xvi. § 2
Lysidice, VIII. xiv. § 2
Lysimache, I. xxvii. § 4
Lysimacheia, I. ix. § 8, xvi. § 2
Lysimachus, I. vi. § 4, 7, vii. § 3, viii. § 1, ix. § 4–xi. § 1, 6, xvi. § 2, VII. iii. § 4, 5
Lysippe, V. ii. § 4
Lysippus, Elean victor, VI. xvi. § 7
Lysis, Pythagorean, IX. xiii. § 1

MACARIA, city, VIII. iii. § 3, xxvii. § 4, xxxvi. § 9
—— spring, I. xxxii. § 6
Macartatus, II. xxix. § 6
Macedonia, history, I. i. § 3, iv. § 1, vi. § 7, x. § 2, xiii. § 3, 4, xxv. § 5, xxix. § 10, II. viii. § 4, 6, III. xxiv. § 6, VII. viii. § 8, 9, x. § 5–7, VIII. xxvii. § 10, IX. xl. § 7, X. iii. § 3, viii. § 2, xix. § 7. See also Philip and other kings
Maceris, X. xvii. § 2
Machaerion, VIII. xi. § 5, 6
Machanidas, tyrant of Sparta, IV. xxix. § 10, VIII. l. § 2
Machaon, II. xi. § 5, xxiii. § 4, xxvi. § 10, xxxviii. § 6, III. xxvi. § 10, IV. iii. § 1, xxx. § 3, xxxi. § 10, 12, cult III. xxvi. § 9, IV. iii. § 2, 9
Macistus, VI. xxii. § 4
Maeander, river, I. xxix. § 7, II. v. § 3, vii. § 9, IV. xxxiv. § 1, 2, V. xiv. § 3, VII. ii. § 11, iv. § 1, VIII. vii. § 3, xxiv. § 11, xli. § 3, X. xxxii. § 13.

GENERAL INDEX

Maenalus, city, VIII. iii. § 4, xxxvi. § 8
—— Mount, VIII. xxxvi. § 7, 8
—— plain, VIII. xxvii. § 3, xxxvi. § 7
Maera, village, VIII. xii. § 7
—— daughter of Atlas, VIII. xii. § 7, xlviii. § 6, liii. § 3
—— daughter of Proetus, X. xxx. § 5
Magas, I. vi. § 8, vii. § 1–3
Magnes, VI. xxi. § 11
Magnesia, in Thessaly, VII. vii. § 6, X. viii. § 2, 3, xx. § 6
—— on Hermus, I. xx. § 5, III. xxii. § 4, X. iv. § 6
—— on Lethaeus, I. i. § 2, xxvi. § 4, xxxv. § 6, III. xviii. § 9, 14, V. xxi. § 10, VI. xvii. § 3, X. xxxii. § 6
Maid, myths, I. xiv. § 2, xxxviii. § 5, xxxix. § 1, xliii. § 2, II. xxiv. § 4, xxxvi. § 7, IV. xxx. § 4, xxxiii. § 4, VIII. xxxi. § 2, xlii. § 2, IX. xxxi. § 9, xxxix. § 2
—— cult, I. xiv. § 1, xxxi. § 4, xxxvii. § 2, xxxviii. § 1, II. iv. § 7, xi. § 3, xiii. § 5, xxii. § 3, xxxiv. § 6, 8, III. xiii. § 2, IV. i. § 8, VII. xxiv. § 2, VIII. ix. § 2, xxiii. § 3, xxxi. § 1, 8, xxxvii. § 9, xliv. § 5, liii. § 7, IX. iv. § 4, viii. § 1, xxii. § 5, xxiii. § 4, xxv. § 5, xxx. § 6, xxxix. § 4
—— representations, I. ii. § 4, xxxvii. § 6, II. xiii. § 5, xviii. § 3, III. xviii. § 8, xix. § 4, xx. § 7, IV. xiv. § 2, xxxiii. § 4, V. xvii. § 3, xx. § 3, xxvi. § 2, VI. xxi. § 2, VIII. xxv. § 3, xxxi. § 5, 8, IX. iv. § 4
—— titles, First-born, I. xxxi. § 4
   Fruit-bringer, VIII. liii. § 7
   Great Goddess, VIII. xxxi. § 1
   Hagne, IV. xxxiii. § 4
   Saviour, VIII. § 2, VIII. xxxi. § 1
Malea, cape, III. xxiii. § 2, xxv. § 2
—— city, VIII. xxvii. § 4
Malians, I. xxiii. § 4, X. viii. § 2, 3, xxiii. § 13
Mallus, I. xxxiv. § 3
Maloetas, river, VIII. xxxvi. § 1, 2
Maltho, gymnasium, VI. xxiii. § 5, 6
Malus, river VIII. xxxv. § 1
Maneros. song, IX. xxix. § 7
Maniae, VIII. xxxiv. § 1, 5
Manius, VIII. li. § 4
Manthuric Plain, VIII. xliv. § 7
Manthyrenses, VIII. xlv. § 1, xlvii. § 1
Manticlus, IV. xxi. § 2, 12, xxiii. § 10, xxvi. § 3

Mantinea, Mantineans, I. xxix. § 13, II. viii. § 6, xxv. § 1, V. xii. § 8, xxvi. § 6, VI. ii. § 4, VIII. iii. § 4, vi. § 4, 6, vii. § 1, 4, viii. § 4–ix. § 10, x. § 9, xi. § 1, 5–9, 15, xii. § 2–xiii. § 1, IX. xiii. § 1, 6, xiv. § 4, xv. § 5, x. xiii. § 6, xx. § 1
—— battle of, I. iii. § 4, VIII. viii. § 10, ix. § 8, xi. § 5–9, IX. xv. § 5
Manto, daughter of Polyeidus, I. xliii. § 5
—— daughter of Teiresias, VII. iii. § 1, 2, IX. x. § 3, xxxiii. § 2
Maratha, VIII. xxviii. § 1
Marathon, I. xiv. § 5, xv. § 3, xvii. § 6, xxi. § 2, xxv. § 2, xxvii. § 10, xxviii. § 2, 4, xxix. § 4, xxxii. § 3–xxxiii. § 2, II. xxix. § 4, III. iv. § 7, IV. xxv. § 5, V. xi. § 6, VII. xv. § 7, VIII. ix. § 10, x. § 9, liii. § 1, IX. i. § 3, iv. § 1, 2, xxxii. § 9, X. x. § 1, xi. § 5, xix. § 4, xx. § 2
—— Attic hero, I. xv. § 3, xxxii. § 4
—— son of Epopeus, II. i. § 1, vi. § 5
Marble, Parian, I. xiv. § 7, xxxiii. § 2, xliii. § 5, II. ii. § 8, xiii. § 4, xxix. § 1, xxxv. § 3, IV. xxxi. § 6, 11, V. xi. § 10, xii. § 6, VIII. xxv. § 6, IX. xx. § 4
—— Pentelic, I. xix. § 6, xxxii. § 1, V. vi. § 6, VI. xxi. § 2, VII. xxiii. § 5, xxv. § 9, xxvi. § 4, xxxii. § 1, VIII. § 1. xxx. § 10, xlvii. § 1, IX. ii. § 7, iv. § 1, xi. § 6, xxv. § 3, xxvii. § 3, X. iv. § 4, xxxii. § 1, xxxiii. § 4, xxxv. § 10
—— Phrygian, I. xviii. § 8, 9
—— Thasian, I. xviii. § 6
Mardonius, I. i. § 5, xxvii. § 1, III. xi. § 3, VI. iii. § 8, IX. ii. § 2, xxiii. § 6. xxv. § 9
Marion, Alexandrian victor, V. xxi. § 10
Marius, city, III. xxi. § 7, xxii. § 8
Market-places, I. i. § 3, xvii. § 1, xliii. § 8, xliv. § 2
   II. ii. § 6–iii. § 6, vii. § 6, 7, ix. § 6, x. § 1, xiii. § 5–7, xxi. § 1, 4, 5, xxxi. § 1, 7, xxxiv. § 1
   III. xi. § 2–4, 9, xii. § 1, 10, xxi. § 8, xxii § 7, 13, xxv. § 3
   IV. xxxi. § 6, xxxiv. § 6
   V. xii. § 6
   VI. xi. § 2, 3, xxiv. § 1–xxvi. § 1
   VII. xx. § 3–7, xxi. § 6, xxii. § 2, 3, xxvii. § 4
   VIII. ix. § 9, xiii. § 2, xix. § 1, xxv

GENERAL INDEX

§ 3, xxx. § 2–xxxi. § 8, xxxviii. § 8,
xl. § 1, xli. § 1, 9, xlvi. § 4, xlviii. § 1–
xlix. § 1
   IX. v. § 14, xii. § 3, xxvii. § 5,
xxxiv. § 3
   X. xxxii. § 10, xxxiii. § 4, 6, xxxiv.
§ 6, xxxv. § 6, xxxvi. § 4, 8, 10,
Ionian VI. xxiv. § 2, gods of, I. xv.
§ 1, II. ix. § 8, III. xi. § 9, 11, V. xv.
§ 4, VII. xxii. § 2, IX. xvii. § 2, xxv.
§ 4

Maron, III. xii. § 9
Marpessa, daughter of Evenus, IV. ii.
§ 7, V. xviii. § 2
—— Choera, VIII. xlvii. § 2, xlviii. § 5
Marpessus, X. xii. § 3, 4, 7.
Marriage, ritual, I. xliii. § 4, II. xxi.
§ 7, xxxii. § 1, xxxiii. § 1, xxxiv. § 12
Marsyas, I. xxiv. § 1, II. vii. § 9, xxii.
§ 9, VIII. ix. § 1, X. xxx. § 9
—— river, X. xxx. § 9
Mases, port, II. xxxv. § 11, xxxvi. § 1–3
Masistius, I. xxvii. § 1
Massiliots, X. viii. § 6, 7, xviii. § 7
Mathia, mountain, IV. xxxiv. § 4
Mausolus, VIII. xvi. § 4
Mecisteus, I. xxviii. § 7, II. xx. § 5,
xxx. § 10, IX. xviii. § 1, X. xxv.
§ 6
Medea, II. iii. § 6–11, xii. § 1, V. xviii.
§ 3, VIII. xi. § 2
—— town, II. xxv. § 9
Medeon, X. iii. § 2, xxxvi. § 6
Medes, I. i. § 5, xvii. § 6, xviii. § 2,
xxv. § 1, xxvii. § 2, xxxii. § 5, IV.
xxxvi. § 6, VII. x. § 1, 2, IX. xxxii.
§ 9, named after Medea II. iii. § 8
Medon, king of Argos, II. xix. § 2
—— king of Aᵗhens, VII. ii. § 1
—— son of Pylades, II. xvi. § 7
Medontidae, IV. v. § 10, xiii. § 7
Medus, II. xii. § 8
Medusa, I. xxi. § 3, xxii. § 7, xxiii. § 7,
xxiv. § 7, II. xx. § 7, xxi. § 5, 6, 7,
xxvii. § 2, III. xvii. § 3, xviii. § 11,
V. x. § 4, xii. § 4, xviii. § 5, VIII.
xlvii. § 5, IX. xxxiv. § 2
Megalopolis, history II. vii. § 4, ix. § 2,
IV. xxix. § 7, VI. xii. § 8, VIII. xxvii.
§ 7–16, xlix. § 4, lii. § 4, IX. xiv. § 4,
description VIII. xxx. § 1–xxxii.
§ 5, boundaries VIII. xxvi. § 8,
xxvii. § 17, xxxiv. § 6, xxxv. § 2,
xxxvi. § 4, xliv. § 5, statue of VIII.
xxx. § 10

Megapenthes, son of Menelaus, II. xviii.
§ 6, III. xviii. § 13, xix. § 9
—— son of Proetus, II. xvi. § 3, xviii.
§ 4
Megara, wife of Heracles, I. xli. § 1, IX.
xi. § 2, X. xxix. § 7
—— city, description, I. xl. § 1–xliv.
§ 3, history, I. v. § 3, xxix. § 13,
xxxvi. § 3, xxxix. § 4–6, xl. § 3, 4,
xli. § 5, II. viii. § 5, xxxiv. § 7, III.
iv. § 6, V. xxvi. § 7, VI. xix. § 13, VII.
v. § 8, 11, VIII. l. § 4, X. xv. § 1, xx.
§ 4
Megarians, I. xxxvi. § 3, xxxix. § 5,
xliii. § 2, 3, V. xiii. § 5, VI. xix. § 12–
14, X. xv. § 1
Megaris, I. xxix. § 4, xlii. § 2, xliv. § 4,
IV. xxxix. § 1, boundaries I. xxxix.
§ 4, xliv. § 4, 10
Meiganitas, river, VII. xxiii. § 5
Meilichus, river, VIII. xix. § 6, xx. § 1,
xxii. § 11
Melaeneae, v. vii. § 1, VIII. iii. § 3,
xxvi. § 8
Melampodidae, II. xxiii. § 2, VI. xvii.
§ 6
Melampus, son of Amythaon, I. xliii.
§ 5, xliv. § 5, II. xviii. § 4, IV. xxxvi.
§ 3, V. v. § 10, VI. xvii. § 6, VIII. xviii.
§ 7, 8, xlvii. § 3, IX. xxxi. § 5
—— Cephallenian, V. ix. § 4
Melangeia, VIII. vi. § 4, 5
Melanion, III. xii. § 9, V. xvii. § 10, xix.
§ 2
Melanippus, son of Ares, VII. xxii. § 8
—— lover of Comaetho, VII. xix. § 2–5
—— son of Theseus, X. xxv. § 7†
—— Theban, IX. xviii. § 1
Melanopus, Athenian, I. xxix. § 6
—— Cymaean poet, V. vii. § 8
Melanthus, I. iii. § 3, xix. § 5, II. xviii.
§ 8, 9, IV. v. § 10, VII. i. § 9, ii. § 3,
iii. § 6, xxv. § 2, VIII. lii. § 1, X. § 1
Melas, son of Antasus, II. iv. § 4, v.
xviii. § 9
—— river in Boeotia, IX. xxxviii. § 6
—— river in Pamphylia, VIII. xxviii.
§ 3
—— son of Oenopion, VII. iv. § 8
—— son of Ops, VIII. xxviii. § 5
—— son of Poseidon, VII. iv. § 8
Meleager, I. xlii. § 6, II. vii. § 9, IV. ii.
§ 7, VIII. iv. § 10, xlv. § 6, X. xxxi.
§ 3, 4
Meles, Athenian, I. xxx. § 1

GENERAL INDEX

Meles, river, VII. v. § 2, 12
Melesander, admiral, I. xxix. § 7
Melia, IX. x. § 5, xxvi. § 1
Meliastae, VIII. vi. § 5
Meliboea, II. xxi. § 9
Melicertes, I. xliv. § 7, 8, II. i. § 3, IX. xxxiv. § 7
Melissa, II. xxviii. § 8
Melitian gate, I. xxiii. § 9
Melpeia, VIII. xxxviii. § 11
Meltas, king of Argos, II. xix. § 2
Memnon, I. xlii. § 3, III. iii. § 8, xviii. § 12, V. xix. § 1, xxii. § 2, X. xxxi. § 5–8
Memphis, I. vi. § 3, vii. § 1, xviii. § 4
Men, created VIII. xxix. § 4, X. iv. § 4, changed into birds I. xxx. § 3, xli. § 9, X. iv. § 8, into wolves VI. viii. § 2, VIII. ii. § 3, 6
Menalces, Elean victor, VI. xvi. § 5
Menalcidas, VII. xi. § 7–xiii. § 8, xvi. § 6
Menander, I. ii. § 2, xxi. § 1
Mende, V. x. § 8, xxv. § 7, xxvi. § 1, xxvii. § 12
Menelaus, I. xxxiii. § 8, II. xiii. § 3, xvii. § 3, xviii. § 6, xxii. § 6, III. i. § 5, xii. § 6, xiv. § 6, xviii. § 13, 16, xix. § 9, xxii. § 2, 10, IV. i. § 4, V. viii. § 3, xviii. § 3, xxii. § 2, VI. xxv. § 3, VII. xxi. § 8, VIII. xxiii. § 4, liii. § 5, X. xv. § 4, xxv. § 2, 3, xxvi. § 3, 7, 8, xxxiii. § 2, cult III. xix. § 9
Meneptolemus, victor, of Apollonia, VI. xiv. § 13
Menestheus, I. i. § 2, iii. § 3, xvii. § 5, 6, xxiii. § 8, II. xxv. § 6, III. xviii. § 5
Menestratus, IX. xxvi. § 7
Menius, river, V.i. § 10, VI. xxvi. § 1
Menoecus, father of Creon, IX. v. § 13
—— son of Creon, IX. xxv. § 1, 2
Menophanes, III. xxiii. § 2–5
Mercy, altar of, I. xvii. § 1
Meriones, III. iii. § 8
Mermerus, II. iii. § 6, 9
Meroe, I. xxxiii. § 4, V. vii. § 4
Mesate, cape, VII. v. § 6
Mesatis, VII. xviii. § 4–6, xix. § 1, xxi. § 14
Mesoa, in Laconia. III. xvi. § 9
—— in Achaia, VII. xx. § 8
Mesoboa, VIII. xxv. § 2
Messa, III. xxv. § 9
Messapius, Mount, IX. xxii. § 5
Messene, daughter of Triopas, IV. i.

§ 1–ii. § 1, 6, iii. § 9, xxvi. § 8, xxvii. § 6, xxxi. § 11
—— city in Messenia, IV. i. § 3, xxxi. § 4–xxxiii. § 2, foundation IV. xxvii. § 5–7, VIII. lii. § 4, IX. xiv. § 5, xv. § 6, X. x. § 5, later history IV. xxix. § 1–5, VIII. l. § 5, walls IV. xxxi. § 5
—— in Sicily, IV. xxiii. § 9, xxvi. § 3, V. xxv. § 2, 11, xxvi. § 5, VI. ii. § 10
Messenia, boundary II. ii. § 6, IV. i. § 1, xx. § 2, xxxvi. § 7, V. vi. § 3, VIII. i. § 1, xxxiv. § 6, xxxv. § 2, safety dependent on secret thing IV. xx. § 4, xxvi. § 7
Messenians, history, I. xxv. § 4, II. xviii. § 7, 8, III. iii. § 1–4, vii. § 6, xi. § 8, xiii. § 2, IV. iii. § 4–8, iv. § 4–xxiii. § 9, xxiv. § 5–7, xxv. § 1–5, xxvii. § 9, xxviii. § 2, 3, xxix. § 6–9, xxxi. § 1, 7, 11, xxxiii. § 2, xxxiv. § 5, V. xxvi. § 1, VIII. v. § 3, IX. ix. § 2, X. xxxviii. § 10, religion IV. iv. § 1, xxvii. § 6, V. xxv. § 2, dedications V. xxv. § 4, xxvi. § 1, not victorious at Olympia VI. ii. § 10, dialect IV. xxvii. § 10
Metanastes, VII. i. § 6
Metaneira, I. xxxix. § 1, 2
Metapontium, V. xxii. § 5, VI. xix. § 1
Metellus, ambassador, VII. viii. § 6, ix. § 1
—— general, VII. xiii. § 1–xvi. § 1
Methana, II. xxxiv. § 1–4
Methapus, IV. i. § 7, 8
Methydrium, VIII. iii. § 3, xii. § 2, xxvii. § 4, 7, xxviii. § 3, xxxv. § 5, 9, xxxvi. § 1–4
Methymna, IX. xxx. § 2, X. xix. § 3
Metion, II. vi. § 5
Metionidae, I. v. § 3, 4, VII. iv. § 5
Metroum, V. xx. § 9, xxi. § 2
Micon, orator, II. ix. § 4
Micythus, V. xxiv. § 6, xxvi. § 2–7
Midas, I. iv. § 5
Mideia, in Argolis, II. xvi. § 2, xxv. § 9, VI. xx. § 7
—— in Boeotia, IX. xxxviii. § 9, xxxix. § 1
Migonium, II. xxii. § 1
Miletus, I. xvi. § 3, xxxv. § 6, II. v. § 3, x. § 5, VII. ii. § 4–11, xxiv. § 5, VIII. xxiv. § 11, xlvi. § 3, X. xxx. § 2, xxxiii. § 2, xxxviii. § 11
Milo, VI. xiv. § 5–9

GENERAL INDEX

Miltiades, son of Cimon, VI. x. § 8, xix. § 6
—— younger, I. xv. § 3, xvii. § 6, xviii. § 3, xxviii. § 3, xxix. § 8, 15, xxxii. § 4, II. xxix. § 4, III. iii. § 7, iv. § 7, xii. § 7, IV. xxiv. § 6, VII. xv. § 7, VIII. viii. § 9, lii. § 1, 2, X. x. § 1
—— archon, IV. xxiii. § 10, VIII. xxxix. § 3
Mimas, Mount, II. i. § 5, VII. iv. § 1, X. ix. § 9
Mimnermus, IX. xxix. § 4
Minoa, cape, III. xxiii. § 11
—— island, I. xliv. § 3
Minos, I. i. § 2, 4, xvii. § 3, xix. § 4, xxii. § 5, xxiv. § 1, xxvii. § 9, 10, xxxix. § 5, II. xxx. § 3, xxxi. § 1, xxxiv. § 7, III. ii. § 4, xviii. § 11, 16, V. xxv. § 9, VII. ii. § 5, iii. § 7, iv. § 5, 6, VIII. liii. § 4, 8, IX. xi. § 4, xvi. § 4
Minotaur, I. xxii. § 5, xxiv. § 1, xxvii. § 10, III. xviii. § 11, 16
Minyae, II. xxix. § 3, IV. xxvii. § 10, VII. ii. § 2, iii. § 6, IX. ix. § 1, xxx. § 1, xxxvi. § 4, 8, xxxvii. § 2, 7, xxxviii. § 4
Minyas, king of Orchomenus IX. xxxvi. § 4–6, xxxviii. § 2, X. xxix. § 6, grave IX. xxxviii. § 3
—— poem, IV. xxxiii. § 7, IX. v. § 9, X. xxviii. § 2, 7, xxxi. § 3
Minyeius, V. vi. § 2, 3
Mirror, VII. xxi. § 12, VIII. xxxvii. § 7
Mistress, daughter of Demeter, V. xv. § 4, 10, VIII. x. § 10, xxvii. § 6, xxxv. § 2, xxxvi. § 9, xxxvii. § 1–10, xxxviii. § 2, xlii. § 1
Mithridates, I. xx. § 4–6, III. xxiii. § 3, 5, IX. vii. § 4, 5, xl. § 7, X. xxxiv. § 2–4
Mitylene, VI. xv. § 1, VIII. xxx. § 2, X. xxiv. § 1
Mnaseas, Cyrenian victor, VI. xiii. § 7, xviii. § 1
Mnasinus, II. xxii. § 5, III. xviii. § 13.
Mneme, Muse, IX. xxix. § 2
Mnemosyne, I. ii. § 5, VIII. xlvii. § 3, IX. xxxix. § 8, 13
Mnesibulus, Elatean victor, X. xxxiv. § 5
Mnesitheus, I. xxxvii. § 4
Modesty, altar of I. xvii. § 1, image of III. xx. § 10, 11
Moline, v. ii. § 1, 2, VIII. xiv. § 9

Molionidae, v. ii. § 1, 2, 5, VIII. xiv. § 9
Molossus, son of Pyrrhus, I. xi. § 1, 2
Molottus, Athenian general, I. xxxvi. § 4
Molpadia, Amazon, I. ii. § 1
Molpia, IX. xiii. § 5
Molpion, VI. iv. § 8
Molurian rock, I. xliv. § 8, 7
Moon, III. xxvi. § 1, v. i. § 4, xi. § 8, VI. xxiv. § 6
Mopsus, son of Ampyx, V. xvii. § 10
—— son of Rhacius, VII. iii. § 2
Moschion, VI. xii. § 6, xvii. § 5
Mother, II. iii. § 4, VII. xvii. § 9, xx. § 3, X. xii. § 10, xxxii. § 3
—— of Gods, I. iii. § 5, xxxi. § 1, II. iv. § 7, xi. § 8, III. xxii. § 4, IV. xxxi. § 6, v. xiv. § 9, xx. § 2, 9, VIII. xxx. § 4, 5, xliv. § 3, X. xxvi. § 1
—— Athena, v. iii. § 2
—— Dindymene, VII. xvii. § 9, xx. § 3, VIII. xlvi. § 4, IX. xxv. § 3
—— Earth, X. xii. § 10
—— Great, III. xii. § 9, VIII. xxxvii. § 2, 3
Mothone, III. x. § 10, xviii. § 1, xxiii. § 1, xxiv. § 4, xxvii. § 8, xxxv. § 1– xxxvi. § 1, VIII. i. § 1
Motye, V. xxv. § 5
Mud, smeared on face, VI. xxii. § 9
Mules, v. v. § 2, ix. § 2, xi. § 8, xix. § 9
Mummius, II. i. § 2, ii. § 2, V. x. § 5, xxiv. § 4, 8, VII. xvi. v. § 1–xvi. § 10
Munychia, I. i. § 4, xxv. § 5, xxvi. § 3, II. viii. § 6
Musaea, festival, IX. xxxi. § 3
Musaeus, I. xiv. § 3, xxii. 7, xxv. § 8, IV. i. § 5, X. v. § 6, vii. § 2, ix. § 11, xii. § 11
Muses, myths, IV. xxxiii. § 7, V. xviii. § 4, IX. xii. § 3, xxix. § 1–6, xxx. § 4, xxxiv. § 3
—— cult, I. xix. § 5, xxx. § 2, II. xxxi. § 3, III. xvii. § 5, v. xiv. § 10, VIII. xxxii. § 2, IX. xxvii. § 5, xxix. § 1–6, xxxi. § 4.
—— representations, I. ii. § 5, xliii. § 6, II. iii. § 1, III. xix. § 5, IV. xxxi. § 10, v. xviii. § 4, VIII. ix. § 1, xxxi. § 5, xxxii. § 2, xlvii. § 3, IX. xxvii. § 5, xxx. § 1, xxxiv. § 4, X. xix. § 4
—— titles, Ardalides, II. xxxi. § 3
Ilisian, I. xix. § 5
Libethrian, IX. xxxiv. § 4

GENERAL INDEX

Museum, hill, I. xxv. § 8–xxvi. § 2, III. vi. § 6

Music, IV. xxvii. § 7, IX. v. § 7, xii. § 5, xxix. § 6, xxx. § 2, X. ix. § 2, xxx. § 7, competitions II. xxxv. § 1, IV. xxxiii. § 2, IX. xxxi. § 3, X. vii. § 2–7

Music-hall, *see* Odeum

Myanians, VI. xix. § 4, 5, X. xxxviii. § 8

Mycale, I. xxv. § 1, III. vii. § 9, V. vii. § 5, VII. iv. § 1, VIII. lii. § 3

Mycalessus, I. xxiii. § 3, IX. xix. § 4, xx. § 2

Mycenae, II. iv. § 2, vi. § 7, xv. § 4, xvi. § 3–xvii. § 1, xviii. § 1, V. xxiii. § 2, 3, VII. xxv. § 5, 6, VIII. v. § 4, xxvii. § 1, xxxiii. § 2, IX. xxxiv. § 6, X. xx. § 1, 2

Mycon, VI. ii. § 9

Mygdon, X. xxvii. § 1

Mylaon, VIII. xxxvi. § 1, 2, xxxviii. § 9

Myles, king of Laconia. III. i. § 1, xii. § 5, xx. § 2, IV. i. § 1

Myonia, X. xxxviii. § 8

Myro, poetess, IX. v. § 8

Myron, historian, of Priene, IV. vi. § 1–4

—— tyrant of Sicyon, II. viii. § 1, VI. xix. § 1, 2, 4

Myropolis, portico, VIII. xxx. § 7

Myrrhinus, I. xxxi. § 4, 5

Myrtilus, II. xviii. § 2, V. i. § 7, x. § 6, VI. xx. § 17, VIII. xiv. § 10–12

Myrtle, I. xxii. § 2, xxvii. § 1, II. xxii. § 3, 4, III. xxii. § 12, IV. xxvi. § 7, V. xiii. § 7, VI. xxiv. § 6, 7, VIII. xxvi. § 1, IX. xxviii. § 3

Myrto, VIII. xiv. § 12

Mys, of Europus, IX. xxiii. § 6

Mysaeum, VII. xxvii. § 9

Mysia, in Asia, I. iv. § 6, v. § 5, xxv. § 2, III. ii. § 1, VII. viii. § 9, IX. v. § 14, xviii. § 4

—— in Argolis, II. xviii. § 3

Mysius, II. xviii. § 3, xxxv. § 4, VII. xxvii. § 9

Mysteries, I. ii. § 5, xxxvii. § 4, xxxviii. § 3, II. xii. § 5, xiv. § 1, xxvi. § 8, xxx. § 2, xxxvi. § 7, xxxvii. § 2, xxxviii. § 3, IV. i. § 5–8, ii. § 6, xxvi. § 7, xxxiii. § 1, V. x. § 1, VIII. xv. § 1, 2, xxix. § 1, X. xxxi. § 11, xxxviii. § 7

Myus, VII. ii. § 10, 11

NABIS, IV. xxix. § 10, 11, VII. viii. § 4, 5, ix. § 2, VIII. l. § 5–li. § 2

Naia, spring, III. xxv. § 4

Naiads, III. xxv. § 2, VIII. iv. § 2, X. xxxiii. § 4

Naliphus, river, VIII. xxxviii. § 9

Names, Greek and Roman, VII. vii. § 8

Narcaeus, V. xvi. § 7

Narcissus, IX. xxxi. § 7, 9, xli. § 7

Narycidas, Phigalean victor, VI. vi. § 1

Nasamones, I. xxxv. § 5, 6

Nasi, xxiii. § 2, 8, xxv. § 2

Naupactia, poem, II. iii. § 9, IV. ii. § 1, X. xxxviii. § 11

Naupactus, IV. xxiv. § 7, xxvi. § 1–3, xxxi. § 7, V. iii. § 6, xxvi. § 1, VI. xvi. § 2, IX. xxv. § 9, xxxi. § 6–9, xxxviii. § 3, X. xxxviii. § 9–13

Nauplia, I. xxii. § 6, II. xxxviii. § 2, IV. xxiv. § 4, xxvii. § 8, xxxv. § 2, VIII. xlviii. § 7

Nausicaa, I. xxii. § 6, v. xix. § 9, VIII. xlviii. § 3

Naxos, island, I. xxvii. § 5, v. x. § 3, xxiii. § 2, VI. xvi. § 5, VII. iii. § 3, IX. xxii. § 6

—— in Sicily, VI. xiii. § 8

Necessity, sanctuary of, II. iv. § 6

Necklaces, v. xvii. § 7, xxii. § 1, VIII. xxiv. § 10, IX. xli. § 2–5, X. xxix. § 7

Neda, nymph, IV. xxxiii. § 1, VIII. xxxi. § 4, xxxviii. § 3, xlvii. § 3

—— river, IV. xx. § 1–6, xxxiii. § 1, xxxvi. § 7, v. v. § 3, vi. § 3, VIII. xxxviii. § 3, xli. § 2–4

Neileus, VII. ii. § 1–10

Neleids, II. xviii. § 4, 9, IV. iii. § 6

Neleus, king of Pylus, II. ii. § 2, IV. ii. § 5, iii. § 1, 3, xv. § 8, xxxvi. § 1–5, V. viii. § 2, IX. xxxvi. § 8, X. x. § 1, xxix. § 5, xxxi. § 10

—— son of Codrus, VII. ii. § 1, 6, X. x. § 1

Nemea, I. xxii. § 7, xxvii. § 9, II. xv. § 2, 3, xix. § 5, V. xi. § 5, xxii. § 6, xxv. § 7, xxvi. § 7, VI. i. § 7, ii. § 11, iii. § 9, 11, V. § 5, xx. § 19

Nemean games, instituted X. xxv. § 7, winter celebration II. xv. § 3, VI. xvi. § 4, crown VIII. xlviii. § 2

Nemesis, I. xxxiii. § 2–8, VII. v. § 2, 3, xx. § 9, IX. xxxv. § 6

Neocles, Boeotarch, IX. i. § 6

Neolaidas, victor, of Pheneus, VI. i. § 3

Neon, X. ii. § 4, iii. § 2, xxxii. § 9

GENERAL INDEX

Neoptolemus, II. xxix. § 9, III. xx. § 8,
IV. xvii. § 4, X. xvi. § 4, xxiv. § 4,
xxv. § 9, xxvi. § 4, xxvii. § 1, 2,
cult. I. iv. § 4, X. xxiv. § 6. *See also*
Pyrrhus
Nereus and daughters, II. i. § 8, xxi.
§ 9, xxvi. § 7, V. xix. § 8
Neris, II. xxxviii. § 6
Nero, II. xxxvii. § 5, VII. xvii. § 3, 4,
IX. xxvii. § 4, dedications II. xvii.
§ 6, V. xii. § 8, carries off statues V.
xxv. § 8, xxvi. § 3, IX. xxvii. § 3,
X. vii. § 1, xix. § 2
Nessus, III. xviii. § 12, X. xxxviii. § 2
Nestane, VIII. vii. § 4, viii. § 1
Nestor, II. ii. § 2, xviii. § 7, 8, III. xxvi.
§ 8, 10, IV. iii. § 1–7, xxxi. § 11,
xxxvi. § 2–5, V. xxv. § 8, X. xxv. § 2,
11, xxvi. § 1, 4, xxix. § 10
Nicagora, II. x. § 3
Nicander, king of Sparta, II. xxxvi.
§ 4, III. iii. § 2, vii. § 4, 5, xvi. § 6,
IV. iv. § 4, vii. § 7
—— Elean victor, VI. xvi. § 5
Nicasylus, Rhodian victor, VI. xiv.
§ 1, 2, 4
Nicias, general, I. xxix. § 12, II. ii. § 5
Nicocles, victor, of Acriae, III. xxii. § 5
—— tyrant of Sicyon, II. viii. § 3
—— of Tarentum, I. xxxvii. § 2
Nicomachus, IV. iii. § 10, xxx. § 3
Nicomedes, king of Bithynia, V. xii. 7
Nicomedia, III. iii. § 8, xix. § 4, V. xii.
§ 7, VIII. xi. § 11
Nicopolis, V. xxiii. § 3, VII. xviii. § 8, 9,
X. viii. § 3–5, xxxviii. § 4
Nicostratus, son of Menelaus, II. xviii.
§ 6, III. xviii. § 13, xix. § 9
—— Argive, II. xxii. § 3
—— Cilician, victor, V. xxi. § 10, 11
—— Heraean victor, VI. iii. § 11
Night, I. xl. § 6, xliv. § 2, V. xviii. § 1,
VII. v. § 3, X. xxxviii. § 6
Nightingales, I. xli. § 9, IX. xxx. § 6
Nile, river, I. xxxiii. § 4, 6, xlii. § 3, II.
v. § 3, IV. xxxiv. § 2, 3, V. vii. § 4,
xiv. § 3, xxi. § 9, xxvi. § 9, VIII. ix.
§ 7, xxiv. § 12, IX. xl. § 6, X. xxxii. § 18
Nineveh, VIII. xxxiii. § 2
Niobe, daughter of Phoroneus, II. xxii.
§ 5
—— daughter of Tantalus, I. xxi. § 3,
II. xxi. § 9, 10, xxxiv. § 4, 5, III. iv.
§ 1, V. xi. § 2, xvi. § 4, VIII. ii. § 5, 7,
xxxviii. § 10

Nisaea, I. xix. § 4, xxxix. § 4, xliv. § 3,
II. xxxiv. § 7, X. xv. § 1
Nisus, I. xix. § 4, xxxix. § 4–6, xli.
§ 5, 6, xliv. § 3, II. xxxiv. § 7
Nomia, nymph, VIII. xxxviii. § 11, X.
xxxi. § 10
Nonacris, VIII. xvii. § 6–xviii. § 7,
xxxi. § 4
Nora, in Sardinia, X. xvii. § 5
North Wind, *see* Boreas
Nycteus, II. vi. § 1, 2, IX. v. § 4, 5
Nymphaeum, harbour, III. xxiii. § 2
Nymphas, VIII. xxxiv. § 6
Nymphasia, VIII. xxxvi. § 4
Nymphon, II. xi. § 3
Nymphs, myths III. xvii. § 3, IV.
xxvii. § 4, VI. xxii. § 7, 9, VIII. iv. § 2,
xxxviii. § 3, xli. § 2, X. x. § 8, xii. § 3–
11, xxiv. § 7, xxxi. § 10, xxxii. § 9,
cult I. xxxi. § 4, xxxiv. § 3, xl. § 1,
xliv. § 2, III. x. § 7, V. xiv. § 10, xv.
§ 3, 10, VI. xxii. § 7, VIII. iv. § 2, xx.
iii. § 9, xxiv. § 4, X. xxiv. § 7, xxxii.
§ 7, representations III. xvii. § 3, V.
xx. § 3, VIII. xxxi. § 4, xxxvii. § 2,
IX. xxxiv. § 4
—— titles, Acmenae, V. xv. § 6
Anigrid, V. v. § 11
Arcadian, VIII. xxxi. § 4
Of Beautiful Crowns, V. xv. § 3
Cithaeronian, IX. iii. § 9
Corician, X. xxxii. § 7
Ionian, VI. xxii. § 7
Ismenian, I. xxxi. § 4
Libethrian, IX. xxxiv. § 4
Sithnid, I. xl. § 1

Oaks, II. xi. § 4, III. x. § 6, IV. i. § 6, v.
xii. § 8, VII. xxvi. § 10, VIII. i. § 6,
xi. § 1, xii. § 1, xxiii. § 8, xxv. § 1,
xxxvii. § 10, xlii. § 12, liv. § 5, IX.
iii. § 4, xxiv. § 5, X. xxxii. § 9, in cult
I. xvii. § 5, VII. xxi. § 2, VIII. xxiii.
§ 5, xxxviii. § 4, liv. § 4, images of
oak VIII. xvii. § 2, IX. iii. § 2–5,
pillars V. xvi. § 1, VI. xxiv. § 9,
sanctuary VIII. x. § 2
Oaths, II. ii. § 1, V. xxiv. § 9–11, VI.
xx. § 3, VII. xxiv. § 9, xxv. § 2,
IX. xxxiii. § 3, X. xxvi. § 3, on pieces
of animal III. xx. § 9, IV. xv. § 8, v.
xxiv. § 9, 11
Ocean, I. xiv. § 3, xxxiii. § 3–5, xxxv.
§ 7, xxxviii. § 7, II. i. § 1, IV. xxx. § 4,

VII. v. § 3, VIII. xviii. § 1, 2, xli. § 5, 6,
IX. x. § 5, X. xx. § 3
Ocnus, X. xxix. § 1, 2
Octavia, II. iii. § 1
Odeum, I. viii. § 6, xiv. § 1, II. iii. § 6,
VII. xx. § 6, IX. xxxv. § 6
Odrysae, I. ix. § 6, x. § 4, IV. xxxiii. § 3
Odyssey, I. xii. § 5, II. xvi. § 4, III.
xviii. § 16, IV. i. § 3, VIII. xxix. § 2,
IX. v. § 7, 10, ix. § 5, xxxiii. § 2, xli.
§ 3, X. iv. § 5
Odysseus, I. xxii. § 6, xxxv. § 4, II. iii.
§ 3, xiii. § 3, III. xii. § 1, 4, xx. § 10,
11, xxiv. § 11, IV. xii. § 2, v. xix. § 7,
xxv. § 3. VI. vi. § 7, 8, VIII. iii. § 7,
xii. § 6, xix. § 5–7, xxix. § 2, xlviii.
§ 3–6, IX. v. § 2, xli. § 4, x. viii. § 8,
xxv. § 1, 3, 4, xxvi. § 3, 7, 8, xxvii.
§ 1, 3, xxviii. § 1, 7, xxix. § 1, 8–10,
xxxi. § 2, pictures I. xxii. § 6, II. iii.
§ 3, v. xix. § 7, IX. iv. § 2, x. xxvi. § 3,
xxviii. § 1, xxix. § 8, statues v. xxii.
§ 2, xxv. § 8
Oeanthea, X. xxxviii. § 9
Oebalus, son of Cynortas, II. ii. § 3,
xxi. § 7, III. i. § 3, 4, xv. § 10, IV. ii.
§ 4
—— Spartan, IV. xii. § 9
Oebotas, Dymaean victor, VI. iii. § 8,
VII. xvii. § 6, 7, 13, 14
Oechalia, in Euboea, IV. ii. § 3
—— in Messenia, IV. ii. § 2, 3, iii. § 10,
xxvi. § 6, xxxiii. § 4
Oedipodia, poem, IX. v. § 11
Oedipus, I. xxviii. § 7, xxx. § 4, II. xx.
§ 5, xxxvi. § 8, IV. iii. § 4, viii. § 8,
v. xix. § 6, IX. ii. § 4, v. § 10–12, ix.
§ 5, xviii. § 3–6, xxv. § 2, xxvi. § 2, 4,
X. v. § 3, 4, xvii. § 4, shrine I. xxx. § 4
Oeneus, son of Pandion, I. v. § 2
—— son of Porthaon, II. xiii. § 8,
xxiii. § 5, xxv. § 2, IV. ii. § 7, xxxv.
§ 1, VII. iv. § 1, xviii. § 10, X. x. § 3,
xxxi. § 3, xxxviii. § 5
Oeniadae, I. xi. § 4, IV. xxv. § 1–10, v.
xxvi. § 1
Oenobius, I. xxiii. § 9
Oenoe, in Argolis, I. xv. § 1, II. xxv.
§ 2, 3, X. x. § 4
—— in Attica, I. xxxiii. § 8
—— fountain, VIII. xv. § 6
—— nymph, VIII. xxx. § 3, xlvii. § 3
Oenomaus, v. i. § 6, 7, x. § 6, xi. § 6,
xiv. § 6, 7, xvii. § 7, xxii. § 6, VI. xx.
§ 17, 18, xxi. § 3–10, xxii. § 4, VIII.

xiv. § 10, 11, xx. § 2, 3, house v.
xiv. § 7, xx. § 6, pillar V. xx. § 6–8,
VI. xviii. § 7, stables VI. xxi. § 3
Oenone, II. v. § 2, xxix. § 2
Oenopion, VIII. iv. § 8, 9, v. § 13
Oenotrus, VIII. iii. § 5
Oenussae islands, IV. xxxiv. § 12
Oeoclus, IX. xxix. § 1
Oeolycus, III. xv. § 8, IV. vii. § 8
Oeonus, III. xv. § 4, 5
Oeroe, IX. iv. § 4
Oeta, I. i. § 3, iv. § 2, II. xxiii. § 5, III.
iv. § 8, v. i. § 2, VII. vi. § 3, v. § 4,
X. xx. § 1, xxii. § 1, 8, xxiv. § 1
Oetylus, III. xxi. § 7, xxv. § 9, xxvi. § 1
Ogygus, I. xxxviii. § 7, IX. v. § 1, xix.
§ 6, xxxiii. § 5
Oicles, III. xii. § 5, VI. xvii. § 6, VIII. ii.
§ 4, xxxvi. § 6, xlv. § 7
Oil, IV. xxxv. § 8, X. xxxii. § 19, in
cult I. xxvi. § 7, II. vi. § 3, v. xi. § 10,
VIII. xix. § 2, xlii. § 11, IX. xxxix.
§ 7, X. xxiv. § 6
Olbius, river, VIII. xiv. § 3
Olen, Hyperborean, X. v. § 7, 8
—— Lycian poet, I. xviii. § 5, II. xiii.
§ 3, v. vii. § 8, 9, VIII. xxi. § 3, IX.
xxvii. § 2
Olenius, VI. xx. § 16
Olenus, V. iii. § 3, VII. vi. § 1, xviii. § 1,
xix. § 9, xxii. § 1
Olidas, Elean victor, VI. xv. § 2
Olives, I. xxiv. § 3, xxvii. § 2, xxx. § 2,
xlii. § 7, II. xxviii. § 2, 7, xxix. § 8,
xxxii. § 10, xxxviii. § 4, III. xxiii. § 7,
v. xi. § 1, xv. § 3, 10, xvi. § 3, VIII.
xxiii. § 5, xxxvii. § 10, X. xix. § 3
Olmius, river, IX. xxxi. § 7
Olmones, IX. xxiv. § 3, xxxiv. § 10
Olympia, v. i. § 7, vii. § 1, x. § 1–VI.
xxi. § 3, Lacedaemonian attack III.
viii. § 3, 4
Olympiads not recorded by Eleans,
VI. iv. § 2, viii. § 3, xxii. § 2, X.
xxxvi. § 9
Olympias, mother of Alexander, I. xi.
§ 1–4, xxv. § 6, IV. xiv. § 7, v. xvii.
§ 4, xx. § 10, VIII. vii. § 7, IX. vii. § 2
—— spring, VIII. xxix. § 1
Olympic council, VI. iii. § 7, vi. § 6
Olympic games, III. viii. § 1, v. iv. § 5,
vi. § 7, vii. § 6–ix. § 6, x. § 1, xii. § 5,
xv. § 3, 12, xxi. § 2–18, xxiv. § 9,
VI. iv. § 2, vi. § 3, viii. § 1, ix. § 1,
xxii. § 2, 3, VIII. ii. § 2, xlviii. § 1, 2,

GENERAL INDEX

record of victories III. xxi. § 1, v.
xxi. § 9, VI. ii. § 3, vi. § 3, viii.
§ 1, xiii. § 10, X. xxxvi. § 9

Olympiodorus, I. xxv. § 2–xxvi. § 4,
xxix. § 13, X. xviii. § 7, xxxiv. § 3

Olympus, mountain in Thessaly, VI.
v. § 5, IX. xxx. § 9, 11, xl. § 8

—— in Arcadia, VIII. xxxviii. § 2

Olynthus, I. xxix. § 7, III. v. § 9

Omens, *see* Divination

Omphace, VIII. xlvi. § 2, IX. xl. § 4

Omphale, I. xxxv. § 8, xxi. § 3

Omphalos, II. xiii. § 7, X. xvi. § 3

Onchestus, I. xxxix. § 5, xlii. § 1, IX.
xxvi. § 6

Oncium, VIII. xxv. § 4

Onomacritus, poet, I. xxii. § 7, VIII.
xxxi. § 3, xxxvii. § 5, IX. xxxv. § 5

Onomarchus, X. ii. § 5, 6

Onomastus, Smyrnaean victor, v.
viii. § 7

Onugnathus, cape, III. xxii. § 10, 11,
xxiii. § 1

Opheltes, II. xv. § 2, 3

Ophioneus, IV. x. § 5, 6, xii. § 10. xiii.
§ 3

Ophis, river, VIII. viii. § 4, 7

Ophitea, X. xxxiii. § 10

Opis, I. xliii. § 4, v. vii. § 8

Opportunity, altar of, V. xiv. § 9

Opus, IX. xxiii. § 7, X. i. § 2, xxxv. § 1,
5

Oracles, of Ammon III. xviii. § 3, VIII.
xi. § 11, Amphiaraus I. xxxiv. § 4,
Amphilochus I. xxxiv. § 3, Apollo
II. xxiv. § 1, III. iv. § 4, IV. xxxii.
§ 5, VII. ii. § 6, iii. § 1, v. § 2, xxi. § 13,
VIII. xxix. § 4, IX. xxxiii. § 6, X. v.
§ 5–8, xxxv. § 1, Dionysus IX. xxx.
§ 9, X. xxxiii. § 11, Earth v. xiv. § 10,
X. v. § 5, Heracles VII. xxv. § 10,
Hermes VII. xxii. § 2, Ino III. xxvi.
§ 1, VI. xiii. § 3, Nymphs IX. iii. § 9,
Poseidon X. v. § 6, Sibyls, X. xii.
§ 1–9, Trophonius IX. xxxvii. § 5,
xxxix. § 4–xl. § 2, Zeus VII. xxi.
§ 2–4, xxv. § 1, VIII. xi. § 12, xxviii.
§ 6

—— responses I. xliv. § 6
II. xviii. § 2, xx. § 10, xxvi. § 7
III. iii. § 6, 7, viii. § 9, xi. § 8, 10
IV. ix. § 3, xii. § 1, 4, 7, xx. § 1,
xxvi. § 4, xxxii. § 3, 5, xxxiv. § 9
V. iii. § 1, 5, iv. § 3, 4, vii. § 3,
xxvii. § 10

Oracles, responses, VI. iii. § 8, vi. § 8,
viii. § 3, ix. § 8, xi. § 8, xx. § 7
VII. i. § 8, ii. § 1, v. § 2, xvii. § 6,
13, xix. § 4–8, xxi. § 3, xxv. § 1, 2
VIII. i. § 6, v. § 4, viii. § 4, ix. § 3,
xi. § 10, 12, xxiii. § 7, xxix. § 8, 14,
xxix. § 4, xxxvi. § 8, xliii. § 6
IX. v. § 10, vii. § 6, xii. § 2, xvi. § 3,
xviii. § 5, xxvi. § 3, xxx. § 9, xxxii.
§ 10, xxxviii. § 3, 5, xxxix. § 4
X. i. § 4, vi. § 7, x. § 6–8, xiv. § 5,
xxiv. § 2, xxxvii. § 6, ambiguous
VIII. xi. § 10. *See also* Divination

Orchomenus, in Arcadia, V. xxiii. § 2,
VII. xiv. § 1, VIII. iii. § 3, v. § 11 xii.
§ 5–xiii. § 6, xxiii. § 2, xxvii. § 4, 7,
xxxvi. § 4, xlvii. § 6, IX. xxxvi. § 6,
X. xx. § 1

—— in Boeotia, I. ix. § 3, xxiv. § 2,
xliv. § 7, II. xxix. § 3, IV. xxvii. § 10,
VII. ii. § 3, iii. § 6, VIII. xxxiii. § 2,
IX. iii. § 6, xv. § 3, xvii. § 1, 2, xxiv.
§ 3, xxv. § 4, xxvi. § 1, xxix. § 2,
xxx. § 1, xxxii. § 5, xxxiii. § 6,
xxxiv. § 6, xxxv. § 3, xxxvi. § 2–
xxxix. § 1, X. iv. § 1, xxix. § 5,
xxxv. § 1

Oreithyia, I. xix. § 5, xxxviii. § 2, v.
xix. § 1

Orestes, I. xxii. § 6, xxviii. § 5, xxxiii.
§ 8, xli. § 2, II. xvi. § 7, xviii. § 5, 6,
xxix. § 9, xxxi. § 4, 8, 9, III. i. § 5, 6,
ii. § 1, iii. § 6, 7, xi. § 10, xvi. § 7,
xix. § 9, xxii. § 1, V. iv. § 3, VII. i.
§ 7, vi. § 2, xxv. § 7, VIII. iii. § 2, v.
§ 1, 4, xxxiv. § 1–4, liv. § 4, IX. xvi.
§ 4, bites off finger VIII. xxxiv. § 2,
bones III. iii. § 6, xi. § 10, VIII. liv.
§ 4, statue II. xvii. § 3

—— Roman, VII. xiv. § 1–3, xvi. § 1

Oresthasium, VI. x. § 9, VIII. iii. § 1, 2,
xxvii. § 3, xxxix. § 4, xli. § 1, xliv. § 2

Oreus in Euboea, VII. xxvi. § 4

Orgies, IV. i. § 5, ii. § 6, xiv. § 1, xv.
§ 7, VIII. vi. § 5, xxvi. § 2, xxxvii. § 5,
IX. xx. § 4, xxv. § 7, X. iv. § 3, xxxii.
§ 7, xxxiii. § 11. *See also* Mysteries

Orion, IX. xx. § 3

Orneae, II. xii. § 5, xxv. § 5, 6, VIII.
xxvii. § 1, X. xviii. § 5

Ornytion, II. iv. § 3, xxix. § 3, IX.
xvii. § 6, X. i. § 1, iv. § 10

Ornytus, VIII. xxviii. § 4

Orontes, river, VI. ii. § 7, VIII. xx. § 2,
xxix. § 3, 4, xxxiii. § 3, X. xx. § 5

Oropus, I. xxxiii. § 2, xxxiv. § 1–4, VII. xi. § 4–xii. § 3

Orpheus, I. xiv. § 3, II. xxx. § 2, III. xiii. § 2, xiv. § 5, xx. § 5, v. xxvi. § 3, VI. xx. § 18, IX. xvii. § 7, xxvii. § 2, xxx. § 4–12, X. vii. § 2, xxx. § 6–8

Orphica, I. xxxvii. § 4

Orphondas, Theban victor, X. vii. § 7

Orsippus, Megarian victor, I. xliv. § 1

Orthia, in Elis, v. xvi. § 7

Orthopolis, II. v. § 8

Ortilochus, IV. i. § 4, xxx. § 2

Ortygia, v. vii. § 2, 3, VIII. liv. § 3

Orus, II. xxx. § 5

Oryx, VIII. xxv. § 2

Oryxis, Mount, VIII. xiv. **§ 1**

Osiris, X. xxxii. § 18

Osogoa, VIII. ix. § 4

Ostracina, VIII. xii. § 2, **3**

Ostriches, IX. xxxi. § 1

Othryadas, II. xx. § 7

Otilius, VII. vii. § 8, 9, X. xxxvi. § 6

Otus, IX. xxix. § 1

Outrage, stone of, I. xviii. § 5

Oxen, I. xiv. § 4, xxiv. § 4, xxviii. § 10, IV. xxxi. § 9, v. xxvii. § 9, 10, VII. xx. § 3, IX. xii. § 1, X. xv. § 1, xvi. § 6, xxxii. § 16, used for barter III. xii. § 3. *See also* Bull, Cow

Oxylus, v. iii. § 6–iv. § 4, viii. § 5, ix. § 4, xvi. § 1, xviii. § 6, VI. xxiii. § 8, 9, xxiv. § 9

PACTYES, IV. xxxv. § 10

Paeanieus, I. xxiii. § 10

Paeanius, Elean victor, VI. xv. § 10, xvi. § 9

Paedize, II. x. § 1

Paeon, son of Antilochus, II. xviii. § 8
—— son of Endymion, v. i. § 4, 5

Paeonaeus, Dactyl, v. vii. § 6, xiv. § 7

Paeonia, v. i. § 5, IX. xxi. § 2, x. xiii. § 1, xix. § 7, 12

Pagae, I. xli. § 8, xliv. § 4, IX. xix. § 2

Pagondas, Theban victor, v. viii. § 7

Pagus, mountain, III. v. § 2

Paideros, plant, II. x. § 5

Palaea, III. xxii. § 6

Palaemon, I. xliv. § 8, II. i. § 8, ii. § 1, iii. § 4, VIII. xlviii. § 2

Palamedes, II. xx. § 3, X. xxxi. § 1–3

Palatium, VIII. xliii. § 2

Palestine, I. xiv. § 7, IX. xix. § 8, X. xii. § 9

Paliscius, VIII. xxxvi. § 7

Palladium, I. xxviii. § 8, 9, II. xxiii. § 5

Pallantium, v. i. § 8, VIII. iii. § 1, xi. § 5, xxvii. § 3, 7, xliii. § 1–xliv. § 5

Pallas, Athenian, I. xxii. § 2, xxviii. § 10
—— Arcadian, VIII. iii. § 1, xliv. § 5, 6
—— Titan, VII. xxvi. § 12, VIII. xviii. § 1, 2

Palms, I. xxvi. § 7, VI. xxiii. § 5, VIII. xlviii. § 1–3, IX. xix. § 8, X. xv. § 4, 5

Pamisus, river, IV. iii. § 10, xxxi. § 4, xxxiv. § 1–4

Pammerope, I. xxxviii. § 3

Pamphos, poet, I. xxix. § 2, xxxviii. § 3, xxxix. § 1, VII. xxi. § 9, VIII. xxxv. § 8, xxxvii. § 9, IX. xxvii. § 2, xxix. § 8, xxxi. § 9, xxxv. § 4

Pamphylia, VII. iii. § 7, VIII. xxviii. § 3

Pamphylus, II. xxviii. § 6

Pan, myths, I. xxviii. § 4, VIII. xxxvi. § 8, xxxviii. § 11, xlii. § 3, liv. § 6, X. xxiii. § 7, 10
—— cult, I. xxviii. § 4, xxxii. § 7, xxxiv. § 3, II. xi. § 1, xxiv. § 6, v. xv. § 6, 8, 9, VIII. xxiv. § 4, xxvi. § 2, xxxi. § 3, xxxvi. § 8, xxxvii. § 2, 11, xxxviii. § 5, 11, liii. § 11, liv. § 4, 7, X. xxxii. § 7
—— representations, I. xxxvi. § 2, xliv. § 9, II. x. § 2, xxxix. § 4, xxxi. § 3, xxxvii. § 2

Panacea, I. xxxiv. § 3

Panathenaea, I. xxix. § 1, VIII. ii. § 1

Pancratium, at Olympia v. viii. § 8, 11, victors in both pancratium and wrestling v. xxi. § 9–11

Pandareos, X. xxx. § 1–3

Pandion, I. v. § 2–4, xix. § 3, xxxix. § 4, 6, xli. § 6–8, IV. i. § 6–8, ii. § 6, xx. § 4, IX. xxxiii. § 1, X. x. § 1, xii. § 11

Pandora, I. xxiv. § 7

Pandrosus, I. ii. § 6, xviii. § 2, xxvii. § 2, IX. xxxv. § 2

Panhellenius, Mount, II. xxx. § 4

Panopeus, IX. xl. § 12, X. iii. § 1, iv. § 1–7, xxxiii. § 1, xxxv. § 8

Panormus, in Achaia, VII. xxii. § 10
—— in Ionia, v. vii. § 5
—— Messenian, IV. xxvii. § 1, 2

GENERAL INDEX

Pantaleon, VI. xxi. § 1, xxii. § 2–4

Pantarces, Elean victor, V. xi. § 3, VI. x. § 6, xv. § 2

Panyasis, IX. xi. § 2, X. viii. § 9, xxix. § 9

Paphos, I. xiv. § 7, VIII. v. § 2, xxiv. § 6, liii. § 7

Paraballon, Elean victor, VI. vi. § 3

Paraebasium, VIII. xxviii. § 7

Parapotamii, X. iii. § 1, xxxiii. § 7, 8

Paris, III. xxii. § 1, V. xix. § 5, X. xxxi. § 8. *See also* Alexander, son of Priam

Parium, IX. xxvii. § 1

Parnassus, I. iv. § 4, II. xxix. § 2, 3, IV. xxiii. § 3, xxxiv. § 9–11, V. i. § 2, VII. iii. § 10, VIII. iv. § 6, X. iv. § 3, 10, vi. § 1, 2, viii. § 9, xix. § 7, xxiii. § 4, 5, xxiv. § 7, xxxii. § 1–xxxiii. § 5, xxxvi. § 3

Parnes, Mount, I. xxxii. § 1, 2

Parnon, Mount, II. xxxviii. § 7

Paroria, VIII. xxvii. § 3, xxxv. § 6, 7

Paros, I. xxxii. § 4, II. xxvii. § 2, III. xviii. § 8, V. xx. § 2, VIII. xlv. § 5, xlvii. § 1, IX. xxii. § 6, xxxv. § 7, X. xxviii. § 3

Parrhasia, VI. viii. § 2, VIII. xxvii. § 2, 4, xxxviii. § 3

Parrots, II. xxviii. § 1

Parthenias, river, VI. xxi. § 7

Parthenius, Mount, I. xxviii. § 4, VIII. vi. § 4, xlviii. § 7, liv. § 6, 7

Parthenon, I. i. § 2, xxiv. § 5, VIII. xli. § 9

Parthenopaeus, son of Melanion, III. xii. § 9

—— son of Talaus, II. xx. § 5, IX. xviii. § 6, xix. § 2

Paseas, tyrant of Sicyon, II. viii. § 2, 3

Pasiphae, III. xxvi. § 1, V. xxv. § 9

Pasithea, IX. xxxv. § 4

Pataecus, Achaean victor, V. ix. § 1

Patrae, II. ix. § 2, III. ii. § 1, IV. xxxi. § 7, VI. iv. § 6, xxv. § 6, VII. vi. § 2–5, xvii. § 5, xviii. § 2–xxii. § 1, 6, 10, 11, xxiii. § 2, IX. xli. § 1, X. xxii. § 6, xxxviii. § 9

Patroclus, III. xix. § 13, xxiv. § 10, IV. xxviii. § 7, V. viii. § 3, xi. § 8, X. iv. § 2, xiii. § 5, xxvi. § 6, xxx. § 3, 6

—— Macedonian, I. i. § 1, xxxv. § 1, III. vi. § 4, 5

Paus, VIII. xxiii. § 9

Pausanias, son of Cleombrotus, I. xiii. § 4, III. iv. § 9, 10, xiv. § 1, xvii. § 7–xviii. § 1, VIII. lii. § 2

—— son of Pleistoanax, I. xiii. § 4, II. ix. § 1, III. v. § 1–7, ix. § 11, VIII. viii. § 7

—— the author, life I. xiv. § 4, xxxviii. § 7, V. i. § 2, xii. § 3, xiii. § 7, VII. xx. § 6, VIII. ix. § 7, IX. xxi. § 1, X. xxxiv. § 5, work I. xxvi. § 4, xxxix. § 3, III. xi. § 1, views of myths II. xvii. § 4, III. xxv. § 5, VIII. viii. § 3

Peace, I. viii. § 2, xviii. § 3, VI. ix. § 3, IX. xvi. § 2

Peacock, II. xvii. § 6

Pear-tree, II. xvii. § 5, IV. xvi. § 5

Pedestals without statues, VIII. xxx. § 5, xxxviii. § 5, xlix. § 1

Pediments, I. xxiv. § 5, II. xi. § 8, v. x. § 6–8, VII. xxvi. § 6, VIII. xlv. § 6, IX. xi. § 6, X. xix. § 4

Pegae, VIII. xliv. § 4, liv. § 3

Pegasus, II. i. § 9, iii. § 5, iv. § 1, xxxi. § 9, IX. xxxi. § 3

—— of Eleutherae, I. ii. § 5

Peiraeus, I. i. § 2, 3, ii. § 2, xxv. § 5, 8, xxvi. § 3, xxviii. § 11, xxix. § 10, 16, II. viii. § 6, III. v. § 1

Peirasus, II. xvi. § 1, xvii. § 5

Peirene, II. ii. § 3, iii. § 2, 3, v. § 1, xxiv. § 7

Peirithous, I. ii. § 1, xvii. § 4, xviii. § 4, xxx. § 4, xli. § 5, II. xxii. § 6, III. xviii. § 15, xxiv. § 11, V. x. § 8, xi. § 5, VIII. xlv. § 7, IX. xxxi. § 5, X. xxvi. § 2, xxviii. § 2, xxix. § 9, 10

Peirus, river, VII. xviii. § 1, 2

Peisander of Cameirus, poet, II. xxxvii. § 4, VIII. xxii. § 4

Peisistratus, tyrant, I. iii. § 3, xiv. § 1, xxiii. § 1, xxix. § 15, III. iv. § 2, VII. xxvi. § 13, IX. vi. § 2

Peisodorus, Rhodian victor, V. vi. § 8, VI. vii. § 2–4

Pelagon, VI. xxi. § 11, IX. xii. § 1

Pelagus, oak-wood, VIII. xi. § 1, 5, 10

Pelanoi, VIII. ii. § 3

Pelarge, IX. xxv. § 7, 8

Pelasgia, VIII. i. § 6, iv. § 1

Pelasgians, I. xxviii. § 3, III. xx. § 5, IV. xxxvi. § 1, VII. ii. § 2

GENERAL INDEX

Pelasgus, Arcadian, II. xiv. § 4,
VIII. i. § 4–ii. § 1, xxii. § 2
—— son of Triopas, I. xiv. § 2,
II. xxii. § 1, xxiv. § 1
Peleae, X. xii. § 10
Peleus, I. xxxvii. § 3, II. xxix. § 2,
4, 9, III. xviii. § 12, v. xvii. § 10,
xviii. § 5, VIII. xlv. § 6, X. xxx. § 4
Pelias, II. iii. § 9, IV. ii. § 5, v. viii.
§ 2, xvii. § 9, 11, VIII. xi. § 1–3,
X. xxx. § 8
Pelium, Mount, VII. vii. § 6, X. xix.
§ 2
Pellana, III. i. § 4, xxi. § 2, 3, xxvi.
§ 2, VI. viii. § 5
Pellene, II. vii. § 4, viii. § 5, xii. § 2,
VI. viii. § 1, xiii. § 11, VII. vi. § 1,
vii. § 1, 3, xvii. § 14, xxvi. § 12–
xxvii. § 12, VIII. xv. § 5, 8, xvii.
§ 5, xviii. § 14, IX. xv. § 4, X. xi.
§ 6
Pelopidas, IX. xiii. § 1, xv. § 1, 2
Pelopium, v. xiii. § 1, 2, 8, xiv. § 10,
xxiv. § 5, xxvii. § 1
Peloponnesus, geography, II. xiii.
§ 7, III. xxi. § 6, v. i. § 1, ii. § 5,
VIII. i. § 1–3, xxxviii. § 7
Pelops, son of Agamemnon, II. xvi.
§ 6
—— Lydian, I. xli. § 5, II. v. § 7, vi.
§ 5, xiv. § 4, xv. § 1, xviii. § 2,
xxii. § 3, xxvi. § 2, xxx. § 8, xxxiii.
§ 1, v. i. § 6, 7, viii. § 2, x. § 6–8,
xiii. § 1–7, xiv. § 10, xxiv. § 4, xxvii.
§ 7, xxiv. § 7, xxv. § 10, xxvii.
§ 1, VI. xix. § 6, xx. § 7, 17–19,
xxi. § 6, 9, 11, xxii. § 1, 8, VIII.
xiv. § 2, 11, 12, IX. xl. § 11, X.
xviii. § 2
Pencalas, river, VIII. iv. § 3, X. xxxii.
§ 3
Peneius, river in Thessaly, I. xxvii.
§ 6, II. xvi. § 2, xxiv. § 1, VI. v. § 5,
IX. xxxiv. § 6
—— in Elis, VI. xxii. § 5
Peneleos, VII. ii. § 3, 10, IX. v. § 15, 16
Penelope, III. xii. § 1, 3, xiii. § 6,
xx. § 10, 11, VIII. xii. § 5, 6, IX.
xli. § 5, X. xxx. § 1
Pentathlum, I. xxxv. § 5, II. xxix. § 9,
III. xi. § 6, v. vii. § 10, viii. § 7, ix.
§ 1, 3, xvii. § 10
Pentathlus, X. xi. § 3
Pentelicus, Mount, I. xxxii. § 1, 2
Penthesilea, v. xi. § 6, X. xxxi. § 8, 9

Pentheus, I. xx. § 3, II. ii. § 7, IX. ii.
§ 4, v. § 4
Penthilus, II. xviii. § 6, 8, III. ii. § 1,
v. iv. § 3, VII. vi. § 2
Pephnus, III. xxvi. § 2–4
Peraethenses, VIII. iii. § 4, xxvii.
§ 3, xxxvi. § 7
Perdiccas, I. vi. § 3
Pergamus, son of Neoptolemus, I. xi.
§ 1, 2, III. xx. § 8
—— city, I. iv. § 5, 6, x. § 4, II. xi.
§ 2, 7, xxvi. § 8, 9, III. xxvi. § 10,
v. xiii. § 3, 8, VI. xxiv. § 8, VII. ii.
§ 11, viii. § 9, xvi. § 1, 8, VIII. iv.
§ 9, xlii. § 7, IX. xxxv. § 6, X. xv.
§ 3, xviii. § 6, xxv. § 10
Periander, I. xxiii. § 1, II. xxviii. § 8,
X. xxiv. § 1
Periboea, I. xvii. § 3, xlii. § 2, 4
Pericles, I. xxv. § 1, xxviii. § 2, xxix.
§ 3, 16, VIII. xli. § 9
Periclymenus, II. xviii. § 8, IX. xviii.
§ 6
Periclytus, Tenedian, x. xiv. § 1
Perieres, II. xxi. § 7, III. i. § 4, xi. § 11,
xxvi. § 4, IV. ii. § 2, 4, iii. § 7, v.
xvii. § 9, VI. xxii. § 2
Perilaus, Argive victor, II. xx. § 7
—— accuser of Orestes, VIII. xxxiv.
§ 4
—— tyrant of Argos, II. xxiii. § 7
Perinthus, I. xxix. § 10
Periphetes, son of Hephaestus, II. i.
§ 4
—— son of Nyctimus, VIII. xxiv. § 1
Persaeus, II. viii. § 4, VII. viii. § 3
Persea, fountain, II. xvi. § 6
Persephone, V. xx. § 3, VIII. xxxi.
§ 2, xxxvii. § 9, xlii. § 2, IX. xxiii.
§ 3, 4, X. xxx. § 6. See also Maid
Perseus, II. xv. § 3, 4, xvi. § 2, 3,
xx. § 4, xxi. § 5–7, xxii. § 1, xxiii.
§ 7, III. i. § 4, ii. § 2, xx. § 6, IV.
ii. § 4, xxix. § 1, xxxv. § 9, cult
xviii. § 1, representations I.
xxii. § 7, xxiii. § 7, II. xxvii. § 2,
III. xvii. § 3, xviii. § 11, v. xviii.
§ 5, x. x. § 5
—— Macedonian king, I. xxxvi. § 6,
II. ix. § 5, VII. x. § 5–10, xiii. § 1,
VIII. viii. § 11
Persian Colonnade, III. xi. § 3
Persians, II. xxix. § 5, xxxi. § 5, III.
ix. § 6, xi. § 7, xiv. § 1, xx. § 4,
v. iv. § 7, VII. vi. § 6, VIII. l. § 1.

247

GENERAL INDEX

X. ii. § 1, **xiv**. § 5, xix. § 4, figures
I. xviii. § 8, III. xi. § 3, law IX. xxxii.
§ 10

Persians, ode by Timotheus, VIII. l. § 3

Persuasion, I. xxii. § 3, xliii. § 6,
II. vii. § 7, 8, viii. § 1, V. xi. § 8,
IX. xxxv. § 5

Pessinus, I. iv. § 5, VII. xvii. § 10, 11

Petra, place near Elis, VI. xxiv. § 5

—— spring, IX. xxxiv. § 4

Petrachus, IX. xli. § 6

Petroma, VIII. xv. § 1, 2

Petrosaca, VIII. xii. § 4

Phaeacians, III. xviii. § 11, VIII. xxix.
§ 2, X. xxix. § 10

Phaedimus, Aeolian victor, V. viii. § 11

Phaedra, I. xviii. § 5, xxii. § 1, 2,
II. xxxii. § 3, 4, IX. xvi. § 4, X.
xxix. § 3, 5

Phaedrias, VIII. xxxv. § 1

Phaenna, III. xviii. § 6, IX. xxxv.
§ 1

Phaennis, X. xii. § 10, xv. § 2

Phaestus, son of Heracles, II. vi.
§ 6, 7, x. § 1

Phaethon, I. iii. § 1, iv. § 1, II. iii. § 2

Phalaecus, X. ii. § 7

Phalaesiae, VIII. xxxv. § 3

Phalanthus, in Arcadia, VIII. xxxv. § 9

—— founder of Tarentum, X. x. § 6–8,
xiii. § 10

Phalces, son of Temenus, II. vi. § 7,
xi. § 2, xiii. § 1, xxviii. § 3, 5

Phalerum, I. i. § 2–5, xxviii. § 9,
xxxvi. § 4, VIII. x. § 4, X. xxxv.
§ 2

Phalysius, X. xxxviii. § 13

Phanas, Messenian victor, IV. xvii.
§ 9

Pharae, in Achaia, VII. vi. § 1, xxii.
§ 1–6

—— in Messenia, IV. iii. § 2, 10, xvi.
§ 8, xxx. § 2, 3, xxxi. § 1

Pharos, V. vii. § 4, VI. xxiii. § 6

Phaselis, III. iii. § 8

Phasis, river, IV. xxxiv. § 2

Phayllus, Crotonian victor, X. ix.
§ 2

—— Phocian general, X. ii. § 6, 7

Phegeus, VI. xvii. § 6, VIII. xxiv. § 2,
8, 10, IX. xli. § 2

Pheiditia, VII. i. § 8

Pheidolas, Corinthian victor, VI.
xiii. § 9, 10

Pheidon, tyrant of Argos, VI. xxii. § 2

Phellia, river, III. xx. § 3

Phelloe, VII. xxvi. § 10

Phemonoe, X. v. § 7, vi. § 7, xii. § 10

Pheneus, v. xxvii. § 8, VI. i. § 3,
VIII. xiii. § 5–xvi. § 1, xvii. § 5, 6,
xviii. § 7, xix. § 3, 4, xx. § 1, xxii.
§ 1

Pherae, I. xiii. § 2, II. x. § 7, xxiii. § 5

Pherecydes, I. xx. § 7

Pherenice, V. vi. § 7

Pherenicus, Elean victor, VI. xvi.
§ 1

Pherias, Aeginetan victor, VI. xiv.
§ 1

Phialo, VIII. xii. § 3

Phialus, VIII. iii. § 3, v. § 7, 8, xxxix.
§ 2

Phigalia, III. xvii. § 9, IV. xxiv. § 1,
v. v. § 4, VI. vi. § 1, VIII. iii. § 1, 2,
v. § 7, 8, xxvii. § 11, xxx. § 3, 4,
xxxix. § 1–xlii. § 13

Philaeus, I. xxxv. § 2

Philammon, II. xxxvii. § 2, 3, IV.
xxxiii. § 3, IX. xxxvi. § 2, X. vii.
§ 2

Philander, X. xvi. § 5

Philanorium, II. xxxvi. **§ 3**

Philanthus, V. ii. § 4

Philetaerus, I. viii. § 1, x. **§ 4**

Philetas, victor, of Sybaris, V. viii. § 9

Philinus, Coan victor, VI. xvii. § 2

Philip, son of Amyntas, I. iv. § 1,
ix. § 4, 5, xxv. § 3, xxix. § 10,
xxxiv. § 1, II. xx. § 4, 5, IV. xxix.
§ 1–3, xxxii. § 2, VI. xvi. § 3, VII.
vii. § 4–viii. § 9, ix. § 7, x. § 6, xiii.
§ 1, xvii. § 5, VIII. vii. § 11, l. § 4,
X. xxxiii. § 3, xxxiv. § 3, xxxvi. § 6

—— Azanian victor, VI. viii. § 5

—— portico of, VIII. xxx. § 6

Philippeum, V. xvii. § 4, xx. § 9, 10

Philippides, I. xxviii. § 4, VIII. liv. § 6

Philistus, I. xiii. § 9, xxix. § 12, v.
xxiii. § 6

GENERAL INDEX

Philles, Elean victor, VI. ix. § 4

Philoctetes, I. xxii. § 6, xxiii. § 4, v. xiii. § 4, VIII. viii. § 5, xxxiii. § 4, X. xxviii. § 1

Philogenes, VII. ii. § 4, iii. § 10

Philomela, I. v. § 4, xiv. § 7, xli. § 8, X. iv. § 9

Philomelus, X. ii. § 2–5, viii. § 7, xxxiii. § 2, xxxvii. § 2

Philon, Corcyraean victor, VI. ix. § 9, xiv. § 13

Philonides, VI. xvi. § 5

Philopappus, I. xxv. § 8

Philopoemen, son of Craugis, IV. xxix. § 8, 10, 12, VII. ix. § 4, 6, VIII. xxvii. § 15, 16, xlix. § 1, lii. § 1, 6

—— general of Attalus, VII. xvi. § 1, 8

Philotas, VII. ii. § 3, 10

Philoxenus, poet, I. ii. § 3

Phineus, III. xviii. § 15, v. xvii. § 11

Phintas, descendant of Androcles, IV. xvi. § 2, xvii. § 9

—— son of Sybotas, IV. iv. § 1

Phlegra, IX. xxxvi. § 2

Phlegyans, VIII. iv. § 4, IX. ix. § 2, xxxvi. § 2, 3, X. iv. § 1, vii. § 1, xxxiv. § 2

Phlegyas, II. xxvi. § 3, 4, IX. xxxvi. § 1–4

Phlias, son of Dionysus, II. vi. § 6, vii. § 6, xii. § 6

Phlius, I. xxv. § 4, II. v. § 2, 3, x. § 1, xi. § 3, xii. § 3–xv. § 1, xxv. § 5, 6, v. xxii. § 1–6, xxiii. § 2, VII. iii. § 9, xxvi. § 6, X. vii. § 7, xiii. § 6, xx. § 1

Phlya, I. xxxi. § 4

Phocaea, I. i. § 5, II. xxxi. § 6, IV. xxxiii. § 7, VII. iii. § 8, 10, v. § 4, X. viii. § 6

Phocians, I. xxv. § 4, III. v. § 3, ix. § 9, 10, x. § 3, 4, IV. v. § 4, xxviii. § 1, v. xxv. § 6, VI. vi. § 2, VII. ii. § 4, iii. § 10, VIII. iv. § 4, xxvii. § 9, IX. vi. § 4, X. i. § 3–iii. § 4, iv. § 1, v. § 1, vii. § 1, viii. § 2, xiii. § 4, 6, 7, xv. § 1, 7, xx. § 1, 3, xxiii. § 3, 5, 9, xxxiii. § 1

Phocicum, X. v. § 1

Phocis, X. boundaries II. xxix. § 3, X. i. § 2, xiii. § 4, xxxvii. § 2, xxxviii. § 1

Phocus, son of Aeacus, II. xxix. § 2–10, X. i. § 1, 10, xxx. § 4, xxxii. § 10, xxxiii. § 12

—— son of Ornytian, II. iv. § 3,

xxix. § 3, IX. xvii. § 5, 6, X. i. § 1, iv. § 10, xxxii. § 11

Phoebaeum, III. iv. § 9, 10, xx. § 2

Phoebe, II. xxii. § 5, III. xvi. § 1, IV. xxxi. § 9, 12

Phoebia, IX. xv. § 4

Phoenicians, I. vi. § 4, 5, xii. § 5, xiv. § 7, III. xxi. § 6, v. xii. § 4, xxv. § 5, 6, 12, VI. xix. § 7, VII. v. § 5, xxiii. § 7, 8, IX. v. § 1, xii. § 2, xix. § 8, xxviii. § 2, X. xi. § 3, xxxii. § 18

Phoenicus, harbour, IV. xxxiv. § 12

Phoenix, poet, I. ix. § 7

—— river, VII. xxiii. § 5

Phoezon, VIII. xi. § 4

Pholoe, mountain, VI. xxi. § 5, VIII. xxiv. § 4, xxvii. § 17

Pholus, III. xviii. § 10

Phormio, Athenian admiral, I. xxiii. § 10, xxix. § 3, X. xi. § 6

—— Erythraean, VII. v. § 7

—— Spartan, III. xvi. § 2, 3

—— victor, of Halicarnassus, v. xxi. § 3

Phormis, v. xxvii. § 1–8

Phoroneus, I. xxxix. § 5, 6, II. xv. § 5, xix. § 5, xx. § 3, xxi. § 1

Phrasycleides, archon, VI. v. § 3, VIII. xxvii. § 8

Phreattys, law-court, I. xxviii. § 11

Phrixa, city, VI. xxi. § 6

—— nymph, VIII. xlvii. § 3

Phrixus, son of Athamas, I. xxiv. § 2, xliv. § 7, IX. xxxiv. § 5–8, xxxvii. § 1

—— river, II. xxxvi. § 6, xxxviii. § 1

Phrontis, pilot, X. xxv. § 2

Phruria, III. xii. § 8

Phrygia, I. iv. § 5, xiv. § 2, xxix. § 10, II. v. § 3, v. xxv. § 6, VIII. xxiv. § 11, X. xxvii. § 1, xxxi. § 7, xxxii. § 3, 4, xxxvi. § 1, music XV. xvii. § 9, IX. xii. § 5

Phryne, I. xx. § 1, 2, IX. xxvii. § 3, 5, X. xv. § 1

Phrynichus, X. xxxi. § 4

Phthia, VI. xi. § 5

Phthiotis, VII, i. § 6, X. viii. § 2, 3, xx. § 6

Phylace, VIII. liv. § 1, 2

Phylacides, X. xvi. § 5

Phylactris, hill, VIII. xlviii. § 4

Phylacus, X. viii. § 7, xxiii. § 2

Phylas, king of Dryopians, I. v. § 2, IV. xxxiv. § 9, X. x. § 1

249

GENERAL INDEX

Phylas, son of Antiochus, II. iv. § 3, III. xiii. § 4, IX. xl. § 5, 6

Phyleus, Athenian, X. x. § 1

—— Messenian, IV. xiii. § 5, 6

—— son of Augeas, V. i. § 10, iii. § 1, 3

Phylodamia, IV. xxx. § 2, VII. xxii. § 5

Physcoa, V. xvi. § 6, 7

Phytalus, I. xxxvii. § 2, 4

Pielus, I. xi. § 1, 2

Piera, fountain, V. xvi. § 8

Pieria, mountain, IX. xxix. § 3, xxx. § 7, X. xiii. § 7

Pierus, IX. xxix. § 3, 4, xxx. § 4

Pigs, II. xi. § 7, V. xvi. § 8, VI. ii. § 5, VII. xvii. § 10, VIII. i. § 5, IX. viii. § 1

Pillars, I. xviii. § 9, II. xi. § 2, xvii. § 3, III. xix. § 2, xx. § 9, V. xxvi. § 1, VIII. xxvi. § 2, xxx. § 4, xxxviii. § 7, xliv. § 2, xlv. § 5, V. v. § 2, wooden V. xvi. § 1, xx. § 6, VI. xxiv. § 9

Pindar, I. ii. § 1, xli. § 5, II. xxvi. § 8, xxx. § 3, III. xxv. § 2, IV. ii. § 7, xxx. § 6, V. x. § 1, xiv. § 6, xxii. § 6, VI. ii. § 5, VII. ii. § 7, xxvi. § 8, IX. xvi. § 1, xvii. § 2, xxii. § 3, 6, 7, xxiii. § 2–4, xxx. § 2, X. v. § 12, xvi. § 3, xxii. § 9, chair X. xxiv. § 5, house IX. xxv. § 3, statue I. viii. § 4, tomb IX. xxiii. § 2–4

Pine-trees, II. i. § 3, 7, x. § 3, V. vi. § 4, VIII. xlviii. § 2, X. xxxviii. § 9

Pioniae, IX. xviii. § 4

Pipe, VIII. xxxviii. § 11. *See also* Flute

Pisa, V. i. § 6, 7, iii. § 1, iv. § 7, vi. § 4, viii. § 6, x. § 2, xiii. § 4, xvi. § 5, 6, VI. iv. § 2, xxi. § 1–xxii. § 4, 6, VIII. xx. § 2, liv. § 3

Pitane, III. xiv. § 2, xvi. § 9

Pitch, I. xv. § 4, IV. xxxv. § 8

Pittacus, I. xxiii. § 1, X. xxiv. § 1

Pittheus, I. xxii. § 2, xxvii. § 7, xxxvii. § 4, II. xxx. § 8—xxxi. § 9, V. xix. § 3

Pits, sacrificial, II. xii. § 1, xxii. § 3, V. xiii. § 2

Pityussa, island, II. xxxiv. § 8

Plagues, I. iii. § 4, xliv. § 7, II. vii. § 7, xxxii. § 6, III. ix. § 2, IV. ix. § 1, V. iv. § 6, xiii. § 6, VII. vii.

§ 1, x. § 3, xvii. § 2, VIII. xli. § 2, 8, IX. v. § 1, 9, viii. § 2, xxii. § 1, xxxvi. § 3, xxxviii. § 3, X. xi. § 5

Plane-trees, II. xxxvii. § 1, 4, III. xi. § 2, xiv. § 8, IV. xxxiv. § 4, V. xxvii. § 11, VI. xxiii. § 1, VII. v. § 2, xxii. § 1, VIII. xix. § 2, xxiii. § 4, IX. xix. § 7

Plataea, I. xxxviii. § 8, II. vi. § 1, IX. i. § 1–iv. § 3, history I. xv. § 3, xxix. § 12, xxxii. § 3, III. vii. § 10, ix. § 3, IV. xxvii. § 9, 10, IX. i. § 2–8, dedication at Delphi X. xv. § 1

—— battle of I. xxvii. § 1, III. iv. § 10, xi. § 7, VI. iii. § 8, x. § 6, xiv. § 13, VII. vi. § 4, VIII. vi. § 1, IX. i. § 3, ii. § 6, vi. § 1, X. ii. § 1, xv. § 1, monuments of V. xxiii. § 1, X. xiii. § 9

Plastene, V. xiii. § 7

Platanistas, grove at Sparta, III. xi. § 2, xiv. § 8, 10, xv. § 1, xx. § 8

Plataniston, river, IV. xxxiv. § 4, VIII. xxxix. § 1

Platanistus, cape, III. xxiii. § 1

Plato, I. xxx. § 3, IV. xxxii. § 4, VII. xvii. § 3, X. xxiv. § 1

Pleiades, VIII. iii. § 7

Pleistaenus, Thespian victor, VI. xvi. § 1

Pleistoanax, I. xiii. § 4, III. v. § 1

Pleistus, river, X. viii. § 8, xxxvii. § 7

Plemnaeus, II. v. § 8, xi. § 2

Pleuron, III. xiii. § 8

Plutarch, Euboean, I. xxxvi. § 4

Pluto, mother of Tantalus, II. xxii. § 3

—— god of underworld, I. xxviii. § 6, xxxviii. § 5, II. xviii. § 3, xxxv. § 10, xxxvi. § 7, III. xix. § 4, V. xx. § 3

Plutus, I. viii. § 2, IX. xvi. § 2, xxvi. § 8

Podaleirius, III. xxvi. § 10, IV. iii. § 2, xxxi. § 10, 12

Podares, VIII. ix. § 9, 10, x. § 5

Poemander, IX. xx. § 1

Polemocrates, II. xxxviii. § 6

Polichne, IV. xxxiii. § 6

Polites, Carian victor, VI. xiii. § 3, 4

Polus, Arcadian, VIII. xxxi. § 7, xxxv. § 10

—— in Boeotia, IX. xx. § 3

Polybius, VIII. ix. § 1, 2, xxx. § 8, 9, xxxvii. § 2, xliv. § 5, xlviii. § 8

250

GENERAL INDEX

Polyboea, III. xix. § 4
Polybotes, I. ii. § 4
Polybus, II. vi. § 6
Polycaon, son of Butas, IV. ii. § 1, 2
—— son of Lelex, III. i. § 1, IV. i. § 1–ii. § 1, iii. § 9
Polychares, Messenian victor, IV. iv. § 5–v. § 2, 6
Polycles, Cyrenaean victor, X. iii. § 1
—— victor, surnamed Polychalcus, VI. i. § 7
Polycrates, rhetorician, VI. xvii. § 9
—— tyrant, I. ii. § 3, VIII. xiv. § 8
Polyctor, Elean wrestler, V. xxi. § 16, VI. xxiii. § 4
Polydectes, king of Sparta, II. xxxvi. § 4, III. vii. § 2, 3, IV. iv. § 4
Polydeuces, III. xii. § 8, xiv. § 7, xviii. § 14, xx. § 1, xxiv. § 7, IV. iii. § 1, V. xvii. § 9, VIII. ii. § 4, xlv. § 6. See also Dioscuri
Polydeucia, fountain, III. xx. § 1
Polydorus, king of Sparta, III. iii. § 1–4, xi. § 10, xii. § 3, IV. vii. § 7, 8, viii. § 10, xv. § 3, VIII. lii. § 1
—— son of Cadmus, II. vi. § 2, IX. v. § 3, 4, xii. § 4
Polyeidus, I. xliii. § 5
Polyneices, Elean victor, V. viii. § 9
—— son of Oedipus, II. xix. § 8, xxv. § 1, xxxvi. § 8, IV. iii. § 4, viii. § 8, V. xix. § 6, VII. iii. § 1, IX. v. § 12–14, viii. § 7, ix. § 5, 4, xxv. § 1, 12, xxxiii. § 1, statues I. xx. § 5, X. x. § 3
Polypeithes, Laconian victor, VI. xvi. § 6
Polyphemus, X. xxix. § 10
Polysperchon, V. vi. § 1
Polyxena, I. xxii. § 6, X. xxv. § 10
Polyxenus, son of Jason, II. iii. § 8
Polyxo, III. xix. § 9
Pomegranate, II. xvii. § 4, V. xix. § 6, VI. ix. § 1, xiv. § 6, VIII. xxxvii. § 7, IX. xxv. § 1
Pompus, king of Arcadia, VIII. v. § 8
Pontinus, river, II. xxxvi. § 8–xxxvii. § 2
Poplar, black V. xiv. § 3, X. xxx. § 6, white II. x. § 6, V. v. § 5, xiii. § 3, xiv. § 2
Porinas, VIII. xv. § 8
Porticoes, I. i. § 3, ii. § 4, 5, iii. § 1, 3,

xiv. § 6, xv. § 1–xvi. § 1, II. ix. § 6, xxvii. § 6, xxxi. § 7, xxxv. § 10, III. xi. § 3, xiii. § 6, xv. § 1, xvii. § 4, V. xi. § 6, xv. § 6, xxi. § 17, VI. xx. § 10, 13, xxi. § 2, xxiv. § 2–5, 10, xxv. § 1–4, VII. xx. § 9, xxiii. § 5, VIII. xxx. § 6–10, xxxi. § 1, 9, IX. xxii. § 2, X. xi. § 6, xxi. § 6, xxxiv. § 7, xxxv. § 6
Poseidon, myths I. xxiv. § 5, xxvi. § 5, xxvii. § 6, xxxvii. § 2, II. i. § 6, iv. § 6, xv. § 5, xx. § 6, xxii. § 4, xxxiii. § 1, IV. xxiv. § 6, V. xxii. § 6, VI. xxv. § 3, VII. iv. § 8, xx. § 4, xxiv. § 6, xxv. § 8, VIII. viii. § 2, x. § 8, xxv. § 5–8, xlii. § 1, 2, IX. xxxi. § 6, X. v. § 6, xxix. § 5, children I. v. § 2, xiv. § 3, 6, xvii. § 3, xxi. § 4, xxxviii. § 2, xxxix. § 3, 5, xliv. § 3, II. i. § 3, iv. § 3, v. § 7, xii. § 4, xxx. § 5, 8, IV. ii. § 5, v. i. § 8, xvii. § 9, VII. iv. § 1, VIII. xxxvii. § 9, IX. xx. § 1, xxii. § 5, xxvi. § 5, xxix. § 1, 6, xxxvi. § 4, xxxviii. § 9, xxxix. § 1, X. vi. § 1, x. § 8, xii. § 1, xiv. § 1
—— cult, I. xxvi. § 5, xxx. § 4, xxxviii. § 6
  II. i. § 7, ii. § 1, 3, ix. § 6, xii. § 2, xxii. § 4, xxxii. § 8, xxxiii. § 2, xxxiv. § 10, 11, xxxvi. § 3, xxxviii. § 1–4
  III. xi. § 9, xii. § 5, xiv. § 2, 7, xv. § 7, 10, xx. § 2, xxi. § 5, xxv. § 4
  IV. xxxi. § 6
  V. xxiv. § 4, xv. § 5, xxiv. § 1
  VI. xx. § 18
  VII. xxi. § 7–10, xxiv. § 2–12, xxv. § 3, 12, xxvii. § 8
  VIII. v. § 5, vii. § 2, x. § 2–xi. § 1, xiii. § 2, xxiii. § 3, xxx. § 1, xxxv. § 6, xxxvi. § 2, xxxvii. § 10, xliv. § 4
  IX. xxvi. § 5, xxxvii. § 1
  X. v. § 6, ix. § 4, xi. § 6, xxiv. § 4, xxxvi. § 8, xxxviii. § 8, 12
—— representations, I. ii. § 4, xxiv. § 3, 5, II. i. § 7, ii. § 1, 8, iii. § 4, xxxv. § 1, xxxvi. § 3, III. xvii. § 3, xviii. § 10, xix. § 3, xxi. § 8, xxiii. § 5, 8, xxiii. § 2, xxv. § 4, v. xi. § 8, xxvi. § 2, VI. xxv. § 6, VII. xxi. § 7–10, xxiii. § 10, VIII. xiv. § 5, xxxi. § 7, xxxv. § 6, IX. xxvi. § 5, X. ix. § 7, xxxvi. § 8, xxxviii. § 12

GENERAL INDEX

Poseidon, titles, Asphalius, III. xi. § 9, VII. xxi. § 7
    Earth-embracer, III. xx. § 2, xxi. § 8
        Father, I. xxxviii. § 6
        Genesius, II. xxxviii. § 4
        Heliconian, VII. xxiv. § 5, 6
        Hippocurius, III. xiv. § 2
        Horse-god, I. xxx. § 4, v. xv. § 5, VI. xx. § 18, VII. xxi. § 7–9, VIII. x. § 2–5, xiv. § 5, xxv. § 7, xxxvi. § 2, xxxvii. § 10
        of House, III. xiv. § 7
        Isthmian, II. ix. § 6
        of Kin, II. xv. § 10
        King, II. xxx. § 6
        Laoetas, v. xiv. § 4, xxiv. § 1
        Onchestian, IX. xxvi. § 5, xxxvii. § 1
        Overseer, VIII. xxx. § 1
        Pelagaeus, VII. xxi. § 7
        Phytalmius, II. xxxii. § 8
        Prosclystius, II. xxii. § 4
        of Taenarum, III. xii. § 5
Poseidonias, II. xxx. § 8
Potami, I. xxxi. § 3, VII. i. § 5
Potidaea, v. xxiii. § 2, 3, X. xi. § 5
Potniae, IX. viii. § 1–3
Prasiae, I. xxxi. § 2
Pratinas, poet, II. xiii. § 6
Praxidamas, Aeginetan victor, VI. xviii. § 7
Praxidicae, III. xxii. § 2, IX. xxiii. § 3
Praxilla, poetess, III. xiii. § 5
Presbon, IX. xxxiv. § 8, xxxvii. § 1
Preugenes, III. ii. § 1, VII. vi. § 2, xviii. § 5, xx. § 7–9
Priam, I. xxix. § 5, II. xxiii. § 5, 6, xxiv. § 3, xxv. § 6, III. ix. § 4, xix. § 6, xxvi. § 5, IV. xvii. § 4, v. iii. § 6, xix. § 5, VII. xxiv. § 2, IX. xviii. § 5, X. xxv. § 5, 9, xxvi. § 1, 9, xxvii. § 2
Priapus, IX. xxxi. § 2
Priene, IV. vi. § 1, 3, VII. ii. § 9, 10, v. § 5, VIII. xxiv. § 11, X. xxiv. § 1
Priests, boys VII. xxiv. § 4, VIII. xlvii. § 3, X. xxxiv. § 8, annual VIII. xiii. § 1, IX. xl. § 12, for life II. xxxii. § 1, resign if child dies IV. xii. § 6, of Artemis at Aricia II. xxvii. § 4, part in ritual I. xxiv. § 4, xxviii. § 10, II. xxxv. § 5
Priestesses, girls II. xxxiii. § 2, VII.

xix. § 1, xxvi. § 5, bound to chastity VII. xviii. § 12, xxv. § 13, VIII. v. § 11, xiii. § 1, statues of II. xvii. § 3, 7, xxxv. § 8, VII. xxv. § 7, part in ritual I. xxvii. § 3, II. xvii. § 3, 7, xxxv. § 7, III. xvi. § 10, IV. xvii. § 1, VI. xx. § 3, 9, VII. xxv. § 7
Prinus, VIII. vi. § 4
Processions, I. ii. § 4, xxix. § 1, 16, II. vii. § 5, 8, xxxv. § 5, VI. xx. § 7, VII. xviii. § 12, VIII. xxxix. § 5, X. xviii. § 5, xxxii. § 17
Procles, Andrian victor, VI. xiv. § 13
—— Carthaginian author, II. xxi. § 6, IV. xxxv. § 4
—— Spartan, III. i. § 7, 8, vii. § 1
—— tyrant of Epidaurus, II. xxviii. § 8
Procne, I. v. § 4, xxiv. § 3, xli. § 8, 9, X. iv. § 9
Proconnesus, I. xxiv. § 6, v. vii. § 9, VIII. xlvi. § 4
Procris, I. xxxvii. § 6, IX. xix. § 1, X. xxix. § 6
Procrustes, I. xxxviii. § 5
Prodicus, poet, IV. xxxiii. § 7
Prodomeis, I. xlii. § 1
Proedria, V. xv. § 4
Proetus, son of Abas, II. iv. § 2, vii. § 8, ix. § 8, xii. § 2, xvi. § 2–5, xxv. § 7, 9, V. v. § 10, VIII. xviii. § 7, 8, X. x. § 3
Promachus, son of Heracles, VIII. xxiv. § 2, 7, IX. xi. § 4
—— Pellenian victor, VI. viii. § 5, 6, VII. xxvii. § 5–7
—— son of Parthenopaeus, II. xx. § 5, IX. xix. § 2, X. x. § 4
Prometheus, son of Iapetus, I. xxx. § 2, II. xiv. § 4, xix. § 5, 8, V. xi. § 6, X. iv. § 4
—— one of Cabeiri, IX. xxv. § 6
Pron, mountain, II. xxxiv. § 11, xxxv. § 4, xxxvi. § 1, 2
Pronomus, IV. xxvii. § 7, IX. xii. § 5, 6
Prorus, Cyrenaean victor, X. ii. § 3
Prospalta, I. xxxi. § 1
Prosymna, II. xvii. § 1
Protesilaus, I. xxxiv. § 2, III. iv. § 6, IV. ii. § 7, xxxvi. § 3, V. xvii. § 10, X. xiv. § 2, xxx. § 3
Proteus, III. xviii. § 16, xix. § 1–4, VIII. liii. § 5
Protolaus, Mantinean victor, VI. vi. § 1

GENERAL INDEX

Protophanes, Magnesian victor, I.
xxxv. § 6, V. xxi. § 10

Prusias, VIII. xi. § 11

Prytaneum, I. v. § 1, xviii. § 3, xx.
§ 1, xxvi. § 3, xxviii. § 10, xlii.
§ 7, xliii. § 2, II. iv. § 4, v. xiii. § 11,
xv. § 12, xx. § 10, IX. xxxii. § 8

Prytanis, boxer, of Cyzicus, V. xxi. § 3

—— son of Eurypon, II. xxxvi. § 4,
III. vii. § 2, IV. iv. § 4

Psamathe, I. xliii. § 7, 8, II. xix. § 8

Psamathus, harbour, III. xxv. § 4

Psila, Doric word for wings, III. xix.
§ 6

Psophis, V. xxiv. § 2, VI. xvi. § 5–7,
VIII. xxiii. § 9–xxv. § 1

Psyttalea, I. xxxvi. § 2, IV. xxxvi. § 6

Ptolemy I, son of Lagus, I. i. § 1, v.
§ 5, vi. § 1–8, viii. § 6, ix. § 1, 6,
x. § 2, xi. § 5, xvi. § 1, VI. iii. § 1,
xv. § 10, xvi. § 3, 9, xvii. § 3, IX. xvi.
§ 1, X. x. § 2

—— II, Philadelphus, I. i. § 1, v. § 5,
vi. § 8–vii. § 3, viii. § 6, xvii. § 2,
xviii. § 4, VI. xvii. § 3, IX. xxxi. § 1,
X. vii. § 8

—— III, Euergetes, II. viii. § 5,
ix. § 3

—— VIII, Philometor, I. viii. § 6,
ix. § 1–3

—— called Thunderbolt, I. xvi. § 2,
X. xix. § 7

Ptous, Mount, IX. xxiii. § 5–7

Pulydamas, victor, of Scotussa,
VI. v. § 1–vii. § 1, VII. xxvii. § 6

Pulytion, I. ii. § 5

Pure Gods, VIII. xliv. § 6

Purification, I. xxii. § 2, xxxiv. § 5,
xxxvii. § 4, xliii. § 5, II. vii. § 7,
xvii. § 1, xx. § 2, xxx. § 3, xxxi. § 4,
8, xxxviii. § 2, III. xv. § 3, V. v. § 10,
xvi. § 8, xxvii. § 10, VII. xxvi. § 7,
VIII. xiii. § 1, xviii. § 7, xli. § 2,
IX. xx. § 4, xxxix. § 5

Purple dye III. xxi. § 6, X. xxxvii. § 3,
robes II. xvii. § 6, V. xii. § 4, VII.
xxii. § 7, X. xxv. § 5

Pygmies, I. xii. § 4

Pylades, son of Strophius, I. xxii.
§ 6, II. xvi. § 7, xxix. § 4, 9, III. i. § 6

—— Megalopolitan musician, VIII.
l. § 3

Pylas, king of Megara, I. v. § 3,
xxxix. § 4, 6, IV. xxxvi. § 1, VI.
xxii. § 5

Pylos, in Elis, IV. xxxvi. § 1, V. iii.
§ 1, xviii. § 6, VI. xxii. § 5, 6, xxv.
§ 2, 3

—— in Messenia, II. xviii. § 7, III.
xxvi. § 8, IV. i. § 3, ii. § 5, iii. § 7,
xviii. § 1, xxiii. § 1, xxxi. § 11,
xxxvi. § 1–7, VII. xxii. § 6, VII. ii.
§ 3, VIII. i. § 1, IX. xxxvii. § 8, xli.
§ 4

Pyraea, grove, II. xi. § 3

Pyraechmes, Aetolian slinger, V. iv.
§ 2

Pyrcon, X. v. § 6

Pyrilampes, Ephesian victor, VI. iii.
§ 13

Pyrrha, daughter of Creon, IX. x. § 3

Pyrrhichus, III. xxi. § 7, xxv. § 1–4

Pyrrhon, VI. xxiv. § 5

Pyrrhus, son of Achilles, I. iv. § 4,
xi. § 1, xiii. § 9, xxxiii. § 8, II. v. § 5,
xxiii. § 6, III. xxv. § 1, xxvi. § 7,
X. vii. § 1, xxiii. § 2, xxvi. § 4. See
also Neoptolemus

—— son of Aeacides, I. vi. § 8,
ix. § 7, 8, x. § 1, 2, xi. § 1–xiii. § 9,
II. xxi. § 4, III. vi. § 3, IV. xxix. § 6,
xxxv. § 3, 4, VI. iii. § 12, xii. § 3,
xiv. § 9, VII. viii. § 5

—— king of Pisa, VI. xxii. § 4

—— shepherd, VII. v. § 11

—— son of Ptolemy, IV. xxxv. § 3

Pythaeus, II. xxiv. § 1, xxxv. § 2

Pythagoras, philosopher, II. xiii.
§ 2, IX. xiii. § 1

Pytharatus, IV. vii. § 4, viii. § 10

Pytharchus, Mantinean victor, VI. vii.
§ 1

Pytheas, Boeotarch, VII. xiv. § 6,
xv. § 10

Pythes, of Abdera, VI. xiv. § 12

Pythian games, II. xxxii. § 2, VI. vii.
§ 4, xiv. § 9, VIII. xviii. § 8, X. vii.
§ 2–8, xxxiii. § 8, xxxvii. § 4

Pythian flute-tune, II. xxii. § 8, V. vii.
§ 10

Pythionice, I. xxxvii. § 5

Pytho, II. xxxiii. § 2, V. iii. § 1,
VI. i. § 7, iii. § 4–11, X. vi. § 5, xviii.
§ 2. See also Delphi

—— dragon, II. vii. § 7, xxx. § 3,
X. vi. § 5

Pythocles, Elean victor, VI. vii. § 10

Pythocritus, Sicyonian musician, VI.
xiv. § 10

Pyttalus, Elean victor, VI. xvi. § 8

GENERAL INDEX

QUARRIES, I. xix. § 6, xxxii. § 1, III. xxi. § 4, V. viii. § 8

Quoits, I. xxxv. § 5, II. xvi. § 2, xxix. § 9, V. iii. § 7, xx. § 1, VI. xiv. § 6, xix. § 4, invented II. xvi. § 2

RAIN, I. xxiv. § 3, xxxii. § 3, II. xix. § 8, xxv. § 10, xxix. § 7, xxx. § 4, xxxiv. § 3, VII. xxiv. § 7, VIII. xxxviii. § 4, IX. xxxix. § 4

Rams, I. xxiv. § 2, II. iii. § 4, xviii. § 1, IV. xxxiii. § 4, V. xxvii. § 8, VIII. xi. § 2, xxxii. § 1, IX. xxii. § 1, X. xvii. § 12, in cult I. xxxiv. § 5, IV. xiii. § 1, V. xiii. § 2, IX. xxii. § 1, xxxiv. § 5, xxxix. § 6, X. xxix. § 1

Red, statues painted, II. ii. § 6, VII. xxvi. § 11, VIII. xxxix. § 6

Rexibius, Opuntian victor, VI. xviii. § 7

Rhacius, VII. iii. § 1, 2, IX. xxxiii. § 2

Rhacos, kind of olive, II. xxxii. § 10

Rhadamanthys, VII. iii. § 7, VIII. liii. § 4, 5

Rhadine, VII. v. § 13

Rhaeteae, VIII. xxviii. § 4

Rhamnus, I. xxxii. § 2, VII. v. § 3

Rharium, plain, I. xxxviii. § 6

Rhea, I. xviii. § 7, V. vii. § 6, VII. viii. § 2, x. § 1, xxxii. § 5, xxxvi. § 2, 3, xli. § 2, xlvii. § 3, IX. ii. § 7, xli. § 6

Rhegium, IV. xxiii. § 6, xxvi. § 2, V. xxv. § 2, xxvi. § 3, 4, § 5, VI. vi. § 4

Rhegnidas, II. xiii. § 1

Rheiti, I. xxxviii. § 1, II. xxiv. § 6

Rhianus, poet, IV. i. § 6, vi. § 1, xv. § 2, xvii. § 11

Rhinocerus, V. xii. § 1, IX. xxi. § 2

Rhipe, VIII. xxv. § 12

Rhium, VII. xxii. § 10, VIII. v. § 6, X. xi. § 6

Rhodes, I. vi. § 6, xxxvi. § 5, II. vii. § 1, IV. xxiv. § 2, 3, VI. vii. § 6, VIII. xliii. § 4, athletes V. xxi. § 8, VI. vii. § 1, colossus I. xviii. § 6, dedication at Delphi X. xviii. § 4, cult of Helen III. xix. § 10, tomb of Rhodian I. xxxvii. § 5, walls IV. xxxi. § 5

Rhodos, place in Laconia, III. xxvi. § 9

Rhopalus, son of Phaestus, II. vi. § 7

Rhus, at Megara, I. xli. § 2

Rhypes, VII. vi. § 1, xviii. § 7, xxiii. § 4

Ribbons, IV. xvi. § 6, V. xi. § 1, VI. i. § 7, ii. § 2, xx. § 19, VIII. xxxi. § 8, IX. xxxix. § 8, X. xxxv. § 10

Rivers, cold VIII. xxviii. § 2, curing skin diseases V. v. § 11, curing love VII. xxiii. § 3, harbouring dangerous creatures IV. xxxiv. § 2, 3, flowing through lakes V. vii. § 3, VIII. liv. § 3, underground II. v. § 3, VIII. xliv. § 4, liv. § 1, IX. xxx. § 8, winding VIII. xli. § 3, bringing down mud VII. ii. § 11, VIII. xxiv. § 8, 11

——cult, I. xxxiv. § 3, xxxvii. § 3, xli. § 2, IV. iii. § 10, VIII. xx. § 3, xxiv. § 12, xli. § 3, IX. xxx. § 8, X. viii. § 10

Rock, stuck with arrows I. xliv. § 4, of Sibyl X. xii. § 1

Romans, history I. ix. § 5, xii. § 1, 2, xiii. § 1, xx. § 4–7, xxix. § 14, xxxvi. § 6, II. i. § 2, III. xxiii. § 5, VI. iii. § 12, xii. § 3, VII. vii. § 7–xvi. § 10, VIII. xxx. § 8, li. § 4, IX. vii. § 4, xl. § 7, X. xxxiv. § 2, 4, xxxv. § 2, colonies II. i. § 2, VII. xviii. § 7, governors v. xv. § 2, VII. xvi. § 10, names VII. vii. § 8, tongue II. iv. § 5. *See also* Senate, Hadrian, Antoninus, Emperors

Rome, founded VIII. xliii. § 2, fora v. xii. § 6, VIII. xlvi. § 4, X. v. § 11, other places and objects II. xxvii. § 5, IV. xxxv. § 10, V. xii. § 6, VI. ix. § 3, VIII. xvii. § 4, xlvi. § 5, IX. xxi. § 1, statues taken to v. xxv. § 9, VI. ix. § 3, VII. xxii. § 5, 9, VIII. xlvi. § 1, 4, IX. xxxiii. § 6

Roses, VI. xxiv. § 6, 7, IX. xli. § 7

Roxana, I. vi. § 3, IX. vii. § 2

Rumour, altar of, I. xvii. § 1

Ruthlessness, stone of, I. xxviii. § 5

SABBE, sibyl, X. xii. § 9

Sacadas, VI. xiv. § 9, 10, IX. xxx. § 2, X. vii. § 4, 5

Sacred War, VIII. xxvii. § 9, IX. vi. § 4, x. iii. § 1, xiii. § 6

Sacrifices, burnt II. x. § 1, 5, xi. § 7, IV. xxxi. § 9, v. xiii. § 3, 9, xiv. § 2, xv. § 10, VI. xx. § 3, VII. xviii. § 11–13, VIII. xxxviii. § 8, IX. iii. § 8, xviii.

GENERAL INDEX

§ 3, X. xxxii. § 16, buried X. xxxii.
§ 14, consumed II. x. § 1, xxvii.
§ 1, V. xiii. § 2, xvi. § 3, VIII. xxxviii.
§ 8, X. iv. § 10, xxxviii. § 8, thrown
into pit I. xviii. § 7, V. xiii. § 2,
thrown into water I. xxxiv. § 4,
III. xxiii. § 8, VII. xxiv. § 3, VIII. vii.
§ 2, X. viii. § 10, annual I. xlii. § 6,
II. iii. § 7, xii. § 1, III. i. § 8, IV. iii.
§ 10, VI. xx. § 7, VII. xix. § 10, xx.
§ 9, VIII. xiv. § 11, xxxvi. § 6, xli.
§ 1, IX. xxxviii. § 5, X. xxiv. § 6,
daily II. xxxv. § 11, V. xii. § 10,
X. iv. § 10, monthly II. xxiv. § 1,
V. xv. § 10, at midday X. xxxii. § 16,
after sunset II. xi. § 7, at night
II. xxiv. § 1, III. xiv. § 9, VIII. xiv.
§ 11, IX. xxxix. § 6, X. xxxviii. § 8,
secret II. xvii. § 1, III. xx. § 3, VIII.
xxxviii. § 7, for rain II. xxv. § 10,
xxix. § 8, VIII. xxxviii. § 4, of all
kinds of animals IV. xxxi. § 9, VII.
xviii. § 11–13, IX. xix. § 7, X. xxxii.
§ 12, bears VII. xviii. § 12, birds
II. xi. § 7, IV. xxxi. § 9, VII. xviii.
§ 12, X. xxxii. § 16, blood VIII. ii.
§ 3, X. iv. § 10, bloodless I. xxvi.
§ 5, fruit VII. xviii. § 12, VIII. xxxvii.
§ 7, IX. xix. § 5, geese X. xxxii. § 6,
grapes VII. xlii. § 11, meal I. xviii.
§ 7, money I. xxxiv. § 4, VII. xxii.
§ 3, oil VIII. xlii. § 11, pregnant
victims II. xi. § 4, IX. xxv. § 8,
puppies III. xiv. § 9, wheat V. xv.
§ 10, wineless I. xxvi. § 5, V. xv.
§ 10, wolf-cubs VII. xviii. § 12, wool
VIII. xlii. § 11, to lake III. xxiii.
§ 8, to lightning VIII. xxix. § 1,
to rivers I. xxxvii. § 3, IV. iii. § 10,
VIII. xli. § 3, to sceptre IX. xl.
§ 12, to serpents II. xi. § 8, to springs
I. xxxiv. § 4, X. viii. § 10, to winds
II. xii. § 1, VIII. xxix. § 1, xxxvi.
§ 6. *See also* Heroes, Marriage,
Barley, Boars, Bulls, Cakes, Cows,
Deer, Goats, Hair, Honey, Horses,
Human, Incense, Oxen, Pigs, Rams,
Sheep, Thighs
Sacrilege punished, III. iv. § 5, IV.
xxiv. § 5, VII. xix. § 2–4, xxiv.
§ 6, xxv. § 3, VIII. v. § 11, x. § 3,
IX. xxxix. § 12, X. ii. § 4–7, xxviii.
§ 5
Salamis, island off Attica, I. iii. § 2,
xiv. § 5, xxv. § 6, xxxv. § 2–xxxvi.

§ 2, xl. § 5, II. viii. § 6, xxix. § 10,
III. xi. § 3, xvi. § 6, IV. xxxvi.
§ 6, V. xi. § 5, VII. vi. § 3, VIII. x.
§ 9, X. xiv. § 5, xxxi. § 1
—— in Cyprus, VIII. xv. § 7
Samicum, v. v. § 3–vi. § 3, VI. xxv. § 6
Samos, II. iii. § 2, xxxi. § 6, III. xii.
§ 10, VI. ii. § 9, iii. § 14–16, xiii.
§ 5, VII. ii. § 8, 9, iv. § 1–7, v. § 4,
13, x. § 1, X. ix. § 10, xii. § 5
Samothrace, VII. iv. § 3
Sandion, I. xliii. § 3
Saon, IX. xl. § 2
Sapaeans, VII. x. § 6
Sappho, I. xxv. § 1, xxix. § 2, VIII.
xviii. § 5, IX. xxvii. § 3, xxix. § 8
Sarapammon, Egyptian boxer, v.
xxi. § 15
Sarapion, Alexandrine victor, v.
xxi. § 18, VI. xxiii. § 6
Sardes, III. ix. § 5, 8, IV. xxiv. § 2,
v. vi. § 5
Sardinia, I. xxix. § 5, IV. xxiii. § 5,
VII. ii. § 2, xvii. § 3, IX. xxiii. § 1,
X. xvii. § 1–13, xviii. § 1
Saron, II. xxx. § 7
Saronia, festival, II. xxxii. § 10
Sarpedon, VII. iii. § 7, X. xxxi. § 5, 8
Satrap, VI. xxv. § 6
Satyrides, islands, I. xxiii. § 6
Satyrs, I. xxiii. § 5, II. xiii. § 6,
statues I. xxx. § 1, 2, xlii. § 5
Satyrus, Elean victor, VI. iv. § 5
Saunium, spring, X. xxxvii. § 3
Sauromatae, I. xxi. § 5, VIII. xliii. § 6
Saurus, VI. xxi. § 3, 4
Scaeus, Samian victor, VI. xiii. § 5
Scambonidae, I. xxxviii. § 2
Scandeia, III. xxiii. § 1
Scarphea, II. xxix. § 3, VII. xv. § 3,
4, 9, X. i. § 2
Scedasus, IX. xiii. § **5, 6**
Scenoma, III. xvii. § 6
Scephrus, VIII. liii. § 2, 3
Sceptres, II. x. § 3, V. xi. § 1, VIII.
xxxvii. § 4, IX. xxxix. § 3, xl. § 11,
12, xli. § 1, 5
Schedius, X. iv. § 2, xxx. § 8, xxxvi.
§ 10
Schoenus, VIII. xxxv. § 10
Sciadis, VIII. xxxv. § 5
Scias, at Sparta, III. xii. § 10, xiii. § 1
Sciathis, mountain, VIII. xiv. § 1
Scieria, festival, VIII. xxiii. § 1
Scillus, V. vi. § 4–7, xvi. § 1, VI. xxii. § 4

GENERAL INDEX

Sciron, robber, I. iii. § 1, xliv. § 8
—— son of Pylas, I. xxxix. § 6, xliv.
§ 6, II. xxix. § 9
Scirus, I. xxxvi. § 4
Scolitas, hill, VIII. xxx. § 6
Scolus, IX. iv. § 4
Scope, VIII. xi. § 7
Scorpion, IX. xxi. § 6
Scotane, VIII. xxiii. § 8
Scotitas, III. x. § 6
Scotussa, VI. v. § 2, 3, VII. xxvii. § 6
Scourging, III. xvi. § 10, VIII. xxiii.
§ 1
Sculpture, history of, V. xx. § 2, xxiii.
§ 3
Scyllaeum, cape, II. xxxiv. § 7, 8
Scyllis, diver, X. xix. § 1
Scyras, river, III. xxv. § 1
Scyros, I. xvii. § 6, xxii. § 6, III. iii.
§ 7, xxv. § 1
Scyrus, river, VIII. xxxv. § 1
Scythians, I. xxxi. § 2, xliii. § 1, III.
ix. § 6, VI. xxvi. § 9, VIII. xliii.
§ 3, bow X. xxxi. § 8
Sea, images of II. i. § 7–9, old man of
III. xxi. § 9
Seasons, I. xl. § 4, II. xiii. § 3, xx. § 5,
xxx. § 5, III. xviii. § 10, xix. § 4,
v. xv. § 3, xvii. § 1, IX. xxxv. § 2,
representations I. xl. § 4, II. xvii.
§ 4, III. xviii. § 10, xix. § 4, 5, v.
xi. § 7, xvii. § 1, VII. v. § 9, VIII.
xxxi. § 3
Sebrus, III. xv. § 1, 2
Seleadas, Elean victor, VI. xvi. § 6
Selemnus, river, VII. xxiii. § 1–3
Seleucus, I. vi. § 4, 7, vii. § 3, viii.
§ 1, x. § 2, 4, 5, xvi. § 1–3, III. xvi.
§ 8, VI. xi. § 1, xv. § 7, xvi. § 2,
3, VIII. xxxiii. § 3, xlvi. § 3, li. § 4,
X. xix. § 7
Selinus, in Sicily, VI. xix. § 10, 11
—— in Laconia, III. xxii. § 8
—— Seleadas, Elean victor, VII. i. § 3, 4
—— river, V. vi. § 6, VII. xxiv. § 5
Sellasia, II. vii. § 4, ix. § 2, III. x. § 7,
IV. xxix. § 9, VII. vii. § 4, VIII. xlix. § 5
Semele, I. xxxi. § 2, xxxvii. § 5,
III. xix. § 3, xxiv. § 3, IX. ii. § 3,
v. § 2, xii. § 3, 4, xvi. § 6, 7
Semnae, I. xxviii. § 6, xxxi. § 4, II.
xi. § 4, VII. xxv. § 2
Senate, Roman VII. vii. § 9, ix. § 1–6,
xi. § 3–5, xiv. § 1, Spartan II. ix. § 1,
III. v. § 2, xi. § 2

Sepia, mountain, VIII. xvi. § 2
Seps, snake, VIII. iv. § 7, xvi. § 2
Serapis, I. xviii. § 4, II. iv. § 6, xxxiv.
§ 10, III. xiv. § 5, xxii. § 13, xxv.
§ 10, IV. xxxii. § 6, VII. xxi. § 13,
xxvi. § 7, IX. xxiv. § 1
Seres, VI. xxvi. § 6–9
Serpents, I. xxi. § 6, II. xxviii. § 1,
III. xxiii. § 7, VIII. iv. § 7, xvi. § 2,
IX. xxi. § 6, xxxviii. § 1, X. xvii.
§ 12, in myth IV. xiv. § 7, v. xviii.
§ 5, VI. xx. § 5, VII. xviii. § 3, VIII.
viii. § 4, xxix. § 3, IX. x. § 1, X.
xxxiii. § 9, in cult I. xxiv. § 7,
xxxvi. § 1, II. x. § 3, xi. § 8, xxvii.
§ 2, xxviii. § 1, IV. xiv. § 7, VI.
xx. § 5, IX. x. § 5, xxxi. § 7, xxxix.
§ 3, X. vi. § 6, representations I.
xxiv. § 7, V. xix. § 1, VI. xix. § 8,
VIII. xi. § 8, xxxvii. § 4, IX. xxxix.
§ 3, X. xiii. § 9, xxvi. § 3
Sesostris, I. xlii. § 3
Seven against Thebes, II. xx. § 5, X. x.
§ 3
Seven wise men, I. xxiii. § 1, X. xxiv.
§ 1
Shamefastness, I. xvii. § 1, III. xx.
§ 10
Sheep, II. xi. § 4, 7, xv'i', § 1, xxiv. § 1,
VI. ii. § 5, IX. xiii. § 4, xxii. § 1, X.
xxxii. § 16
Shell-fish, III. xxi. § 6, X. xxxvii.
§ 3
Shields, first used II. xxv. § 7, race with
II. xi. § 8, III. xiv. § 3, V. viii. § 10,
xii. § 8, bronze I. xv. § 4, II. xxi. § 4,
V. xii. § 8, VI. xix. § 4, IX. xvi.
§ 5, X. xi. § 6, gilded V. x. § 5,
golden I. xxv. § 7, V. x. § 4, X.
viii. § 7, xix. § 4, Amazonian I. xli.
§ 7, Argolic II. xxv. § 7, VIII. l. § 1,
Celtic VIII. l. § 1, Gallic X. xix.
§ 4, xxi. § 3, Persian VIII. l. § 1,
X. xix. § 4, of Aristomenes IV. xvi.
§ 5, 7, xxxii. § 5, 6, IX. xxxix. § 14,
of Athena I. xxiv. § 7, of Epaminondas VIII. xi. § 8, of Menelaus X.
xxvi. § 3, blazons IV. xvi. § 7, xxviii.
§ 5, V. xix. § 4, xxv. § 9, VIII. xi.
§ 8, X. xxvi. § 3
Ship, Panathenaic, I. xxix. § 1
Sibyls, II. vii. § 1, VIII. viii. § 8, 9,
X. ix. § 11–xii. § 10
Sicania, V. xxv. § 6, VIII. xxiv. § 2,
xlvi. § 2

GENERAL INDEX

Sicily, races of **V.** xxv. § 6, history
I. ii. § 3, xii. § 5, xxix. § 11–13,
II. xxii. § 9, III. xvi. § 4, 5, IV. xxxvi.
§ 4, V. xxvii. § 1, VI. ii. § 10, vi.
§ 7, ix. § 4, xii. § 3, xix. § 10, VII.
iv. § 6, 7, X. xv. § 5

Sicyon, history I. xxv. § 4, xxvii.
§ 5, II. i. § 1, ii. § 2, v. § 6–vii. § 1,
viii. § 3, 4, IV. xi. § 1, xv. § 7, VI.
iii. § 3, VII. vii. § 2, xi. § 4, xxvi.
§ 2, X. xv. § 8, description II. vii.
§ 4–xi. § 2, old city II. v. § 6, vii.
§ 1, harbour II. xii. § 2, tombs II.
vii. § 2, 4, treasuries v. xiv. § 9,
VI. xix. § 1–6, X. xi. § 1

Sicyonia, II. vi. § 5, VII. i. § 1, vi. § 1,
VIII. i. § 2, X. xxxii. § 19

Side, III. xxii. § 11

Sidon, man of, VII. xxiii. § 7

Silence, street of, VI. xxiii. § 8

Silenus, I. iv. § 5, xxiii. § 5, xxiv. § 1,
II. vii. § 9, xxii. § 9, III. xxv. § 2, 3,
VI. xxiv. § 8, oldest Satyrs called
Sileni I. xxiii. § 5

Silphium, III. xvi. § 3

Silver, uncoined III. xii. § 3, image of
I. v. § 1, nails of I. xxiv. § 3

Simonides, II. ii. § 3, III. viii. § 2,
VI. ix. § 9, IX. ii. § 5, X. xxvii. § 4

Simus, king of Arcadia, VIII. v. § 8

Sinis, I. xxxvii. § 4, II. i. § 4, X. xxv. § 7

Siphnus, X. xi. § 2

Sipylus, Mount, I. xx. § 5, xxi. § 3,
xxiv. § 8, II. xxii. § 3, III. xxii. § 4,
v. xiii. § 7, vi. xxii. § 1, VII. xxiv.
§ 13, xxvii. § 12, VIII. ii. § 7, xvii.
§ 3, xxxviii. § 10

Sirens, I. xxi. § 1, IX. xxxiv. § 3, X.
v. § 12, vi. § 5

Sisyphus, II. i. § 3, ii. § 2, iii. § 11,
iv. § 3, v. § 1, VI. xx. § 19, IX. xvii.
§ 6, xxiv. § 3, xxxiv. § 7, 10, X.
iv. § 10, xxx. § 5, xxxi. § 10

Sithnid nymphs, I. xl. § 1

Sixteen women, at Elis, V. xvi. § 2,
6, 8, VI. xxiv. § 10

Skins, worn, IV. xi. § 3, VI. vi. § 11,
VIII. i. § 5, X. xxxviii. § 3

Slaves, sold III. xii. § 3, X. xxxii. § 15,
of god X. xxxii. § 12, allowed
sanctuary II. xiii. § 4, freed III. xv.
§ 7, xvi. § 8, used in war I. xxxii.
§ 3, II. xx. § 9, IV. vii. § 3, VII. xvi.
§ 8, given public burial I. xxix.
§ 7, xxxii. § 3

Sleep, II. xxxi. § 3, X. xxxv. § 4, images
II. x. § 2, III. xviii. § 1, V. xviii.
§ 1, cult II. xxxi. § 3

Smenus, river, III. xxiv. § 9

Smyrna, I. xxxiii. § 7, II. xxvi. § 9,
IV. xxi. § 5, xxx. § 6, V. viii. § 7,
VI. xiv. § 3, VII. v. § 1, 9, 12, IX.
xi. § 7, xxix. § 4, xxxv. § 6

Snakes, *see* Serpents

Socrates, son of Sophroniscus, I.
xxii. § 8, xxx. § 3, IX. xxxv. § 7

—— Pellenian victor, VI. viii. § 1

—— Theban sculptor, IX. xxv. § 3

Sodamas, Argive, III. xviii. § 8

—— victor, of Assus, VI. iv. § 9

Solon, I. xvi. § 1, xviii. § 3, xl. § 5,
X. xxiv. § 1, xxxvii. § 6, 7, statue
I. xvi. § 1

Sophanes, Athenian general, I. xxix.
§ 5

Sophius, Messenian victor, VI. iii.
§ 2

Sophocles, poet, I. xxi. § 1, xxviii.
§ 7

—— torch-bearer, I. xxxvii. § 1

Soron, forest, VIII. xxiii. § 8, 9

Sosander, fined at Olympia, V. xxi.
§ 16, VI. xxiii. § 4

Sosipolis, VI. xx. § 2–5, xxv. § 4

Sostratus, of Dyme, VII. xvii. § 8

—— of Pellene, victor, VII. xviii. § 14

—— of Sicyon, victor, VI. iv. § 1

Sotades, Cretan victor, VI. xviii. § 6

Soteria, VII. xxi. § 7, xxiv. § 3

Sparta, III. xi. § 1–xviii. § 5, history
III. i. § 1–x. § 5, walls III. xii. § 8,
xv. § 3, VII. viii. § 5, ix. § 5, VIII. li.
§ 3, distance from Olympia VI. xvi.
§ 8, statue of Spartan people III.
xi. § 10, training of boys III. xi.
§ 9, xiv. § 6–10, xvi. § 9, VII. viii.
§ 5, VIII. xxiii. § 1, li. § 3. *See also*
Lacedaemonians

Sparti, VIII. xi. § 8, IX. v. § 3, x. § 1

Spears, I. xxiv. § 7, xxviii. § 2, III.
iii. § 8, xxiv. § 2, IX. xl. § 11

Spercheus, river, I. xxxvii. § 3, VII.
xv. § 3, X. xx. § 6–9, xxii. § 3,
xxiii. § 13

Sphacteria, I. xiii. § 5, xv. § 4, III.
v. § 5, IV. xxvi. § 1, 2, xxxvi. § 6,
V. xxvi. § 1, VI. xxii. § 6

Sphaereis, Spartan youths, III. xiv.
§ 6

Sphaerus, II. xxxiii. § 1, V. x. § 7

GENERAL INDEX

Sphettus, II. xxx. § 9

Sphinx, I. xxiv. § 5, III. xviii. § 14, v. xi. § 2, IX. xxvi. § 2–4

Sphragidium, IX. iii. § 9

Spiders, IX. vi. § 5

Springs and fountains, with peculiar water III. xxiii. § 2, xxiv. § 7, IV. xxxv. § 8–12, IX. xxxiv. § 4, flowing every other year VIII. xxix. § 1, flowing from tree IV. xxxiv. § 4, dripping II. vii. § 4, healing IV. xxxi. § 4, VI. xxii. § 7, VIII. xix. § 2, oracular VII. xxi. § 11, 13

Stadium, I. xix. § 6, xliv. § 1, II. i. § 7, xxiv. § 2, xxvii. § 5, xxix. § 11, xxxii. § 3, xxxiv. § 10, III. xiv. § 3, xxi. § 1, IV. iv. § 5, v. § 10, xiii. § 7, xxxii. § 6, V. xix. § 9, xvi. § 3, xxi. § 2, 15, xxii. § 1, xxiii. § 4, VI. xix. § 15, xx. § 8, 10, VIII. x. § 1, 2, xii. § 5, xiv. § 9, xxxii. § 3, xxxvi. § 8, xxxviii. § 5, xlvii. § 4, IX. xi. § 6, xxiii. § 1, 2, X. xxxii. § 1, usual form II. xxvii. § 5, IX. xxiii. § 1

Statues, *see* Images

Stenyclerus, IV. iii. § 7, vi. § 6, xv. § 8, xvi. § 6, xxvii. § 1

Stesichorus, II. xxii. § 7, III. xix. § 13, VIII. iii. § 2, IX. ii. § 3, xi. § 2, X. xxvi. § 1, 9

Steunus, cave, VIII. iv. § 3, X. xxxii. § 3

Sthenelus, II. xviii. § 5, xx. § 5, xxii. § 8, 9, xxiv. § 3, xxx. § 10, VIII. xlvi. § 2, X. x. § 4

Stiris, X. iii. § 2, xxxv. § 8–xxxvi. § 1

Stoai, see Porticoes

Stomius, Elean victor, VI. iii. § 2

Stones, in myth I. xxi. § 3, xxiii. § 5, xxxv. § 3, xlii. § 2, II. xxv. § 8, xxxi. § 4, III. xxii. § 1, IX. x. § 3, xi. § 2, 7, xvi. § 7, xix. § 1, xxxiv. § 2, X. xxxi. § 10, 12, swallowed by Cronus VIII. viii. § 2, xxxvi. § 3, IX. ii. § 7, xli. § 6, X. xxiv. § 6, in cult I. xxviii. § 5, xliv. § 2, III. xii. § 1, VII. xxii. § 4, 5, ix. xxiv. § 3, xxvii. § 1, xxxiv. § 2, xxxviii. § 1, X. xxv. § 6, unwrought II. xxv. § 8, xxxiv. § 10, xxxvi. § 3, III. xxii. § 1, VII. xxii. § 5, VIII. xiii. § 3, xviii. § 2, IX. xvii. § 7, xviii. § 2, xix. § 3, xxiv. § 3,

xxvii. § 1, xxxviii. § 1, X. v. § 4, xxxvi. § 8

Stoning festival, II. xxxii. § 2

Straight Street, I. xliv. § 2

Straton, victor of Aegium, VII. xxiii. § 5

—— Alexandrine victor, V. xxi. § 9

Strife, figure of, V. xix. § 2

Strings of lyre, III. xii. § 10, IX. v. § 7, viii. § 4

Struggle, figure of, V. xx. § 3, xxvi. § 3

Struthus, cape, II. xxxvi. § 3

Stymphalian birds, V. x. § 9, VIII. xxii. § 4–6, IX. xi. § 6

Stymphalus, II. iii. § 5, xxiv. § 6, V. x. § 9, VI. vii. § 10, VIII. iv. § 4, 6, 7, v. § 4, xiii. § 5, xvi. § 1, xxii. § 1–9, IX. xi. § 6

Styra, IV. xxxiv. § 11, v. xxiii. § 2

Styx, river, VIII. xvii. § 6, xviii. § 1–6, xix. § 3

Sulla, I. xx. § 4–7, IX. vi. § 5, vii. § 4, 5, xxx. § 1, xxxiii. § 6, xl. § 7, X. xxi. § 6

Sun, I. iv. § 1, xxxiii. § 4, II. i. § 1, 6, iii. § 10, xi. § 5, V. i. § 9, VI. xxv. § 2, IX. xxxv. § 5, cult II. iv. § 6, xi. § 1, xviii. § 3, xxxi. § 5, xxxiv. § 10, III. xx. § 4, V. xxv. § 9, VIII. ix. § 4, X. xi. 5, representations II. iii. § 2, v. § 1, III. xxvi. § 1, V. xi. § 8, VI. xxiv. § 6, VIII. xxxi. § 7, X. xix. § 4,

—— titles, Eleutherius II. xxxi. § 5

Heracles, VIII. xxxi. § 7

Saviour, VIII. xxxi. § 7

Sunium, cape, I. i. § 1, xxviii. § 2, xxxv. § 1, II. viii. § 6, X. xxv. § 2

Suppliants, protected by gods, I. xx. § 7, III. iv. § 1, 5, xvii. § 9, IV. xxiv. § 5, VII. xxiv. § 6, xxv. § 1–4

Susa, I. xlii. § 3, III. ix. § 5, xvi. § 8. IV. xxxi. § 5, VI. v. § 7, X. xxxi. § 7

Swans, I. xxx. § 3

Sybariades, Lacedaemonian victor, V. viii. § 10

Sybaris, V. viii. § 9, treasury VI. xix. § 9

Sybotas, king of Messenia, IV. iii. § 10, iv. § 1

Syene, I. xxxiii. § 4, V. vii. § 4, VI. xxvi. § 2, VIII. xxxviii. § 6

Symbola, VIII. liv. § 1, 2

Symmachus, Elean victor, VI. i. § 3

—— Messenian victor, VI. ii. § 10

GENERAL INDEX

Syracuse, I. ii. § 3, xii. § 5, xxiii. § 3, xxix. § 13, II. xxii. § 9, V. vii. § 2, 3, viii. § 8, VI. ix. § 5, xii. § 1–4, vii. § 9, xix. § 7, X. xxviii. § 6

Syrians, I. v. § 5, vi. § 4, 5, 8, xxv. § 8, III. xvi. § 8, xxvi. § 10, VI. ii. § 7, VII. viii. § 3, 4, VIII. xx. § 2, xxiii. § 5, xxix. § 3, 4, xliii. § 4, li. § 4, X. xx. § 5

Sys, river, IX. xxx. § 11

Sythas, river, II. vii. § 8, xii. § 2, VII. xxvii. § 12

TABLES, I. xxxiii. § 4, V. xii. § 5, xx. § 1–3, VI. xxvi. § 2, VIII. xxx. § 2, xxxi. § 3, IX. xl. § 12

Taenarum, II. xxxiii. § 2, III. xiv. § 2, xxi. § 7, xxv. § 4–9, IV. xxiv. § 5, VII. xxv. § 3

Talaus, II. vi. § 6, xx. § 5, xxi. § 2, IX. xviii. § 6, X. xiii. § 6

Taletum, mountain, III. xx. § 4, 5

Talos, VIII. liii. § 5

Talthybius, II. xxvi. § 10, III. xii. § 7, V. xxiv. § 11, VII. xxiv. § 1

Talus, VII. iv. § 8

Tanagra, I. xxix. § 6, 13, xxxiv. § 1, III. xi. § 8, V. x. § 4, xxvi. § 7, VIII. xxxvi. § 10, IX. iii. § 6, vi. § 3, xix. § 4–xxii. § 3, X. xxviii. § 6

Tanaus, river, II. xxxviii. § 7

Tantalus, son of Thyestes, II. xviii. § 2, xxii. § 3

—— son of Zeus, II. xxii. § 2, 3, III. xxii. § 4, V. xiii. § 7, VIII. ii. § 5, IX. v. § 7, X. xxx. § 2, xxxi. § 12

Taras, X. x. § 8, xiii. § 10

Taraxippus, VI. xx. § 15–19, X. xxxvii. § 4

Tarentum, I. xii. § 2, xiii. § 1, III. x. § 5, xii. § 5, VI. iii. § 2, offerings at Delphi X. x. § 6, xiii. § 10

Tartarus, VIII. xxxvii. § 5, IX. xxvii. § 2

Tartessus, VI. xix. § 2, 3

Tauri, I. xxxiii. § 1, xliii. § 1, III. xvi. § 7, 8, 11

Taurosthenes, Aeginetan victor, VI. ix. § 3

Taxilus, I. xx. § 6, IX. xl. § 7, X. xxxiv. § 2–6

Taygete, III. i. § 2, xviii. § 10, xx. § 2, IX. xxxv. § 1

Taygetus, Mount, III. i. § 2, xx. § 2–7, IV. vii. § 2, VIII. xxiv. § 4

Tegea, description VIII. xliv. § 1–xlix. § 1, liii. § 1–liv. § 7, history III. iii. § 5, vii. § 3, xi. § 7, VIII. iii. § 4, iv. § 3, X. ix. § 6, xx. § 1, offerings at Delphi X. ix. § 5, tribes VIII. liii. § 6, road from Argos II. xxiv. § 5–7

Tegeates, VIII. iii. § 4, xlv. § 1, xlviii. § 6, liii. § 2–4

Teiresias, VII. iii. § 1, IX. x. § 3, xi. § 3, xvi. § 1, viii. § 4, xix. § 3, xxxiii. § 1, 2, X. xxviii. § 1, xxix. § 8

Telamon, I. v. § 2, xxviii. § 11, xxxv. § 2, 3, xlii. § 4, II. xxix. § 2–10, III. xix. § 13, V. xxii. § 2, VIII. xv. § 6, 7, xlv. § 6

Telchines, IX. xix. § 1

Teleclus, III. ii. § 6, 7, vii. § 4, xv. § 10, IV. iv. § 2–4, v. § 1, 9, xxxi. § 3

Telemachus, son of Odysseus, IX. xli. § 4, X. xxv. § 2

—— Elean victor, VI. xiii. § 11

Telephus, I. iv. § 6, III. xxvi. § 9, 10, V. xiii. § 3, VIII. xlv. § 7, xlviii. § 7, liv. § 6, IX. v. § 14, 15, xxxi. § 2, xli. § 1

Telesarchus, X. xx. § 5, xxii. § 1

Telesilla, II. xxx. § 8, 9, xxviii. § 2, xxxv. § 2

Telestas, Messenian victor, VI. xiv. § 4

Telete, IX. xxx. § 4

Tellias, X. i. § 8, 10, 11, xiii. § 7

Tellon, Oresthasian victor, VI. x. § 9

Temenus, son of Aristomachus, II. vi. § 7, xiii. § 1, xviii. § 7, xix. § 1, xxi. § 3, xxvi. § 2, xxviii. § 3, 4, xxxviii. § 1, III. i. § 5, IV. iii. § 3–8

—— son of Pelasgus, VIII. xxii. § 2

Temesa, VI. vi. § 7–11

Temples, oldest II. xxxi. § 6, V. xvi. § 1, double I. xxvi. § 5, II. x. § 2, xxv. § 1, VI. xx. § 3, VIII. ix. § 1, with upper story III. xv. § 1, unfinished VII. v. § 4, IX. ii. § 1, iv. § 4, xxxix. § 4, burnt I. i. § 5, II. v. § 5, VII. v. § 4, X. xxxv. § 2, without roof I. i. § 5, xl. § 6, xliv. § 3, II. vii. § 6, xi. § 2, xii. § 2, xv. § 2, xxiv. § 3, xxxiv. § 10, xxxvi. § 2, III. xxi. § 8, xxii. § 10, VI. xxv. § 1, VIII. xli. § 10, xliv. § 3, IX.

259

xxxiii. § 3, in ruins II. ix. § 7, xi. § 1, xxxvi. § 8, VI. xx. § 6, xxi. § 3, 4, 6, VIII. ix. § 6, xii. § 9, xiv. § 4, xv. § 5, xvii. § 1, xxiv. § 6, xxv. § 3, xxxi. § 2, xxx. § 4, 6, xxxi. § 9, xxxii. § 2, 3, xxxiv. § 5, xxxvi. § 8, xliv. § 2, 4, liii. § 11, liv. § 5, IX. xxxiii. § 7, X. viii. § 8, xxxv. § 3. *See also* Corinthian, Doric, Ionic, Back-chamber, Fore-temple

Tenea, II. v. § 4

Tenedos, II. v. § 4, VI. xvii. § 1, X. xiv. § 1, 3, 4

Tenerus, IX. x. § 6, xxvi. § 1

Teos, VII. iii. § 6, 10, v. § 11, xxiv. § 5

Tereus, I. v. § 4, xli. § 8, 9, IX. xvi. § 4, X. iv. § 8, 9

Termesus, river, IX. xxix. § 5

Terra-cotta, I. iii. § 1

Terror, figure of, II. iii. § 7

Teucer, I. iii. § 2, xxiii. § 8, xxviii. § 11, II. xxix. § 4, VIII. xv. § 6, 7

Teumessus, IX. xix. § 1–3

Teuthis, VIII. xxvii. § 4, 7, xxviii. § 4–6

Teuthrone, III. xxi. § 7, xxv. § 4

Thalamae, III. xxi. § 7, xxvi. § 1

Thales, of Gortyna, I. xiv. § 4

—— of Miletus, X. xxiv. § 1

Thalia, Grace, IX. xxxv. § 5

Thaliades, VIII. xxv. § 2

Thallo, IX. xxxv. § 2

Thalpius, V. iii. § 3, 4

Thamyris, IV. xxxiii. § 3, 7, IX. v. § 9, xxx. § 2, X. vii. § 2, xxx. § 8

Thasos, V. xxv. § 12, 13, VI. xi. § 2, X. xxvii. § 4, xxviii. § 3

Thaumasius, Mount, VIII. xxxvi. § 2

Theagenes, tyrant of Megara, I. xxviii. § 1, xl. § 1, xli. § 2

—— Thasian victor, VI. vi. § 5, 6, xi. § 2–9, xv. § 3

Theano, X. xxvii. § 3

Theantus, Leprean victor, VI. vii. § 8

Theatres, I. xx. § 3, 4, xxi. § 1, 3, 4, xxix. § 16, II. i. § 7, iv. § 5, vii. § 5, xiii. § 5, xx. § 7, 8, xxvii. § 5, xxix. § 11, xxxi. § 4, III. xiv. § 1, xv. § 1, IV. xii. § 6, xxxii. § 6, v. xii. § 6, VI. xiii. § 11, xxvi. § 1, VII. xx. § 9, xxi. § 6, xxiii. § 9, VIII. ix. § 2, 5, 6, xxxii. § 1, 3, xlix. § 1, l. § 3, IX. xvi. § 6, xxii.

§ 2, xxvii. § 5, X. xxxii. § 1, 10, xxxiii. § 4, xxxiv. § 6, xxxv. § 4, 6

Thebais, poem, VIII. xxv. § 8, IX. ix. § 5, xviii. § 6

Thebe, II. v. § 2, v̄. xxii. § 6, IX. v. § 6, xv. § 6

Thebes, in Egypt, I. ix. § 3, xlii. § 3, VIII. xxxiii. § 2

—— in Greece, description IX. viii. § 4–xii. § 6, xvi. § 1–xviii. § 6, gates IX. viii. § 4–7, foundation II. vi. § 4, IX. v. § 6, attacked by Seven I. xxxix. § 2, II. xx. § 5, VIII. xxv. § 4, X. x. § 3, taken by Epigoni I. xliii. § 1, xliv. § 4, II. xx. § 5, VII. iii. § 1, IX. xxv. § 7, xxxiii. § 1, later history I. xxv. § 4, xxxiv. § 1, II. vi. § 2, 4, III. ix. § 3, 13, IV. xxxii. § 4–6, VI. iii. § 3, VII. ii. § 3, x. § 2, xv. § 9, VIII. viii. § 10, xi. § 9, xxxiii. § 2, l. § 3, IX. i. § 4–8, v. § 1–vii. § 6, viii. § 6, ix. § 1, 4, xiii. § 3–12, xvii. § 1, 3, xix. § 3, xxxvii. § 1, X. x. § 5, xx. § 1, sacked by Alexander IV. xxvii. § 10, VII. vi. § 9, xvii. § 2, IX. vi. § 5, xxiii. § 5, xxv. § 10, restored by Cassander IV. xxvii. § 10, VII. vi. § 9, IX. iii. § 6, vii. § 1, 2, 4, dedication at Delphi X. xiii. § 6, treasury X. xi. § 5, image of city IV. xxxi. § 10

Theecoleon, V. xv. § 8, 10

Theganussa, island, IV. xxxiv. § 12

Theisoa, on Mount Lycaeus, VIII. xxvii. § 4, xxxvii. § 3, 9

—— near Methydrium, VIII. xxvii. § 4, 7, xxviii. § 3

Theius, river, VIII. xxxv. § 3

Thelpusa, VIII. xxiv. § 4, xxv. § 1–12, xlii. § 1

Themides, II. xxxi. § 5

Themis, I. xxii. § 1, II. xxvii. § 5, xxxi. § 5, V. xiv. § 10, xvii. § 1, VIII. xxv. § 7, IX. xxxi. § 1, xxxv. § 4, X. v. § 6

Themiscyra, I. ii. § 1, xv. § 2, xli. § 7

Themisonium, X. xxxii. § 4

Themisto, mother of Homer, X. xxiv. § 3

Themistocles, son of Neocles, I. i. § 2, ii. § 2, xviii. § 2, 3, xxvi. § 4, xxxvi. § 1, xxxvii. § 1, VII. vi. § 3, VIII. l. § 3, lii. § 2, X. xiv. § 5, 6, grave I. i. § 2

GENERAL INDEX

Themistocles, son of Poliarchus, I. xxxvii. § 1

Theocrestus, Cyrenian victor, VI. xii. § 7

Theoclus, seer, IV. xvi. § 1, 5, xx. § 1, 3, xxi. § 2, 5, 10, 11

Theodorus, Elean victor, VI. xvi. § 8
—— actor, I. xxxvii. § 3

Theognetus, Aeginetan victor, VI. ix. § 1

Theomelida, place in Sparta, III. xiv. § 2

Theophilus, archon, X. iii. § 1

Theopompus, son of Damaretus, VI. x. § 4, 5
—— son of above, Heraean victor, VI. x. § 4, 5
—— historian, III. x. § 3, VI. xviii. § 5
—— Spartan king, III. iii. § 2, vii. § 5, xvi. § 6, IV. iv. § 4, vi. § 4, 5, vii. § 7–9, viii. § 9, x. § 3
—— Theban, VI. vi. § 2

Theotimus, Elean victor, VI. xvii. § 5

Theoxenia, games, VII. xxvii. § 2, 4

Thera, III. i. § 7, 8, xiv. § 3, xv. § 6, VII. ii. § 2, X. xv. § 6

Therapne, III. xiv. § 9, xix. § 7, 9, xx. § 1, 2

Theras, III. i. § 7, 8, xv. § 6, IV. iii. § 4, VII. ii. § 2

Thermodon, river in Asia, I. ii. § 1, III. xxv. § 3, VII. ii. § 7
—— in Boeotia, IX. xix. § 3

Thermopylae, I. i. § 3, iv. § 1–4, III. iv. § 7, 8, xiv. § 1, IV. xxxv. § 9, VII. xxiv. § 4, IX. xxxii. § 9, X. xx. § 1–xxii. § 12

Thero, nurse of Ares, III. xix. § 8
—— daughter of Phylas, IX. xl. § 5, 6

Thersander, son of Polyneices, II. xx. § 5, VII. iii. § 1, IX. v. § 14, 15, viii. § 7, ix. § 4, X. x. § 4

Thersilium, VIII. xxxii. § 1

Thersilochus, Corcyraean victor, VI. xiii. § 6

Thersius, Thessalian victor, V. ix. § 1

Thersites, X. xxxi. § 1

Theseus, birth I. xvii. § 3, xli. § 5, II. xxx. § 9, xxxii. § 9, V. x. § 8, VII. xvii. § 7, X. xxv. § 7, exploits I. iii. § 1, xii. § 3, 6, xix. § 1, xxii. § 2, 5, xxvii. § 7, 8, 9, xxviii. § 10, xxxi. § 1, xxxii. § 6, xxxvii. § 4,

xxxviii. § 5, xxxix. § 2, 3, xli. § 3, 4, xliv. § 8, II. i. § 3, 4, xxvii. § 4, xxxi. § 1, xxxii. § 7, III. xviii. § 5, VIII. ii. § 1, xlv. § 6, xlviii. § 3, IX. xl. § 4, X. xxv. § 7, xxix. § 4, Amazons I. ii. § 1, xv. § 2, xli. § 7, II. xxxii. § 9, v. xi. § 4, 7, Minotaur I. i. § 2, xxii. § 5, xxiv. § 1, xlii. § 2, III. xviii. § 16, with Helen I. xviii. § 4, II. xxii. § 6, xxxii. § 7, III. xviii. § 15, xxiv. § 11, with Peirithous I. xvii. § 2, 4, xviii. § 4, xli. § 5, II. xxii. § 6, V. x. § 8, IX. xxxi. § 5, X. xxix. § 9, Athenian institutions I. iii. § 3, xxii. § 3, VIII. ii. § 1, bones III. iii. § 7, cult I. xvii. § 2, 6, xxx. § 4, X. xi. § 6, cult of his children I. i. § 4, representations I. iii. § 1, 3, viii. § 4, xv. § 2, 3, xvii. § 2, 3, xxiv. § 1, xxvii. § 8, III. xviii. § 15, 16, IV. xxxii. § 1, V. x. § 8, xi. § 4, 5, 7, xix. § 1, VIII. xlv. § 6, X. x. § 1, xxix. § 9

Thespiae, VI. xvi. § 1, VII. ii. § 2, IX. iii. § 6, xiii. § 8, xiv. § 2, 4, xx. § 2, xxiii. § 1, 2, xxvi. § 6, 7, xxvii. § 1–6, xxix. § 3, xxxi. § 3, 7, X. xvii. § 5, xx. § 2

Thesprotia, I. vi. § 8, xvii. § 4, 5, xviii. § 4, II. xxii. § 6, III. xviii. § 5, IV. xxxiv. § 3, V. xiv. § 2, xxiii. § 2, IX. xxxvi. § 3

Thesprotis, poem, VIII. xii. § 5, 6

Thessalonice, VIII. vii. § 7, IX. vii. § 3

Thessaly, I. iv. § 1, xiii. § 2, xxv. § 4, xxix. § 6, 9, VII. viii. § 9, ix. § 12, IV. ii. § 3, xxxvi. § 3, V. xxiv. § 2, VII. x. § 2, IX. iv. § 2, X. i. § 3–11, viii. § 2, xxiii. § 13, grave of Thessalians at Athens I. xxix. § 6, dedication at Olympia V. xxiv. § 1

Thestius, III. xiii. § 8, xix. § 5, VIII. xlv. § 6, IX. xxvii. § 6, 7

Thetis, III. xxi. § 9, xxii. § 2, V. xviii. § 5, xix. § 8, xxii. § 2, VIII. xli. § 5, 6, sanctuary III. xiv. § 4, 5

Thighs, burnt in sacrifice, I. xxiv. § 2, II. x. § 1, 5, xi. § 7, III. ix. § 4, V. xiii. § 8, 9, xiv. § 2, VIII. xxxviii. § 8

Thisbe, IX. xxxii. § 2, 3, X. xxxvii. § 2

GENERAL INDEX

Thoas, son of Andraemon, v. iii. § 6, X. xxxviii. § 5

Thocnia, VIII. iii. § 2, xxix. § 5

Tholos, at Athens I. v. § 1, at Epidaurus II. xxvii. § 3

Thornax, in Argolis, II. xxxvi. § 1
—— in Laconia, III. x. § 8, xi. § 1

Thrasybulus, Athenian, I. xxix. § 3, III. v. § 1, 4, IX. xi. § 6
—— Elean soothsayer, VI. ii. § 4–6, xiv. § 9, VIII. x. § 5

Thrasydaeus, III. viii. § 4, 5

Thrasyllus, VII. vii. § 7

Thrasymedes, son of Nestor, II. xviii. § 8, IV. xxxi. § 11, xxxvi. § 2

Thrones, II. iv. § 7, xvii. § 4, xix. § 5, xxvii. § 2, III. xviii. § 1–xix. § 1, v. xi. § 1–8, xii. § 5, xiii. § 7, VII. v. § 9, VIII. xxxvii. § 3, IX. xxv. § 3

Thronium, v. xxii. § 3, 4

Thucydides, I. xxiii. § 9, VI. xix. § 5

Thuria, IV. xxxi. § 1, 2

Thyestes, II. xviii. § 1–3, xxii. § 3, IX. xl. § 11

Thyia, daughter of Castalius, X. vi. § 4, xxix. § 5
—— festival, VI. xxvi. § 1, 2

Thyiades, X. iv. § 3, vi. § 4, xix. § 4, xxxii. § 7

Thymoetes, II. xviii. § 9

Thyraeum, VIII. iii. § 3, xxxv. § 7

Thyrea, II. xxix. § 5, xxxviii. § 5, III. vii. § 5, VIII. iii. § 3, liv. § 4, X. ix. § 12

Thyrides, cape, III. xxv. § 9

Tiasa, river, III. xviii. § 6

Tiger, IX. xxi. § 4

Tilphusa, spring, IX. xxxiii. § 1

Timaenetus, Phliasian victor, X. vii. § 7

Timagoras, I. xxx. § 1

Timalcus, I. xli. § 3, 4, xlii. § 4

Timanthes, victor, of Cleonae, VI. viii. § 4

Timasitheus, victor, of Croton, VI. xiv. § 5
—— Delphian victor, VI. viii. § 6

Timocleidas, tyrant of Sicyon, II. viii. § 2

Timon, Athenian, I. xxx. § 4
—— Elean victors, v. ii. § 5, VI. ii. § 8, xii. § 6, xvi. § 3

Timosthenes, Elean victor, VI. ii. § 6

Timotheus, son of Conon, I. iii. § 2, xxiv. § 3, xxix. § 15, VI. iii. § 16

Timotheus, musician, III. xii. § 10, VIII. l. § 3

Tipha, IX. xxxii. § 4

Tiryns, I. xxxii. § 6, II. xvi. § 2, 5, v. ii. § 2, xxiii. § 2, destroyed by Argives II. xvii. § 5, xxv. § 8, v. xxiii. § 3, VIII. xxvii. § 1, xlvi. § 3, walls II. xvi. § 5, xxv. § 8, VII. xxv. § 6, VIII. xxxiii. § 3, IX. xxxvi. § 5

Tisamenus, Iamid, III. xi. § 5–9, VI. xiv. § 13
—— son of Orestes, II. xviii. § 6–8, xxxviii. § 1, III. i. § 5, 6, IV. iii. § 3, VII. i. § 7, 8, vi. § 2
—— son of Thersander, III. xv. § 6–8, IX. v. § 15

Tisander, Naxian victor, VI. xiii. § 8

Tisias, rhetorician, VI. xvii. § 8

Tisicrates, victor, of Croton, VI. ix. § 5

Tisis, diver, IV. ix. § 3, 4

Titan, brother of Sun, II. xi. § 5

Titane, II. xi. § 3, 5, xii. § 1–3, xxiii. § 4, xxvii. § 1, VII. xxiii. § 8

Titans, v. vii. § 10, VII. xviii. § 4, xxvi. § 12, xxvii. § 11, VIII. xxxvii. § 5

Tithorea, II. iv. § 3, xxix. § 3, IX. xvii. § 4, 5, X. i. § 1, xxxii. § 8–xxxiii. § 1

Tithronium, X. iii. § 2, xxxiii. § 12

Tithraustes, III. ix. § 7

Titthium, mountain, II. xxvi. § 4, xxvii. § 7

Tityus, III. xviii. § 15, X. iv. § 2–6, xi. § 1, xxix. § 3

Tlepolemus, son of Heracles, II. xxii. § 8, III. xix. § 9
—— Lycian, v. viii. § 11

Tolmides, I. xxvii. § 5, xxix. § 14

Tombs, remarkable I. xxxvii. § 5, II. vii. § 2, VIII. xvi. § 4, in market-place I. xliii. § 8, xliv. § 1, III. xii. § 7, VI. xxiv. § 9, VII. xxiv. § 1, IX. v. § 14, secret II. ii. § 2, xxix. § 8, xxxii. § 1, cult I. xliii. § 4, II. xii. § 5, xxxiii. § 1, xxxviii. § 1, IV. xxxii. § 3, IX. xviii. § 3, 4, X. iv. § 10

Torches, I. xxxvii. § 1, II. vii. § 5, xxii. § 3, VII. xxiii. § 6, xxvii. § 3, VIII. xxv. § 7, xxxvii. § 3, 4, IX. xxvii. § 2, X. xxxvii. § 1

Torch-race, I. xxx. § 2

Tortoises, I. xliv. § 8, II. xix. § 7, VIII. xvii. § 5, xxiii. § 9, liv. § 7, figures of II. xix. § 7, VI. xxv. § 1, VIII. xxx. § 6

Town-hall, see Prytaneum

Trachis, at foot of Mount Oeta, I. iv. § 2, xxxii. § 6, II. xxiii. § 5, III. iv. § 8, X. xxiii. § 1, 8

—— in Phocis, X. iii. § 2

Trachy, Mount, VIII. xiii. § 4

Tragus, river, VIII. xxiii. § 2

Trajan, IV. xxxv. § 3, V. xii. § 6

Trapezus, IV. xvii. § 2, VIII. iii. § 3, v. § 4, xxvii. § 4–6, xxix. § 1, xxxi. § 5

Treasuries, at Delphi X. xi, at Olympia VI. xix, of Atreus II. xvi. § 6, of Minyas IX. xxxvi. § 5, xxxviii. § 2

Trees, oldest VIII. xxiii. § 5, worshipped II. ii. § 7

Tretus, II. xv. § 2, 4

Tricca, IV. iii. § 2

Tricoloni, VIII. iii. § 4, xxvii. § 3, 5, xxxv. § 5–xxxvi. § 1

Tricolonus, son of Lycaon, VI. xxi. § 10, VIII. iii. § 4, xxxv. § 6

Tricrana, island, II. xxxiv. § 8

Tricrena, mountain, VIII. xvi. § 1, 2

Trident, I. xxvi. § 5, II. xxx. § 6, X. xxxvi. § 8

Trimarcisia, Gallic word, X. xix. § 11

Trinasus, III. xxii. § 3

Triopas, founder of Cnidus, X. xi. § 1

—— son of Phorbas, II. xvi. § 1, IV. i. § 1

Triphylia, V. v. § 3, vi. § 4, xvi. § 1, xxiii. § 2, VI. xv. § 1, xxii. § 4, xxv. § 6

Tripodisci, I. xliii. § 8

Tripods, I. xx. § 1, xxi. § 3, xliii. § 8, IV. xii. § 8–10, xiv. § 2, xxxii. § 1, V. xvii. § 11, VII. iv. § 10, IX. x. § 4, xxxi. § 3, X. vii. § 6, xiii. § 7–9, bronze I. xviii. § 8, xx. § 1, III. xviii. § 7, 8, IV. xiv. § 2, V. xii. § 5, IX. x. § 4, X. vii. § 8, clay IV. xii. § 9, without fire IV. xxxii. § 1, golden X. xiii. § 9, contest of Heracles for tripod III. xxi. § 8, VIII. xxxvii. § 1, X. xiii. § 7, 8

Triptolemus, I. xiv. § 1–4, xxxviii. § 6, II. xiv. § 3, VII. xviii. § 2, 3, VIII. iv. § 1

Triteia, VI. xii. § 9, VII. vi. § 1, xxii. § 6–9

Triton, river, VIII. xxvi. § 6, IX. xxxiii. § 7

Tritonis, lake, I. xiv. § 6, II. xxi. § 5, 6 IX. xxxiii. § 7

Tritons, II. i. § 7, 8, III. xviii. § 10, VIII. ii. § 7, IX. xx. § 4, xxi. § 1

Troezen, I. ii. § 1, viii. § 2, xxii. § 1, 2, xxv. § 4, xxvii. § 7, 8, II. i. § 4, viii. § 5, xxx. § 5–xxxiv. § 3, 12, v. x. § 7, xxiii. § 2, VI. viii. § 4, VIII. i. § 1, x. v. § 6, ix. § 8, 10

Troilus, Elean victor, VI. i. § 4, 6

Trojan War, II. xvii. § 3, III. iv. § 7, IV. vi. § 1, xxxv. § 1, v. iv. § 7, xiii. § 4

Tropaea, VIII. xxv. § 1

Trophies, I. xv. § 1, xxxii. § 5, xxxvi. § 1, II. xx. § 1, xxi. § 4, 8, III. ii. § 6, x. § 6, xiv. § 7, xxiv. § 6, IV. viii. § 13, xxxii. § 5, 6, V. xxvii. § 11, VI. ii. § 8, iii. § 2, xxi. § 2, VIII. x. § 5, 8, lii. § 6, IX. ii. § 6, xl. § 7–9, X. xix. § 1

Trophonius, I. xxxiv. § 2, IV. xvi. § 7, xxxii. § 5, 6, VIII. x. § 2, IX. xi. § 1, xxxvii. § 4–6, xxxix. § 2– xl. § 3, X. v. § 13

Troy, II. iv. § 2, IV. xxxv. § 1, X. xxxiii. § 2, in Pausanius' time I. xxxv. § 4, VIII. xii. § 9, capture I. xxviii. § 9, IV. xxxv. § 1, in art I. xv. § 2, II. xvii. § 3, X. xxv. § 2– xxvii. § 4, in literature X. xxv. § 5, xxvi. § 1, xxvii. § 2

Trumpet, II. xxi. § 3, V. xxii. § 1

Trygon, VIII. xxv. § 11

Tunic, building, III. xvi. § 2, 3

Tuthoa, river, VIII. xxv. § 12

Twelve Gods, I. iii. § 3, xl. § 3, VIII. xxv. § 3

Twins, place in Argolis, II. xxxvi. § 3

Tyche, see Fortune

Tydeus, son of Oeneus, III. xviii. § 12, IX. xviii. § 1, 2, X. x. § 3

—— Athenian general, X. ix. § 11

Tyndareus, I. xvii. § 5, xxxiii. § 7, 8, II. i. § 9, xviii. § 2, 6, 7, xxxiv. § 10, III. i. § 4, 5, xii. § 5, xiii. § 1, 8, xv. § 11, xvi. § 2, xvii. § 2–4, xviii. § 11, 14, xx. § 9, xxi. § 2, xxiv. § 7, 10, IV. xxvii. § 1, xxxi. § 9, v. viii. § 4, VIII. v. § 1, xxxiv. § 4

263

GENERAL INDEX

Typaeus, Mount, V. vi. § 7
Typhos, III. xviii. § 10
Tyrbe, festival, II. xxiv. § 6
Tyre, V. xxv. § 12, VII. v. § 5, IX. xxvii. § 8
Tyro, II. xvi. § 4
Tyrrhenians, IV. xxxv. § 12, V. xii. § 5, VII. x. § 11, VIII. vii. § 3, X. xi. § 3, xvi. § 7
Tyrtaeus, IV. vi. § 5, xiii. § 6, xiv. § 5, xv. § 2, 6, xvi. § 2, 6, xviii. § 3

Udaeus, IX. v. § 3
Umpires, V. ix. § 5, xvi. § 8, VI. i. § 5, ii. § 2, vi. § 6, xx. § 10, xxiii. § 2, xxiv. § 1–3
Underground folk, VIII. xv. § 3
Underworld gods, II. xxxi. § 2, X. xxxii. § 13
Unknown gods, I. i. § 4, V. xiv. § 8
Untilled Plain, VIII. vii. § 1, 4, viii. § 1
Urania, IX. xxix. § 6
Uranus, VII. xxiii. § 4, IX. xxix. § 4

Vengeance, I. xliii. § 7, 8
Vespasian, VII. xvii. § 4
Victory, I. i. § 3, xxii. § 4, xxiv. § 7, xxix. § 16, xxxiii. § 3, II. xi. § 8, III. xvii. § 4, IV. xxxvi. § 6, V. x. § 4, xi. § 1, 2, xvii. § 3, xxvi. § 1, 6, VI. xii. § 6, xviii. § 1, IX. xxvii. § 5, X. ix. § 5, 6, Athena I. xlii. § 4, Wingless I. xxii. § 4, II. xxx. § 2, III. xv. § 7, V. xxvi. § 6
Vines, II. xiii. § 6, xxxiv. § 2, xxxviii. § 3, VI. xxii. § 1, VII. xxvi. § 10, IX. xxv. § 1, X. xxxvi. § 1, xxxviii. § 1

Walls, of Acropolis I. xxviii. § 3, of Tiryns II. xxv. § 8, of Messene IV. xxxi. § 5, brick strongest VIII. viii. § 8, wooden I. xviii. § 2
Washing, in ritual, I. xxxviii. § 9, II. xxxviii. § 2, V. v. § 11, VI. xx. § 2, VIII. xiii. § 1, xvi. § 1, xxviii. § 2, IX. xxxix. § 7, X. xxxiv. § 8
Water, in ritual II. vii. § 1, V. xi. § 10, with peculiar properties I. xxvi. § 5, II. xxxiv. § 1, IV. xxxv. § 8, 12, V. v. § 8, 9, vii. § 5, VII. xxiii. § 3, VIII. vii. § 2, 3, x. § 4, X. xi. § 4, prophetic III. xxiii. § 8,

VII. xxi. § 12, IX. ii. § 1, X. xxiv. § 7, healing v. v. § 11, VI. xxii. § 7, VIII. xix. § 3
Wayside Goddess, III. xiv. § 9
Wheat, burnt in sacrifice, v. xv. § 10
Wheel, in Argolis, II. xxiv. § 7
White Island, III. xix. § 11–13
Widows, II. xxi. § 7, pray for husbands X. xxxviii. § 12, sacrifice before remarriage II. xxxiv. § 12, Hera VIII. xxii. § 2
Willows, III. xvi. § 10, VII. iv. § 4, VIII. xxiii. § 5, X. xxx. § 6
Winds, cult, II. xii. § 1, xxxiv. § 2, IV. xxxv. § 8, VIII. xxix. § 1, IX. xxxiv. § 3
Wine, V. xv. § 10, VI. xxvi. § 2, VII. xxvii. § 3, IX. iii. § 8, xx. § 5. See also Sacrifices
Wolf, II. ix. § 7, xix. § 4, 7, IV. xi. § 3, VI. vi. § 11, xiv. § 8, VII. xii. § 2, xviii. § 12, X. vi. § 2, xvii. § 12, xxxiii. § 9, bronze x. xiv. § 7, man changed into VI. viii. § 2, VIII. ii. § 3, 6
Women, in ritual II. xi. § 6, xxi. § 7, xxiv. § 1, xxxiv. § 12, xxxv. § 7, IV. xvii. § 1, V. xvi. § 2–6, VI. xx. § 2, 3, VII. xxv. § 13, xxvii. § 10, VIII. xxiii. § 1, xlviii. § 5, X. xii, excluded II. xxvii. § 6, III. xxii. § 7, V. vi. § 7, VII. v. § 8, brave deeds II. xx. § 9, IV. xvii. § 1, xxi. § 6, VIII. v. § 9, xlviii. § 4, X. xxii. § 5, superfluous VII. xxi. § 14
Wood, burnt in sacrifice V. xiii. § 3, xiv. § 2, VII. xviii. § 11, 13, used for images VIII. xvii. § 2. See also Images, Cedar, Box, etc.
Wool, in ritual V. xii. § 4, VI. xxv. § 5, VIII. xlii. § 11, X. xxiv. § 6, spinning VIII. iv. § 1
Workers, gods called, VIII. xxxii. § 4. See also Athena
Wrestling, I. xxxix. § 3, V. viii. § 7, 9, xxi. § 9–12
—— ground, I. xxxix. § 3, IV. xxxii. § 1, V. xv. § 8, VI. xxi. § 2, xxiii. § 4, 5

Xanthippus, I. xxv. § 1, xxviii. § 2, xxix. § 16, III. vii. § 9, VIII. lii. § 3
Xanthus, son of Erymanthus, VIII. xxiv. § 1

Xanthus, son of Ptolemy, IX. v. § 16

Xenarches, Acarnanian victor, VI. ii. § 1

—— Laconian victor. VI. ii. § 2

Xenias, Elean traitor. III. viii. § 4, v. iv. § 7, VI. i. § 3, VII. x. § 2

Xenocles, Maenalian victor, VI. ix. § 2

—— torch-bearer, I. xxxvii. § 1

Xenodamus, victor, of Anticyra, X. xxxvi. § 9

Xenodicus, victorious boxer, VI. xiv. § 12

Xenodocus, Messenian victor, IV. v. § 10

Xenombrotus, Coan victor, VI. xiv. § 12

Xenon, Achaean, VII. x. § 9

—— Leprean victor, VI. xv. § 1

Xenophon, Athenian, I. iii. § 4, xxii. § 4, v. vi. § 5, 6, VIII. ix. § 5, 10, IX. xv. § 5

—— Corinthian victor, IV. xxiv. § 5

—— victor of Aegium, VI. iii. § 13

Xerxes, I. viii. § 2, 5, xvi. § 3, xx. § 4, xxvii. § 6, xxxvi. § 2, xxxvii. § 1

II. xxxi. § 5

III. iv. § 7, 8, ix. § 6, xi. § 3, xii. § 6

VI. v. § 4

VII. vi. § 3, x. § 2

VIII. xlii. § 8, xlvi. § 3, lii. § 2

IX. i. § 3, vi. § 1, xxv. § 9, xxxii. § 5, 9

X. iii. § 2, vii. § 1, xiv. § 5, xix. § 2, xx. § 1, xxxiii. § 5, 8, xxxv. § 2, 6

Xuthus, I. xxxi. § 3, II. xiv. § 2, xxvi. § 1, VII. i. § 2, iv. § 2, xxv. § 8

Xystus, VI. xxiii. § 1

YEARNING, image of, I. xliii. § 6

Yew, IV. xxvi. § 7, VIII. xvii. § 2

ZACYNTHUS, IV. xxiii. § 5, VIII. xxiv. § 3

Zancle, IV. xxiii. § 6–9, v. xxv. § 11

Zanes, v. xxi. § 2, VI. xx. § 8

Zarax, I. xxxviii. § 4, III. xxi. § 7, xxiv. § 1

Zeno, I. xxix. § 15, II. viii. § 4

Zephyrium, cape, III. iii. § 1, VI. vi. § 4, xix. § 6

Zephyrus, I. xxxvii. § 2, III. xix. § 5

Zetes, III. xviii. § 15

Zethus, II. vi. § 4, IX. v. § 6, 9, viii. § 4, xvii. § 4, 5, X. xxxii. § 11

Zeugma, X. xxix. § 4

Zeus, birth and childhood IV. xxxiii. § 1, v. vii. § 6, VIII. viii. § 2, xxviii. § 2, xxxvi. § 2, 5, xxxviii. § 2, IX. ii. § 4, xli. § 6, X. xxiv. § 6, other myths I. xix. § 3, xxiv. § 2, xxv. § 1, xxxiii. § 7, xl. § 1

II. i. § 1, v. § 1, vi. § 4, vii. § 1, xvii. § 4, xxii. § 2–5, xxiv. § 4, xxv. § 8, xxvi. § 2, xxix. § 2, xxx. § 3–6, xxxiv. § 5, xxxvi. § 1

III. i. § 2, ii. § 4, xxiv. § 3

v. i. § 3, vii. § 10, x. § 8, xi. § 7, xiv. § 9, xviii. § 3, xxii. § 6, xxiv. § 5, 6

VI. xxv. § 3

VII. xvii. § 9, 10, 12, xix. § 6

VIII. ii. § 3, iii. § 6, viii. § 2, xviii. § 3, xxii. § 2, xxiv. § 14, xxxii. § 4, xli. § 2, xlii. § 3

IX. iii. § 1, v. § 2, xix. § 1, xxv. § 2, xxvi. § 8, xxix. § 4, xxxv. § 5, xl. § 11

X. xxx. § 2

—— cult, I. i. § 4, iv. § 5, xiii. § 3, xvi. § 1, xvii. § 5, xviii. § 6–9, xxiv. § 2–4, xxvi. § 2, 5, xxviii. § 10, xxxi. § 4, xxxii. § 2, xxxiv. § 3, xxxvii. § 4, xl. § 4–6, xliv. § 9

II. iv. § 5, v. § 5, xv. § 2, 3, xix. § 5, 8, xx. § 3, 6, xxi. § 2, xxiv. § 2, 3, xxv. § 10, xxix. § 8, xxx. § 3–6, xxxi. § 10, xxxii. § 7, xxxiv. § 6, xxxvi. § 2

III. ix. § 2, x. § 6, xi. § 9, xii. § 9, xiii. § 6, 8, xiv. § 5, xvii. § 4, xix. § 7, xx. § 3, xxii. § 1, xxiii. § 10, xxv. § 1

IV. iii. § 9, xxii. § 7, xxxiii. § 1, 2

v. v. § 1, 5, viii. § 2, x. § 1–xi. § 10, xii. § 5, xiii. § 1–3, 8, 11, xiv. § 1–9, xv. § 4–10, xxiv. § 1

VI. viii. § 2, xxiv. § 3

VII. xx. § 3, xxiii. § 9, xxiv. § 2–4, xxv. § 1, xxvi. § 4, 10

VIII. ii. § 2–6, ix. § 2, xii. § 1, xxvi. § 6, xxx. § 2, 8–10, xxxi. § 4, xxxviii. § 2–7, xlii. § 8, xliv. § 6, xlviii. § 6, liii. § 9, 11

IX. ii. § 4–7, viii. § 5, xix. § 3, xxv. § 4, xxxiv. § 5, xxxix. § 4–5, xl. § 11

Zeus, cult, X. xii. § 10, xxi. § 5, 6,
xxviii. § 6, xxxviii. § 8
—— representations, as stone III.
xxii. § 1, as child VII. xxiv. § 4,
beardless V. xxiv. § 6, with three
eyes II. xxiv. § 3, others I. i. § 3,
ii. § 5, iii. § 2, 5, xvii. § 2, xviii.
§ 6, xxiv. § 4, xxxii. § 2, xl. § 4,
xliii. § 6
II. ii. § 8, iv. § 5, ix. § 6, xvii.
§ 3, xix. § 7, xx. § 1, xxii. § 2, xxiv.
§ 3, xxvii. § 2
III. xi. § 11, xii. § 11, xvii. § 6,
xviii. § 10, xix. § 3, xxi. § 4, xxvi.
§ 6
IV. xxxi. § 6, xxxiii. § 2, xxxiv. § 6
V. ii. § 3, x. § 2, 6, xi. § 1–10,
xvii. § 1, xx. § 2, xxi. § 2–17,
xxii. § 1–7, xxiii. § 1, 4, xxiv. § 6, 9,
11, xxv. § 1, xxvi. § 3
VI. vii. § 2, x. § 6, xix. § 4–12,
xxiii. § 4
VII. xx. § 3, xxiii. § 9, 10, xxiv.
§ 2, xxvi. § 4
VIII. xiv. § 7, xxxi. § 4, xxxvii.
§ 1, xlvi. § 2, xlvii. § 3
IX. ii. § 4–7, xix. § 3, xxv. § 4,
xxvi. § 7, xxxiv. § 1–5, xxxix. § 4,
xli. § 6
X. v. § 2, ix. § 7, xiii. § 6, xiv.
§ 5, xxiv. § 4
—— titles, Anchesmius I. xxxii. § 2
Apemius, I. xxxii. § 2
Apesantius II. xv. § 3
Aphesius, I. xliv. § 9
Averter of Flies, V. xiv. § 1
Capitoline, II. iv. § 5
Cappotas, III. xxii. § 1
Charmon, VIII. xii. § 1
Child, VIII. xlvii. § 3
Chthonius, II. ii. § 8, V. xiv. § 8
Cithaeronian, IX. ii. § 4
Clarian, VIII. liii. § 9
Coccygius, II. xvii. § 4, xxxvi. § 2
Conius, I. xl. § 6
Coryphaeus, II. iv. § 5
Cosmetas, III. xvii. § 4
Counsellor, I. iii. § 5, III. xiii. § 6
Croceatas, III. xxi. § 4
Ctesius, I. xxxi. § 4
Descender, V. xiv. § 10
at Dodona, I. xvii. § 5
of Fair Wind, III. xiii. § 8
of Freedom, I. iii. § 2, xxvi.
§ 2, IX. ii. § 5–7, X. xxi. § 5, 6

Zeus, titles, Friendly, VIII. xxxi. § 4
Giver, VIII. ix. § 2
Greatest, X. xxxvii. § 3
Guide of Fate, V. xv. § 5, VIII.
xxxvii. § 1, X. xxiv. § 4
Heliconian, VII. xxiv. § 5
Herceius, IV. xvii. § 4, V. xiv. § 7,
VIII. xlvi. § 2, X. xxvii. § 2
Homagyrius, VII. xxiv. § 2, 3
Hospitable, III. xi. § 11
Hymettian, I. xxxii. § 2
Ithomatas, III. xxvi. § 6, IV. iii.
§ 9, xii. § 7, 8, xiii. § 1, xix. § 3,
xx. § 4, xxiv. § 7, xxvi. § 3, xxvii.
§ 6, xxxiii. § 1, 2
King, IX. xxxix. § 4, 5
Laoetas, V. xiv. § 4, xxiv. § 1
Laphystius, V. xiv. § 2, IX. xxxiv.
§ 5
Larisaeus, II. xxiv. § 3
Lecheates, VIII. xxvi. § 6
Leucaeus, V. v. § 5
Lycaeus, IV. xxii. § 7, VI. viii.
§ 2, VIII. ii. § 1, 3, 6, xxx. § 2, 8,
xxxviii. § 4–7, xliv. § 6, liii. § 11
of Market-place, III. xi. § 9,
V. xv. § 4, IX. xxv. § 4
Mechaneus, II. xxii. § 2
Meilichius, I. xxxvii. § 4, II. ix.
§ 6, xx. § 1, 2
Messapeus, III. xx. § 3
Most High, I. xxvi. § 5, II. ii.
§ 8, III. xvii. § 6, V. xv. § 5, VIII.
ii. § 3, xiv. § 7, IX. viii. § 5, xix.
§ 3
Nemean, II. xv. § 2, 3, xx. § 3,
xxiv. § 2, IV. xxvii. § 6
Oath-god, V. xxiv. § 9
Olympian, I. xvii. § 2, xviii.
§ 6, 8, xix. § 1, II. v. § 5, xxvii.
§ 2, III. ix. § 2, xii. § 11, xiv. § 5,
IV. xxxi. § 6, V. viii. § 2, x. § 1–
xi. § 10, xii. § 5, xiii. § 8, 11, xiv.
§ 2–9, xxi. § 8, xxiv. § 3, VI. xix.
§ 6, 10, VII. xx. § 3, VIII. xlii. § 8, 9,
X. xxviii. § 6
Panhellenius, I. xviii. § 9, xliv.
§ 9, II. xxx. § 8, xxx. § 3, 4
Parnethius, I. xxxii. § 2
Phyxius, II. xxi. § 2, III. xvii.
§ 9
Polieus, I. xxiv. § 4, xxviii. § 10
Purifier, V. xiv. § 8
Rain-god, I. xxxii. § 2, II. xix.
§ 8, IX. xxxix. § 4

GENERAL INDEX

Zeus, titles, Saotes, IX. xxvi. § 7, 8
  Saviour, II. xx. § 6, xxxi. § 10,
III. xxiii. § 10, IV. xxxi. § 6, xxxiv.
§ 6, V. v. § 1, VII. xxiii. § 9, VIII. ix.
§ 2, xxx. § 10
  Scotitas, III. x. § 6
  in Sea, II. xxiv. § 4
  Semaleus, I. xxxii. § 2
  Sthenius, II. xxxii. § 7, xxxiv. § 6
  god of Suppliants, I. xx. § 7,
III. xvii. § 9, VII. xxv. § 1
  Teleius, VIII. xlviii. § 6

Zeus, titles, of Thunderbolt, V. xiv. § 7
  Tropaean, III. xii. § 9
  of Underworld, II. xxiv. § 4
  Warlike, V. xiv. § 6
  Wealthy, III. xix. § 7
Zeuxidamus, king of Sparta, III. vii.
  § 6, 10, IV. xv. § 3
Zeuxippus, king of Sicyon, II. vi. § 7
Zoetia, VIII. xxvii. § 3, xxxv. § 6, 7
Zoster, I. xxxi. § 1
Zypoetes, founder of Astacus, V.
  xii. § 7

INDEX OF ARTISTS

ACESTOR, VI. xvii. § 4, X. xv. § 6

Ageladas, of Argos, IV. xxxiii. § 2, VI. viii. § 6, x. § 6, xiv. § 11, VII. xxiv. § 4, VIII. xlii. § 10, X. x. § 6, xiii. § 10

Agoracritus, of Athens, IX. xxxiv. § 1

Alcamenes, I. i. § 5, viii. § 4, xix. § 2, xx. § 3, xxiv. § 3, II. xxx. § 2, V. x. § 8, VIII. ix. § 1, IX. xi. § 6

Alypus, of Sicyon, VI. i. § 3, viii. § 5, X. ix. § 10

Amphion, of Cnossus, VI. iii. § 5, X. xv. § 6

Amyclaeus. of Corinth, X. xiii. § 7

Anaxagoras, of Aegina, V. xxiii. § 3

Andreas, of Argos, VI. xvi. § 7

Androsthenes, of Athens, X. xix. § 4

Angelion, II. xxxii. § 5, IX. xxxv. § 3

Antenor, I. viii. § 5

Antiphanes, of Argos, V. xvii. § 4, X. ix. § 6, 8, 12

Antiphilus, architect, VI. xix. § 7

Apelles, painter, IX. xxxv. § 6

—— sculptor, VI. i. § 6

Arcesilaus, painter, I. i. § 3

Aristander, of Paros, III. xviii. § 8

Aristocles, son of Cleoitas, V. xxiv. § 5

—— Cydonian, V. xxv. § 11

—— of Sicyon, VI. iii. § 11, ix. § 1

Aristogeiton, X. x. § 4

Aristomedes, of Thebes, IX. xxv. § 3

Aristomedon, of Argos, X. i. § 10

Ariston, Laconian, V. xxiii. § 7

Aristonus, of Aegina, V. xxii. § 5

Ascarus, of Thebes, V. xxiv. § 1

Asterion, VI. iii. § 1

Athenodorus, of Cleitor, X. ix. § 8

Attalus, of Athens, II. xix. § 3

BATHYCLES, of Magnesia, III. xviii. § 9, 11, 14, xix. § 2

Boethus, of Chalcedon, V. xvii. § 4

Broteas, III. xxii. § 4

Bryaxis, I. xl. § 6

Bupalus, architect and sculptor, IV. xxx. § 6, IX. xxxv. § 6

CALAMIS, I. iii. § 4, xxiii. § 2, II. x. § 3, V. xxv. § 6, xxvi. § 6, VI. xii. § 1, IX. xvi. § 1, xix. § 4, xx. § 4, xxii. § 1, X. xvi. § 4

Callicles, of Megara, VI. vii. § 2, 9

Callimachus, I. xxvi. § 6, 7, IX. ii. § 7

Calliphon, of Samos, painter, V. xix. § 2, X. xxvi. § 6

Callistonicus, of Thebes, IX. xvi. § 2

Calliteles, V. xxvii. § 8

Callon, of Aegina, II. xxxii. § 5, III. xviii. § 8, VII. xviii. § 10

—— of Elis, V. xxv. § 4, xxvii. § 8

Calynthus, X. xiii. § 10

Canachus, of Sicyon, brother of Aristocles, II. x. § 5, VI. ix. § 1, VII. xviii. § 10, IX. x. § 2

—— pupil of Polycleitus, VI. xiii. § 7, X. ix. § 10

Cantharus, of Sicyon, VI. iii. § 6, xvii. § 7

Cephisodotus, of Athens, I. viii. § 2, VIII. xxx. § 10, IX. xvi. § 2, xxx. § 1

Chartas, Spartan, VI. iv. § 4

Cheirosophus, of Crete, VIII. liii. § 8

Chionis, of Corinth, X. xiii. § 7

Chrysothemis, of Argos, VI. x. § 5

INDEX OF ARTISTS

Clearchus, of Rhegium, III. xvii. § 6, VI. iv. § 4

Cleoitas, I. xxiv. § 3, V. xxiv. § 5, VI. xx. § 14

Cleon, of Sicyon, V. xvii. § 3, 4, xxi. § 3, VI. i. § 5, iii. § 10, viii. § 5, ix. § 2, x. § 9

Colotes, V. xx. § 2

Cratinus, Spartan, VI. ix. § 4

Critius, of Athens, I. viii. § 5, xxiii. § 9, VI. iii. § 5

DAEDALUS, of Athens, I. xxi. § 4, xxvi. § 4, xxvii. § 1, II. iv. § 5, xv. § 1, III. xvii. § 6, V. xxv. § 13, VII. iv. § 4–7, VIII. xvi. § 3, xxxv. § 2, xlvi. § 2, liii. § 8, IX. iii. § 2, 3, xi. § 4, 5, xxxix. § 8, xl. § 3, 4, X. xvii. § 4

Daetondas, of Sicyon, VI. xvii. § 5

Daippus, VI. xii. § 6, xvi. § 5

Dameas, of Cleitor, X. ix. § 8

—— of Croton, VI. xiv. § 5

Damocritus, of Sicyon, VI. iii. § 5

Damophon, of Messene, IV. xxxi. § 6, 7, 10, VII. xxiii. § 6, 7, VIII. xxxi. § 2, 6, xxxvii. § 3

Deinomenes, I. xxv. § 1

Dionysicles, of Miletus, VI. xvii. § 1

Dionysius, of Argos, V. xxvi. § 3, 4, 7, xxvii. § 2

Dipoenus, II. xv. § 1, xxii. § 5, xxxii. § 5, III. xvii. § 6, V. xvii. § 1, 2. VI. xix. § 14

Diyllus, of Corinth, X. xiii. § 7

Dontas, Lacedaemonian, VI. xix. § 14

Dorycleidas, Lacedaemonian, V. xvii. § 1, 2

ENDOEUS, of Athens, I. xxvi. § 4, VII. v. § 9, VIII. xlvi. § 5

Eubius, of Thebes, IX. xi. § 4

Eubulides, of Athens, I. ii. § 5, VIII. xiv. § 10

Eucadmus, X. xix. § 4

Eucheir, of Athens, VIII. xiv. § 10

Eucheirus, of Corinth, VI. iv. § 4

Eucleides, of Athens, VII. xxv. § 9, xxvi. § 4

Euphranor, painter, I. iii. § 4

Eupolemus, architect, of Argos, II. xvii. § 3

Eutelidas, of Argos, VI. x. § 5

Eutychides, of Sicyon, VI. ii. § 7, iii. § 6

GITIADUS, Laconian, III. xvii. § 2, xviii. § 8

Glaucias, of Aegina, VI. ix. § 5, 9, x. § 3, xi. § 9

Glaucus, of Argos, V. xxvi. § 2, 4, 6

—— of Chios, worker in iron, X. xvi. § 1

HEGIAS, of Athens, VIII. xlii. § 10

Hermogenes, of Cythera, II. ii. § 8

Hermon, architect, VI. xix. § 8

—— of Troezen, II. xxxi. § 6

Hippias, VI. xiii. § 5

Hypatodorus, VIII. xxvi. § 7, X. x. § 4

ICTINUS, architect, VIII. xli. § 9

LACRATES, architect, VI. xix. § 8

Laphaes, of Phlius, II. x. § 1, VII. xxvi. § 6

Leochares, I. i. § 3, iii. § 4, xxiv. § 4, V. xx. § 10

Libon, architect, of Elis, V. x. § 3

Locrus, of Paros, I. viii. § 4

Lycius, son of Myron, I. xxiii. § 7, V. xxii. § 3

Lysippus, of Sicyon, I. xliii. § 6, II. ix. § 6, 8, xx. § 3, VI. i. § 5, ii. § 1, 7, iv. § 7, v. § 1, xiv. § 12, xvii. § 3, IX. xxvii. § 3, xxx. § 1

Lyson, I. iii. § 5

Lysus, of Macedon, VI. xvii. § 1

MAESIS, architect, III. xv. § 8

Medon, Laconian, V. xvii. § 2, VI. xix. § 14

Megacles, architect, VI. xix. § 7

Menaechmus, of Naupactus, VII. xviii. § 10

Menodorus, of Athens, IX. xxvii. § 4

Micon, painter, of Athens, I. xvii. § 3, xviii. § 1, II. ix. § 4, VI. vi. § 1, VIII. xi. § 3

—— of Syracuse, VI. xii. § 4

Musus, V. xxiv. § 1

Myron, of Eleutherae, I. xxiii. § 7, II. xxx. § 2, V. xxii. § 3, VI. ii. § 2, viii. § 4, 5, xiii. § 2, IX. xxx. § 1

Mys, engraver, I. xxviii. § 2

NAUCYDES, of Argos, II. xvii. § 5, xxii. § 7, VI. i. § 3, vi. § 2, viii. § 4, ix. § 3

Nicias, painter, I. xxix. § 15, III. xix. § 4, IV. xxxi. § 12, VII. xxii. § 6

270

INDEX OF ARTISTS

Nicodamus, of Maenalus, V. xxv. § 7, xxvi. § 6, VI. iii. § 9, vi. § 1, 3

Olbiades, painter, I. iii. § 5
Olympiosthenes, IX. xxx. § 1
Olympus, VI. iii. § 13
Omphalion, painter, IV. xxxi. § 12
Onaethus, V. xxiii. § 5
Onasias, painter, IX. iv. § 2, v. § 11
Onasimedes, IX. xii. § 4
Onatas, of Aegina, V. xxv. § 10, 13, xxvii. § 8, VI. xii. § 1, VIII. xlii. § 7–12, X. xiii. § 10

Paeonius, of Mende, V. x. § 8, xxvi. § 1
Panaenus, painter, of Athens, V. xi. § 5, 6
Pantias, of Chios, VI. iii. § 11, ix. § 3, xiv. § 12
Parrhasius, designer, I. xxviii. § 2
Pasiteles, V. xx. § 2
Patrocles, of Crotona, VI. xix. § 6
—— of Sicyon, VI. iii. § 4, X. ix. § 10
Pausanias, of Apollonia, X. ix. § 6
Pausias, painter, II. xxvii. § 3
Peisias, I. iii. § 5
Pheidias, of Athens, I. iii. § 5, xiv. § 7, xxiv. § 8, xxviii. § 2, xxxiii. § 3, 8, xl. § 4, V. x. § 2, 8, xi. § 3–9, xiv. § 5, xv. § 1, VI. iv. § 5, x. § 6, xxv. § 1, xxvi. § 3, VII. xxvii. § 2, IX. iv. § 1, x. § 2, xxxiv. § 1, X. x. § 2
Philesius, of Eretria, V. xxvii. § 9
Philotimus, of Aegina, VI. xiv. § 12
Phradmon, of Argos, VI. viii. § 1
Phylacus, V. xxiii. § 5
Pison, of Calauria, VI. iii. § 5, X. ix. § 8
Polycleitus, of Argos, (2), II. xvii. § 4, xx. § 1, xxii. § 7, xxiv. § 5, III. xviii. § 8, VI. ii. § 7, iv. § 11, vi. § 2, vii. § 10, ix. § 2, xiii. § 6
—— architect, II. xxvii. § 5
Polycles, Athenian, VI. iv. § 5, xii. § 9, X. xxxiv. § 8
Polygnotus, painter, of Thasos, I. xviii. § 1, xxii. § 6, IX. iv. § 2, X. xxv. § 1–xxxi. § 12
Pothaeus, architect, VI. xix. § 7
Praxias, of Athens, X. xix. § 4
Praxiteles, of Athens, I. ii. § 3, 4, viii. § 4, xx. § 1, 2, xxiii. § 7, xl. § 3, xliii. § 5, 6, xliv. § 2, II. xxi. § 8, V. xvii. § 3, VI. xxvi. § 1, VIII. ix. § 1, 3, IX. ii. § 7, xi. § 6, xii. § 4,

xxvii. § 3–5, xxxix. § 4, X. xv. § 1, xxxvii. § 1
Protogenes, painter, of Caunus, I. iii. § 5
Pteras, architect, of Delphi, X. v. § 10
Ptolichus, of Aegina, VI. ix. § 1, x. § 9
—— of Corcyra, VI. iii. § 5
Pyrilampes, of Messene, VI. iii. § 13, xv. § 1, xvi. § 5
Pyrrhus, architect, VI. xix. § 8
Pythagoras, painter, of Paros, IX. xxxv. § 1
—— of Rhegium, VI. iv. § 4, vi. § 1, 6, vii. § 10, xiii. § 1, 7, xviii. § 1
Pythodorus, of Thebes, IX. xxxiv. § 3

Rhoecus, of Samos, VIII. xiv. § 8, IX. xli. § 1, X. xxxviii. § 6

Samolas, Arcadian, X. ix. § 6
Scopas, of Paros, I. xliii. § 6, II. x. § 1, xxii. § 7, VI. xxv. § 1, VIII. xxviii. § 1, xliv. § 5, xlvii. § 1, IX. x. § 2, xvii. § 1
Scyllis, see Dipoenus
Serambus, of Aegina, VI. x. § 9
Silanion, of Athens, VI. iv. § 5, xiv. § 4, 11
Simon, of Aegina, V. xxvii. § 2
Soidas, of Naupactus, VII. xviii. § 10
Somis, VI. xiv. § 13
Sostratus, of Chios, VI. ix. § 3
Spintharus, architect, of Corinth, X. v. § 13
Stadieus, VI. iv. § 5
Sthennis, of Olynthus, X. xvi. § 8 xvii. § 5
Stomius, VI. xiv. § 13
Straton, II. xxiii. § 4
Strongylion, I. xl. § 3, IX. xxx. § 1
Syadras, Spartan, VI. iv. § 4
Synnoon, of Aegina, VI. ix. § 1

Tectaeus, II. xxxii. § 5, IX. xxxv. § 3
Telestas, Laconian, V. xxiii. § 7
Theocles, Lacedaemonian, V. xvii. § 2, VI. xix. § 8
Theocosmus, of Megara, I. xl. § 4, VI. vii. § 2, X. ix. § 8
Theodorus, of Samos, III. xii. § 10, VIII. xiv. § 8, IX. xli. § 1, X. xxxviii. § 6
Theomnestus, of Sardes, VI. xv. § 2
Theopropus, of Aegina, X. ix. § 3

INDEX OF ARTISTS

*Printed in Great Britain by
Richard Clay (The Chaucer Press), Ltd.,
Bungay, Suffolk*

THE LOEB CLASSICAL LIBRARY

VOLUMES ALREADY PUBLISHED

Latin Authors

AMMIANUS MARCELLINUS. Translated by J. C. Rolfe. 3 Vols.

APULEIUS: THE GOLDEN ASS (METAMORPHOSES). W. Adlington (1566). Revised by S. Gaselee.

ST. AUGUSTINE: CITY OF GOD. 7 Vols. Vol. I. G. E. McCracken. Vol. II. W. M. Green. Vol. VI. W. C. Greene.

ST. AUGUSTINE, CONFESSIONS OF. W. Watts (1631). 2 Vols.

ST. AUGUSTINE, SELECT LETTERS. J. H. Baxter.

AUSONIUS. H. G. Evelyn White. 2 Vols.

BEDE. J. E. King. 2 Vols.

BOETHIUS: TRACTS and DE CONSOLATIONE PHILOSOPHIAE. Rev. H. F. Stewart and E. K. Rand.

CAESAR: ALEXANDRIAN, AFRICAN and SPANISH WARS. A. G. Way.

CAESAR: CIVIL WARS. A. G. Peskett.

CAESAR: GALLIC WAR. H. J. Edwards.

CATO: DE RE RUSTICA; VARRO: DE RE RUSTICA. H. B. Ash and W. D. Hooper.

CATULLUS. F. W. Cornish; TIBULLUS. J. B. Postgate; PERVIGILIUM VENERIS. J. W. Mackail.

CELSUS: DE MEDICINA. W. G. Spencer. 3 Vols.

CICERO: BRUTUS, and ORATOR. G. L. Hendrickson and H. M. Hubbell.

[CICERO]: AD HERENNIUM. H. Caplan.

CICERO: DE ORATORE, etc. 2 Vols. Vol. I. DE ORATORE, Books I. and II. E. W. Sutton and H. Rackham. Vol. II. DE ORATORE, Book III. De Fato; Paradoxa Stoicorum; De Partitione Oratoria. H. Rackham.

CICERO: DE FINIBUS. H. Rackham.

CICERO: DE INVENTIONE, etc. H. M. Hubbell.

CICERO: DE NATURA DEORUM and ACADEMICA. H. Rackham.

CICERO: DE OFFICIIS. Walter Miller.

CICERO: DE REPUBLICA and DE LEGIBUS; SOMNIUM SCIPIONIS. Clinton W. Keyes.

1

CICERO: DE SENECTUTE, DE AMICITIA, DE DIVINATIONE. W. A. Falconer.

CICERO: IN CATILINAM, PRO FLACCO, PRO MURENA, PRO SULLA. Louis E. Lord.

CICERO: LETTERS to ATTICUS. E. O. Winstedt. 3 Vols.

CICERO: LETTERS TO HIS FRIENDS. W. Glynn Williams. 3 Vols.

CICERO: PHILIPPICS. W. C. A. Ker.

CICERO: PRO ARCHIA POST REDITUM, DE DOMO, DE HARUSPICUM RESPONSIS, PRO PLANCIO. N. H. Watts.

CICERO: PRO CAECINA, PRO LEGE MANILIA, PRO CLUENTIO, PRO RABIRIO. H. Grose Hodge.

CICERO: PRO CAELIO, DE PROVINCIIS CONSULARIBUS, PRO BALBO. R. Gardner.

CICERO: PRO MILONE, IN PISONEM, PRO SCAURO, PRO FONTEIO, PRO RABIRIO POSTUMO, PRO MARCELLO, PRO LIGARIO, PRO REGE DEIOTARO. N. H. Watts.

CICERO: PRO QUINCTIO, PRO ROSCIO AMERINO, PRO ROSCIO COMOEDO, CONTRA RULLUM. J. H. Freese.

CICERO: PRO SESTIO, IN VATINIUM. R. Gardner.

CICERO: TUSCULAN DISPUTATIONS. J. E. King.

CICERO: VERRINE ORATIONS. L. H. G. Greenwood. 2 Vols.

CLAUDIAN. M. Platnauer. 2 Vols.

COLUMELLA: DE RE RUSTICA. DE ARBORIBUS. H. B. Ash, E. S. Forster and E. Heffner. 3 Vols.

CURTIUS, Q.: HISTORY OF ALEXANDER. J. C. Rolfe. 2 Vols.

FLORUS. E. S. Forster; and CORNELIUS NEPOS. J. C. Rolfe.

FRONTINUS: STRATAGEMS and AQUEDUCTS. C. E. Bennett and M. B. McElwain.

FRONTO: CORRESPONDENCE. C. R. Haines. 2 Vols.

GELLIUS, J. C. Rolfe. 3 Vols.

HORACE: ODES AND EPODES. C. E. Bennett.

HORACE: SATIRES, EPISTLES, ARS POETICA. H. R. Fairclough.

JEROME: SELECTED LETTERS. F. A. Wright.

JUVENAL and PERSIUS. G. G. Ramsay.

LIVY. B. O. Foster, F. G. Moore, Evan T. Sage, and A. C. Schlesinger and R. M. Geer (General Index). 14 Vols.

LUCAN. J. D. Duff.

LUCRETIUS. W. H. D. Rouse.

MARTIAL. W. C. A. Ker. 2 Vols.

MINOR LATIN POETS: from PUBLILIUS SYRUS to RUTILIUS NAMATIANUS, including GRATTIUS, CALPURNIUS SICULUS, NEMESIANUS, AVIANUS, and others with " Aetna " and the " Phoenix." J. Wight Duff and Arnold M. Duff.

OVID: THE ART OF LOVE and OTHER POEMS. J. H. Mozley.

2

OVID: FASTI. Sir James G. Frazer.
OVID: HEROIDES and AMORES. Grant Showerman.
OVID: METAMORPHOSES. F. J. Miller. 2 Vols.
OVID: TRISTIA and EX PONTO. A. L. Wheeler.
PERSIUS. Cf. JUVENAL.
PETRONIUS. M. Heseltine; SENECA; APOCOLOCYNTOSIS. W. H. D. Rouse.
PLAUTUS. Paul Nixon. 5 Vols.
PLINY: LETTERS. Melmoth's Translation revised by W. M. L. Hutchinson. 2 Vols.
PLINY: NATURAL HISTORY.
10 Vols. Vols. I.–V. and IX. H. Rackham. Vols. VI.– VIII. W. H. S. Jones. Vol. X. D. E. Eichholz.
PROPERTIUS. H. E. Butler.
PRUDENTIUS. H. J. Thomson. 2 Vols.
QUINTILIAN. H. E. Butler. 4 Vols.
REMAINS OF OLD LATIN. E. H. Warmington. 4 Vols. Vol. I. (ENNIUS AND CAECILIUS.) Vol. II. (LIVIUS, NAEVIUS, PACUVIUS, ACCIUS.) Vol. III. (LUCILIUS and LAWS OF XII TABLES.) Vol. IV. (ARCHAIC INSCRIPTIONS.)
SALLUST. J. C. Rolfe.
SCRIPTORES HISTORIAE AUGUSTAE. D. Magie. 3 Vols.
SENECA: APOCOLOCYNTOSIS. Cf. PETRONIUS.
SENECA: EPISTULAE MORALES. R. M. Gummere. 3 Vols.
SENECA: MORAL ESSAYS. J. W. Basore. 3 Vols.
SENECA: TRAGEDIES. F. J. Miller. 2 Vols.
SIDONIUS: POEMS and LETTERS. W. B. ANDERSON. 2 Vols.
SILIUS ITALICUS. J. D. Duff. 2 Vols.
STATIUS. J. H. Mozley. 2 Vols.
SUETONIUS. J. C. Rolfe. 2 Vols.
TACITUS: DIALOGUES. Sir Wm. Peterson. AGRICOLA and GERMANIA. Maurice Hutton.
TACITUS: HISTORIES AND ANNALS. C. H. Moore and J. Jackson. 4 Vols.
TERENCE. John Sargeaunt. 2 Vols.
TERTULLIAN: APOLOGIA and DE SPECTACULIS. T. R. Glover. MINUCIUS FELIX. G. H. Rendall.
VALERIUS FLACCUS. J. H. Mozley.
VARRO: DE LINGUA LATINA. R. G. Kent. 2 Vols.
VELLEIUS PATERCULUS and RES GESTAE DIVI AUGUSTI. F. W. Shipley.
VIRGIL. H. R. Fairclough. 2 Vols.
VITRUVIUS: DE ARCHITECTURA. F. Granger. 2 Vols.

Greek Authors

ACHILLES TATIUS. S. Gaselee.

AELIAN: ON THE NATURE OF ANIMALS. A. F. Scholfield. 3 Vols.

AENEAS TACTICUS, ASCLEPIODOTUS and ONASANDER. The Illinois Greek Club.

AESCHINES. C. D. Adams.

AESCHYLUS. H. Weir Smyth. 2 Vols.

ALCIPHRON, AELIAN, PHILOSTRATUS: LETTERS. A. R. Benner and F. H. Fobes.

ANDOCIDES, ANTIPHON, Cf. MINOR ATTIC ORATORS.

APOLLODORUS. Sir James G. Frazer. 2 Vols.

APOLLONIUS RHODIUS. R. C. Seaton.

THE APOSTOLIC FATHERS. Kirsopp Lake. 2 Vols.

APPIAN: ROMAN HISTORY. Horace White. 4 Vols.

ARATUS. Cf. CALLIMACHUS.

ARISTOPHANES. Benjamin Bickley Rogers. 3 Vols. Verse trans.

ARISTOTLE: ART OF RHETORIC. J. H. Freese.

ARISTOTLE: ATHENIAN CONSTITUTION, EUDEMIAN ETHICS, VICES AND VIRTUES. H. Rackham.

ARISTOTLE: GENERATION OF ANIMALS. A. L. Peck.

ARISTOTLE: METAPHYSICS. H. Tredennick. 2 Vols.

ARISTOTLE: METEOROLOGICA. H. D. P. Lee.

ARISTOTLE: MINOR WORKS. W. S. Hett. On Colours, On Things Heard, On Physiognomies, On Plants, On Marvellous Things Heard, Mechanical Problems, On Indivisible Lines, On Situations and Names of Winds, On Melissus, Xenophanes, and Gorgias.

ARISTOTLE: NICOMACHEAN ETHICS. H. Rackham.

ARISTOTLE: OECONOMICA and MAGNA MORALIA. G. C. Armstrong; (with Metaphysics, Vol. II.).

ARISTOTLE: ON THE HEAVENS. W. K. C. Guthrie.

ARISTOTLE: ON THE SOUL. PARVA NATURALIA. ON BREATH. W. S. Hett.

ARISTOTLE: CATEGORIES, ON INTERPRETATION, PRIOR ANALYTICS. H. P. Cooke and H. Tredennick.

ARISTOTLE: POSTERIOR ANALYTICS, TOPICS. H. Tredennick and E. S. Forster.

ARISTOTLE: ON SOPHISTICAL REFUTATIONS.
On Coming to be and Passing Away, On the Cosmos. E. S. Forster and D. J. Furley.

ARISTOTLE: PARTS OF ANIMALS. A. L. Peck; MOTION AND PROGRESSION OF ANIMALS. E. S. Forster.

ARISTOTLE: PHYSICS. Rev. P. Wicksteed and F. M. Cornford. 2 Vols.

ARISTOTLE: POETICS and LONGINUS. W. Hamilton Fyfe; DEMETRIUS ON STYLE. W. Rhys Roberts.

ARISTOTLE: POLITICS. H. Rackham.

ARISTOTLE: PROBLEMS. W. S. Hett. 2 Vols.

ARISTOTLE: RHETORICA AD ALEXANDRUM (with PROBLEMS. Vol. II.) H. Rackham.

ARRIAN: HISTORY OF ALEXANDER and INDICA. Rev. E. Iliffe Robson. 2 Vols.

ATHENAEUS: DEIPNOSOPHISTAE. C. B. GULICK. 7 Vols.

ST. BASIL: LETTERS. R. J. Deferrari. 4 Vols.

CALLIMACHUS: FRAGMENTS. C. A. Trypanis.

CALLIMACHUS, Hymns and Epigrams, and LYCOPHRON. A. W. Mair; ARATUS. G. R. MAIR.

CLEMENT of ALEXANDRIA. Rev. G. W. Butterworth.

COLLUTHUS. Cf. OPPIAN.

DAPHNIS AND CHLOE. Thornley's Translation revised by J. M. Edmonds; and PARTHENIUS. S. Gaselee.

DEMOSTHENES I.: OLYNTHIACS, PHILIPPICS and MINOR ORATIONS. I.–XVII. AND XX. J. H. Vince.

DEMOSTHENES II.: DE CORONA and DE FALSA LEGATIONE. C. A. Vince and J. H. Vince.

DEMOSTHENES III.: MEIDIAS, ANDROTION, ARISTOCRATES, TIMOCRATES and ARISTOGEITON, I. AND II. J. H. Vince.

DEMOSTHENES IV.–VI.: PRIVATE ORATIONS and IN NEAERAM. A. T. Murray.

DEMOSTHENES VII.: FUNERAL SPEECH, EROTIC ESSAY, EXORDIA and LETTERS. N. W. and N. J. DeWitt.

DIO CASSIUS: ROMAN HISTORY. E. Cary. 9 Vols.

DIO CHRYSOSTOM. J. W. Cohoon and H. Lamar Crosby. 5 Vols.

DIODORUS SICULUS. 12 Vols. Vols. I.–VI. C. H. Oldfather. Vol. VII. C. L. Sherman. Vol. VIII. C. B. Welles. Vols. IX. and X. R. M. Geer. Vol. XI. F. Walton.

DIOGENES LAERTIUS. R. D. Hicks. 2 Vols.

DIONYSIUS OF HALICARNASSUS: ROMAN ANTIQUITIES. Spelman's translation revised by E. Cary. 7 Vols.

EPICTETUS. W. A. Oldfather. 2 Vols.

EURIPIDES. A. S. Way. 4 Vols. Verse trans.

EUSEBIUS: ECCLESIASTICAL HISTORY. Kirsopp Lake and J. E. L. Oulton. 2 Vols.

GALEN: ON THE NATURAL FACULTIES. A. J. Brock.

THE GREEK ANTHOLOGY. W. R. Paton. 5 Vols.

GREEK ELEGY AND IAMBUS with the ANACREONTEA. J. M. Edmonds. 2 Vols.

THE GREEK BUCOLIC POETS (THEOCRITUS, BION, MOSCHUS). J. M. Edmonds.

GREEK MATHEMATICAL WORKS. Ivor Thomas. 2 Vols.

HERODES. Cf. THEOPHRASTUS: CHARACTERS.

HERODOTUS. A. D. Godley. 4 Vols.

HESIOD AND THE HOMERIC HYMNS. H. G. Evelyn White.

HIPPOCRATES and the FRAGMENTS OF HERACLEITUS. W. H. S. Jones and E. T. Withington. 4 Vols.

HOMER: ILIAD. A. T. Murray. 2 Vols.

HOMER: ODYSSEY. A. T. Murray. 2 Vols.

ISAEUS. E. W. Forster.

ISOCRATES. George Norlin and LaRue Van Hook. 3 Vols.

ST. JOHN DAMASCENE: BARLAAM AND IOASAPH. Rev. G. R. Woodward and Harold Mattingly.

JOSEPHUS. 9 Vols. Vols. I.–IV.; H. Thackeray. Vol. V.; H. Thackeray and R. Marcus. Vols. VI.–VII.; R. Marcus. Vol. VIII.; R. Marcus and Allen Wikgren. Vol. IX. L. H. Feldman.

JULIAN. Wilmer Cave Wright. 3 Vols.

LUCIAN. 8 Vols. Vols. I.–V. A. M. Harmon. Vol. VI. K. Kilburn. Vol. VII. M. D. Macleod.

LYCOPHRON. Cf. CALLIMACHUS.

LYRA GRAECA. J. M. Edmonds. 3 Vols.

LYSIAS. W. R. M. Lamb.

MANETHO. W. G. Waddell: PTOLEMY: TETRABIBLOS. F. E. Robbins.

MARCUS AURELIUS. C. R. Haines.

MENANDER. F. G. Allinson.

MINOR ATTIC ORATORS (ANTIPHON, ANDOCIDES, LYCURGUS, DEMADES, DINARCHUS, HYPERIDES). K. J. Maidment and J. O. Burrt. 2 Vols.

NONNOS: DIONYSIACA. W. H. D. Rouse. 3 Vols.

OPPIAN, COLLUTHUS, TRYPHIODORUS. A. W. Mair.

PAPYRI. NON-LITERARY SELECTIONS. A. S. Hunt and C. C. Edgar. 2 Vols. LITERARY SELECTIONS (Poetry). D. L. Page.

PARTHENIUS. Cf. DAPHNIS and CHLOE.

PAUSANIAS: DESCRIPTION OF GREECE. W. H. S. Jones. 4 Vols. and Companion Vol. arranged by R. E. Wycherley.

PHILO. 10 Vols. Vols. I.–V.; F. H. Colson and Rev. G. H. Whitaker. Vols. VI.–IX.; F. H. Colson. Vol. X. F. H. Colson and the Rev. J. W. Earp.

PHILO: two supplementary Vols. (*Translation only.*) Ralph Marcus.

PHILOSTRATUS: THE LIFE OF APOLLONIUS OF TYANA. F. C. Conybeare. 2 Vols.

PHILOSTRATUS: IMAGINES; CALLISTRATUS: DESCRIPTIONS. A. Fairbanks.

PHILOSTRATUS and EUNAPIUS: LIVES OF THE SOPHISTS. Wilmer Cave Wright.

PINDAR. Sir J. E. Sandys.

PLATO: CHARMIDES, ALCIBIADES, HIPPARCHUS, THE LOVERS, THEAGES, MINOS and EPINOMIS. W. R. M. Lamb.

PLATO: CRATYLUS, PARMENIDES, GREATER HIPPIAS, LESSER HIPPIAS. H. N. Fowler.

PLATO: EUTHYPHRO, APOLOGY, CRITO, PHAEDO, PHAEDRUS. H. N. Fowler.

PLATO: LACHES, PROTAGORAS, MENO, EUTHYDEMUS. W. R. M. Lamb.

PLATO: LAWS. Rev. R. G. Bury. 2 Vols.

PLATO: LYSIS, SYMPOSIUM, GORGIAS. W. R. M. Lamb.

PLATO: REPUBLIC. Paul Shorey. 2 Vols.

PLATO: STATESMAN, PHILEBUS. H. N. Fowler; ION. W. R. M. Lamb.

PLATO: THEAETETUS and SOPHIST. H. N. Fowler.

PLATO: TIMAEUS, CRITIAS, CLITOPHO, MENEXENUS, EPISTULAE. Rev. R. G. Bury.

PLUTARCH: MORALIA. 15 Vols. Vols. I.–V. F. C. Babbitt. Vol. VI. W. C. Helmbold. Vol. VII. P. H. De Lacy and B. Einarson. Vol. IX. E. L. Minar, Jr., F. H. Sandbach, W. C. Helmbold. Vol. X. H. N. Fowler. Vol. XI. L. Pearson and F. H. Sandbach. Vol. XII. H. Cherniss and W. C. Helmbold.

PLUTARCH: THE PARALLEL LIVES. B. Perrin. 11 Vols.

POLYBIUS. W. R. Paton. 6 Vols.

PROCOPIUS: HISTORY OF THE WARS. H. B. Dewing. 7 Vols.

PTOLEMY: TETRABIBLOS. Cf. MANETHO.

QUINTUS SMYRNAEUS. A. S. Way. Verse trans.

SEXTUS EMPIRICUS. Rev. R. G. Bury. 4 Vols.

SOPHOCLES. F. Storr. 2 Vols. Verse trans.

STRABO: GEOGRAPHY. Horace L. Jones. 8 Vols.

THEOPHRASTUS: CHARACTERS. J. M. Edmonds. HERODES, etc. A. D. Knox.

THEOPHRASTUS: ENQUIRY INTO PLANTS. Sir Arthur Hort, Bart. 2 Vols.

THUCYDIDES. C. F. Smith. 4 Vols.

TRYPHIODORUS. Cf. OPPIAN.

XENOPHON: CYROPAEDIA. Walter Miller. 2 Vols.

XENOPHON: HELLENICA, ANABASIS, APOLOGY, and SYMPOSIUM. C. L. Brownson and O. J. Todd. 3 Vols.

XENOPHON: MEMORABILIA and OECONOMICUS. E. C. Marchant.

XENOPHON: SCRIPTA MINORA. E. C. Marchant.

IN PREPARATION

ARISTOTLE: HISTORIA ANIMALIUM **(Greek).** A. L. Peck.
PLOTINUS **(Greek).** A. H. Armstrong.
BABRIUS **(Greek)** AND PHAEDRUS **(Latin).** Ben E. Perry.

DESCRIPTIVE PROSPECTUS ON APPLICATION

London   WILLIAM HEINEMANN LTD
Cambridge, Mass.   HARVARD UNIVERSITY PRESS